westermann

CAMDEN TOWN

5

Erarbeitet von
Pamela Hanus
Robin Kiso
Christoph Reuter
Sylvia Wauer
sowie: Ilka Kratz

Berater der Fachredaktion Gymnasium
Florian Nuxoll

Fachliche Beratung
Roswitha Henseler
Thomas Rahn
Ulrike Selz
Günther Sommerschuh
Prof. Dr. Karin Vogt

Zusatzmaterialien zu Camden Town 5

Für Lehrerinnen und Lehrer:

Textbook 5 für Lehrkräfte	978-3-14-149252-1
Workbook 5 mit Lösungen	978-3-14-149259-0
Teacher's Manual 5	978-3-14-149245-3
Differenzierungsmaterial 5	978-3-14-149323-8
Vorschläge für Lernerfolgskontrollen 5	978-3-14-149266-8
Audio-CD 5 mit DVD für Lehrkräfte	978-3-14-149273-6
BiBox für Lehrerinnen und Lehrer (Einzellizenz)	WEB-14-149287
BiBox für Lehrerinnen und Lehrer (Kollegiumslizenz)	WEB-14-149294
Online-Diagnose zu Camden Town 5	www.onlinediagnose.de

Für Schülerinnen und Schüler:

Workbook 5	978-3-14-149227-9
Klassenarbeitstrainer 5	978-3-7426-0321-0
Vocab Practice 5	978-3-14-149238-5
Lektüre Klasse 5	978-3-14-149337-5
Interaktive Übungen	WEB-14-149348
BiBox (Einzellizenz für 1 Schuljahr)	WEB-14-149301
BiBox (Einzellizenz für 4 Schuljahre)	WEB-14-103352
BiBox (Einzellizenz PrintPlus für 1 Schuljahr)	WEB-14-149308
Westermann Vokabeltrainer-App	www.westermann.de/vokabeltrainer
Grammatiktrainer App	www.westermann.de/ctg-grammatiktrainer
Zoom App	www.zoom-app.de

westermann GRUPPE

© 2020 Bildungshaus Schulbuchverlage Westermann Schroedel Diesterweg Schöningh Winklers GmbH
Braunschweig, www.westermann.de

Das Werk und seine Teile sind urheberrechtlich geschützt. Jede Nutzung in anderen als den gesetzlich zugelassenen bzw. vertraglich zugestandenen Fällen bedarf der vorherigen schriftlichen Einwilligung des Verlages. Nähere Informationen zur vertraglich gestatteten Anzahl von Kopien finden Sie auf www.schulbuchkopie.de.

Für Verweise (Links) auf Internet-Adressen gilt folgender Haftungshinweis: Trotz sorgfältiger inhaltlicher Kontrolle wird die Haftung für die Inhalte der externen Seiten ausgeschlossen. Für den Inhalt dieser externen Seiten sind ausschließlich deren Betreiber verantwortlich. Sollten Sie daher auf kostenpflichtige, illegale oder anstößige Inhalte treffen, so bedauern wir dies ausdrücklich und bitten Sie, uns umgehend per E-Mail davon in Kenntnis zu setzen, damit beim Nachdruck der Verweis gelöscht wird.

Druck A^2 / Jahr 2021
Alle Drucke der Serie A sind im Unterricht parallel verwendbar.

Redaktion: Bettina Hammersen-Schiffner, Kerstin Klemm, Linda Knief, Lucas Mees,
 Dr. Heike Michaelis, Thorsten Schimming
Layout: LIO Design GmbH, Braunschweig
Illustrationen: Ulf Marckwort, Kassel
Umschlaggestaltung: LIO Design GmbH, Braunschweig
Druck und Bindung: Westermann Druck GmbH, Braunschweig

ISBN 978-3-14-**149220**-0

Welcome!

Herzlich willkommen in deinem neuen Englischbuch! Es soll dir beim Englischlernen helfen. Deshalb ist es wichtig, dass du dich gut darin zurechtfindest.

Beantworte die folgenden Fragen und lerne dein Buch kennen. Die Buchstaben ergeben einen Lösungssatz.

1 Das sind Gillian, George, Charlie, Caroline, Emma und Rajiv. Sie wohnen in einem Stadtteil von London. Er heißt Camden
   H Town.
   A Market.

2 Hinten im Buch gibt es einen roten Teil mit Übungen. Wie heißt er?
   E *Skills pages*
   A *Diff and train*

3 Bei vielen Aufgaben findest du kleine Hinweise, die dir beim Bearbeiten der Aufgabe helfen. Was bedeutet dieser Hinweis?
   ▶ Writing | p. 173
   V Auf Seite 173 finde ich Hilfen, um einen Text zu schreiben.
   S Auf Seite 173 finde ich Hilfen, um Vokabeln zu lernen.

4 Hilfen zur englischen Grammatik findest du im *Grammar*-Teil. Er befindet sich auf den Seiten
   E 180-197.
   P 166-179.

5 In den *Wordbanks* findest du viele Wörter und Redewendungen, die zu bestimmten Themen passen. Wo steht die *Wordbank* zum Thema „Essen und Trinken"?
   M Auf Seite 200
   F Auf Seite 203

6 In den Wortlisten ab Seite 206 kannst du die Wörter nachschlagen, die im Buch vorkommen. Die fett gedruckten Wörter in den Wortlisten
   T sind besonders selten.
   U solltest du dir merken.

7 Auf den Seiten 268/269 kannst du häufige Arbeitsanweisungen nachschlagen. *Choose the best answer* bedeutet
   A „Schreibe eine passende Antwort."
   N „Wähle die passendste Antwort aus."

8 In den *Reading tours* ...
   ! findest du spannendes Lesefutter.
   ? bekommst du englische Buchtipps.

Und jetzt kann es losgehen! Höre dir den *Camden Town Song* an und versuche, den Refrain mitzusingen. 🔊 L 1/1 | S 1

Viel Spaß beim Englischlernen!

Inhalt

		Lernziele	Kompetenzen
	Welcome to Camden Town!		
10		Einander begrüßen	sich vorstellen	Vorwissen sammeln	**Listening:** Geräusche zuordnen	einen Text verstehen
	Theme 1	**New in Camden**	
18	Intro: A new house	Räume und Gegenstände in einem Haus benennen	das eigene Zimmer beschreiben	**Listening:** einem Monolog folgen **Speaking:** das eigene Zuhause beschreiben	das eigene Zimmer beschreiben
20	Part A: Around Camden	Gefühle ausdrücken	Bilder beschreiben	über neue Erfahrungen sprechen	Camden kennenlernen **Target task:** Einen Handy-Chat vervollständigen 23	**Listening:** kurzen Dialogen folgen **Speaking:** Gefühle ausdrücken	Bilder beschreiben	einen Dialog laut lesen **Reading:** einen Dialog lesen
24	Target task tools	Unterstützendes Übungsangebot zur Erarbeitung der Target task	
26	Part B: At the corner shop	Über Freunde und Familie sprechen	Fragen stellen und beantworten **Target task:** Über Familien berichten 29	**Listening:** einem Dialog folgen **Speaking:** Fragen stellen und beantworten	andere nach ihren Familien befragen	Ergebnisse präsentieren	einen Dialog vortragen
30	Target task tools	Unterstützendes Übungsangebot zur Erarbeitung der Target task	
32	Photo tour	Around Camden: Fotomaterial und Informationen über den Londoner Stadtteil Camden Town	
34	I can	Selbsteinschätzung nach Abschluss des Kapitels	
	Theme 2	**At school**	
36	Intro: A new friend	Einen Comic vortragen	Zahlen anwenden	**Listening:** einem Telefongespräch zuhören **Speaking:** ein Zahlenspiel spielen
38	Part A: At William Ellis School	Den Schulalltag in Großbritannien kennenlernen	Fähigkeiten ausdrücken **Target task:** Verrückte Klassenregeln schreiben und präsentieren 41	**Listening:** einem Rap zuhören **Speaking:** einen Rap nachsprechen	Fähigkeiten ausdrücken	über Klassenregeln diskutieren	Ergebnisse präsentieren **Reading:** einen Dialog lesen
42	Target task tools	Unterstützendes Übungsangebot zur Erarbeitung der Target task	
44	Part B: At Camden School for Girls	Über den eigenen Schulalltag sprechen **Target task:** ein Poster über die eigene Schule erstellen und präsentieren 47	**Listening:** einem Monolog folgen	einem Dialog Informationen entnehmen **Speaking:** Besitzverhältnisse ausdrücken	über den eigenen Stundenplan sprechen	eine Mini-Präsentation halten
48	Target task tools	Unterstützendes Übungsangebot zur Erarbeitung der Target task	
50	Reading tour	Poems	
52	I can	Selbsteinschätzung nach Abschluss des Kapitels	

	Sprachliche Mittel
Speaking: ein Bild beschreiben	einen Dialog vorspielen	sich vorstellen **Reading:** einen Dialog lesen	Farben 11 • Buchstabieren 12 • Sich vorstellen 14 • Zahlen 14 • Zustimmen/ablehnen 15
Mediation: einer Textnachricht Informationen entnehmen DIFF **Writing:** Aussagen zu einem Bild verfassen **Media:** Medien benennen	**WORTSCHATZ:** *There is … / there are …* 18 • Räume 18 • Gegenstände 18/19 • Präpositionen 19 • Zustimmen/ablehnen 19 **STRUKTUREN:** Regelmäßiger Plural 18 • Artikel *a/an* 19
Viewing: einen Videoclip über Camden Town ansehen **Writing:** einen Handy-Chat vervollständigen	Fragen stellen und beantworten	Gefühle ausdrücken	**WORTSCHATZ:** Gefühle ausdrücken 20 • Stadt 22 • Positive Adjektive 22 **STRUKTUREN:** Personalpronomen und *to be* 21 • Fragen und Kurzantworten mit *to be* 23
Reading: einen Dialog lesen **Writing:** über die eigene Familie berichten **Media:** einen Dialog aufnehmen **CULTURE BOX** *Corner shops*	**WORTSCHATZ:** Familie 26, 28 • R: Präpositionen 27 **STRUKTUREN:** Fragen mit Fragewörtern und *to be* 27 • Possessivbegleiter 29
Reading: einen Comic lesen	**WORTSCHATZ:** Zahlen 37
Mediation: einem Schild Informationen entnehmen DIFF **Media:** einen Rap aufnehmen **Viewing:** einen Videoclip ansehen **Writing:** ein Poster erstellen **CULTURE BOX** Schulalltag in Großbritannien	**WORTSCHATZ:** R: *There is … / there are …* 38 • Schulsachen 38 • R: Präpositionen 38 • Charaktereigenschaften 39 • Classroom phrases 39 • Classroom rules 40 **STRUKTUREN:** Imperativ 40 • *Can/can't* 41
Reading: einen Dialog lesen **Writing:** einen Speiseplan erstellen	über die eigene Schule schreiben	**WORTSCHATZ:** Räume in der Schule 44 • Schulfächer 45 • Lebensmittel 46 • Vorlieben und Abneigungen 47 **STRUKTUREN:** *Have got/has got* 45

Inhalt

		Lernziele	Kompetenzen
	Theme 3	**Hobbies and activities**	
54	Intro: Free time	Über Hobbys sprechen	**Viewing:** einen Videoclip ansehen **Speaking:** die Uhrzeit nennen | das eigene Hobby vorstellen
56	Part A: The bake-off	Über Haushaltstätigkeiten sprechen | Fragen stellen und beantworten **Target task:** eine Geschichte zu Ende schreiben **61**	**Listening:** einem Dialog folgen | einen *chant* hören | einen Monolog verstehen **Speaking:** über Haushaltstätigkeiten sprechen | Fragen stellen und beantworten | Feedback geben | eine eigene Geschichte vorlesen
60	Target task tools	*Unterstützendes Übungsangebot zur Erarbeitung der Target task*	
62	Part B: The talent show	Fragen stellen und beantworten | Gefühle ausdrücken **Target task:** ein Interview vorbereiten und führen **65**	**Listening:** einem Dialog folgen **Speaking:** Fragen stellen und beantworten | Gefühle ausdrücken | ein Interview führen | Feedback geben **Mediation:** Fragen beantworten
66	Target task tools	*Unterstützendes Übungsangebot zur Erarbeitung der Target task*	
68	Photo tour	*Hobbies: Fotomaterial und Informationen über Hobbys britischer Schülerinnen und Schüler*	
70	I can	*Selbsteinschätzung nach Abschluss des Kapitels*	
	Theme 4	**Birthdays**	
72	Intro: Birthday plans	Über den eigenen Geburtstag sprechen	**Listening:** einen Song hören | einem Dialog folgen **Speaking:** über den eigenen Geburtstag sprechen | über eine ideale Geburtstagsparty sprechen
74	Part A: Saturday afternoon	Ausdrücken, was jemand gerade tut **Target task:** ein Telefongespräch vorspielen **77**	**Listening:** einem Telefongespräch folgen **Reading:** eine Geschichte lesen | einen Dialog lesen
78	Target task tools	*Unterstützendes Übungsangebot zur Erarbeitung der Target task*	
80	Part B: The party	Einen Einkaufsdialog führen | eine längere Geschichte lesen **Target task:** eine Geschichte zu Ende schreiben **83**	**Listening:** einem Dialog folgen **Speaking:** einen Einkaufsdialog führen | Ideen sammeln **Mediation:** Informationen entnehmen **DIFF** **Viewing:** einen Videoclip ansehen
84	Target task tools	*Unterstützendes Übungsangebot zur Erarbeitung der Target task*	
86	Reading tour	*Horrid Henry's Birthday Party*	
88	I can	*Selbsteinschätzung nach Abschluss des Kapitels*	

Die Inhalte von Camden Town stellen ein Angebot dar. Die Auswahl der Aufgaben und Übungsteile richtet sich nach dem Lehrplan des jeweiligen Bundeslandes bzw. den Schwerpunkten des schulinternen Curriculums.

Verweise

▶ **DIFF** Training D16 | p. 144	Verweis auf differenzierendes Zusatzangebot
▶ Wordbank 2 | p. 199	Verweis auf eine *Wordbank*
▶ Listening | p. 166	Verweis auf eine *Skills page*
▶ G 16 | p. 192	Verweis auf den Grammatikanhang
🔊 L 1/1, S 1	Verweis auf einen Audio-Track: Track 1 auf der Lehrer-CD 1 bzw. Schüler-Audio-Track 1
	▶ WES-149220-1
▶ WB 5	Verweis auf eine Übung im *Workbook*
▶ WES-149220-2	Verweis auf Online-Materialien

	Sprachliche Mittel
Mediation: Fragen beantworten **Media:** ein Online-Wörterbuch verwenden **Reading:** Kalendereinträge verstehen	**WORTSCHATZ:** Hobbys 54 • Uhrzeit 54 • Wochentage 54
Reading: einem Dialog Informationen entnehmen | eine Geschichte lesen **Writing:** eine Geschichte fortführen	**WORTSCHATZ:** Haushaltstätigkeiten 57 • Hobbys 58 **STRUKTUREN:** *Simple present:* Aussagesätze 57 • Häufigkeitsadverbien 57 • *Simple present:* Fragen und Kurzantworten 58
Reading: einem Poster Informationen entnehmen | einen Dialog lesen | einen Comic lesen | eine Geschichte verstehen **Writing:** Fragen und Antworten notieren	**WORTSCHATZ:** Zustimmen/ablehnen 62 • Gefühle 64 • Vorschläge machen 62 **STRUKTUREN:** R: *Simple present:* Fragen und Kurzantworten 62 • *Simple present:* Fragen mit Fragewörtern 63
Media: ein Online-Wörterbuch verwenden **Reading:** Internetseiten Informationen entnehmen	**WORTSCHATZ:** Datum 72 • Monate 72 • Jahreszeiten 72
Speaking: ein Spiel spielen | Bilder beschreiben | ein Telefongespräch vorspielen **Media:** über Mediennutzung sprechen	**WORTSCHATZ:** Charaktereigenschaften 75 • Telefongespräch 76 • Vorschläge machen 76 • Zustimmen/ablehnen 76 **STRUKTUREN:** *Present progressive* 75 • *Simple present vs. present progressive* 76
Reading: einen Dialog lesen | eine längere Geschichte lesen **Writing:** ein Bilderwörterbuch erstellen | eine Geschichte mit Hilfe von Bildern fortführen **CULTURE BOX** Britisches Geld	**WORTSCHATZ:** Einkaufen 80 • Kleidung 81 • Konjunktionen 83 **STRUKTUREN:** S*ome/any* 81

Symbole

- Diese Aufgabe vermittelt Medienkompetenz.
- ( ) Diese Aufgabe trainiert Sprachmittlung.
- Videoclip auf der DVD für Lehrkräfte
- Partnerarbeit
- Gruppenarbeit

- **A4** Aufgabe A4 ist obligatorisch.
- **A6** Aufgabe A6 ist obligatorisch und dient der Vorbereitung der *Target task* in Part A.
- **A10** Aufgabe A10 ist fakultativ.
- b) Teilaufgabe b) ist fakultativ.

Inhalt

		Lernziele	Kompetenzen
	Theme 5	**Pets and animals**	
90	Intro: Animals	Tiere beschreiben	**Listening:** Tiere identifizieren **Speaking:** ein Spiel spielen | Vorlieben äußern
92	Part A: A new home?	Ratschläge geben | Vorschläge machen | Gefühle ausdrücken **Target task:** einen Dialog fortführen und vorspielen **95**	**Listening:** einem Monolog folgen | einen Dialog anhören **Speaking:** Vermutungen anstellen | Gefühle ausdrücken | einen Dialog vorspielen | Feedback geben **Mediation:** Informationen entnehmen DIFF
96	Target task tools	Unterstützendes Übungsangebot zur Erarbeitung der Target task	
98	Part B: Help the animals	Charaktereigenschaften und Bedürfnisse beschreiben **Target task:** eine Fernsehshow vorspielen **101**	**Listening:** ein Telefongespräch anhören | einem Dialog folgen **Viewing:** einen Videoclip ansehen **Speaking:** Zustimmung/Ablehnung äußern | Präferenzen angeben | eine Fernsehshow vorspielen **Writing:** ein Tier beschreiben
102	Target task tools	Unterstützendes Übungsangebot zur Erarbeitung der Target task	
104	Photo tour	Animals in London: Fotomaterial und Informationen über Tiere in London	
106	I can	Selbsteinschätzung nach Abschluss des Kapitels	
	Theme 6	**Holidays in Britain** OPTIONAL	
108	Intro: Magical Britain	Orte in Großbritannien kennenlernen	**Listening:** einen Dialog anhören **Viewing:** einen Videoclip ansehen
110	Part A: Manchester	Einen Eindruck von Manchester gewinnen **Target task:** einen Flyer erstellen **113**	**Listening:** einem Dialog folgen **Speaking:** ein Bild beschreiben | Gefühle ausdrücken | Präferenzen ausdrücken | einen eigenen Flyer präsentieren
114	Target task tools	Unterstützendes Übungsangebot zur Erarbeitung der Target task	
116	Part B: On the canal	Landeskundliche Informationen über verschiedene Orte gewinnen **Target task:** eine Geschichte schreiben / einen Comic erstellen **120**	**Listening:** einem Dialog folgen **Speaking:** Vorlieben ausdrücken | Feedback geben **Reading:** eine Landkarte erfassen | einen Comic lesen | eine Geschichte lesen
121	Target task tools	Unterstützendes Übungsangebot zur Erarbeitung der Target task	
122	Reading tour	Robin Hood	
124	I can	Selbsteinschätzung nach Abschluss des Kapitels	
	Anhang		
125	Diff and train	*Differenzierungs- und Trainingsanhang* Theme 1 **125** | Theme 2 **133** | Theme 3 **140** | Theme 4 **147** | Theme 5 **155** | Theme 6 **162**	
166	Skills pages	Listening **166** | Reading **167** | Understanding new words **168** | Talking to people **169** | Giving a mini-presentation **170** | Making a page on a computer or tablet **172** | Writing **173** | Memorizing vocabulary **175** | Mediation **177** | Working with others **178** | Writing a grammar card **179**	
180	Grammar	*Erläuterung der grammatikalischen Strukturen*	
198	Wordbanks	1 School **198** | 2 People **199** | 3 Time **200** | 4 At home **201** | 5 Things and places **202** | 6 Clothes **202** | 7 Food and drink **203** | 8 Animals **204** | 9 Hobbies and free time **205**	

Sprachliche Mittel

Reading: Broschüren Informationen entnehmen

WORTSCHATZ: Tiere 90 • Körperteile 90 • Fähigkeiten 90
STRUKTUREN: R: *Simple present:* Fragen und Kurzantworten 91

Reading: einen Dialog lesen | einem Flyer Informationen entnehmen | eine Rollenkarte lesen
Writing: einen Flyer erstellen | einen Dialog schreiben

WORTSCHATZ: Ratschläge 93 • Vorschläge 93 • Gefühle 94
STRUKTUREN: Modalverben 93

Mediation: Informationen entnehmen DIFF
Media: einen Videoclip erstellen
Reading: einer Internetseite Informationen entnehmen | einen Dialog lesen

WORTSCHATZ: Zustimmen/ablehnen 98 • *This/that* 99 • *These/those* 99 • Charaktereigenschaften 100 • Lebensmittel 100
STRUKTUREN: Satzstellung 99

Speaking: Vorlieben angeben
Reading: eine Karte und Sachtexte lesen

WORTSCHATZ: Aktivitäten 108 • Vorlieben 108

Reading: eine Geschichte lesen | Broschüren Informationen entnehmen
Media: ein Computerprogramm verwenden
Writing: einen Sachtext verfassen
CULTURE BOX Manchester

WORTSCHATZ: Gefühle 111 • Werbesprache 112
STRUKTUREN: R: *Simple present:* Fragen mit Fragewörtern 111

Writing: ein Bild erstellen und beschriften | eine Geschichte planen und schreiben | einen Comic planen und erstellen

WORTSCHATZ: Vorlieben 116
STRUKTUREN: R: *Simple present:* Fragen mit Fragewörtern 116 • R: Fragen mit *to be* 117 • R: *Present progressive* 117

206	Word lists	Wortlisten zu den Kapiteln
238	English-German dictionary	Wörterbuch Englisch-Deutsch
257	German-English dictionary	Wörterbuch Deutsch-Englisch
263	Names	Eigennamen
265	The English alphabet / English sounds	Alphabet und Lautschrift

266	Numbers	Kardinal- und Ordinalzahlen
267	Ähnliche Wörter	Ähnliche Wörter im Englischen und Deutschen
268	Class instructions	Arbeitsanweisungen
270	Quellenverzeichnis	

Welcome to Camden Town!

1 What can you see? ▶ WB 1 | p. 3 — A car. / I can see …

2 What can you hear? 🔊 L 1/2 — I can hear cars. / I can hear …

3 Where is …?
👥 Work with a partner. Find the children.

Where is Charlie? / Charlie is in the road. / Where is …?

Charlie Batson · Emma Butler · Caroline McBride · George McBride · Gillian Collins · Rajiv Khan

in the road · in a car · in his room · in front of a shop

10   ten

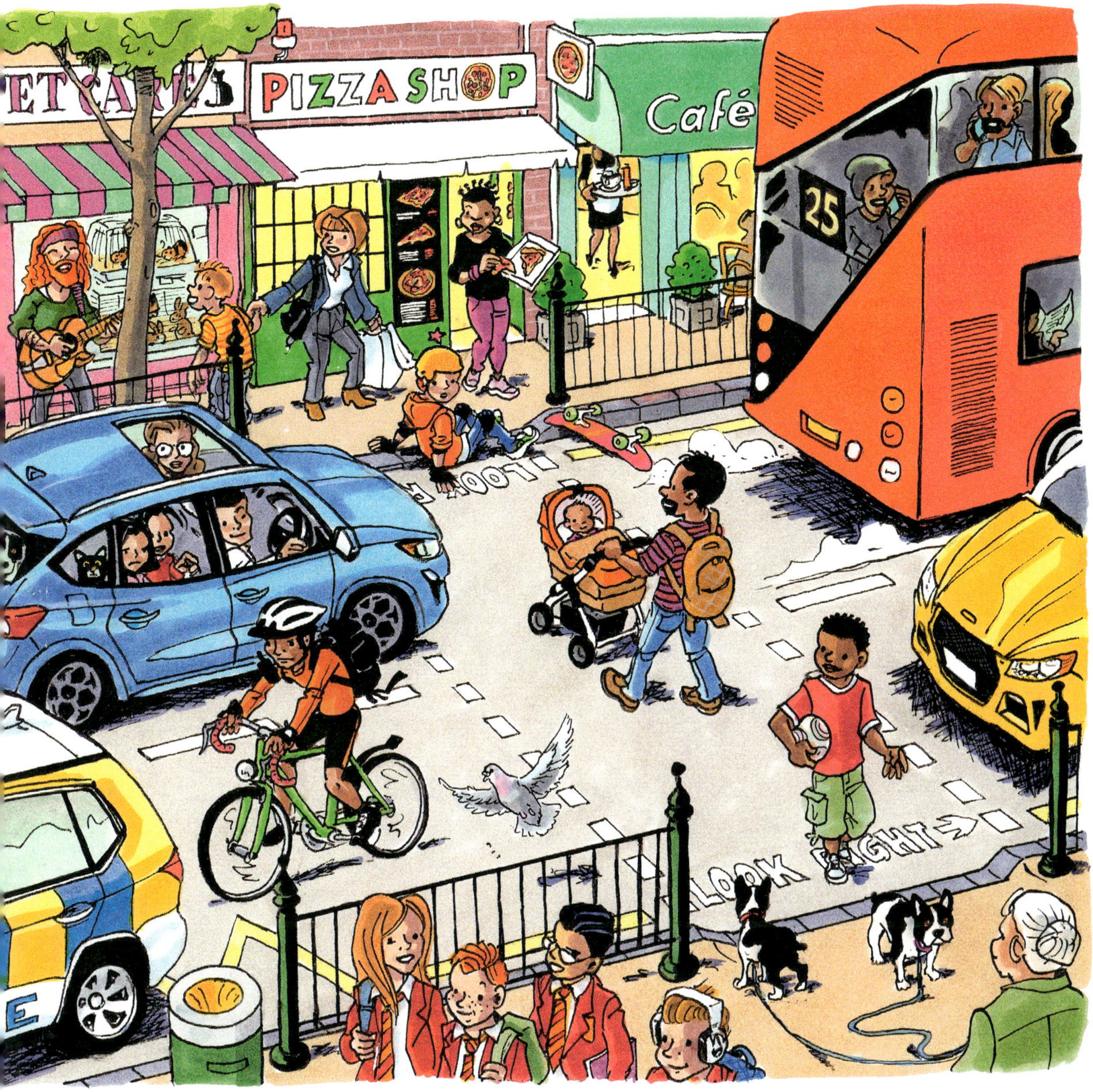

4 Colours ▶ WB 2, 3 | pp. 3, 4

Work with a partner. Play "I spy with my little eye ..."

I spy with my little eye something **red**.

The bus?

Yes.

I spy with my little eye something **green**.

orange | yellow | green | blue | grey | black | white | brown | pink | purple | red

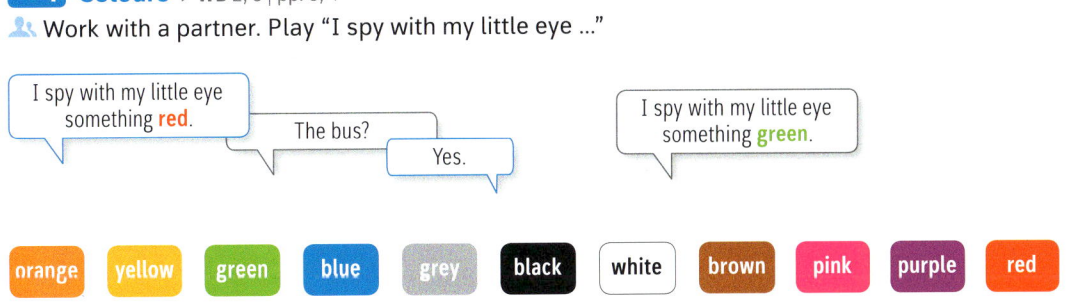

Welcome to Camden Town!

5 The song of the ABC 🔊 L 1/3

Listen to the song and sing along.

The song of the ABC

Come on children, sing it out.
Come on children, sing it loud.
Come on children, sing with me.
This is the song of the ABC.

5 A B C D – E F and a G,
H I J K – oh, so far[1] it is OK.
L M N O P – Q R S and T,
U V W – X Y Z.
That's the alphabet.

10 Hey everybody, sing once more[2].
Sing it as we've done before[3].
Come on, everybody now, don't forget[4]
this rock song of the alphabet.

---

1 so far – *bisher* | **2** once more – *noch einmal* |
3 as we've done before – *wie wir es vorher gemacht haben* | **4** don't forget – *vergesst nicht*

6 Spell your name 🔊 L 1/4

ⓐ) Listen to the CD. Write down the names.
ⓑ) 👥 Work with a partner. Spell your name.
▶ WB 4 | p. 4

7 Play 'hangman'
Play 'hangman'.

My name is **Martin**:
M-A-R-T-I-N

My name is …
What's your last name?

My last name is **Mertens**:
M-E-R-T-E-N-S

My last name is
…

Is there an 'a' in your word?

12 twelve

Welcome to Camden Town!

8 On Albert Street 🔊 L 1/5 | S 2

a) Gillian, Emma, Caroline and George are on Albert Street. Listen and read.

b) 👥 Work in groups (4). ▶ WB 5 | p. 4
- Choose Gillian, Emma, Caroline or George.
- Read the dialogue.
- Learn "your" sentences.
- Act out the dialogue.

thirteen 13

Welcome to Camden Town!

9 "Hi, my name is ..." ▶ WB 6, 7 | p. 5

Talk to a partner like this.

Hi, my name is **Anna**. What's your name?

I'm from **Wuppertal**, too. How old are you?

I'm **twelve**.

My favourite ... is ... What's your favourite ...?

I'm **Jonas**. I'm from **Wuppertal**.

I'm **eleven**. What about you?

What's your favourite **colour/song/film/...**?

10 Number rap L 1/6, 7 | S 3, 4 ▶ WB 8, 9 | pp. 5, 6

Listen to the song and sing along.

NUMBER RAP

One – two – three,
this is fun, do you agree?

Four – five – six and seven,
a rap in English, I'm in heaven!

It's time for eight and then for nine,
up till now we're doing fine!

Next is ten, yes ten is next.
We are the champions,
we are the best!

Now what about eleven?
That's two and two and seven.

Hey, twelve at last
and we're rapping, rapping,
rapping, rapping very fast!

Twelve – eleven – ten – nine – eight.
We like to rap with Camden Town – great!

Seven – six – five – four – three – two – one.
Let's start again! This rap is fun.

Welcome to Camden Town!

11 Emma, Caroline and George

a) Listen to Emma, Caroline and George. 🔊 L 1/8 | S 5

b) Read the dialogue.

Emma: Is that your cat, Caroline?
Caroline: Yes, her name is Socks.
Emma: Hello, Socks. You are sweet.
Caroline: And clever. Socks can do tricks.
5 **George:** Ha! Dogs are much better. My dog Patch can play football. Cats can't play football.
Caroline: Oh, you and your football! What's your hobby, Emma?
Emma: Skateboarding.
10 **Caroline:** Oh, great! It's my hobby, too.
Emma: There's a skateboarding club at my school.
Caroline: What's the name of your school?
Emma: I'm at Camden School for Girls.
Caroline: Cool, that's my school, too. We can go
15 to school together.
George: I'm at William Ellis. William Ellis is a school for boys with a great football team.
Caroline: Oh, George!
Emma: My brother is at William Ellis, too. Jack
20 is 16.
George: Is he a football fan?
Emma: Yes. He's an Arsenal fan.
George: Oh no!

c) Read the statements. Are the statements right or wrong?
Example: *Patch is Caroline's cat. — That's wrong.*

1 George's dog can play football.
2 Emma and Caroline's hobby is in-line skating.
3 Caroline is at Camden School for Girls.
4 Jack is at William Ellis School.
5 Jack and George are Arsenal fans.

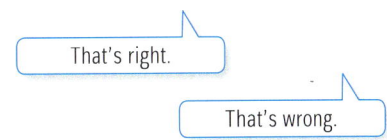

d) Work in groups (3). Read the dialogue out loud. ▶ WB 10, 11 | p. 6

fifteen 15

Welcome to Camden Town!

12 A house in Manchester 🔊 L 1/9

a) Listen to Caroline and look at the pictures of three houses in Manchester. Choose the picture of Caroline's old house.

1

2

3

b) Listen again. Choose the right answers.

1 Caroline's old house is …
   a) big.
   b) small.
   c) boring.

2 The houses in Caroline's old street in Manchester are …
   a) yellow or white.
   b) yellow or red.
   c) red or white.

3 The cats in the street like …
   a) the garden.
   b) the bushes.
   c) the trees.

4 The old blue car is …
   a) in London.
   b) in Dover.
   c) in Manchester.

16   sixteen

1

New in Camden

In diesem *Theme* wirst du ...

- den Stadtteil Camden Town kennenlernen
- dein Zimmer beschreiben
- ausdrücken, wo sich etwas befindet
- über Gefühle sprechen
- lernen, Fragen zu stellen
- einen Chat vervollständigen
- über deine Familie schreiben

1 A new house   Intro

1 A new house ▶ DIFF Support D1, D2, Training D3 | p. 125

Look at the picture. Say what you can see.

- There's a lamp.
- There are doors.
- There's a …
- There are …

one book → two book**s**
one room → two room**s**
▶ G1 | p. 181

2 Listen to George L 1/10 | S 6 ▶ Listening | p. 166

George makes a video for his friends in Manchester.

a) Listen to George. Point at the rooms.
b) Listen again. Finish the sentences.
▶ DIFF Easy alternative D4 | p. 125
  1. Dad's favourite room is the …
  2. The TV is in the …
  3. Mum is in the …
  4. Upstairs, there are the bedrooms and the …
  5. George's room is …

▶ DIFF Training D5-D7 | pp. 125-126   ▶ WB 1 | p. 7

c) Tell a partner about your house/flat.
- There's a kitchen downstairs.
- There are two bedrooms.

d) Look at the picture again. How many examples of media can you find? ▶ DIFF Extra D8 | p. 126
▶ WES-149220-2

book • computer • magazine • newspaper • radio • tablet • TV • phone • poster • laptop

Intro 1

3 Help Caroline

Caroline can't find her things.
Can you help her?

▶ **DIFF** Support D9 | p. 126   ▶ **WB** 2 | p. 7

> The phone is under the bed.

> The … is …

> The shoes are …

in • on • under • between • next to • behind • in front of

> Oh no! I can't find my phone … pencil case … shoes … school bag … laptop … yellow elephant … Manchester T-shirt …

Labels: shelf, books, bed, T-shirt, wardrobe, phone, shoes, school bag, pencils, chair, elephant, desk, pencil case, laptop

4 A quiz for your partner   ▶ WB 3, 4, 22 | pp. 8, 15

a) Write five sentences about Caroline's room. They can be right or wrong.
   Example: *There is a pink school bag on the desk.*
            There are pencils …

▶ **DIFF** Training D10–D12 | pp. 126–127

b) Close your books. Read out your sentences to your partner. Right or wrong?

> There are books on the shelf.

> There is an elephant under the bed.

> There are …

> That's wrong.

> That's right.

a book
an elephant
▶ G2 | p. 182

5 Choose Your room   ▶ Wordbank 4 | p. 201   ▶ WB 5 | p. 9

a) Draw your room and write six sentences about it. **OR**
b) Tell your partner about your room. He/She draws your room.

nineteen 19

1 Around Camden   Part A

A1 In a new city ▶ WB 6 | p. 9

Imagine you live in a new city. Say how you feel.
Example: *I'm happy because my new school is cool.*

I'm happy		my friends are not here.
I'm sad		my new room is great.
I'm excited	because	so many things are new.
I'm worried		my new school is so big.
I'm lonely		my new school is cool.
		…

A2 Emma and Caroline 🔊 L 1/11 | S 7 ▶ Listening | p. 166

a) Write one word on a piece of paper: *happy, sad, excited, worried* or *lonely*. Close your book and listen to Emma and Caroline. When you hear your word, stand up and show it.

b) 👥 Read the dialogue out loud with your partner.

▶ **DIFF** Training D13, D14 | p. 127

Emma: Hi Caroline!
Caroline: Oh, hi Emma …
Emma: Caroline, are you OK?
Caroline: Well, I'm a bit sad.
5   Grandma and Grandpa are in Manchester. And my friend Sophie. We're best friends. And now she's in
10 Manchester and I'm here. Mum and Dad aren't at home. They're very busy. Well … I'm a bit lonely. It isn't easy.
15 **Emma:** What about your brother?

Caroline: Oh, George! He isn't sad. He's happy. A house in London! A garden! George is excited. But I'm not really happy.
Emma: Well, so many things are new for you. A new home, a new 20 school, new friends …
Caroline: Yeah, and I'm a bit worried about school. And Camden … 25
Emma: What's wrong with Camden? It's a fantastic place! Hey, I can show you Camden … Let's play a game!
Caroline: A game? 30
Emma: Yes, a game with photos of Camden! Can I call you back in ten minutes?

c) Read the dialogue again. Say eight things about the people. ▶ Reading | p. 167 ▶ WB 7 | p. 9
Example: *George is happy. Mr and Mrs McBride are …*

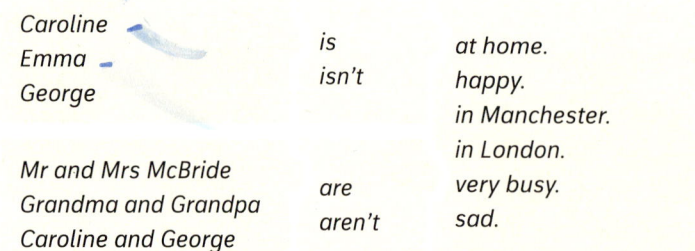

20   twenty

Part A 1

A3 Grammar card Personal pronouns and *to be*

Write a grammar card for personal pronouns and *to be*.
1 Copy the grid.
  Find the missing short forms of *to be* in
  Emma and Caroline's dialogue on page 20.
2 Complete the grid.
3 Read G3 on page 182. Add examples of
  negative sentences to your grammar card.
  ▶ G3, G4 | p. 182, 183   ▶ Grammar card | p. 179   ▶ WB 8 | p. 10

to be	long forms	short forms
singular	I am	I'XXX
	you are	you're
	he is	he'XXX
	she is	she'XXX
	it is	it'XXX
plural	we are	we'XXX
	you are	you're
	they are	they'XXX

A4 Personal pronouns   ▶DIFF Training D15 | p. 127, Extra D16 | p. 128   ▶ WB 9, 10 | p. 10

Read the sentences and choose the right word.
1 Caroline: "**I** / **She** am from Manchester."
2 Caroline is a twin. **He** / **She** is eleven.
3 The new house is on Albert Street. **It** / **She** is big.
4 Caroline: "Emma, **you** / **she** are my new friend!"
5 George is a boy. **He** / **It** is a football fan.
6 George: "Hi Emma and Jack! **They** / **You** are nice!"
7 The McBrides are from Manchester. **We** / **They** are in London now.
8 The McBrides say: "**They** / **We** love the new house!"

A5 George and Caroline   ▶DIFF Training D17 | p. 128   ▶ WB 11 | p. 10

Read the comic. Choose the right short forms from your grammar card (A3) and
write the sentences down.

What's up?
Nothing. I **1** a bit sad.

Why?
Because of Sophie. She **2** in Manchester. And Mum and Dad? They **3** busy.

Yes, that's right. And Mum – she **4** very excited about her new job.
I know. But it **5** easy for me.

But it **6** so cool here! And my new room is super!
Yeah. I love my room, too.

And what about Emma? She **7** nice.
Yes, she is. Oh, that's Emma!

Can I come, too?

1 Part A

A6 Emma's game

a) Emma sends photos of Camden to Caroline. Look at the photos and say what you can see.

> I can see …

> There's … / There are …

café • canal • shop • sign • underground station

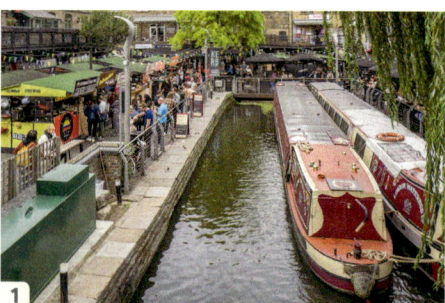

b) Listen to Caroline and George. There are four short dialogues. After each dialogue,
- say where Caroline and George go and
- find the right photo. 🔊 L 1/12 ▶ Listening | p. 166 ▶ WB 12 | p. 11

> They go to the underground station. That's photo number 2.

c) Read the dialogue. Find the English sentences for: 🔊 L 1/13 | S 8 ▶ Reading | p. 167

Mir geht es gut. • Ich hasse Einkaufen! • Halt den Mund! • Meinst du das ernst? • Du bist die Beste!

Caroline: OK, here is the café. But where is Emma? Is she in the café?
George: No, she isn't – look, she's there! Hi Emma!
5 **Emma:** Hi!
Caroline: Emma, you are the best! There are so many great places here in Camden!
George: Yes, the shoe shop is so cool.
Emma: Are you serious? Are you mad about
10   shopping, George?
George: No, I'm not! I hate shopping! But the shoe shop is amazing.

Caroline: I love the canal. It's my favourite place. And the shops are great. There's a really nice little shop on Inverness Street.
15 **Emma:** Oh yes, I know! It's fantastic!
George: Girls, YOU are mad about shopping!
Caroline: No, we aren't. Shut up, George!
Emma: Are you hungry?
Caroline: Yes, I am! Your ice cream looks good.
20   Is it chocolate?
Emma: Yes, it is. Let's get ice cream for you, too. Caroline, are you still sad?
Caroline: No, I'm not. I'm fine. Camden is cool!

d) Collect adjectives from the dialogue and note them down in a list. Example: *great, …* Keep your list for later. ▶ Vocabulary | p. 175

22   twenty-two

Part A 1

A7 Choose the right answers
Look at the photos and the dialogue on page 22. Choose the right answers.
1 Is the underground station red? — Yes, it is. / No, it isn't.
2 Are the shoes in photo number 4 yellow? — Yes, they are. / No, they aren't.
3 Is George in the shoe shop? — Yes, he is. / No, he isn't.
4 Is Emma on a boat? — Yes, she is. / No, she isn't.
5 Are the twins sad? — Yes, they are. / No, they aren't.

A8 Grammar card — Questions and short answers with *to be* ▶ DIFF Training D18 | p. 128
Write a grammar card for questions with *to be* and short answers.
1 Look at this question and this answer from the dialogue on page 22: *Are you hungry? — Yes, I am!*
  Find the answers to the following questions from the dialogue:
  a. *Is she in the café?*   b. *Are you still sad?*
2 Read G5 on page 183/184. On your grammar card, copy the grid with questions and short answers. Write down the rules for questions with *to be* and short answers.
3 Add three questions with *to be* and short answers to your grammar card.
▶ G5 | p. 183 ▶ Grammar card | p. 179 ▶ WB 13 | p. 11

A9 Questions ▶ DIFF Training D19 | p. 129
👤 Write down five questions with *is* or *are*.
Then ask your partner.
▶ DIFF Training D19–D21 | pp. 129–130, Extra D22 | p. 130

	you	good at football?
Are	your friends	eleven?
Is	your sister	at your new school?
	...	...

Is your sister eleven?
Yes, she is. / No, she isn't.

A10 Your favourite place
a) Watch the video about Camden. What is your favourite place?
▶ WB Media 5

b) 👤 Tell your partner in German what you can see and buy at Camden Market.

A11 Target task — Complete the chat
This is Caroline's chat with her old friend Sophie in Manchester.

1 Read Sophie's questions.
2 What can Caroline answer?
   Write 1 or 2 sentences for each answer.
   You can use …
   • the adjectives for feelings from A1,
   • the adjectives from exercise A6d).
3 You can add one question from Sophie and answer it.
▶ Wordbank 2 | p. 199 ▶ WB 14 | p. 12

1 Hi Caroline! How are you? — Hi Sophie! I'm …
2 We miss you! 😢 What about George? Is he sad? — No, George is …
3 What about your new room? — …
4 Please send photos! Is Camden a cool place? — …
5 What is your favourite place in Camden? — …
6 That's great! I miss you! BFF! Bye! — …

💡 **Media**
In Textnachrichten werden häufig Abkürzungen verwendet (z. B. BFF = best friends forever).

Need help? Look at pages 24/25: T1 T2 T3 T4 T5 T6 T7

twenty-three 23

Part A: Target task tools

Target task tools for A 11: Complete the chat

T1 Grammar: Personal pronouns ▶ G4 | p. 183

Copy the grid. Sort the words into the grid.

he	she	it	they
…	…	a fish	…
…	…	…	…

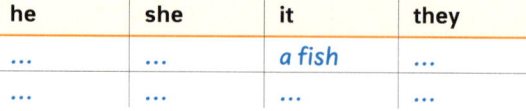

1 a fish
2 Grandpa Butler
3 Mrs Smith
4 Grandma Miller and Rob
5 James
6 an ice cream
7 Tim and Ben
8 Louise
9 Mrs Rice
10 Harry Wells
11 David and Hoover
12 a football

T2 Grammar: Short forms and long forms of *to be* ▶ G3 | p. 182

a) Find the long forms and write them down.

1 it's
2 they're
3 he's
4 we're
5 I'm
6 she's
7 you're

b) Choose five long forms and write sentences.
Example: *I am from Braunschweig. …*

T3 Grammar: Sentences with *to be* ▶ G3 | p. 182

Right or wrong? Correct the wrong sentences.
Example: George is sad. → *George isn't sad. Caroline is sad.*

1 George and Sophie are friends.
2 Caroline and Jack are twins.
3 Emma is lonely.
4 Mr and Mrs McBride are very busy.
5 Sophie is in London.
6 George is a Tottenham fan.
7 Patch is a cat.

Part A: Target task tools

T4 Words: Phrases (1)

Match the German and the English sentences.

1. Wie geht es dir?
2. Es ist nicht einfach.
3. Emma geht es gut.
4. Ich liebe mein neues Zimmer!
5. Emma ist nett.

A It isn't easy.
B Emma is fine.
C I love my new room!
D Emma is nice.
E How are you?

T5 Grammar: Short answers with *to be* ▶ G5 | p. 183

a) Here are questions for Caroline from her friends in Manchester.
What are Caroline's answers? Use short answers.
Example: Are you OK in London? → *Yes, I am.*

1. Is Emma your new best friend?
2. Is George at the same school?
3. Are Patch and Socks with you?
4. Is your grandma in London, too?
5. Are the shops in Camden cool?

b) There is a new pupil in your class. Write down five questions for the new pupil with *is* or *are*.
Example: *Are you new here?*

T6 Words: Phrases (2)

George and Jack are in Albert Street. Read the dialogue. Add phrases from the box.

That's perfect. • *It's great.* • *I'm fine.* • *I love it!* • *It's not bad.* • *What about* • *My favourite place is*

Jack: Hi, George. How are you?
George: 1
Jack: Is the new house OK?
George: Yes, it is. 2
Jack: 3 your new room?
George: It's great. 4
Jack: What about Camden?
George: Camden is so cool! 5 Camden High Street.

Jack: Are you at William Ellis School, too?
George: Yes, I am. Is it a good school?
Jack: Yes, it is. 6
George: A school is a school. Homework and tests.
Jack: But no girls.
George: 7 No school with my sister!

T7 Media: Text messages

Match the words with the emojis.

thanks • *happy* • *OK* • *love* • *cool* • *sad* • *oh no!* • *I don't like it*

1 At the corner shop — Part B

B1 At the shop

a) Look at the pictures. Where are the children? Where is Patch?

b) Listen to the dialogue. What is the problem?
🔊 L 1/14 | S 9 ▶ DIFF Easy alternative D23 | p. 131
▶ Listening | p. 166

c) Read the dialogue and finish the sentences.
▶ DIFF Easy alternative D24, Training D25 | p. 131
▶ Reading | p. 167   ▶ WB 15 | p. 12

1 Rajiv is …
2 Sheree is …
3 There is a noise behind …
4 There is a mouse on …

Mrs Khan: Hello! Can I help you?
George: Yes, please. We'd like some white chocolate.
Mrs Khan: Hm … Where is the white chocolate?
5   Ah, yes … Are you new in Camden?
George: Yes, we are. I'm George, and this is my twin sister Caroline.
Mrs Khan: Ah, twins! That's nice. How old are you?
10 **Caroline:** We're eleven.
Mrs Khan: My son, Rajiv, is eleven, too. My daughter Sheree is 18. Where are you from?
George: We're from Manchester. It's a cool place. And …
15 **Caroline:** Oh! There's a funny noise. What is it?
Mrs Khan: A funny noise?
Caroline: It's behind the newspapers!
George: It's a little mouse!
Caroline: A mouse! Where is it now?
20 **George:** It's on the shelf.
Mrs Khan: Oh, no! Why is there a mouse in my shop?

George: Patch can help!
Mrs Khan: Who is Patch?
25 **George:** He's my dog. Patch can find the mouse! He's in front of the shop.
Caroline: Can my brother bring Patch in?
Mrs Khan: Yes, please. A mouse in the shop isn't good!

Corner shops — Culture box

Ein *corner shop* ist ein kleiner Laden, in dem man fast alles für den täglichen Bedarf kaufen kann, z. B. Lebensmittel, Zeitungen, Süßigkeiten. Viele dieser Läden haben sehr lange Öffnungszeiten. „Corner shop" bedeutet eigentlich „Eckladen", dabei befinden sich viele dieser Läden gar nicht an einer Straßenecke.

Wo kauft ihr ein, wenn ihr schnell etwas braucht?

Part B 1

B2 Dramatic reading ▶ Dramatic reading | p. 178

1 Group work (3): Choose a person each (Mrs Khan, George or Caroline). Look at your person's sentences. Think about your person's feelings when he/she speaks.
2 Practise your part. Example: Be excited when your person is excited. You can record your sentences and hear how you sound.
3 Read the dialogue together.

> **Media**
> Wenn du dich aufnimmst, sprich langsam und deutlich.
> ▶ WB Media 3
> ▶ WES-149220-2

B3 Where's the mouse?

Work with a partner. Look at the pictures.
Where is the mouse now? Where is Patch now?
Ask and answer questions. Take turns.

▶ DIFF Extra D26 | p. 131

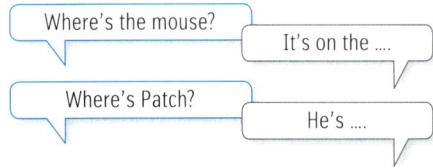

Where's the mouse? — It's on the ….
Where's Patch? — He's ….

1

2

3

4

B4 Grammar card Questions with question words and *to be*

Look at the dialogue on page 26 again.
Find questions with *what, where, how, who* and *why* in the text.
Example: *Where is the white chocolate?*
Check G6 on page 184. Find out how to form questions.
Write a grammar card.

▶ G6 | p. 184   ▶ Grammar card | p. 179   ▶ WB 16 | p. 13

> who = wer
> where = wo

B5 What are the questions?   ▶ DIFF Training D27 | p. 131   ▶ WB 17 | p. 13

a) Look at the answers. What are the questions?

What is …? — My favourite book is *Harry Potter*.
…? — My best friend is Karl.
…? — My house is in Birkenweg.
…? — I'm eleven.

b) Work with a partner. Ask and answer the questions from a). Take turns.

B6 Ask three classmates

Ask three classmates about their families, houses/flats and rooms.
• What is …?   • Who is …?   • Where is …?   • How many …?
Example: *Who is in your family? How many lamps are in your room?*

twenty-seven 27

1 Part B

B7 A new friend 🔊 L 1/15 | S 10

a) Read the dialogue. What is it about?
Choose the correct words from the box. ▶ Reading | p. 167

> The dialogue is about ..., ... and ....

friends • houses • shopping • hobbies • sports • rooms • books • school • classmates • families

Mrs Khan: Ah, Rajiv, can you look after the shop for a minute? I need a cup of tea. Oh, and this is Caroline, this is George.
Rajiv: OK, Mum. – Hi, are you new here?
⁵ **Caroline:** Yes, we are. We live on Albert Street.
Rajiv: We live in the flat upstairs. My mother and father are always in the shop. Their days are very long.
George: Where is your family from?
¹⁰ **Rajiv:** My parents are from Camden, but my grandparents are Indian. My grandmother and grandfather live in Mumbai. And my aunts and uncles are in India, too.
George: Wow, you must speak Indian then!
¹⁵ **Rajiv:** Well, it's Hindi. My sister Sheree and I speak Hindi with our parents at home. But we are English, really.
Caroline: Where's Sheree now?
Rajiv: She's with her best friend, Maya. The girls
²⁰ are always together.
George: Like you and Sophie, Caroline. We're from Manchester. Her best friend there is Sophie.
Rajiv: And who is your best friend, George?
²⁵ **George:** His name is Tom. He lives in Manchester, too.
Rajiv: What's your favourite place in Camden?
Caroline: The canal!
George: My favourite place is my room in our
³⁰ new house. There's a really big desk for my computer.

Rajiv: I like computers, too. *Super Sylvio* is my favourite computer game.
Caroline: That's a good computer game!
³⁵ **George:** I like *FootballWorld* because I like football. I'm a Man United fan.
Rajiv: Hockey is my favourite game. I'm in the school team. But I like *FootballWorld*, too.
George: Cool! We can play together. What's the
⁴⁰ name of your school?
Rajiv: William Ellis. Our hockey team is the best.
George: William Ellis! My new school is William Ellis, too. What about their football team?
Rajiv: They're great, too.

b) Right or wrong? Correct the wrong statements about Rajiv.
Example: His aunts and uncles are in London. → *His aunts and uncles are in India.*
1. His parents are from Mumbai.
2. His room is upstairs.
3. His grandparents are in Camden.
4. His sister is Maya.
5. His favourite game is football.
6. His school is Camden School for Boys.

▶ WB 18 | p. 13

c) Collect the family words from B1 and B7 and write them down.
Keep your list for later.

▶ DIFF Extra D28 | p. 132   ▶ Vocabulary | p. 175

Part B 1

B8 Possessive determiners

a) Copy the grid and complete it. Find the words in B7.

▶ G4 | p. 183, G7 | p. 184   ▶ WB 19 | p. 14

	personal pronoun	possessive determiner
singular	I	my
	...	your
	he	...
	...	her
	...	its
plural	we	...
	you	...
	...	their

b) George writes a text message to his friend Tom. Copy the message and fill in the correct determiner.

▶ DIFF Easy alternative D29, Extra D30 | p. 132   ▶ WB 20 | p. 15

my (2x) • your • his (2x) • her • our (2x) • their

Hi, Tom. How are you? Camden is cool and **1** new house is cool, too. **2** room is really great. Caroline is happy now because Emma is **3** new friend. **4** new friend is Rajiv. **5** family is from India. Rajiv and **6** family live near **7** new house, on Albert Street. **8** flat is above a shop. Say hi to **9** family.
Bye! George

B9 Target task Your family   ▶ Writing | p. 173   ▶ WB 21 | p. 15

1 Write about your family. Say ...
- where you are from,
- who is in your family,
- how old they are,
- their favourite things.

- Use the family words from exercise B7c) and the wordbanks "People" and "Hobbies and free time" on pages 199 and 205.
- Use possessive determiners: *my, our, their, ...*
- Check your work for spelling mistakes.
- You can add pictures, too.

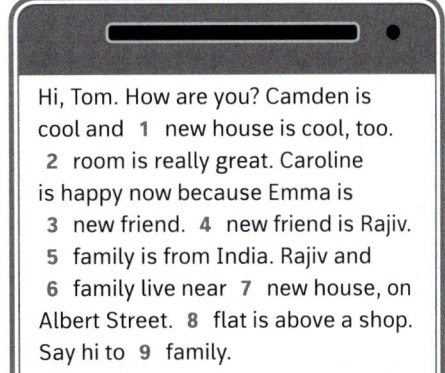

My name is Leon. My family is from Dortmund. There are five people in my family. My mother is called Maria and my father is called Michael. They are from Berlin. Their favourite sport is jogging. My brother Mats is 13 years old. His favourite food is pizza. My sister Mila is eight years old. Her favourite book is "Bibi and Tina". My grandparents are from Greece. Their house is in Greece. They are very old.

2 Interview one of your classmates about his/her family. Ask him/her:

- Where is your family from?
- Who is in your family?
- What is his/her name?
- How old is he/she?
- What is his/her favourite thing?

3 Tell the class about your classmate's family.   ▶ Presentation | p. 170

This is Lina. Her family is from Italy. There are three people in her family. Her mother is called Isabella. She's 38. Lina's sister is Mara. She's 14 years old. Her favourite sport is ballet. ...

Need help? Look at pages 30/31: T1 T2 T3 T4 T5 T6

1 Part B: Target task tools

Target task tools for B 9: Your family

T1 Grammar: Questions with question words and *to be* ▶ G6 | p. 184

a) Write down the correct questions.
1. name – What is – your – ?
2. from – you – Where – are – ?
3. old – you – How – are – ?
4. is – What – favourite colour – your – ?
5. your – favourite singer – Who – is – ?

b) Write down your answers.

T2 Grammar: Questions with question words and *to be* ▶ G6 | p. 184

Emma wants to know more about Caroline.
Look at Caroline's answers. Write down Emma's questions.
Example: My favourite colour is green. → *What is your favourite colour?*

1. My favourite singer is Taylor Swift.
2. My favourite person is my aunt. Her name is Lizzie.
3. Lizzie is 45 years old.
4. She is from Manchester.

T3 Words: Family words

Find the family words and write them down.
Example: *aunt, …*

T4 Grammar: Possessive determiners ▶ G7 | p. 184

Write down what George tells Mrs Khan about his family and friends.
Use the words from the box.

his (2x) • *her* (3x) • *their* (2x) • *our* (2x)

Example: My dog is great at football.   name / Patch
→ *My dog is great at football. His name is Patch.*

1. Dad is a pilot.   favourite room / the kitchen
2. Mum is a doctor.   favourite sport / yoga
3. Caroline is my twin sister.   cat / Socks
4. My grandparents live in Manchester.   house / very nice
5. Grandma is happy.   garden / great
6. My best friend is Tom.   parents / teachers
7. We like Camden.   new house / on Albert Street
8. My aunt and uncle live in the USA.   children / Danny and Lara
9. We like America.   favourite food / hamburgers

Part B: Target task tools

T5 Words: Sports and hobbies

Finish the sentences.
Use the words in the box.
Example: *Mel's hobby is riding.*

*hockey • dancing • reading • football •
skateboarding • riding • playing computer games •
tennis • basketball*

1 Alex's hobby is _____ .

2 Ben's favourite sport is _____ .

3 Jake's hobby is _____ .

4 Emily's favourite sport is _____ .

5 Penny's hobby is _____ .

6 Harry's hobby is _____ .

7 Cara's favourite sport is _____ .

8 Tom's hobby is _____ .

T6 Writing: Write about Emma's family

Write a text about Emma's family.
Use the words in the box.

*80 • Susan • spaghetti • Jack • Scotland • 44 (2x) • 16 •
playing computer games • Camden (2x) • four • Sam*

My name is Emma.

I'm from **1** .
There are **2** people in my family.
My brother is called **3** .
He is **4** years old.
His hobby is **5** .
His favourite food is **6** .
My mother is called **7** and my father is called **8** .
They are from **9** , too.
My mum is **10** years old. My dad is **11** years old, too.
My grandparents are from **12** .
They are **13** years old.

thirty-one 31

1 Around Camden   Photo tour

A Camden Town is a really fantastic place to visit. That is why you can see lots of tourists there every day of the week. The best way to get there is by tube on the Northern Line. Get out at Camden Town underground station and follow[1] the crowds[2].

B Many tourists who come to Camden want to go shopping. There are some fantastic shops in Camden High Street and you can buy trendy clothes and shoes.

C Camden has also got some attractive markets. You can buy all kinds of things[3] there: handbags, sunglasses, jewellery[4] and clothes. A very popular[5] market is *The Stables*[6]. You can still see some model horses there.

D There are some really great places to eat and drink in Camden. You can find food from many different countries[7].

E In Camden Town you can go for long walks along Regent's Canal or take a boat tour on the waterbus to Little Venice and back. It is a lovely trip.

F Camden Town is also a great place to live. It has got some lovely houses and lots of good schools. There are some beautiful parks nearby where you can have picnics and play football and tennis.

---

1 follow – *folgen* | **2** crowds – *Menschenmassen* |
3 all kinds of things – *alle möglichen Sachen* |
4 jewellery – *Schmuck* | **5** popular – *beliebt* |
6 stables – *Ställe* | **7** countries – *Länder*

Photo tour 1

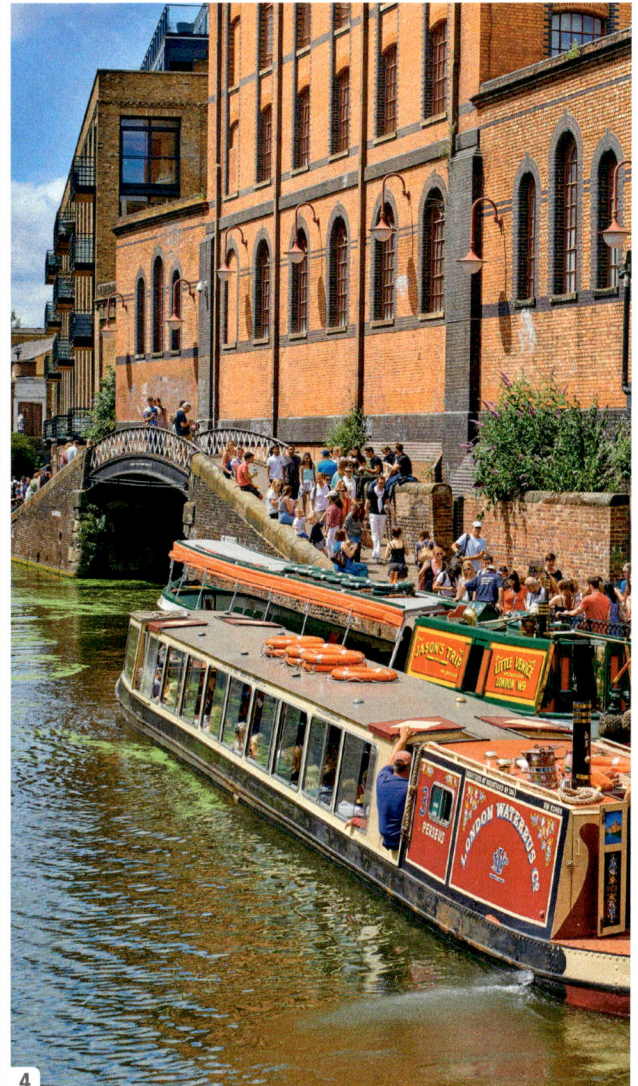

P1
Look at the photos and read the texts.
Match the photos to the texts.

P2
Find captions for the photos.

P3
Look at the photos and play "I spy with my little eye" with a partner.

P4
Choose a photo of a place where you live and write some sentences about it.

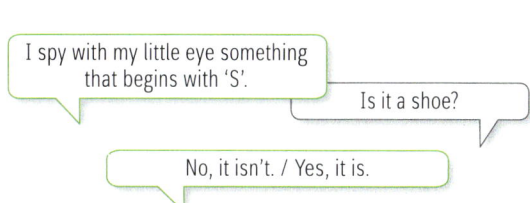

I spy with my little eye something that begins with 'S'.

Is it a shoe?

No, it isn't. / Yes, it is.

thirty-three 33

1 I can ...

Was hast du alles neu gelernt? Diese Seite hilft dir dabei, das zu erkennen. Falls du Hilfe benötigst, etwas nachlesen oder noch ein paar Übungen machen möchtest, findest du hier passende Hinweise.

WORTSCHATZ

Ich kann ...	Aufgaben	Übungen/Hilfen
Räume und Gegenstände in einem Haus benennen *bathroom • bedroom • kitchen • garden • window • bed • desk*	1-5	▶ DIFF D3, D5-D6 ▶ Wordbank 4 | p. 201 ▶ WB 1, 3, 5
mithilfe von *there is/are* sagen, was zu sehen ist *There are doors. • There is a pink school bag on the desk.*	1, 4, A6	▶ DIFF D1, D10 ▶ WB 5
mit Präpositionen beschreiben, wo sich etwas befindet *The phone is under the bed. • There are books on the shelf.*	3-5, B3	▶ DIFF D9, D26 ▶ WB 2, 3, 5
über Gefühle sprechen *I'm happy because my new school is cool. • Mr and Mrs McBride are ...*	A1, A2	▶ T4, T6 | p. 25 ▶ Wordbank 2 | p. 199 ▶ WB 6
Familie und Verwandte benennen *His aunts and uncles are in India. • Her mother is called Isabella.*	B7, B9	▶ DIFF D28 ▶ T6 | p. 31 ▶ Wordbank 2 | p. 199

SKILLS

Ich kann ...	Aufgaben	Übungen/Hilfen
verstehen, worum es in einem Gespräch geht LISTENING	A2, A6, B1	▶ DIFF D4, D23 ▶ WB 12
einem Partner mein Zimmer beschreiben SPEAKING	5	▶ DIFF D1, D9, D10
Fragen zu einem Video über Camden Market beantworten VIEWING	A10	▶ Listening | p. 166
einen Dialog gemeinsam laut lesen READING	B2	▶ Dramatic reading | p. 178
sagen, worum es in einem Dialog geht READING	B7	▶ WB 18
einen Chat vervollständigen WRITING • MEDIA	A11	▶ T1-T7 | pp. 24-25
über meine Familie schreiben *My family is from Dortmund. • My brother Mats is 13 years old. • His favourite food is pizza. • My grandparents are from Greece.* WRITING	B9	▶ DIFF D28, D30 ▶ T1-T6 | pp. 30-31 ▶ WB 21
den Inhalt einer Textnachricht auf Deutsch wiedergeben MEDIATION	D7	▶ Mediation | p. 177 ▶ WB 14

GRAMMATIK

Ich kann ...	Aufgaben	Übungen/Hilfen
den Plural von Wörtern bilden *book → books • bush → bushes*	1	▶ DIFF D2 ▶ G1
die Formen von *to be* bilden und verneinen *I am • she isn't*	A3-A5	▶ DIFF D17 ▶ T2-T3 | p. 24 ▶ G3 ▶ WB 10, 11
Fragen mit *to be* stellen und beantworten *Are you hungry? • How old are you? • Where's the mouse?*	A8, A9, A11, B4-B6	▶ DIFF D18-D20, D27 ▶ T1-T2 | p. 30 ▶ G5, G6 ▶ WB 13, 17
Possessivbegleiter korrekt verwenden *my • your • his • our*	B8, B9	▶ DIFF D29, D30 ▶ T4 | p. 30 ▶ G7 ▶ WB 19

34 thirty-four

At school

In diesem *Theme* wirst du ...

- etwas über den Alltag an britischen Schulen erfahren
- verrückte neue Regeln für euren Klassenraum aufstellen
- lernen auszudrücken, wer etwas kann
- über Lieblingsfächer sprechen
- sagen, wer etwas besitzt
- über deine Schule schreiben

2 A new friend

Intro

1 On the bus   L 1/16 | S 11   ▶ Reading | p. 167

It is George's first day at William Ellis School for Boys.
Listen and read along. What is George's problem?

A   The bus is late.
B   He is at the wrong school.
C   Charlie isn't his friend.

Intro **2**

2 George's problem ▶ DIFF Training D1 | p. 133   ▶ Reading | p. 167

Answer the questions about George and Charlie.
1 What is Charlie's favourite team?
2 Who are Charlie's friends?
3 What is the name of Charlie's school?
4 What is the name of George's school?
5 Where are George and Charlie at the end?

3 Dramatic reading ▶ Dramatic reading | p. 178
1 Choose your parts (Mr McBride, George, Charlie).
2 Read and look up: practise reading your part.
3 Think of actions to go with your sentences.
4 Read the scene and do the actions.

4 Listen to George
    L 1/17 | S 12   ▶ Listening | p. 166

a) Choose the best title for the phone call.
   A George is late
   B The right bus to William Ellis
   C Caroline's bus
   ▶ WB 1 | p. 22

b) Listen again and point at the bus numbers.
   ▶ DIFF Extra D2 | p. 133   ▶ WB 2 | p. 22

c) Say the numbers of the right buses to William Ellis.

5 Play "Fizz!" ▶ DIFF Extra D3 | p. 133   ▶ WB 3 | p. 22

Say "Fizz!" for numbers with seven: seven, fourteen (= 2x7), seventeen, …

| one | two | three | four | five | six | Fizz! | eight |
| nine | ten | eleven | twelve | thirteen | Fizz! | … | |

2 At William Ellis School — Part A

A1 New at school ▶ WB 4 | p. 22

You are at a new school.
What is new for you?

- There's a new way to school.
- There are new rules.
- My classroom is new.
- ...

A2 A school day in Britain  ▶ WB 5 | p. 23

a) Watch the video. What is it about?

the canteen • school uniforms • lockers •
school bags • registration • school buses •
assembly • classrooms • school clubs

- The video is about ..., ..., and ...
- It isn't about ... or ...

Schulalltag in Großbritannien — Culture box

Ein Schultag dauert etwa von 9 bis 16 Uhr. Häufig beginnt der Tag mit der Überprüfung der Anwesenheit *(registration)*. Oft gibt es auch noch eine Schulversammlung *(assembly)*, in der zum Beispiel Projektwochen, Sportveranstaltungen und Konzerte angekündigt werden. In der Mensa *(canteen)* kann man mittags eine warme Mahlzeit essen. Nach dem Unterricht nehmen viele Schüler an Arbeitsgemeinschaften *(school clubs)* teil. An vielen britischen Schulen trägt man eine Schuluniform.

Wie fändest du es, wenn es an deiner Schule Schuluniformen gäbe?

b) What is different from your school?
Name at least two things.
▶ WB Media 5

- There is no ... at our school, but there's a ... at the British school.

A3 At William Ellis School

a) Look at the picture.
- Who is there?
- Where are they?

▶ WB 6, 7 | p. 23

b) Work with a partner.
Ask and answer questions.
▶ DIFF Support D4, Training D5 | p. 134

- Where's the blue pencil?
- It's on the desk.

pen • school bag • pencil • exercise book • pencil case • rubber • ruler • school book • calculator • scissors • glue • folder • felt tip • pencil sharpener

Part A 2

A4 George, Joe and Ms Jefferson L 1/18 | S 13

a) Read the text and look at the picture on page 38.
What can you say about George, Joe and Ms Jefferson?
▶ DIFF Training D6 | p. 134   ▶ Reading | p. 167   ▶ WB 8 | p. 24

rude • friendly • nice •
excited • worried •
funny • strict

Ms Jefferson: Boys, please be quiet. Let's start.
Open your books at page seven.
(knock, knock) Yes, come in!
George: I'm so sorry! The bus … and Charlie …
5 and then … the wrong school and …
Ms Jefferson: It's OK. I'm Ms Jefferson, the history
teacher. What's your name?
George: My name is George McBride.
I'm new in Camden. Sorry I'm late.
10 **Ms Jefferson:** That's OK. It's your first day.
Welcome to William Ellis School. Tell us about
yourself.
Joe: Oh no! A Man United fan!
Ms Jefferson: Joe, don't talk in class!
15 You know the rules.

George: Well, I'm from Manchester.
It's great.
Joe: *(to Rajiv)* What's so great about Manchester?
Ms Jefferson: Joe! Don't talk in class! – George,
20 please go on.
George: And … um … I like football and my
favourite club is Man United.
Joe: Man United is for losers.
Ms Jefferson: Joe, be quiet. George, sit down
25 there, next to Rajiv. Where is your school tie?
George: In my school bag, Ms Jefferson.
Ms Jefferson: Put it on, please. And no football
scarf in the classroom, OK? Now, open your
books at page seven, boys.

b) Read the dialogue again.
Find the English phrases for:
▶ WB 9 | p. 24

Das ist in Ordnung. • *Entschuldigung, dass ich zu spät komme.* •
Lasst uns anfangen. • *Mach bitte weiter.* • *Öffnet eure Bücher auf Seite 7.*

A5 A school rap L 1/19, 20 | S 14, 15

a) Listen to the rap and say it.
▶ DIFF Support D7 | p. 134

b) 👥 Group work (3): Read the rap
out loud together.
1 Think of actions to go
with the words.

2 Practise your rap:
every group member says
a verse.
Say the chorus together.

3 Present your rap to another
group.

c) Make a recording of your rap.
▶ WB Media 3 ▶ WES-149220-2

1 Come on time and don't be late.
Pay attention, sit up straight.
Put your school bag on the floor.
Don't forget to shut the door!

CHORUS
Rules, rules, lots of rules,
in the classroom, in your school.
Rules, rules and more rules.
Some are stupid, some are cool.

2 Please stop talking and don't shout.
Put your hand up, don't call out.
Listen to the teacher and don't talk.
In the classroom please just walk.

3 In the classroom help your friends.
Bring your school things, books and pens.
Do your homework, learn keywords.
Concentrate on what you learn.

2 Part A

A6 Classroom rules – imperatives ▶ G8 | p. 185 ▶ DIFF Training D8 | p. 135

a) Look at the dialogue and the rap on page 39.
   Find examples of classroom rules.
   Example: *Don't talk in class!*

b) Look at the crazy classroom rules. Can you correct them?
   Example: 1 Don't clean the board. → *Clean the board.*
             2 Talk in class. → *Don't talk in class.*

> Our crazy classroom rules
> 1. Don't clean the board.
> 2. Talk in class.
> 3. Don't listen to the teacher.
> 4. Write on your desk.
> 5. Don't be quiet in class.
> 6. Do your homework in the lesson.

A7 Play a polite game of "Simple Simon says"

- Simple Simon says: "Clean the board, please." → Do it.
- Simple Simon says: "Sit on the floor!" → Don't do it.

▶ DIFF Training D9 | p. 135   ▶ WB 10 | p. 25

A8 George and Joe L 1/21 | S 16

a) Can George and Joe be friends? Have a class vote:
   - who says "Yes."?
   - who says "No."?
   - who says "I'm not sure."?

b) Read the dialogue. Who says what?
   A "Can we be friends?"
   B "Hm, I'm not sure."
   C "Hey, I have an idea!"

▶ DIFF Training D10 | p. 135   ▶ Reading | p. 167

George and Rajiv go to their next lesson.
George: Can we go outside now?
Rajiv: No, we can't. There's no time. And, … I'm sorry about Joe. He is quite nice really.
5 **George:** Sure? Oh no …
George's bag falls down. His school things are on the floor.
Joe: Hi, can I help?
George: Hmmm … Yes, OK. Thanks.
10 **Joe:** Hey George, that's a cool pencil case!
And I have the same homework diary.
Oh! But we have a blue folder for music, not a green folder.
George: OK.
15 **Joe:** Can we talk? I'm sorry for earlier. Can we be friends?
George: Hm, I'm not sure.
Rajiv: Hey, I have an idea! We can have lunch together.
20 **George:** OK.
Rajiv: And we can meet after school, too. Can you play basketball?
George: Yes, I can!
Joe: Well, I can't.
25 **George:** What about football?
Rajiv: Real football or *FootballWorld*?
Joe: I can play both!
Rajiv: Great! Let's meet after school and play *FootballWorld*. Can I be Neymar?
30 **George and Joe:** No, you can't!

c) Are George and Joe friends now? Have a vote.

Part A 2

A9 School words

a) Look at the picture and the dialogue on page 40. Make a word web for school things. You can look at A3b) again and on page 198 for more words.
▶ Wordbank 1 | p. 198   ▶ Vocabulary | p. 175   ▶ WB 11, 12 | p. 25

b) Play "I spy with my little eye" with a partner. Only use things in your classroom.

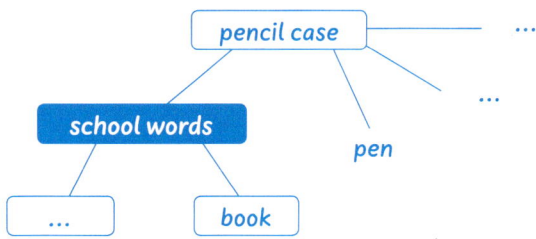

A10 Joe, Rajiv and George can …

Look at the dialogue on page 40.
Say what Joe, Rajiv and George can do and what they can't do.
▶ G9 | p. 185

> Joe can play football.

> George and Rajiv can't go outside.

A11 Can you …?   ▶ G9 | p. 185   ▶ DIFF Training D11 | p. 135   ▶ WB 13 | p. 26

a) Tell your partner three things you can do and three things you can't do.

> I can dance and I can …, but I can't …

b) Find out more about your classmates. What can they do? What can't they do? Write down four questions for your classmates. Example: *Can you play basketball?*

Can you
- play basketball?
- speak French?
- make pizza?
- …?

> Bonjour!

▶ Wordbank 9 | p. 205   ▶ DIFF Easy alternative D12 | p. 136

c) Milling around: Ask your classmates your questions. Answer their questions. Take notes.
▶ Milling around | p. 178

> **Can** you play basketball? 💡
> → Yes, I can.
>   No, I can't.

d) Talk about your classmates. Who can do what?
Example: *Katharina can play tennis. Alex can …*
▶ DIFF Training D13 | p. 136

A12 Target task — Crazy rules for your classroom

Work in groups. Write crazy rules for your classroom.

1 What are your classroom rules? Talk about them.
▶ Talking | p. 169   ▶ Wordbank 1 | p. 198

> I think this rule is OK/boring/stupid/… • I don't think so.
> I like this rule because … • I don't like this rule because …

> Our classroom rule is: "Don't bring a phone." I don't like this rule because …

> Yes, you're right.

> Our classroom rule is: "Be nice to your classmates." I think this rule is OK.

2 Think of five crazy rules and write them down.
Example: *Bring your pet to school.*
3 Present your rules to the class.
4 Choose the top five crazy rules for your classroom.
5 Make a poster with your new classroom rules.

> …

> Well, I'm not sure about that.

Need help? Look at pages 42/43.   T1 T2 T3 T4 T5 T6

2 Part A: Target task tools

Target task tools for A12: Crazy rules for your classroom

T1 Words: School things and colours

a) Write about the school things in the picture.
Example: *The folder is blue.*

  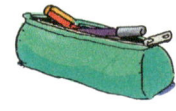 

b) Play a memory game alone or with a partner.
- Look around your classroom for 30 seconds.
- Try to remember as many things as you can.
- Write down all the things in one minute.

Example: *green pen, yellow chair, black pencil case, …*

> **Media**
> Um neue Wörter zu lernen kannst du auch eine Vokabeltrainer-App verwenden.
> ▶ Vocabulary | p. 175

T2 Listening: In the classroom 🔊 L 1/22 | S 17

Listen to the teacher. Note down the missing words.

1 Please be XXX.
2 Don't XXX in class.
3 XXX your books at page eight, please.
4 Now, let's XXX.

T3 Grammar: Imperative ▶ G8 | p. 185

Match the pictures (A–H) and the sentences (1–8). Complete the crazy rules for your home.
Example: *A6 Don't help your parents.*

A B C D

E F G H

Always
Don't

1 XXX keep your shoes on[1].
2 XXX be late for school.
3 XXX eat with your hands.
4 XXX tidy[2] your room.
5 XXX listen to loud music.
6 XXX help your parents.
7 XXX play computer games at night.
8 XXX play with your mobile.

---
1 to keep your shoes on – *die Schuhe anbehalten* | **2** to tidy – *aufräumen*

Part A: Target task tools **2**

T4 Grammar: Imperative ▶ G8 | p. 185
Look at the picture.
Write down what the teacher can say.
Example: *Sit down, please.*

T5 Words: Discussion
Look at these phrases.
Copy them and put them in a grid.

Yes, that's OK. • I'm not sure. • You're right. • I think you're wrong. • No, I don't think so.

+	−
Yes, that's OK.	…
…	…

T6 Words: Adjectives
Match the English and the German adjectives.

1 boring
2 good
3 crazy
4 stupid
5 bad
6 great

A verrückt
B großartig
C schlecht
D langweilig
E blöd
F gut

2 At Camden School for Girls — Part B

B1 Caroline's first day at school L 1/23 ▶ DIFF Training D14 | p. 136 ▶ WB 14 | p. 26

a) Listen to a tour of the school. Point at the rooms when you hear them.

b) Match the words to the rooms.

IT room • canteen • art room • assembly hall • library • science room

> The canteen is picture number …

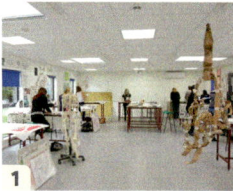
1

2

3

4

5

6

B2 In the classroom L 1/24 | S 18 ▶ WB 15 | p. 26

a) Close your books and listen to the dialogue. Draw Emma's face. Is she happy or not happy?
▶ Listening | p. 166

b) Read the dialogue and answer the questions.
1 Where is Emma's seat?
2 What is Beebee's problem?
3 What colour is Julia's lunchbox?

▶ DIFF Training D15, D16 | p. 136, Extra D17, D18 | pp. 136-137

Mr May: Hello, Jennie. Thank you for the tour. Now, girls, go to your seats. Your names are on the desks.
Caroline: I've got my seat, Emma. But you aren't
5 next to me. It's Beatrice – who is that?
Beebee: Hi, I'm Beatrice. Please call me Beebee.
Caroline: Hi, Beebee. I'm Caroline. Emma, where's your seat?
Emma: Next to Gillian. She's from my old class.
10 **Gillian:** Hi, Emma. I'm next to you! Great!
Emma: Hm. Hi!
Beebee: *(to Caroline)* Oh, Emma is very grumpy!
Mr May: Please listen, girls. First, here is the timetable for today. Please write it down. We
15 have got English in the first lesson. Then you have got two lessons of PE before morning break.
Caroline: Please, Sir. Beebee has got a problem. She hasn't got her PE things.
20 **Mr May:** Well, please talk to Mr Green, your PE teacher. He has got some extra PE things.
Gillian: I haven't got extra shoes but I've got an extra T-shirt for you, Beebee.
Beebee: Thanks, Gillian!
25 **Aisha:** Mr May, Julia has got my lunchbox.
Julia: I haven't got your lunchbox!
Mr May: Girls, please! Now Julia, look again.
Julia: OK … Oh sorry, Aisha, I've got your lunchbox. Our lunchboxes are both green.
30 **Mr May:** Now, after morning break your class has got geography and then music. And now write down the three lessons in the afternoon. Some of you have got French and some have got Spanish. Then all of you have got maths and
35 history.

Part B 2

B3 Who has got what?

Read the dialogue on page 44.
Make sentences about it.

Mr Green		history in the first lesson.
Gillian	has got	her PE things.
Julia	hasn't got	English in the first lesson.
Beebee		extra shoes.
		some extra PE things.
The girls	have got	an extra T-shirt.
	haven't got	Aisha's lunchbox.

> 've got = have got
> 's got = has got !

B4 Grammar card *have got/has got* ▶ DIFF Training D19, Extra D20 | p. 137

a) Write a grammar card for *have got/has got*.
  1 Look at these sentences: I **have got** a dog.   Caroline **has got** a cat.   We **have got** a pony.
    When do you use *have got*? When do you use *has got*?
    Look at page 186 and find the rule.
  2 Write down the rule and find more examples for your grammar card.
  ▶ G10 | p. 186   ▶ Grammar card | p. 179   ▶ WB 16 | p. 27

b) Look at B2 again. Add examples of negative sentences with *have got/has got* to your grammar card.

B5 Gillian's timetable ▶ WB 17 | p. 27

a) What school subjects do you know?
Write them down in a list. Look at B2 for help.
▶ Vocabulary | p. 175

b) Listen to the girls. Raise your hand
when you hear a school subject.
🔊 L 1/25 | S 19   ▶ DIFF Training D21 | p. 138

Caroline: That's a funny timetable.
I can't read it.
Gillian: It's a puzzle. Can you understand it?
Beebee: Your timetable is weird, Gillian. It's not
5 like Caroline's timetable. Why is there a
picture of a crown?
Emma: Well, I think it's very clever! Let me try.
Have we got history on Tuesday?
Gillian: That's right.
10 **Caroline:** Have we got religious education on
Wednesday after morning break?
Gillian: Yes, that's right.
Caroline: And have we got drama on Friday
afternoon?
15 **Emma:** Yes, we have, look at the picture. And on
Friday morning we've got French. The colours
of the flag are red, white and blue.
Caroline: I haven't got French. I've got Spanish
with Beebee.
20 **Emma:** Oh, not French with me?

Caroline: No, sorry.
Beebee: Cool! Caroline, we can sit together again!
Gillian: Emma, I've got French. We can sit
together.
25 **Emma:** OK, Gillian.
Gillian: And what about the first lesson on
Thursday? It's my favourite subject.
Caroline: That's easy. It's art! And now it's time for
Beebee's favourite subject … lunch!
30 **Beebee:** Yes, let's go to the canteen!

c) Read the dialogue and add more subjects
to your list from a).
Which subjects have you got at your school?
Which subjects haven't you got?

Part B

B6 A quiz ▶DIFF Support D22, Training D23 | p. 138 ▶ WB 18 | p. 28

a) Work with a partner. Make a quiz. Ask and answer questions about Gillian's timetable on page 45.

b) Check G10 on pages 186/187. Add questions with *have got/has got* to your grammar card from B4.
▶ G10 | p. 186

B7 Favourite subjects ▶DIFF Training D24, D25 | pp. 138-139 ▶ Wordbank 1 | p. 198 ▶ WB 20 | p. 29

a) Read the dialogue on p. 45 again and find out:
- what is Gillian's favourite subject?
- what is Beebee's favourite "subject"?

b) Milling around ▶ Milling around, p. 178
1. Ask three pupils about their favourite subjects.
2. Report back to the class.
3. Write the favourite subjects on the board.
   - Count the results.
   - Use different colours for the girls' and the boys' favourite subjects.
   - What are the three favourite subjects in your class?

> **The genitive**
> We use 's or s' for people:
> → My *friend's* name is Tom. (one friend)
> → My *friends'* names are Helen and Sam. (two friends)
> We use *of* for things:
> → The *colours of* the flag are red, white and blue.
> ▶ G11 | p. 187

B8 School menu

a) Work with a partner. Look at the menu. Can you work out what the meals are in German? ▶ New words | p. 168

b) Listen to the girls. Who has got what for lunch?
🔊 L 1/26 | S 20 ▶DIFF Easy alternative D26 | p. 139 ▶ Listening | p. 166

> Compare the English words with German words (salad – *Salat*) or words from other languages.

Camden School for Girls

	Monday	Tuesday	Wednesday	Thursday	Friday
Main course	chicken and rice, green salad	lasagne, green salad	lamb kebab, potatoes, green salad	steak with chips, green salad	fish and chips, green salad
Main course (vegetarian)	macaroni cheese, tomato salad	pasta with tomato sauce	pizza with broccoli, green salad	veggie lasagne, green salad	veggie burger, green salad
Dessert	ice cream	muffins	chocolate pudding	ice cream	banana pudding
Fresh fruit	apples	bananas	oranges	kiwis	apples

c) Start a word list about food.
▶ Vocabulary | p. 175
▶ Wordbank 7 | p. 203
▶ WB 21 | p. 29

banana
apple
salad
rice
lasagne
…

Part B 2

B9 Food words
Play a game:
▶ WB 19 | p. 28

> At my birthday party I'd like lasagne. → At my birthday party I'd like lasagne and ice cream. → At my birthday party I'd like lasagne, ice cream and … → …

B10 Your favourite food   ▶ DIFF Training D27 | p. 139

a) Work with a partner.
Talk about your favourite food.
▶ Talking | p. 169   ▶ Wordbank 7 | p. 203

> I like … / I love … / My favourite food is …

> I like that, too! / Oh no, I hate …

b) Write your favourite school menu for a day.
Show it to a partner. Talk about your menus.

> On my menu, there is … • There is … on my menu because it's my favourite food. • … is nice. • … is not very healthy. • I like …, but I don't like …

B11 Camden School for Girls   ▶ Reading | p. 167

a) Read about Camden School for Girls again (on pages 44-47). Take notes on:
- rooms
- timetable
- subjects
- canteen

b) Talk to a partner.

> I like/don't like Camden School for Girls because there's/there are …

> I think it's a good school because they have got/haven't got …

B12 Target task   Make a poster about your school and present it   ▶ Presentation | p. 170   ▶ WB 22 | p. 29

1. Collect words and phrases about your school in a word web. Think about rooms, subjects and people at your school.
   ▶ Wordbank 1 | p. 198
2. Work in groups. Compare your word webs and add new words.
3. In your group, each pupil writes a short text on a piece of paper. Write about …
   - where your school is,
   - your class and teachers,
   - rooms at your school,
   - your timetable,
   - school rules,
   - the canteen and food.

   You can use *has/have got* and *can*.
   ▶ Writing | p. 173
4. Compare your texts and check them. Then put these texts on a poster and add photos.
   ▶ Making a page | p. 172   ▶ WB Media 6   ▶ WES-149220-2
5. Present your poster to your classmates.
6. Give feedback to the other groups. Talk about the text, layout and photos.

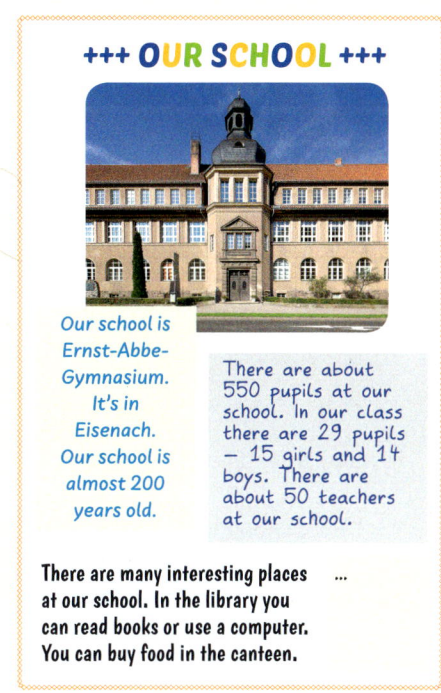

+++ OUR SCHOOL +++

Our school is Ernst-Abbe-Gymnasium. It's in Eisenach. Our school is almost 200 years old.

There are about 550 pupils at our school. In our class there are 29 pupils — 15 girls and 14 boys. There are about 50 teachers at our school.

There are many interesting places at our school. In the library you can read books or use a computer. You can buy food in the canteen.

Need help? Look at pages 48/49.   T1 T2 T3 T4 T5 T6

Part B: Target task tools

Target task tools for B12: Make a poster about your school

T1 Words and phrases: School words (1)

Puzzle out the school rooms and write them down.

TI romo • bralryi • teecann • asebmlys hlla • scnceie moro • ssclarmoo

T2 Grammar: have got/has got (1) ▶ G10 | p. 186

Write down six sentences or more.

| I / You / We / They / My friends | have got / haven't got | a big room. / an Arsenal T-shirt. / an IT room. / a blue school bag. / a green pen. / a skateboard. / a cat. / books. / two brothers. / … |
| He / She / It / My school / My friend | has got / hasn't got | |

T3 Grammar: have got/has got: long forms and short forms ▶ G10 | p. 186

a) Match the short forms to the long forms.
There are more long forms than you need.

1. she's got
2. they haven't got
3. we've got
4. Tom hasn't got
5. I've got

A I have got
B we have got
C Tom has not got
D she has not got
E they have not got
F we have not got
G Tom has got
H I have not got
I she has got

b) Copy what George says about Patch, but use short forms for *has got* and *have got*.

Patch is a border collie. He has got big brown eyes. Patch has got a favourite toy. It's a small ball. I sometimes go to the park with Patch. There are many dogs. The other dogs have not got a Manchester United football. We have got a garden behind our house. I have got a great dog!

forty-eight

Part B: Target task tools

T4 Words and phrases: School words (2)

a) What subjects have the pupils got in these rooms?
There is one more subject than you need.

> In picture 1 they have got …

music • religious education • science • French • geography • history • art

b) Write down more rooms at school.

T5 Grammar: have got/has got (2) ▶ G10 | p. 186

Look at Gillian's timetable on page 45. Compare it with your timetable.
Example: *Gillian has got science on Tuesday and Thursday, but I've got science on Friday.*
I've got PE on Wednesday, but Gillian …

T6 Mediation: Schools in Britain ( ) ▶ Mediation | p. 177

Work with a partner.
Choose one text about a British school.
Read it and tell your partner in German about the school in your text.
Example: *Die Foxhill-Schule ist eine Schule für …*

- Auf der *Skills page Mediation* auf Seite 177 findest du Hilfen.
- Du musst nicht Wort für Wort übersetzen.
  Beispiel: *There is* = Es gibt

Langdon School

Langdon School is a school for boys. There are about 800 pupils at our school. There are no school uniforms. We have a big sports programme. You can play rugby, football, tennis, hockey and cricket. Our pupils often win prizes at sports events. We have a big science room and a theatre.

Welcome to Foxhill School!

We are a school for boys and girls. There are about 1,500 pupils at our school. All pupils wear school uniforms. There is a big sports field and a tennis court. Our canteen offers healthy food and drinks. There is vegetarian and vegan food, too. We have a big library and you can visit our school rabbit Peter there.

2 Poems

Reading tour

R1 Shape poems ▶ Wordbank 1 | p. 198

Look at these shape¹ poems.
Write a shape poem about your school things or what you see and do at school.

---
1 shape – *Form*

R2 I love to do my homework 🔊 L 1/29 | S 23

a) Read the poem. Find the sentence that goes with the picture.
b) Choose another sentence from the poem and draw a picture.
c) 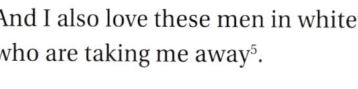 Group work: Act the poem.

▶ Reading | p. 167

I love to do my homework

I love to do my homework,
it makes me feel so good.
I love to do exactly¹
as the teacher says I should².
5 I love to do my homework,
I love it every day³.
And I also love these men in white⁴
who are taking me away⁵.

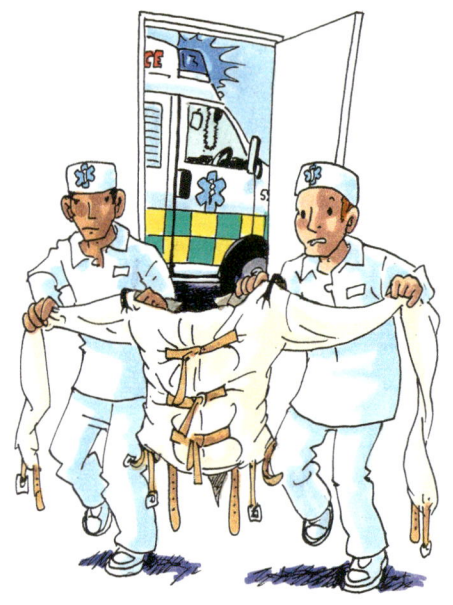

---
1 exactly – *genau*
2 as the teacher says I should – *so wie mein Lehrer es will*
3 every day – *jeden Tag*
4 these men in white – *diese Männer in Weiß*
5 who are taking me away – *die mich wegbringen*

Reading tour 2

R 3 **Two poems** 🔊 L 1/30 | S 24

a) Read the poems on this page. Choose one of them and write it on an A4 page. Draw two or three pictures to illustrate the text.
▶ Reading | p. 167

b) 👥 Learn your poem by heart[1]. Say it to a partner.

1 by heart – auswendig

c) Put up your poems in class.
Your classmates can find out which sentences and pictures go together.

Media
Du kannst dein Gedicht auch aufnehmen und dir die Aufnahme immer wieder anhören. Das hilft dir beim Auswendiglernen.

▶ WB Media 3   ▶ WES-149220-2

Twin tricks

Tim is my twin brother.
We two look the same[1].
So when we're in school uniform
we like playing a game.

5 Let me tell you what we do.
Our trick is very cool.
We go to the wrong lessons
when we are at school!

Tim likes playing the piano[2],
10 but he doesn't like IT.
I like playing computer games,
but music isn't for me.

So when he has IT,
I go and say I'm him[3].
15 And the teachers think[4] I'm great at music.
But I'm not – it's Tim!

1 we two look the same – *wir zwei sehen gleich aus*
2 playing the piano – *Klavier spielen*
3 and say I'm him – *und sage, dass ich er bin*
4 to think – *denken*

Pets at school

Today at our school
it's my favourite day,
because[1] one of your pets
can go in and play!

5 Anne has got a dog
and Tom has got a cat.
And Kate has got a hamster,
that lives in her hat[2].

And what about me?
10 I go with Big Jake.
But my teacher doesn't like it,
because he's a snake[3]!

1 because – *weil*
2 that lives in her hat – *der in ihrem Hut lebt*
3 snake – *Schlange*

2   I can …

Was hast du alles neu gelernt? Diese Seite hilft dir dabei, das zu erkennen. Falls du Hilfe benötigst, etwas nachlesen oder noch ein paar Übungen machen möchtest, findest du hier passende Hinweise.

WORTSCHATZ

Ich kann …	Aufgaben	Übungen/Hilfen
Gegenstände in meiner Schultasche benennen *school bag • pencil • excercise book • calculator • scissors*	A3, A9	▶ DIFF D4, D5 ▶ T1 | p. 42 ▶ Wordbank 1 | p. 198 ▶ WB 6
Redewendungen für den Unterricht verwenden *Open your books at page seven. • Sorry I'm late.*	A4	▶ T2 | p. 42 ▶ Wordbank 1 | p. 198 ▶ WB 8
Räume in einer Schule benennen *IT room • science room • canteen • assembly hall • library*	B1, B12	▶ DIFF D14 ▶ T1 | p. 48 ▶ Wordbank 1 | p. 198 ▶ WB 14
Schulfächer benennen *drama • history • French • art • religious education • English*	B5-B7, B12	▶ DIFF D21 ▶ T4 | p. 49 ▶ Wordbank 1 | p. 198 ▶ WB 17
über Essen und Trinken sprechen *My favourite food is pizza. – I like pizza, too.*	B8-B10, B12	▶ Wordbank 7 | p. 203 ▶ WB 19, 21

SKILLS

Ich kann …	Aufgaben	Übungen/Hilfen
verstehen, wenn jemand ein Problem beschreibt LISTENING	4	▶ DIFF D2 ▶ Listening | p. 166 ▶ WB 1
Zahlen bis 100 verstehen LISTENING	4	▶ DIFF D3 ▶ WB 2, 3
einen Text lebendig vortragen SPEAKING	3	▶ Dramatic reading | p. 178
eine Mini-Präsentation halten SPEAKING • WRITING	B12	▶ Mini-Presentation | p. 170
einem Video über den Schulalltag in Großbritannien folgen VIEWING	A2	▶ WB 5
einen Dialog lesen und Fragen dazu beantworten READING	B2, B5	▶ DIFF D17, D18 ▶ Reading | p. 167 ▶ WB 15
einen Text über meine Schule schreiben WRITING	B12	▶ T1–T6 | pp. 48-49 ▶ Writing | pp. 173-174
jemandem auf Englisch über unsere Schule Auskunft geben MEDIATION	D27	▶ Mediation | p. 177

GRAMMATIK

Ich kann …	Aufgaben	Übungen/Hilfen
Sätze im Imperativ bilden *Clean the board • Don't talk in class. • Be nice to your classmates.*	A6, A7, A12	▶ T3–T4 | pp. 42-43 ▶ DIFF D9 ▶ G8 ▶ WB 10
Fragen und Aussagen mit *can/can't* formulieren *Can you play basketball? – Yes, I can.*	A11	▶ DIFF D11-13 ▶ G9 ▶ WB 13
Sätze mit *have got/has got* bilden und verneinen *I have got a dog • Julia hasn't got history in the first lesson.*	B3, B4	▶ T2, T3, T5 | pp. 48-49 ▶ DIFF D19, D20 ▶ G10 ▶ WB 16
Fragen mit *have got/has got* stellen und beantworten *Has Gillian got art on Monday? – No, she hasn't.*	B6	▶ DIFF D22, D23 ▶ G10 ▶ WB 18
den Genitiv korrekt verwenden *This is Emma's computer. • The colour of the house is green.*	D24, D25	▶ G11 ▶ WB 20

Hobbies and activities

In diesem *Theme* wirst du ...

- über Hobbys sprechen
- die Uhrzeit angeben
- über Haushaltstätigkeiten sprechen
- Fragen stellen
- eine Geschichte zu Ende schreiben
- ein Interview vorbereiten und durchführen

3 Free time — Intro

1 Hobbies ▶ DIFF Support D1 | p. 140 ▶ WB 1 | p. 37

What can you do in your free time?
Make a word web.

▶ Vocabulary | p. 175
▶ Wordbank 9 | p. 205

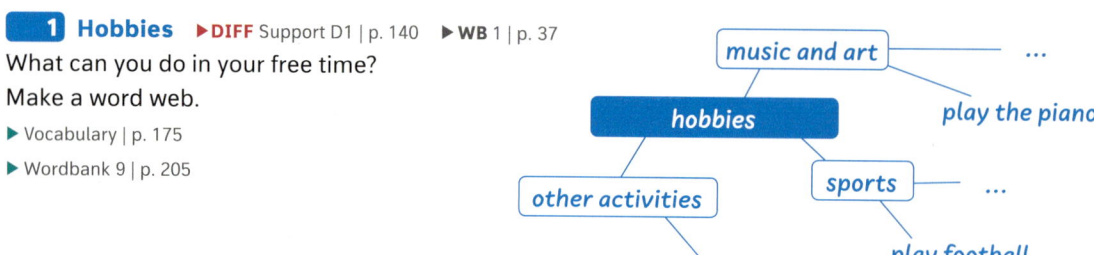

2 A video about hobbies ▶ WB 2 | p. 37

a) Watch the video. What hobbies are there?
Which is the most interesting for you?

b) Watch the video again. Say if the statements are correct. Correct the wrong statements.
▶ WB Media 5   ▶ WES-149220-2

1 Sophia is 14 years old.
2 Hockey is a fast sport.
3 Abby's hobby is scouts.
4 Jake plays golf every weekend with his mum.
5 Amy's favourite sport is hockey.
6 Amy is a goalkeeper.
7 Gracie dances every day.
8 James has got three guitars.

3 Your hobby ▶ WB 3 | p. 37

a) What is your favourite hobby? Make a word list about it.
You can use words from exercise 1 and a dictionary for help.
▶ Vocabulary | p. 175

b) Look at the questions and note down the answers. Then tell your classmates about your hobby.
- What is your hobby?
- When do you do it?
- Where do you do it?
- Why do you like it?

> **Media**
> You can use an online dictionary, too.
> ▶ New words | p. 168   ▶ WB Media 4
> ▶ WES-149220-2

4 What's the time?

Match the times to the clocks.
1 two o'clock
2 quarter past four
3 half past seven
4 quarter to one
5 ten to four

A   B   C   D   E

▶ Box "The time" | p. 219   ▶ Wordbank 3 | p. 200   ▶ WB 4 | p. 37

5 The McBrides' family planner ▶ DIFF Training D2, D3 | p. 140

a) Look at the family planner on page 55. Read the sentences and find out who it is.
Example: He/She has got a lunch date on Tuesday at half past twelve. → That's Mrs McBride.

1 He/She has got a dance class at half past four on Tuesday.
2 He/She has got a yoga class at quarter to eight on Thursday.
3 He/She has got football training at quarter past four on Wednesday.
4 He/She has got a golf lesson on Sunday at twenty past three.

Intro **3**

Our busy week

FAMILY NAME: McBride

Monday	Tuesday	Wednesday	Thursday	Friday	Saturday	Sunday
7:15 pm yoga class (Mum)	12:30 pm lunch date with aunt Lizzy (Mum)	4:15 pm football training (George)	7:45 pm yoga class (Mum)	charity bake-off at school (George)	9 am dance class (Caroline)	3:20 pm golf lesson (Dad)
	4:30 pm dance class (Caroline)	7:30 pm badminton class (Dad)			11 am gym (Mum & Dad)	
	5:45 pm football training (George)					

b) Ask your partner questions about the time. Start at eight o'clock. Take turns.
▶ Wordbank 3 | p. 200   ▶ WB 5 | p. 38

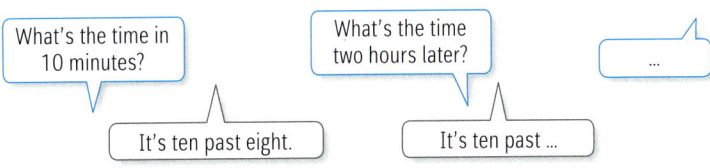

- What's the time in 10 minutes?
- It's ten past eight.
- What's the time two hours later?
- It's ten past …
- …

6 The bake-off flyer ( ) ▶ Mediation | p. 177

a) Look at the flyer. Guess the meaning of these words:

best • baker • bring • cake • winner • sell • information • visit

b) A German friend has some questions about the bake-off. Answer them in German.
1. Was ist das für ein Wettbewerb?
2. Was muss man machen, um teilzunehmen?
3. Was passiert mit den fertigen Backwaren?
4. Was kann man machen, wenn man noch Fragen hat?

Guessing words
- Is it like a German word? (for example *information* → *Information*)
- Is it from a word family? (for example *win* → *winners*)
- Can the other words in the sentence help?
- Can pictures help?

▶ New words | p. 168

3 The bake-off — Part A

A1 What a mess! 🔊 L 1/31 | S 25

a) Look at the picture and listen. Who is in the kitchen?

b) Listen again and answer the questions:
1. Where is the bake-off?
2. What is George's cake for the charity bake-off?
3. Who has got a special recipe for muffins?

▶ DIFF Easy alternative D4 | p. 141

A2 In the kitchen 🔊 L 1/32 | S 26

a) Read the dialogue. What is it about?

> It's about … and …

30 minutes later, Caroline comes into the kitchen.
Caroline: George, what a mess!
George: I know. I want to make a chocolate cake but it's so difficult.
Caroline: A chocolate cake?
5 **George:** It's for the charity bake-off at school tomorrow. I'm in a team with Rajiv.
Caroline: Let me try the cake … Ugh! Horrible!
George: I know. It's really bad. Grandma wants to give me her special muffin recipe. I must call
10 her.
Caroline: What about Rajiv? Is he a good baker?
George: I don't know but he wants to make a banana cake.
Caroline: Sounds good! What about the other
15 boys in your class?
George: Joe and James want to make biscuits. But they don't have a lot of time because they have football training this afternoon. Everyone is really busy. We don't know what the
20 prize is, but we all want to win!
Caroline: Well, good luck then.
George: Thanks. Hey, can you help me? I must clean the kitchen now.

Caroline: No way!
25 **George:** But I always help you!
Caroline: Ha! You never help me. And you never do jobs at home.
George: That's not true!
Caroline: You never empty the dishwasher. And
30 you never lay the table and you never tidy your room and …
George: OK. But I often take out the rubbish and hoover the floor. And I usually walk the dog.
Caroline: Yes, because Patch is YOUR dog! And
35 sometimes Dad walks Patch, too.
George: But he doesn't take out the rubbish.
Caroline: Well, *I* often load the dishwasher.
George: Yeah, and you're really good at it! Why don't you load it now? For me? Please?
40 **Caroline:** No way!

b) 👥 Test your partner. Right or wrong? Correct the wrong sentences.

▶ DIFF Extra D5 | p. 141   ▶ Reading | p. 167   ▶ WB 6, 7 | pp. 38, 39

> That's right.

> That's wrong. George never …

1. George never empties the dishwasher.
2. George always tidies his room.
3. George never hoovers the floor.
4. George often takes out the rubbish.
5. George never walks the dog.
6. Caroline never loads the dishwasher.

Part A 3

A3 Grammar card — Simple present: statements ▶DIFF Training D6, D7 | pp. 141–142 ▶WB 8 | p. 39

1. Copy the grid.
2. Look at the dialogue in A2 again.
   Find sentences with *want* and complete the grid.
3. When do you use *want*? When do you use *want**s***?
   Look at page 188 and start a grammar card for the *simple present*.
4. Find the negative sentences for these sentences in the dialogue:
   I know. → …
   He takes out the rubbish. → …
   We know what the prize is. → …
5. How do you form the negative sentences? Look at page 189 for more information.
   Add the rule to your grammar card. ▶ G12 | p. 188 ▶ Grammar card | p. 179

I	**XXX**
you	**want**
he	**XXX**
she	**XXX**
it	**want**s
we	**XXX**
you	**want**
they	**XXX**

A4 Jobs at home
▶DIFF Support D8 | p. 142

Look at the pictures.
Write down who does what.
Example: *Rajiv makes his bed but he doesn't …*

▶DIFF Training D9, D10 | pp. 142–143

1 Rajiv

2 Charlie

3 Gillian

4 Emma

5 Jack

A5 Jobs, jobs, jobs
▶DIFF Training D11, D12 | p. 143

a) Read the dialogue on page 56 again.
   Make a list of jobs around the house.
   Then add more jobs you know.
   Example: *empty the dishwasher, …*
   ▶ Wordbank 4 | p. 201 ▶ Vocabulary | p. 175

b) What are your jobs at home?
   👥 Talk to a partner.
   ▶ G13 | p. 189 ▶ Talking | p. 169 ▶ WB 9 | p. 40

   "I always make my bed."
   "I sometimes …"

   Im Englischen sagst du:
   I always make my bed.
   Im Deutschen sagst du:
   Ich mache immer mein Bett.

A6 What a hard life! 🔊 L 1/33, 34 | S 27, 28
Listen to the chant and say it. Act out the jobs.

I tidy my room and make my bed,
I tidy so much, it hurts my head.
*What a life, what a life,
What a hard, hard life!*

I empty the dishwasher, I clean my bike,
but it's riding my bike that I really like!
What a life, …

I take out the rubbish, make Mum a cup of tea,
I work really hard, can't you see?
What a life, …

3 Part A

A7 At the supermarket
a) Listen. What is George's idea for the bake-off?
🔊 L 1/35

b) Read the dialogue. Does he tell Emma about his idea?
🔊 L 1/36 | S 29 ▶ Reading | p. 167

George is still at the supermarket when he meets Emma.
Emma: Hi, George! What have you got? Oh, you want to buy muffins! Do you like muffins?
George: Yes, I do.
5 **Emma:** They look delicious! Are they for your family?
George: No, they are for Rajiv and me.
Emma: Really? You must be very hungry! But what about the decorations? Do you always decorate the muffins? Funny!
10 **George:** No, I don't. Er, my mum needs the decorations for a cake.
Emma: Does your mum often bake cakes?
George: Er … yes, she does. Every Friday.
Emma: Mmm … I love cakes! Does Caroline
15 help your mum?
George: No, she doesn't. Sorry, I must go now. Bye!

c) Read again and answer the questions.
1 Do Emma and George meet at the supermarket?   Yes, they do. / No, they don't.
2 Does George like muffins?   Yes, he does. / No, he doesn't.
3 Does George always decorate muffins?   Yes, he does. / No, he doesn't.
4 Does Emma love cakes?   Yes, she does. / No, she doesn't.

A8 Grammar card Simple present: questions with *do/does* and short answers
1 Look at the dialogue in A7. Find questions with *do* or *does*.
Write them down and use colours: **blue** for *do/does*, **red** for the subject and **green** for the infinitive.
Example: **Do you like** muffins?
2 When do you use *do*? When do you use *does*?
Add the rule and the examples to your grammar card for the simple present (A3).
3 Then add positive and negative short answers (for example *Yes, I do. / No, I don't.*) ▶ G14 | p. 190
▶ Grammar card | p. 179   ▶ DIFF Training D13 | p. 144   ▶ WB 10, 12 | pp. 40, 41

A9 Questions, questions ▶ WB 11 | p. 40
a) 👥 Write down six questions. Interview your partner. Note down the answers.
▶ DIFF Training D14, Extra D15 | p. 144

| Do / Does | you / you and your family / your brother/sister / your best friend / … | bake / eat / play / watch / … | cakes every weekend? / pizza on Fridays? / football/tennis/basketball every week? / TV every night? / … |

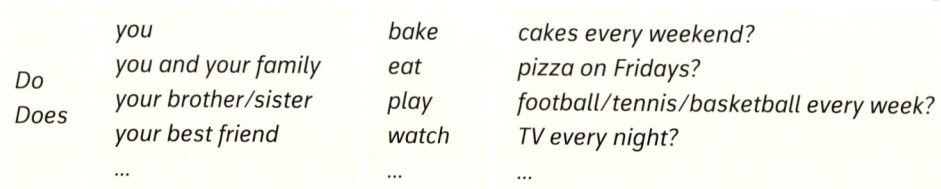

b) Use your notes to write about your partner.
Example: *Antonia eats pizza on Fridays, but she doesn't bake cakes every weekend.*
She and her family watch TV every night. …

c) Read out your texts in class, but don't say your partner's name. The others must guess who it is.

Part A 3

A10 Perfect muffins ▶ DIFF Training D16 | p. 144, Extra D17 | p. 145 ▶ Reading | p. 167 ▶ WB 13 | p. 41

a) Read the story. What is George's problem? 🔊 S 30

George is back from the supermarket. He puts the muffins on the table. They look perfect. Bing! He has got a new message. It is from Rajiv. "Still in the kitchen? Do you need help?" George
5 smiles. Then he sends Rajiv a photo of the muffins and writes: "Yes! Come to my house and help me decorate the muffins."
15 minutes later Rajiv is in the McBrides' kitchen. "Wow! Your muffins look fantastic! My cake isn't
10 perfect but it tastes good. George, we are a great team!"
George smiles but says nothing and begins to decorate the muffins. Suddenly the doorbell rings. "Caroline!" George shouts. "Can you open
15 the door, please?"
Caroline comes downstairs and opens the door. It is Emma.

"Oh no," George says. He looks worried.
20 He tries to hide the muffins. "What's wrong?" Rajiv asks. The girls come into the kitchen. Caroline says:
25 "What a mess! Again!"
She explains to Emma: "There is a charity bake-off at William Ellis tomorrow. The boys want to win but my brother can't bake." When she sees the muffins, she is surprised: "Wow, George,
30 are these the muffins from Grandma's recipe?" George doesn't answer. Caroline is excited. "Emma, look! My brother is a great baker!" Emma looks at the muffins. Then she looks at George.

b) What do you think: What happens next?
1 Emma doesn't say anything.
2 Emma tells Caroline and Rajiv about the muffins.
3 Emma talks to George alone.

c) Listen and check if you are right. 🔊 L 1/37

d) Scan the story and write down other words you can use for *say*. Example: *shout, …*
▶ Vocabulary | p. 175

A11 Target task Write an ending for the story

1 Choose one of the pictures and write an ending for the story.
2 Plan your ending:
 • What happens exactly? How do the characters feel? What do they say?
 • Collect words and phrases for your story.
3 Write the ending. Remember to …
 • use the simple present.
 • use direct speech (for example "The muffins look great," their teacher Mr Woolf says.)
 • use different words for *say*. (→ A10d), T3 on page 60).
 • use words to connect your sentences (connectives). (→ T4 on page 60).
4 👥 Work in groups. Read your stories to your group. Then correct them and choose the one you like best.
Present the story in class and give feedback to the other groups.

▶ Writing | p. 173   ▶ Wordbank 2 | p. 199   ▶ WB 14, 15 | pp. 41, 42

1

2

3

Need help? Look at pages 62–63. T1 T2 T3 T4 T5 T6

3 Part A: Target task tools

Target task tools for A11: Write an ending for the story

T1 Grammar: Simple present (statements) ▶ G12 | p. 188

Write down what Charlie does.
Example: *1 Charlie plays football.*

> Be careful with *do*, *go* and *tidy*.
> Check the spelling on page 188.

1. I play football.
2. I load the dishwasher.
3. I help at home.
4. I go to school.
5. I tidy my room.
6. I make my bed.
7. I do the shopping.
8. I watch TV.

T2 Words: Feelings

Find the words for feelings and write them down.
Example: *sad, …*

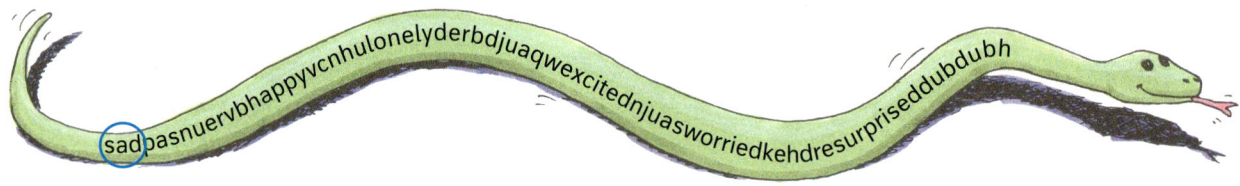

T3 Words: Other words for *say* 🔊 L 1/38 | S 31

Direct speech makes stories more interesting.
But be careful – it is boring if you always use the verb *say*.

a) What are these words? You can use them for *say*.

/ɑːsk/ • /tel/ • /ɪkˈspleɪn/ • /ʃaʊt/ • /ˈɑːnsə/

b) Listen and check your words.
Add the German meaning, too.

> You can use your dictionary or an online dictionary.

T4 Words: Connectives

a) Connectives are words you can use to connect sentences, for example *and* or *but*.
They make a story interesting to read.
Read the text on page 59 again and find
the English words for these connectives:

und • dann • plötzlich • als • aber

b) Use connectives to make this text more interesting.

> Joe and James want to bake biscuits. They meet at Joe's house. Joe has got a dog. His name is Rex. Rex loves cakes. Rex loves biscuits. He wants to be in the kitchen. Joe says: "No, Rex! Go to the living room!" Joe and James read the recipe. They bake the biscuits. Joe and James go into the living room. Rex goes into the kitchen. In the living room, Joe and James start to play computer
> 5 games. There is a noise in the kitchen. Joe goes into the kitchen. He sees Rex. The biscuits aren't there.

Part A: Target task tools 3

T5 Writing ▶ Writing | p. 173

Read this ending of the story about the bake-off. Collect words and phrases you can use for your ending. Note down …
- adjectives to describe feelings (for example *excited*),
- other adjectives for *good* or *nice* (for example *great*),
- verbs and phrases (for example *to try the cake*).

It is the day of the bake-off at William Ellis School. Rajiv and George are at their table with the banana cake and the muffins. Everything looks wonderful. When Mr Woolf comes to their table
5 he tries the cake. "This cake tastes very good," he tells them. Rajiv is very excited. Then Mr Woolf takes a muffin. "Boys, your muffins look fantastic. And they taste great!" he says. George and Rajiv smile. They are very happy. But suddenly George
10 sees his grandmother. What a surprise! She is at the bake-off. George is shocked. He is worried that his grandmother can see that the muffins are from the supermarket. "Hello George," his grandmother smiles. Then she looks at the muffins. She takes one and looks at it. Then she tastes it. She asks: "George, are these muffins from my recipe?" George answers: "No, they aren't." Then Mr Woolf asks George's grandmother: "Are you a good baker, Mrs McBride? Maybe you can help me. George's muffins are wonderful, but Joe's biscuits
15 are great, too. Who should be the winner?" George's grandmother looks at George. Then she answers: "I think Joe is the winner!"

T6 Words: Feedback

Look at these phrases. You can use them to give feedback to the other groups in A11. Copy the grid and fill it in.

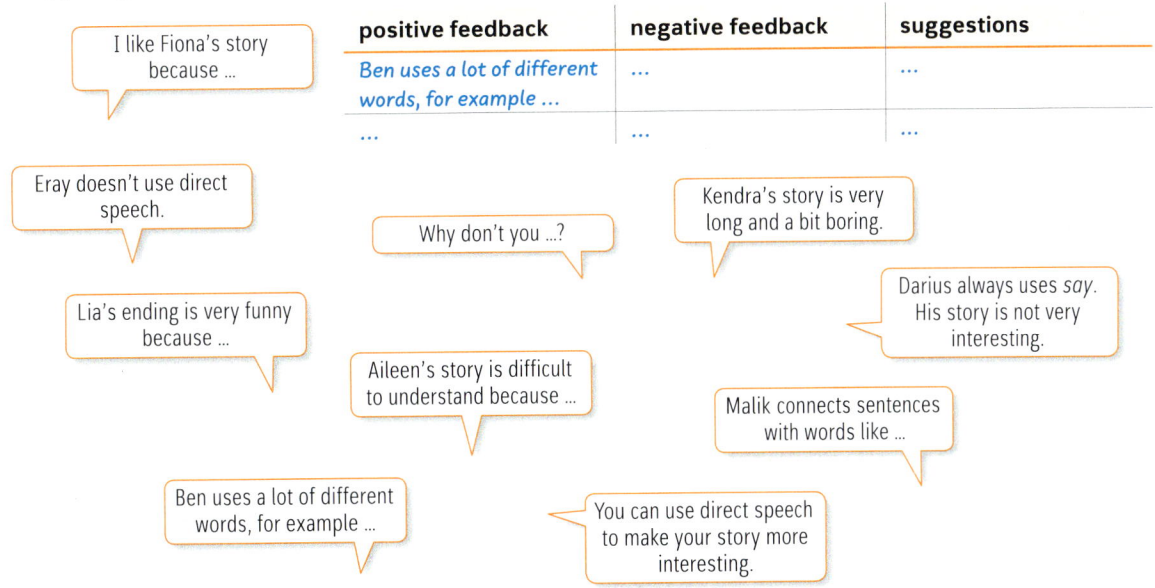

sixty-one 61

3 The talent show — Part B

B1 A school poster ▶ DIFF Training D18 | p. 145

a) Look at the poster.
What is it about?

b) What can you do at a talent show? Collect words in class. You can look at page 205 for help.

B2 At Camden School for Girls 🔊 S 32

a) Read the dialogue. Describe the girls' plan.
▶ Reading | p. 167   ▶ WB 16 | p. 42

Caroline: Look, a talent show! What do you think, girls? Have we got talent?
Beebee: Of course!
Caroline: OK, the audition is next week.
5 **Emma:** That's not much time. And I'm not really good at anything special.
Caroline: That's not true, Emma. You're good at volleyball. And you like reading and dancing.
Emma: But you can't take part in a talent show and
10 read or play volleyball! And I don't want to dance in front of everyone. Why do you want to be in the show, Beebee?
Beebee: Oh come on, Emma. Don't be so boring. Because we can wear beautiful costumes and be
15 the stars of the show, of course!
Gillian: But Beebee, you need more than beautiful costumes to be a star. What do you want to do?
Beebee: I don't know, but …
Caroline: We can be circus clowns and do funny
20 things. How do you like that?
Beebee: No way! I hate clowns!

Caroline: But Beebee, we can't just wear pretty costumes and smile.
Emma: Why don't you do our dance routine?
25 Caroline and I sometimes dance at home. It is quite good, I think.
Caroline: That's a great idea, Emma! But you must dance, too.
Emma: Only if Gillian comes, too.
30 **Gillian:** I'm not sure. I'm very nervous when I'm on a stage.
Caroline: Oh please, Gillian. Why don't you try it?
Gillian: OK. But don't get angry if we don't win. When do we want to meet?
35 **Caroline:** Let's meet at my house on Saturday afternoon.

b) Answer the questions.
1 What does Beebee say to Emma?
2 How does Beebee feel about circus clowns?
3 Why does Beebee want to take part?
4 Where do the girls want to meet?
5 When do the girls want to meet?
▶ DIFF Easy alternative D19, Training D20 | p. 145

c) Scan the dialogue. Find phrases you can use to agree, to disagree or to make suggestions.
Example: *OK, …*
          What do you think?, …
▶ Vocabulary | p. 175   ▶ WB 17 | p. 43

d) 👥 What about you? Do you like talent shows? Have you got a special talent?
Use your list from B1b) and talk to your partner. You can use some phrases from c).
▶ DIFF Training D21 | p. 146

- Do you like talent shows? — Yes, I do. / No, I don't.
- Have you got a special talent? Can you …? — Yes, I do. I can … / No, I …
- Why don't you take part in a talent show? — That's a great idea! / No way!

B3 Grammar card Simple present: questions with question words ▶ Grammar card | p. 179 ▶ WB 19 | p. 44

You know how to ask questions with *do/does* (A8). This is how you can ask questions with question words (for example *what, where, when, why, how, who*) and *do/does*:
*What **do** you think*?
Find more examples in B2. Add them to your grammar card for the simple present.
Use colours for: question word, do/does, subject, infinitive. Check G15 on page 191. ▶ G15 | p. 191

! who = wer
where = wo

B4 Questions about the audition ▶ DIFF Support D22, Training D23, Extra D24 | p. 146 ▶ WB 18, 20 | pp. 43, 44

In the afternoon the girls ask their teacher about the audition.
Look at Mr Green's answers. Complete the girls' questions.
Example: *1 Where does the audition take place?*

1. Where does …?
2. Why …?
3. What …?
4. When …?
5. How many …?

1. The audition takes place in the assembly hall.
2. It takes place in the assembly hall because it's a big room.
3. You wear your PE things for the audition.
4. The audition takes place at 4 pm.
5. We choose three acts for the talent show.

B5 George, Rajiv and Charlie ▶ Reading | p. 167

a) Read the comic. Say what happens.
b) What do Rajiv and George think about dancing?

c) Listen to the dialogue. What is Charlie's problem? ◀)) L 1/39 ▶ Listening | p. 166
d) Imagine you are Charlie. What do you do now?

3 Part B

B6 The auditions at Camden School for Girls ◀)) L 1/40 ▶ Listening | p. 166

On Wednesday the girls go to the auditions at Camden School for Girls.

a) Listen and find out if they can take part in *Camden's Got Talent*.

b) Listen again and say what acts take part.

piano solo • magic tricks • acrobatic routine • comedy • song • dance routine

c) Choose Emma, Caroline, Beebee or Gillian. Say how she feels.

sad • happy • disappointed • glad • angry • worried • excited • …

B7 Mediation ( ) ▶ Mediation | p. 177

Read the poster.
Then answer the questions in German.

1 Wo findet der Wettbewerb statt?
2 Was kann man gewinnen?
3 Wo kann man Eintrittskarten kaufen?
4 Was kosten sie?
5 Was wird geboten?
6 Was sollte man beachten, wenn man hingeht?

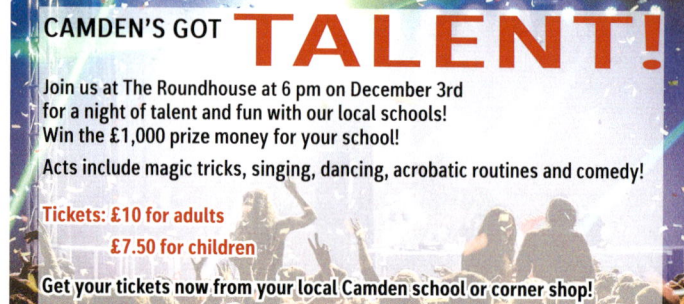

B8 Camden's Got Talent ◀)) S 33

a) Read the story and choose the best title for it. Give reasons. ▶ New words | p. 168
▶ DIFF Training D25 | p. 147   ▶ Reading | p. 167   ▶ WB 21 | p. 45

| 1 An exciting evening | 2 Charlie surprises his friends | 3 Rajiv's special night

On the day of the show Caroline and her friends are at The Roundhouse. They are very excited. They know a lot of the girls from Camden School for Girls. Claire Brown plays a brilliant piano
5 solo and Kira and Sally do a fantastic acrobatic routine. Grace is a bit nervous but the girls clap a lot to support her. There are very good acts from other schools, too. Emma loves the magic tricks and Gillian laughs and laughs at the clowns' act.

10 George is there, too. He is next to Emma. There is too much dancing for him.
15 He only wants to hear Rajiv and

the school band. Unfortunately he hasn't got a friend with him. Rajiv is still behind the stage and Charlie doesn't answer his texts. Charlie is a
20 bit strange at the moment. George doesn't know what is wrong with him. George can see Charlie's family in the audience, but where is Charlie?

The show is very long but then it is time for Rajiv and the William Ellis school band. When the
25 music starts, the audience starts to clap. Rajiv is a really cool guitar player and the band is fantastic. When the band finishes, everyone stands up and claps a lot. The girls and George think they must be the winners.

There is just one more act – dancers from Acland Burghley School. George thinks, "Why isn't Charlie here? He must know some of the dancers. We could laugh at the dancers together!"

Then the music starts, the dancers come on stage and Emma suddenly shouts, "Look, it's Charlie!" George is very surprised. Charlie is on stage – he does a solo. "Wow, look how Charlie moves," says Caroline. George agrees. Charlie is an amazing dancer. His group dances hip hop – it is fantastic.

At the end everyone stands up and cheers and Charlie takes a special bow. Now George understands why Charlie doesn't answer his texts. Then it is time to find out the winners of the competition. Claire and Rajiv and the school band are the winners but Charlie gets a special prize for best dancer.

b) Read the story again and decide if these sentences are right or wrong. Write down the words from the text.
Example: Grace is a bit strange. → *That's wrong. "Grace is a bit nervous." (line 6).*

1. Emma loves the dance routine.
2. Gillian laughs at the magic tricks.
3. George is next to Caroline.
4. Rajiv is a really bad guitar player.
5. Charlie is not a good dancer.
6. Rajiv gets a special prize.

B9 Target task Prepare an interview

1. You are a school reporter from Acland Burghley at Camden's Got Talent. You want to interview Charlie. Look at the reporter's notes. Write down questions for Charlie.
   Example: *How do you feel?*
   You can add more questions.
   Use the simple present.
   ▶ Writing | p. 173

2. Note down what Charlie can answer.
3. 👥 Work with a partner. One of you is the reporter, one of you is Charlie. Act out the interview. ▶ Talking | p. 169
4. Make sure that …
   - the reporter is interested in Charlie,
   - your questions are short and clear,
   - your answers are clear,
   - you answer the questions with more than one or two words.

   - how/feel?
   - why/dance hip hop?
   - when/practise?
   - how often/practise?
   - where/practise?
   - what/your friends think?
   - …

   You can start like this:
   Reporter: Congratulations, Charlie! What a great show!
   Charlie: Thanks.
   Reporter: I'm a reporter for the Acland Burghley school magazine. Can I ask you some questions?
   Charlie: Sure!
   …

   > Your questions are short and clear.

5. Present your interview to another pair. Give feedback. ▶ WB 22 | p. 45

Need help? Look at pages 68/69. T1 T2 T3 T4 T5 T6

3 Part B: Target task tools

Target task tools for B9: Prepare an interview

T1 Simple present: Questions with question words ▶ G15 | p. 191

a) Add *do* or *does* and write down the correct questions.
 1 in the competition / want to do / the girls / What / ?
 2 the girls / want to meet / When / at Caroline's house / ?
 3 take place / Where / the competition / ?
 4 Rajiv / What / do in the competition / ?
 5 Charlie / George's texts / Why / not answer / ?
 6 solo dance / Who / ?

b) Answer the questions.

T2 Simple present: Questions with question words ▶ G15 | p. 191

Write down the questions so that the highlighted parts are the answers.
Example: Charlie wears jeans to school. → *What does Charlie wear to school?*

1 The audience claps when Rajiv plays the guitar.
2 Rajiv and the school band play rock music.
3 Charlie does an amazing solo on stage.
4 George sits next to Emma.
5 Charlie takes a bow because the audience cheers.
6 Claire wins a prize for her performance.

T3 Words: Talent show

Use the words to complete the text.

auditions • prizes • take part • talented • competition • audience • practise • stars • performance

This year Camden School for Girls wants to **1** in a school music **2**. Many of the girls can play a musical instrument and are very **3**. On Friday after school there are **4** so that the music teacher can choose the best girls. The winners must **5** for weeks after school. On the day of the competition the girls' families and friends are in the **6**. The Camden School girls give a fantastic **7** and are the **8** of the show. At the end of the evening they win many **9**.

Part B: Target task tools 3

T4 Words: Talent show
Match the English sentences and the German translations.

1 Herzlichen Glückwunsch!
2 Was für eine fantastische Darbietung!
3 Du bist der Star der Show!
4 Großartige Unterhaltung!
5 Erzähl mir mehr davon!
6 Vielen Dank für das Interview.
7 Bitte schön.
8 Mir geht es großartig.

A What a fantastic performance!
B Congratulations!
C Great entertainment!
D You're the star of the show!
E Thank you for the interview.
F Tell me more about it.
G I feel great.
H You're welcome.

T5 Word order: Adverbs of frequency ▶ G13 | p. 189
Put the words in the right order and write down the sentences.
1 to school / always / goes / George / by bus
2 a cake / Mrs Butler / bakes / on Sundays / sometimes
3 often / football / Gillian / plays / at the weekend
4 in the shop / helps / usually / Rajiv / his parents
5 in the morning / never / Charlie / watches TV
6 a book / Caroline / reads / sometimes / in the evening

T6 Speaking: Interview
A reporter for the William Ellis school magazine interviews Rajiv about the school band.
Complete the reporter's questions.

Reporter: Hi Rajiv! Congratulations, what a fantastic show!
Rajiv: Thanks.
Reporter: Can I ask you some questions?
Rajiv: Of course.
Reporter: How do you **1** ?
Rajiv: I feel great! I always have fun with the band.
Reporter: Tell me more about it. How often **2** ?
Rajiv: We practise every week.
Reporter: Where **3** ?
Rajiv: We meet at school.
Reporter: What kind of music **4** ?
Rajiv: I like rock songs and hip hop.
Reporter: Thank you for the interview.
Rajiv: You're welcome.

3 Hobbies — Photo tour

Many free-time activities in England are the same as in Germany.
British children do sports, play musical instruments or spend time with their friends.
Some of these activities take place at school, usually in the form of school clubs. This is because the school day is long. School usually starts at 9 o'clock in the morning and ends between 3 and 4 o'clock in the afternoon. So there is not much free time during the week.

A Schools offer[1] many different sports and they usually have very good facilities[2], such as sports halls and playing fields. Pupils can play many different sports, such as table tennis, hockey, cricket, football and basketball. They can play in a school team and take part in competitions against other schools.

B Music is also very popular in most British schools. Many schools have a number of different bands, orchestras and choirs that pupils can join. These groups practise at lunchtime or after school and they perform during the school year. Pupils can also have individual lessons to learn different musical instruments, but parents must pay for these.

C Pupils can also do many other activities before and after school and at lunchtime. You can learn how to do pottery[3], write poetry and take part in a poetry slam, and you can do exciting science experiments. Or perhaps you want to join the maths club or learn Mandarin Chinese[4]? School clubs offer you the chance to do many exciting things.

---

1 to offer – *anbieten* | **2** facilities – hier: *Ausstattung* | **3** pottery – *Töpfern* | **4** Mandarin Chinese – *Mandarin (chinesische Sprache)*

Photo tour

P1 Free-time activities L 1/42 | S 35
a) Listen to the pupils and say what their free-time activities are.

  Bertie • Julia • Alexa • Alice • Rocco

  playing the violin • meeting up with friends • trampolining • playing the steel drum • going to a shopping centre

b) Find photos to match the activities.

P2 Activities in British schools
Read the text about free-time activities in British schools and match the other photos to the correct paragraphs (A-C).
▶ Reading | p. 167

P3 An email to a pen friend
Write an email to an English pen friend.
Tell her/him about your free-time activities.
- What are your free-time activities and when and where do you do them?
- What is the same as in Britain, and what is different?

You can use words from exercises 1 and 3 on page 54 for help.
▶ Wordbank 9 | p. 205
▶ Writing | p. 173

Hi ...,
How are you? Let me tell you about my free-time activities. ...
What about your hobbies?
Love, ...

sixty-nine 69

3   I can …

Was hast du alles neu gelernt? Diese Seite hilft dir dabei, das zu erkennen. Falls du Hilfe benötigst, etwas nachlesen oder noch ein paar Übungen machen möchtest, findest du hier passende Hinweise.

WORTSCHATZ

Ich kann …	Aufgaben	Übungen/Hilfen
über Hobbys sprechen *What is your favourite hobby? – My favourite hobby is playing football.*	1, 3, 5	▶ **DIFF** D1 ▶ Wordbank 9 | p. 205 ▶ **WB** 1, 3
die Uhrzeit angeben *What time is it? – It's half past seven.*	4	▶ **DIFF** D2, D3 ▶ Wordbank 3 | p. 200 ▶ **WB** 4, 5
Haushaltstätigkeiten beschreiben *to tidy the room • to walk the dog • to empty the dishwasher*	A2, A4–A6	▶ **DIFF** D8, D10, D11 ▶ Wordbank 4 | p. 201 ▶ **WB** 6
unterschiedliche Wörter für *say* verwenden *to ask • to tell • to explain • to shout • to answer*	A10, A11	▶ T3 | p. 60 ▶ **WB** 14

SKILLS

Ich kann …	Aufgaben	Übungen/Hilfen
heraushören, worum es in einem Gespräch geht LISTENING	A1, A7, B5, B6	▶ **DIFF** D4 ▶ Listening | p. 166
verstehen, worum es in einem Lied geht LISTENING	A6	▶ Listening | p. 166
ein Interview führen, das ich vorbereitet habe SPEAKING • WRITING	B9	▶ T6 | p. 67 ▶ Talking | p. 169
entscheiden, ob Aussagen richtig oder falsch sind, nachdem ich mir ein Video über Hobbys angesehen habe VIEWING	2	▶ **WB** 2
entscheiden, ob Aussagen richtig oder falsch sind, nachdem ich einen Dialog oder eine Geschichte gelesen habe READING	A2, B8	▶ **DIFF** D4 ▶ Reading | p. 167
sagen, worum es in einer Geschichte geht READING	A10, B8	▶ **DIFF** D17 ▶ **WB** 21
Informationen aus einem Dialog herauslesen READING	B2	▶ **DIFF** D19, D20
eine Geschichte zu Ende schreiben WRITING	A11	▶ T1–T6 | pp. 60–61 ▶ Writing | p. 173 ▶ **WB** 15
unbekannte Wörter aus einem Faltblatt erschließen und Fragen zu einem Informationstext auf Deutsch beantworten MEDIATION	6, B7	▶ Understanding new words | p. 168 ▶ Mediation | p. 177

GRAMMATIK

Ich kann …	Aufgaben	Übungen/Hilfen
Aussagesätze im *simple present* formulieren und verneinen *George always makes his bed. • Rajiv doesn't lay the table.*	A3–A5, A11	▶ **DIFF** D6, D7, D9–D12 ▶ T1 | p. 60 ▶ G12 ▶ **WB** 7, 8
die Regel zur Satzstellung in Aussagesätzen verwenden *I always empty the dishwasher.*	A5, A11	▶ **DIFF** D11, D12 ▶ T6 | p. 67 ▶ G13
Entscheidungsfragen im *simple present* bilden und beantworten *Do you like muffins? – Yes, I do.*	A8, A9, A11	▶ **DIFF** D14, D15 ▶ G14 ▶ **WB** 10
Fragen mit Fragewörtern im *simple present* bilden *What do you think? • When does the audition take place?*	B3, B4	▶ **DIFF** D22–D24 ▶ T1, T2 | p. 66 ▶ G15 ▶ **WB** 19

4

Birthdays

In diesem *Theme* wirst du …

- über Geburtstage sprechen
- Daten angeben
- berichten, was gerade passiert
- ein Telefongespräch vorspielen
- ein Einkaufsgespräch führen
- eine Geschichte zu Ende schreiben

4 Birthday plans   Intro

1 The calendar rap   🔊 L 1/43, 44 | S 36, 37   ▶ WB 1, 2 | p. 52

a) Listen to the calendar rap and sing it.

b) Listen again.
Stand up when you hear the month of your birthday.

January • February • March • April • May • June • July • August • September • October • November • December

2 Birthday dates   🔊 L 1/45   ▶ DIFF Support D1 | p. 147

a) Listen and say the dates.

b) Listen again and point at the dates.

1 2 3 4 5 6 7

3 The birthday game

a) Talk about your birthdays in class.   ▶ Wordbank 3 | p. 200   ▶ WB 3 | p. 53

> When is your birthday?

> My birthday is in winter. It's on the 31st of January.

> I think you're in the wrong place. Your birthday is in June/in summer/…

These words can help you:
spring • summer • autumn • winter

b) 1 Make a line from January to December.
   2 One pupil goes out.
   3 Two pupils change places.
   4 The first pupil comes back.
      He/She must say who is in the wrong place.   ▶ WB 4 | p. 53

4 Birthdays in London   ▶ WB 5 | p. 53

It is Caroline and George's first birthday in London. They want to do something special.

a) Read the websites. Which is your favourite birthday party? Say why.   ▶ Reading | p. 167

b) Copy the grid and complete it.

	Trent Park	Kayaking on Regent's Canal	Alexandra Palace
activity	pony riding, party games	kayaking	…
price	…	…	…
food	…	bring your own cake and food	…
decorations	horse theme decorations	…	paper plates, indoor fireworks

c) Make a word web.
You can use the words from b) and add more words you know.
▶ Vocabulary | p. 175

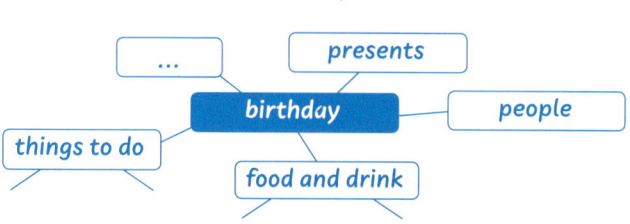

Intro **4**

Pony riding at Trent Park
A fantastic way to celebrate your birthday

Ride with your friends for an hour. Then you can enjoy food and games in our party room with horse theme decorations.

We offer different menus with mini pizzas, sandwiches and ice cream.
- £32 for each pony
- £8 per child

www.trentpark.co.uk/ponyriding

Kayaking on Regent's Canal

Take your friends kayaking on Regent's Canal on your birthday. You can see and do lots of exciting things.
£60 per hour for up to 8 children (8–16 years)
£25 per hour to use the club room for your party after the kayaking.
We decorate the room with balloons and paper chains.
Bring your own birthday cake and party food.

www.alexandrapalace.co.uk/birthdayparties

Birthday parties on ice

Enjoy a wonderful birthday party at Alexandra Palace. Parties include an hour of exciting ice skating and fantastic food in our Ice Café.
The price is £17.50 per child. Parents are free.
You can have special party food for your guests:
- burger, chips and lemonade
- fish fingers, chips and apple juice
- vegetarian buffet

We decorate the table with paper plates and indoor fireworks.

5 Who wants what? L 1/46 ▶ Listening | p. 166

a) Listen to the dialogue and answer the questions:
- Which party does Caroline like?
- Which party does George like?

b) What does Mrs McBride say? Can they have two parties?

c) What party do the twins choose?
A Football party
B Fancy dress party
C Harry Potter party

6 Your dream birthday party

▶ DIFF Support D2 | p. 147, Extra D3-D5 | p. 148

a) Plan your dream birthday party. Note down your ideas.
Think about
- place
- food and drink
- activities
- decorations
- guests

b) Tell your partner about your dream birthday party.

Use your words from exercise 4.
You can also use:
- the wordbank on page 203,
- the dictionary on pp. 257-262,
- or an online dictionary.
▶ New words | p. 168
▶ WB Media 4 ▶ WES-149220-2

seventy-three 73

4 Saturday afternoon — Part A

A1 Saturday afternoon 🔊 S 38

a) Read about the McBrides. Where are Mr and Mrs McBride? Where are Caroline and George?

▶ Reading | p. 167   ▶ **DIFF** Easy alternative D6 | p. 149   ▶ WB 6 | p. 54

It is Saturday afternoon, a week before the party. Mr and Mrs McBride are training at the gym at the moment. They always train at the gym on Saturdays. The twins usually stay at home. Today
5 they want to plan their birthday party.
But right now George is sitting on the sofa. He is watching Arsenal against Manchester United on TV. It is a great football match. George is happy because the Man United players are winning.
10 Patch is sleeping next to George.
Caroline is writing a shopping list for the party. "What about the invitation cards, George?", she asks her brother, but George isn't listening. "And what about the decorations?" No answer.
15 Caroline is angry. George never helps her when there is football on TV.
Suddenly the phone rings. George answers the phone. It is Mrs McBride.
"Is everything OK?", she asks. "What are you
20 doing right now? Are you playing computer games?"
George answers, "No, I'm not. We are writing a shopping list for the party. And we are making the invitation cards and decorations."
25 "That's wonderful," Mrs McBride says.
"Are you coming home now?", George asks.
"No, we're not. We're just having coffee," Mrs McBride answers.

Caroline tries to take the phone from George but
30 he says, "Bye Mum, see you soon!"
Now Caroline is very angry. "You aren't writing a shopping list and you aren't making invitation cards or decorations!", she shouts at George. "You're lazy! And a liar!"
35 George looks at the TV. The match is over. He says, "OK, give me the invitation cards." He sits down. "See? I'm not a liar. I'm helping you now."

b) 👥 Test your partner: Right or wrong? Correct the wrong sentences.

> Caroline is watching a football match.
>
> That's wrong. She is writing a shopping list.
>
> George is watching a football match.
>
> That's right.

George Caroline Patch	is isn't	sitting on the sofa. watching a football match. sitting at the table. sleeping. writing a shopping list. listening. making decorations.
Mr and Mrs McBride The twins	are aren't	playing computer games. training at the gym. coming home now. planning the party.

Media
Sieh dir das Bild an und überfliege den Text noch einmal. Welche Medien verwendet George in seiner Freizeit? Welche Medien verwendest du in deiner Freizeit?
▶ WB Media 2   ▶ WES-149220-2

Part A 4

A2 What do you think of George?
Read A1 again. What do you think of George?

funny • cheeky • lazy • clever • unfair • …

> I think George is cheeky because he doesn't tell his mum what he is doing.

> I think George is lazy because …

A3 Grammar card Present progressive ▶ DIFF Training D7, Support D8 | p. 149   ▶ WB 7 | p. 54

Start a grammar card for the present progressive. You use the present progressive to say what somebody is doing now.

1 Look at these sentences from the text.
  How do you form the present progressive?
  Patch is sleeping next to George.
  Mr and Mrs McBride are training at the gym.

2 Read G16 on pages 192/193.
  Note down how you form …
  • positive statements,
  • negative statements,
  • questions.
  Note down the rules about the spelling, too.
  Find examples in A1 and write them down.

A4 What are they doing now? ▶ DIFF Training D9-D11 | pp. 149-150   ▶ WB 8, 9 | p. 55

Say what the twins' friends and family are doing/not doing now.
Example: *1. Emma and Gillian are talking on the phone. They aren't doing their homework.*

1 Emma and Gillian: talk on the phone / do their homework

2 Charlie: play basketball / watch TV

3 Rajiv: do homework / work in the shop

4 twins' parents: have lunch / wash the car

5 Beebee: read a book / play the guitar

6 Joe: walk his dog / load the dishwasher

A5 A game ▶ DIFF Support D12, Extra D13 | p. 151   ▶ Wordbank 9 | p. 205

a) Group work: Play a game.
  1 Write down activities on cards.
  2 Mix the cards and put them face down.
  3 Take a card. Mime the activity to your group.
  4 Your group must guess the activity.

b) In your group think of an activity to do together. Show it to another group. They must guess it.

> Are you …?

> Yes, we are.

> No, we aren't. We're …

> Are you playing tennis?

> Yes, I am.

> No, I'm not. Try again.

4 Part A

A6 Simple present or present progressive? ▶ G17 | p. 193 ▶ DIFF Training D14, D15 | p. 152 ▶ WB 10, 11 | p. 56

You use the *simple present* to talk about routines:
*They **always** train at the gym on Saturdays.*
You use the *present progressive* to say what somebody is doing now:
***Right now** George is sitting on the sofa.*

Choose the correct verb form.
1 Elizabeth **plays / is playing** the piano right now.
2 Elizabeth **plays / is playing** the piano on Saturday afternoons.
3 Rajiv often **plays / is playing** football in the park at the weekend.
4 Rajiv **plays / is playing** football in the park right now.
5 The girls **eat / are eating** muffins in the café at the moment.
6 The girls **meet / are meeting** at the café every Sunday.
7 My family **goes / is going** to Scotland every summer.
8 We **have / are having** a wonderful holiday in Scotland at the moment.

A7 A phone call ◀)) L 1/47 | S 39 ▶ WB 12 | p. 57

a) Close your books. Listen to George and Charlie.
Say what their plan is. ▶ DIFF Easy alternative D16 | p. 152 ▶ Listening | p. 166

b) Listen again and answer the questions.
1 Why are Charlie and Rajiv looking for more players?
2 Who is Rajiv texting?
3 What are Emma and Gillian doing?

c) Read the dialogue with a partner. ▶ Dramatic reading | p. 178
Imitate the way George and Charlie talk.

George: Hello?
Charlie: Hi, George, it's Charlie.
George: Hey Charlie! What are you doing now?
5 **Charlie:** I'm playing football with Rajiv. But it's boring with just two players. So right now we are looking for more players. Why don't you
10 come along?
George: Sounds good. Where are you playing?
Charlie: We're playing in the park. By the way, what is Caroline doing at the moment?
15 Can she come, too? Emma and Gillian aren't answering their phones. Rajiv is just texting them.

George: Oh man. Why are you asking the girls? Caroline is busy. She's planning our party. 20
Charlie: Oh, come on, please ask her because we need more players. It's much more fun.
George: OK then. When do you want to meet? 25
Charlie: What about 4:30? Oh, just a minute … Rajiv has got a text message from Emma and Gillian. They are shopping at Camden Market right now but we can all 30 meet later. Is five o'clock good for you?
George: Yes, that's fine. See you later.
Charlie: Bye for now.

d) Collect phrases you can use in a phone call:
• to start a phone call, • to end a phone call, • to make suggestions and react to them.
▶ DIFF Training D17 | p. 152 ▶ Vocabulary | p. 175

Part A 4

A8 In the park

a) The friends are now in the park. Look at the pictures.
Say what is happening in each picture.
Write one sentence about each picture.
Use the verbs in the box.
Example: *In picture 1 they are choosing teams.*

*score a goal (2x) •
walk off the field • shout at •
say sorry • choose teams*

b) In picture 3 George says "Girls can't play football!" What do you think: Is he right?

A9 Choose Write or draw ▶ DIFF Training D18 | p. 152
- What is happening? Write about each picture in the comic above.
  Use the present progressive.   **OR**
- Draw a comic and write speech bubbles and captions.
  Use the present progressive.

A10 Target task Act out a phone call

Act out a phone call with your partner.
You want to meet your friend in the afternoon and do something nice.

1 Collect ideas for your phone call and write them down. ▶ Wordbank 9 | p. 205   ▶ Talking | p. 169
Note down …
 • what you are doing at the moment,
 • what your friend is doing,
 • what you want to do together,
 • where you can go,
 • …

2 Use your phrases from A7d) to start and finish the phone call, to make suggestions and to react to them. Remember when to use the present progressive and when to use the simple present.

3 Act out the phone call. You can use your notes.

Media
Tip: You can record your phone call.
▶ WB Media 3   ▶ WES-149220-2

Need help? Look at pages 78/79: T1 T2 T3 T4 T5

4 Part A: Target task tools

Target task tools for A 10: Act out a phone call

T1 Present progressive: Questions ▶ G16 | p. 192

👥 Work with a partner. Look at the picture for a minute, then close your book.
Your partner looks at the picture and asks you questions. Take turns.

- What is ... doing? / ...
- Is Rajiv riding his bike?
- Yes, he is. / No, he isn't.
- Is ...? / Are ...?

T2 Present progressive or simple present? ▶ G17 | p. 193

a) Use the grid and write sentences. What do the people usually do?
What are they doing now?
Example: *1. Grace often plays basketball but now she is reading a book.*

	simple present		present progressive
1	Grace often (play) basketball	but	now she (read) a book
2	Kemi and her father usually (watch) a film on Saturdays	but	today they (make) pizza.
3	Usually Ian (play) football after school	but	now he (buy) a new computer game.
4	Mrs Spencer never (help) at home	but	now she (hoover) the living room.

b) Grace is talking to Kemi on the phone. Copy the text and choose the correct forms.

Grace: "Hi Kemi. Sorry, I can't come, I **1 look / am looking** after my cousin, Ben. He's four. My mum usually **2 does / is doing** it, but today she **3 watches / is watching** a film at the cinema with my aunt. They often **4 go / are going** to the cinema together. Ben is really cute. He **5 goes / is going** to kindergarten every day. Now he **6 draws / is drawing** a picture. He **7 sits / is sitting** on the floor next to me. And you? What **8 do you do / are you doing**? You **9 talk / are talking** to me on the phone? Very funny!"

Part A: Target task tools **4**

T3 Words: Making plans

It is Friday afternoon. Katie phones her friend Lara.

a) Put the sentences in the right order and write down their conversation.

b) Read out the dialogue with a partner.

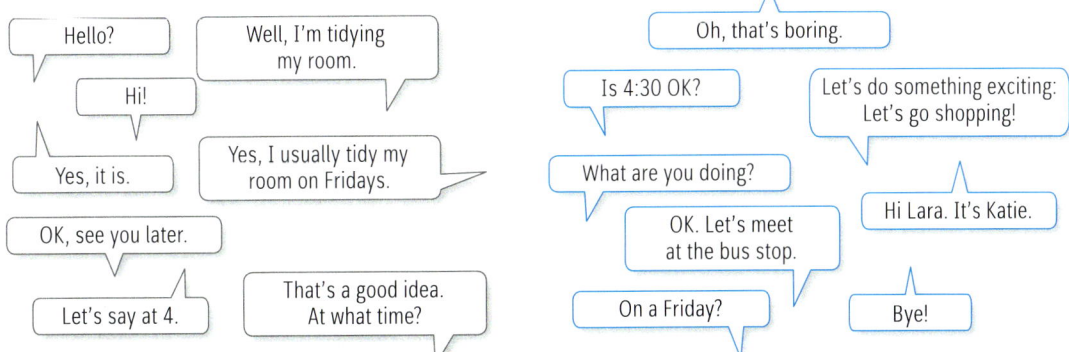

- Hello?
- Well, I'm tidying my room.
- Oh, that's boring.
- Hi!
- Is 4:30 OK?
- Let's do something exciting: Let's go shopping!
- Yes, it is.
- Yes, I usually tidy my room on Fridays.
- What are you doing?
- OK, see you later.
- OK. Let's meet at the bus stop.
- Hi Lara. It's Katie.
- Let's say at 4.
- That's a good idea. At what time?
- On a Friday?
- Bye!

T4 Words: Making a phone call

Copy the grid and fill in the words.

beginning/ending a phone call	making suggestions	reacting to suggestions
Hi	…	…

Hi • Bye for now. • It's Charlie. • No, sorry. • How is it going? • Bye. • Let's … • Hey • Why don't we …? • Great idea! • This is Gillian. • What about …? • What's up? • Is five o'clock good for you? • Sounds good! • Maybe we can … • Hello • See you later.

T5 Media: On the phone

Think about when you use your phone and answer the questions.

1. Who do you talk to on the phone?

   my friends • my parents • my grandparents • a pizza delivery service • …

2. Why do you use the phone to communicate with these people?

   I don't see them very often.
   I need to ask them something.
   I want to tell them about my day.

3. Do you call, send a text message or send a voice message if you want to …
   - ask what's for homework?
   - tell your dad that you are late?
   - go to the cinema with a group of friends?
   - want to say happy birthday to your aunt?

Media

Sprecht darüber, was die Vor- und Nachteile von Telefongesprächen, Textnachrichten und Sprachnachrichten sind. Was verwendet ihr am häufigsten? Warum?

seventy-nine 79

4 The party — Part B

B1 Emma and Gillian 🔊 L 1/48 | S 40

Emma and Gillian are shopping at Camden Market. Close your books and listen. Note down the things they are talking about. What do they buy?   ▶ DIFF Easy alternative D19 | p. 153

▶ Listening | p. 166   ▶ WB 14, 15 | pp. 57, 58

T-shirt • jeans • bag with an elephant • earrings • poster • phone case • balloon • birthday card

Emma: Look, Gillian. This T-shirt is really nice!
Gillian: Yeah, but I don't like the colour.
Emma: Look, there's a bag with an elephant! Perfect for Caroline.
5 **Shop assistant:** Can I help you?
Emma: No, thanks, we're just looking.
Gillian: Excuse me, how much is the elephant bag, please?
Shop assistant: It's £19.99.
10 **Gillian:** Oh, that's a bit expensive. Have you got any other elephant bags?
Shop assistant: No, we haven't. Sorry. But we've got some other nice things. Let me know if you need help.
15 **Emma:** Let's find some earrings for Caroline's birthday.
Gillian: Earrings? Hm! Does Caroline like earrings?
Emma: No idea, but she loves her phone. How
20 about a new phone case?
Gillian: Great idea! – Excuse me, have you got any phone cases?
Shop assistant: Yes, of course. We've got some over there.
25 **Emma:** Thank you. – Gillian, look at this phone case. It looks like an elephant.
Gillian: It's great. But Caroline has got a MyPhone 7. This is for a MyPhone 8. Have you got any elephant cases for a MyPhone 7?
30 **Shop assistant:** Let me check … Yes, here you are!
Emma: How much are they?
Shop assistant: £8.99.
Emma: Oh, that's a good price.
Gillian: Yes, that's cheap. Let's buy one. And we've
35 even got some money left for a funny birthday card. They haven't got any cards here. Let's go to the card shop over there.
Emma: Perfect. I love shopping at Camden Market!

Britisches Geld

Culture box

In Großbritannien wird in *pounds* und *pence* bezahlt. Für das *pound* gibt es dieses Zeichen: £. Ein Pfund hat hundert *pence*. So werden die Preise angegeben: £2.30, aber du sagst: *two pound(s) thirty*. Bei *50p* kannst du *fifty pence* oder *fifty p* sagen.
Sieh dir das Video an und finde heraus:
• Was ist auf den Geldscheinen und Münzen zu sehen?
• Was passiert mit dem Geld, wenn es eine neue Königin oder einen neuen König gibt?
Kannst du herausfinden, wie viel Euro man für ein Pfund bezahlen muss?

B2 In the shop

Read the dialogue and match the sentence halves.

1 Emma wants to find
2 The shop assistant hasn't got
3 The shop assistant shows them
4 Gillian and Emma have got

A some money left for a birthday card.
B some earrings for Caroline.
C any other elephant bags in the shop.
D some phone cases.

Part B 4

B3 *Some or any?* ▶ DIFF Training D20 | p. 153 ▶ WB 16, 17 | pp. 58, 59

a) When do you use *some*, when do you use *any*?
First read the box. You can look at G18 on page 194 for help.

> In positive statements, you use *some*:
> → *We've got some other nice things.*
> In negative statements and questions you use *any*:
> → *They haven't got any cards here.*
> → *Have you got any other bags?*
> ▶ G18 | p. 194

b) Now look at the pictures.
Say what they *have got / haven't got*.

> Lea has got some ...
> but she hasn't got any ...

1 Lea

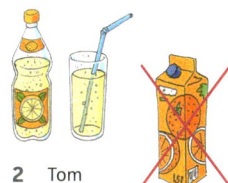
2 Tom

3 Christopher

4 Daniel

B4 *A shopping dialogue* ▶ DIFF Training D21 | p. 153, Support D22, Extra D23 | p. 154 ▶ WB 13 | p. 57

a) Read the dialogue on page 80 and collect shopping phrases in a grid.

Shop assistant	Customer
Can I help you?	*No, thanks, we're just looking.*
...	...

b) Work with a partner.
Write a shopping dialogue and act it out.
One of you is the shop assistant, one of you is the customer.
You can use your phrases from B4a).
Tip: You can record your dialogue.
▶ Wordbank 6 | p. 202 ▶ Talking | p. 169 ▶ WB Media 3
▶ WES-149220-2

B5 *An invitation card* ▶ DIFF Extra D24 | p. 154
Look at the invitation card.
Do you want to go to this party?
Say why or why not.

B6 *Charlie and Rajiv* ▶ DIFF Training D25 | p. 155 ▶ Wordbank 6 | p. 202

a) Read the dialogue. What are the boys talking about? ▶ WB 19 | p. 59

Charlie: Rajiv, have you got a costume for the party?
Rajiv: No. I don't like fancy dress parties.
5 **Charlie:** Why not? Fancy dress parties are fun!
And I've got the best costume.
Guess what it is! I can give you a hint:
My trainers and my socks are white.
10 **Rajiv:** No idea.
Charlie: My trousers are white and my jumper is white, too.
Rajiv: Have you got a white coat, too?
15 Are you a doctor?
Charlie: No, but I've got white gloves, too.
Rajiv: White gloves? Are you a ghost?
Charlie: No! I've got a white helmet, too.
Rajiv: A helmet?
20 **Charlie:** Yes! OK, my last hint is: My costume is from a science fiction film.

b) What is Charlie's costume?
c) Make a picture dictionary for clothes.
d) Describe what somebody in your class is wearing. The class must guess who it is.

eighty-one 81

B7 The birthday party S 41 WB 20 | p. 60

a) Look at the pictures. What do you think is happening?
b) Read the story and find a new title for it.

▶ DIFF Easy alternative D26 | p. 155
▶ New words | p. 168   ▶ Vocabulary | p. 175

It is the day of the twins' party. There are decorations in the living room and there is a big table with delicious food: muffins, sandwiches, hot dogs and a big birthday cake.
5 Stormtrooper Charlie is the DJ. Everyone looks great in their costumes. Even Rajiv has got a cool costume. He is a detective.

Caroline is very happy. She loves the party and the costumes. She says, "Emma, your elf costume
10 is so cool! Please let me take a picture!"
Beebee rolls her eyes. "Pah, elves are for babies!" Beebee is a vampire. She thinks she looks really cool.
Emma is upset but Rajiv says, "You're just jealous,
15 Beebee. Come on, Caroline. Give me your phone. I can take a picture of you and elf Emma. Aaaand smile …!"
Behind the girls ninja George is dancing with a glass of orange juice in his hand. Now he is doing
20 a cool dance move – and spills the juice over Emma's costume.

Emma screams, "Oh, George, look at my costume!"
"Oops, I'm sorry," George says. Emma is upset.
25 "It's ruined now!"
"Don't be a baby," Beebee laughs. "It's just a bit of orange juice. Come on, George, let's get a new drink."
Emma is angry with Beebee and George. She
30 doesn't want to be at the party anymore. When she goes into the garden, Rajiv goes outside, too.
"Don't listen to Beebee," Rajiv says. "You still look great. Come on, let's take a selfie." Emma smiles, but suddenly she says, "Rajiv, look! Behind you!"
35 "What is it?", Rajiv asks.
"There is a ladder at the Jacksons' house next door! Why is there a ladder?"
Rajiv says, "There is no light in the house. The Jacksons aren't at home."
40 Suddenly Emma points at a window. "Look! There's a torch! I think there is a burglar in the house!"
They don't know what to do. Through the window they can see their friends at the party. Everyone is
45 having fun. The twins are opening their presents.

"I've got an idea," Emma says. "Give me your phone." She calls the police. "Hello? This is Emma Butler here. I'm at 153 Albert Street. There is a burglar in the house. My friend and I are
50 watching him but you must be quick!"
Emma and Rajiv are waiting. They can see the torch in the Jacksons' kitchen now. The police aren't there. "We must do something," Rajiv says. "Let's take the ladder away!" They run into the
55 Jacksons' garden. "Shhh, quiet!", Rajiv whispers. The ladder is heavy but together they can move it away from the house. "Good," Emma whispers.

"Now the burglar can't get away." "But what if he just opens the front door and runs away?", Rajiv answers.

"Oh no, you're right!", Emma says.

They go around the house and watch the front door. "Look, what's that?", Emma asks. She points at a bike. "That isn't Mr or Mrs Jackson's bike. It must be the burglar's bike!"

Suddenly a man with a black jumper opens the window upstairs. He looks very nervous. He starts to climb out of the window.

"Rajiv, look!", Emma whispers. "What can we do now?"

c) Read the story again and answer the questions:
1. What is Rajiv's costume?
2. What does Beebee think of her costume?
3. Why is Emma upset?
4. What does Emma see in the garden?
5. What do Emma and Rajiv do together?

B8 Conjunctions ▶ G19 | p. 194 ▶ WB 21 | p. 60

Use the conjunctions (*and, because, ...*) and connect the sentence parts.

There are decorations		they see a ladder.
Caroline is happy		calls the police.
Beebee loves her costume	and	a man opens the window.
Emma is upset	because	Beebee laughs at her.
Rajiv and Emma are in the garden	but	a big table with delicious food.
Emma takes Rajiv's phone	when	she loves her party.
They are watching the house		she thinks Emma's costume is for babies.

B9 Other words for *say* ▶ DIFF Extra D27 | p. 155 ▶ WB 18 | p. 59

a) Scan the story and collect words you can use for *say*.
Example: *scream, ...*

b) Compare your list with a partner's. Add missing words to your list. ▶ Vocabulary | p. 175

B10 Target task Write the ending of the story

1. Work with a partner.
   Look at the pictures and take notes.
   - What happens next?
   - What do the characters say?

   let the air out of the tyres •
   hanging out of the window • jump • Hurry up! •
   run back to George and Caroline's house •
   catch • watch • heroes

2. Write the ending of the story. ▶ Writing | p. 173
   - Use the simple present and the present progressive where necessary.
   - Use direct speech (for example "Good," Emma whispers.).
   - Use conjunctions (→ B8).
   - Use different words for *say* (→ B9).

3. Now check your text and edit it.

Need help? Look at pages 84/85: T1 T2 T3 T4 T5 T6

Part B: Target task tools

Target task tools for B10: Write the ending of the story

T1 Reading (1)

Read the story on pages 82/83 again.
Then put the sentences in the correct order and find the solution.

- T There is a burglar in the house.
- C Emma sees a ladder at the Jacksons' house.
- E Rajiv goes outside, too.
- I Emma calls the police.
- E The burglar opens the window and starts to climb outside.
- E Emma's costume is ruined.
- D It is the day of the twins' party.
- V Emma and Rajiv take the ladder away.
- T Emma is very upset and goes into the garden.

T2 Reading (2) ▶ Reading | p. 167

Read the story on pages 82/83 again. Find the correct answers.

1. Rajiv has got a cool costume. He is a …
   - A stormtrooper.
   - B vampire.
   - C detective.

2. Beebee thinks she looks really …
   - A cool.
   - B nice.
   - C fantastic.

3. George is drinking …
   - A lemonade.
   - B milk.
   - C orange juice.

4. Emma is upset so she goes …
   - A home.
   - B into the garden.
   - C into the kitchen.

5. In the garden next door Emma sees a …
   - A light.
   - B cat.
   - C ladder.

6. Emma and Rajiv decide to …
   - A catch the burglar.
   - B tell their friends.
   - C take the ladder away.

T3 Revision: Personal pronouns and possessive determiners ▶ G4 | p. 183 ▶ G7 | p. 184

Copy the sentences and fill in the correct words.

our • she • her • he • my • his • your • we

1. My brother is eight. **XXX** name is Max. **XXX** can play tennis.
2. **XXX** name is Lea. What's **XXX** name?
3. I've got a lot of friends. **XXX** often play football together. **XXX** favourite place is the park.
4. I've got a cat. **XXX** name is Leonore. **XXX** is a great cat.

Part B: Target task tools **4**

T4 **Words**

a) Unscramble the words and write them down.

licpoe • rglabur • chwat • chcat • imbcl • wdowin • itwa

b) What are the words in German?

T5 **Revision: Simple present** ▶ G12 | p. 188

Write down the correct verb forms in your exercise book.

make • have (2x) • like • buy • love • bake • be (3x)

Gillian's birthday is in February. She usually **1** a birthday party with her family. Her parents **2** divorced, but they **3** friends. Gillian's Dad **4** got a girlfriend. Her name is Carol. Gillian **5** her very much because she **6** funny. Her parents always **7** a great present for Gillian. Her mum always **8** a big cake and her grandmother usually **9** special muffins for Gillian. Gillian **10** her birthday!

T6 **Mediation: A website** ( )

a) Look at this website with tips for editing a story.
Note down the tips in German.
▶ Mediation | p. 177

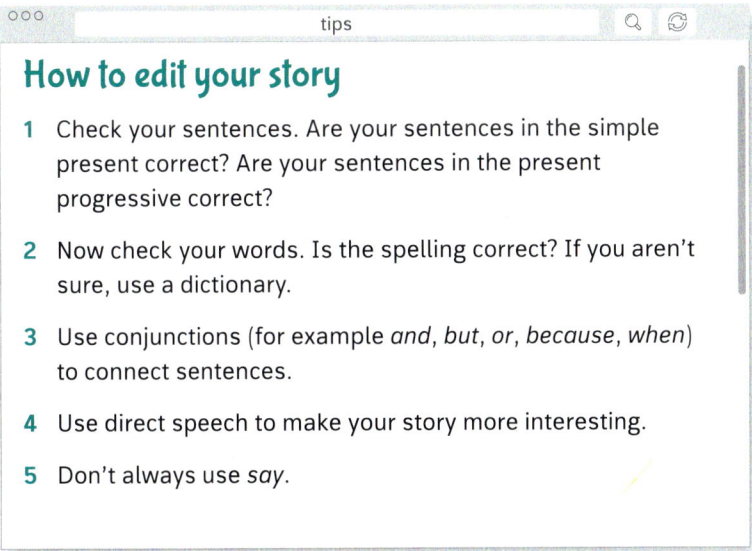

How to edit your story

1. Check your sentences. Are your sentences in the simple present correct? Are your sentences in the present progressive correct?

2. Now check your words. Is the spelling correct? If you aren't sure, use a dictionary.

3. Use conjunctions (for example *and*, *but*, *or*, *because*, *when*) to connect sentences.

4. Use direct speech to make your story more interesting.

5. Don't always use *say*.

b) Now use the tips to edit the ending of your story in B10 on page 83.

Horrid Henry's Birthday Party   Reading tour

R1 **Horrid¹ Henry's Birthday Party**

a) Describe the book cover.

> water blaster = *große Wasserpistole*
> present = *Geschenk*

b) What do you think happens in the story?

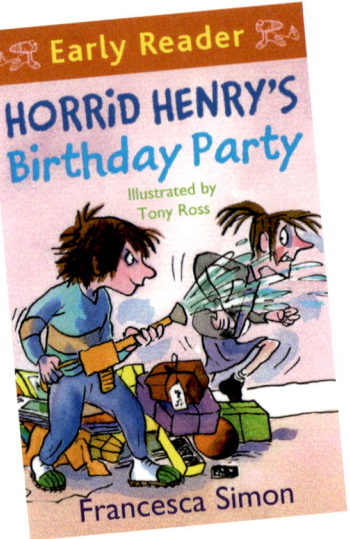

R2 **A special present**

a) Read parts A–D of the story *Horrid Henry's Birthday Party*. Put them in the correct order.

A

Rude² Ralph was the last to arrive³. He handed Henry
a long rectangular package⁴ wrapped in newspaper⁵.
It was a Super Soaker 2000 water blaster.
"Oh," said⁶ Mum.
5 "Put it away," said Dad.
"Thank you, Ralph," beamed⁷ Henry. "Just what I wanted⁸."

B

Ding Dong.
It was the first guest, Sour Susan. She held⁹ a large present.
Henry snatched¹⁰ the package.
10 It was a pad of paper and some felt tips¹¹.
"How lovely¹²," said Mum. "What do you say, Henry?"
"I've already got that," said Henry.
"Don't be horrid, Henry," said Mum.

---

1 horrid – *entsetzlich, grauenhaft* | **2** rude – *unverschämt, unhöflich* | **3** was the last to arrive – *kam als letzter an* | **4** a long rectangular package – *ein langes, rechteckiges Paket* | **5** wrapped in newspaper – *in Zeitung eingepackt* | **6** said – *sagte* | **7** beamed – *strahlte* | **8** just what I wanted – *genau das, was ich wollte* | **9** held – *hielt* | **10** snatched – *schnappte* | **11** a pad of paper and some felt tips – *ein Papierblock und einige Filzstifte* | **12** lovely – *schön*

86 eighty-six

Reading tour 4

C

Then Henry had¹ a wonderful, spectacular idea.
15 He got up and sneaked out² of the room. […]
There was a noise outside.³ Then Henry burst⁴ into the
kitchen, Super Soaker in hand.

D

Henry's birthday arrived⁵ at last.
"Happy birthday, Henry!" said Peter.
20 "Where are my presents?" said Henry.
Dad pointed. Horrid Henry attacked the pile⁶.
Mum and Dad had given him⁷ a first encyclopedia, Scrabble,
a fountain pen⁸, a hand-knitted cardigan⁹, a globe¹⁰ and three sets
of vests and pants¹¹.
25 "Oh," said Henry. He pushed the dreadful presents aside¹².

Happy birthday, Henry!

Happy birthday, Henry!

---

1 had – *hatte* | **2** got up and sneaked out – *stand auf und schlich aus …* | **3** There was a noise outside. – *Draußen gab es ein Geräusch.* |
4 burst – *platzte* | **5** arrived – *kam* | **6** attacked the pile – *stürzte sich auf den Haufen* | **7** had given him – *hatten ihm geschenkt* |
8 fountain pen – *Füller* | **9** hand-knitted cardigan – *selbstgestrickte Strickjacke* | **10** globe – *Globus* | **11** three sets of vests and pants –
drei Unterwäschesätze | **12** he pushed the dreadful presents aside – *er schob die schrecklichen Geschenke auf die Seite*

b) Go to page 270 to find out if you are right.

R 3 **Talk about the story**

a) Read the story in the correct order again. What do you think of the story?

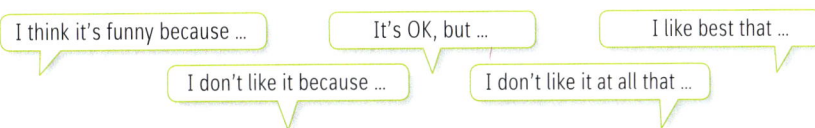

I think it's funny because …   It's OK, but …   I like best that …
I don't like it because …   I don't like it at all that …

b) What can you find out about Henry? What kind of person is he?

He doesn't like …   He is nice/friendly/unfriendly to his parents/to his friends because …
He wants to …

R 4 **What happens next?**

The ending of the story is missing. Now you know Henry a little bit. Guess what happens at Henry's party.
Draw a picture and write down what Henry and the other people do.

These phrases can help you:
I think he plays with the Super Soaker and then …
He gets some … from the kitchen and then …
Rude Ralph … His other friends …
His parents …
Look up words you don't know in the dictionary.

eighty-seven

4 I can ...

Was hast du alles neu gelernt? Diese Seite hilft dir dabei, das zu erkennen. Falls du Hilfe benötigst, etwas nachlesen oder noch ein paar Übungen machen möchtest, findest du hier passende Hinweise.

WORTSCHATZ

Ich kann ...	Aufgaben	Übungen/Hilfen
das Datum angeben *When is your birthday? – My birthday is on the 31st of January.*	1-3	▶ **DIFF** D1 ▶ Wordbank 3 | p. 200 ▶ **WB** 1, 3, 4
über Geburtstage sprechen *My favourite birthday party is ...*	4, 6	▶ **DIFF** D2, D4 ▶ **WB** 5, 14
ein Telefongespräch führen *Hello? – Hi George, it's Charlie. • Bye for now.*	A7	▶ **DIFF** D16 ▶ T5 | p. 79
Kleidungsstücke benennen *trousers • jumper • trainers • coat • socks • gloves*	B6	▶ **DIFF** D25 ▶ Wordbank 6 | p. 202 ▶ **WB** 19

SKILLS

Ich kann ...	Aufgaben	Übungen/Hilfen
einem kurzen Telefongespräch folgen LISTENING	A7	▶ **DIFF** D16 ▶ Listening | p. 166
Schlüsselbegriffe aus einem Gespräch raushören LISTENING	B1	▶ **DIFF** D19
ein Einkaufsgespräch führen SPEAKING	B4	▶ **DIFF** D1, D22 ▶ Wordbank 6 | p. 202 ▶ **WB** 15
beschreiben, was gerade auf einem Bild passiert SPEAKING	A8	▶ G16
ein Telefogespräch führen, wenn ich mich darauf vorbereitet habe SPEAKING • WRITING • MEDIA	A10	▶ **DIFF** D17 ▶ T4, T5 | p. 79 ▶ Talking | p. 169
die richtigen Aussagen zu einem Video auswählen VIEWING	D23	▶ **WB** 13
Informationen auf Webseiten verstehen und in einer Tabelle sammeln READING • MEDIA	4	▶ Reading | p. 167
der Handlung einer Geschichte folgen READING	B7	▶ **DIFF** D26, D27 ▶ T1, T2 | p. 84
einen Einkaufsdialog schreiben WRITING	B4	▶ **DIFF** D22
eine Geschichte zu Ende schreiben WRITING	B10	▶ T1-T6 | pp. 84-85 ▶ Writing | p. 173
den Inhalt einer Webseite auf Deutsch wiedergeben MEDIATION • MEDIA	D24, T6	▶ Mediation | p. 177

GRAMMATIK

Ich kann ...	Aufgaben	Übungen/Hilfen
Fragen und Aussagesätze im *present progressive* bilden und verneinen *Patch is sleeping. • Charlie isn't watching TV.*	A3-A5, A8, A9	▶ **DIFF** D8-D13 ▶ T1, T2 | p. 78 ▶ G16 ▶ **WB** 6, 7, 9
entscheiden, ob ich *simple present* oder *present progressive* verwende *My family goes to Scotland every summer. • Right now George is sitting on the sofa.*	A6	▶ **DIFF** D14-D15 ▶ T3 | p. 79 ▶ G17 ▶ **WB** 10, 11
die Mengenwörter *some* und *any* korrekt verwenden *Have you got any other bags? • We've got some other nice things.*	B3, B4	▶ **DIFF** D20 ▶ G18 ▶ **WB** 16, 17
Sätze mit Konjunktionen verbinden *Caroline is happy because she loves her party.*	B8, B10	▶ G19 ▶ **WB** 21

5

Pets and animals

In diesem *Theme* wirst du ...

- Tiere beschreiben
- Broschüren lesen und auswerten
- über Verhaltensregeln im Umgang mit Haustieren sprechen
- dich in andere Personen hineinversetzen
- einen Dialog fortführen und vorspielen
- über Charaktereigenschaften sprechen
- eine Fernsehshow entwickeln

5 Animals — Intro

1 Animal sounds 🔊 L 2/1 ▶ DIFF Training D1 | p. 155

a) Copy the grid. Then listen to the animal sounds and fill in the grid.

pets	farm animals	wild animals
…	…	…

fish • mouse • cow • pig • sheep • lion • duck • chicken • cat • dog • horse • budgie • hamster • elephant

b) Divide the class into three groups. Listen again. Stand up for animals that …
- have got fur (group 1)
- can fly (group 2)
- can't fly (group 3)

c) Add more animals to your grid from a).
👥 Then compare your list with your partner's.
▶ Wordbank 8 | p. 204   ▶ Vocabulary | p. 175   ▶ WB 1 | p. 67

d) Play a game:
elephant → tiger → rabbit → …

2 Your animal ▶ DIFF Training D2, Extra D3 | p. 156

Choose an animal. Make a word web.
Think of what your animal …
- looks like
- can do
- eats
- needs

▶ Wordbank 8 | p. 204   ▶ Vocabulary | p. 175   ▶ WB 2 | p. 67

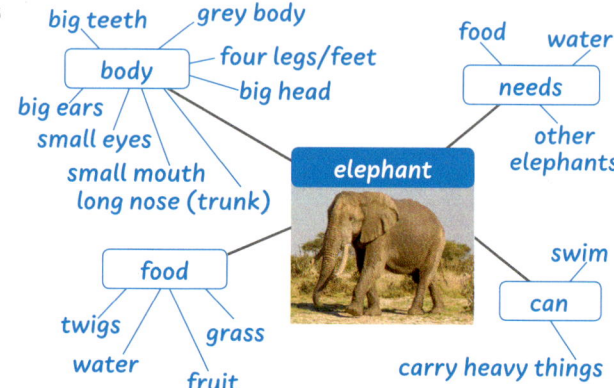

word web: elephant
- body: big teeth, grey body, four legs/feet, big head, big ears, small eyes, small mouth, long nose (trunk)
- needs: food, water, other elephants
- can: swim, carry heavy things
- food: twigs, water, grass, fruit

Battersea Dogs and Cats Home

Battersea Dogs and Cats Home is a famous animal shelter in London. It is open every day from 10.30 am to 4 pm. The
5 home does not have much money, so adults must pay £2 and children £1 when they want to visit. You can look at the animals, but you can also
10 support the work of the home. One of the best days to visit is the first Sunday in September. It is the Dog Reunion Day for all the dogs with a new home.
15 All families and their dogs are welcome. There are games and competitions for the dogs and one dog can even become the Best Battersea Dog of the year.

20 But be careful! You may fall in love with one of the dogs or cats from the shelter!

A

The London Wetland Centre

World Wetlands Day on 2nd February is a good day to visit the London Wetland Centre and find out about all
5 the animals that live close to the water. But you can come on any other day as well from 9.30 am. It is £8.50 for children and £14 for adults.
10 Leave your best clothes at home. If the weather is good, you can watch the otters and many birds or go to a fantastic playground. If it is
15 raining, you can go to the Discovery Centre to play with the digital pond or a high-tech underwater camera.

B

Intro **5**

3 A ten-question game

Group work:
Think of an animal. The others must guess it.
They can only ask ten yes/no questions.

▶ G9 | p. 185, G14 | p. 190   ▶ WB 3, 4 | pp. 67, 68

> Does it live in Africa?
> No, it doesn't.
> Can it fly?
> Yes, it can.
> …

4 Mini-jigsaw   ▶ DIFF Training D4 | p. 156   ▶ Mini-jigsaw | p. 178   ▶ WB 5, 6 | pp. 68, 69

a) Group work:
1. Each group chooses one flyer from pages 90/91.
2. Copy the grid. Read the flyers and fill in the grid.
3. Tell two other groups about your flyer. Then listen to the other groups and complete the grid.

	What animals can you see?	What can you do?	When is a good time to go?	How much is it?
London Zoo	20,000 animals of over 700 kinds	…	…	…
Battersea Dogs and Cats Home		…	…	…
The London Wetland Centre	…	…	…	…

b) Where would you like to go? Give reasons.

c) Put together a flyer for a place in your area where you can see animals. Include information on what animals you can see, what you can do, when it is a good time to go and how much it is.

▶ Making a page | p. 172   ▶ WB Media 6   ▶ WES-149220-2

> I'd like to go to … because you can see/look at …
> I'd like to go to … because you can help with/ work on …
> My favourite place is … because it's fun to …
> I think it's a good idea to go to … because there is/are …

London Zoo

At London Zoo every day is a great day to visit! It is the home of more than 20,000 animals of over 700 different kinds. Ticket
5 prices start at £18 for children. Don't miss the Land of the Lions to find out more
10 about these wild cats. There are not many of them left in the world. Go to Penguin
15 Beach and look at the crazy stunts of the penguins there. Make your visit unforgettable: become a zoo-keeper for a day and help out with some of the animals — you get a special zoo-keeper T-shirt, too!

C

5 A new home? Part A

A1 Oscar L 2/2 | S 45

a) Listen to Oscar. Who is he? What is his situation? ▶ DIFF Easy alternative D5 | p. 157
b) What do you think: How does Oscar feel? ▶ Wordbank 2 | p. 199

I think	Oscar is glad/unhappy/... because ...
I guess	he has/hasn't got a place where he ...
Maybe	his family doesn't ...
Perhaps	life is fun for him because ...

A2 At Regent's Canal L 2/3 | S 46

a) Read the dialogue.
Say what happens in three sentences.
▶ WB 7 | p. 69

Gillian: Oh, look, there's a dog. Isn't he cute?
Charlie: Calm down, Gillian. There are millions of dogs in London.
Gillian: But he is alone. I hope he isn't sick. We
5 must see if he's OK.
Caroline: You shouldn't go near him. You don't know him. Maybe he's dangerous.
George: Don't be a baby, Caroline. You must put your hand in front of his nose. Then he can
10 smell you and find out what you're like.
Gillian: Look, now he's licking my hand. Hey, what's your name?
George: Look, he's got a collar. It says "Oscar" here. Hello, Oscar!
15 **Gillian:** You're a good boy, Oscar. I think he wants your ice cream, Charlie.
Charlie: No way! That's *my* ice cream.
George: Well, dogs mustn't eat ice cream anyway. It isn't good for them. We should get him some
20 dog food.
Gillian: Great idea, George. Do you know where the next pet shop is?
George: Let me think. We can go to "Pet Paradise". They should know what we can do with Oscar.
25 **Gillian:** Can't we keep him?
Caroline: We mustn't keep him, Gillian. Maybe his owners are looking for him. And *we* can't have another pet – we've already got Patch and Socks.
30 **Gillian:** Oh, you needn't worry about it. I can take him home.
Charlie: What about your mum? Shouldn't you ask her first?

Gillian: No, she thinks flats aren't good for dogs.
35 But she can't say no to such a sweet dog. Now, please give him to me, George. Come on, Oscar. Let's get you some food.

b) Read the dialogue again. Complete the sentences. ▶ DIFF Training D6, D7 | p. 157
Read out the sentence in the dialogue that gives you the answer.

1 🐾 is worried that the dog is sick.
2 🐾 is worried that the dog is dangerous.
3 Oscar wants 🐾 's ice cream.
4 🐾 shouldn't eat ice cream.
5 🐾 knows where a pet shop is.
6 Charlie isn't sure that 🐾 wants a dog at home.

c) Look at these sentences from the text.
Use the pronouns from the box to replace the highlighted parts.
▶ DIFF Support D8, Training D9 | p. 157 ▶ G20 | p. 195

them (2x) • her • it • him

1 You must put your hand in front of his nose.
2 They should know what we can do with Oscar.
3 We've already got Patch and Socks.
4 What about your mum?
5 No, she thinks flats aren't good for dogs.

A3 Grammar card | Modal verbs ▶ DIFF Training D10 | p. 158 ▶ WB 8 | p. 70

1 Start a grammar card for modal verbs.
Copy the grid. Complete it with statements from A2.

subject	modal verb	verb		translation
...	must	...	...	...
...	mustn't	...	...	...
You	needn't	worry	about it.	Du brauchst dir darüber keine Sorgen zu machen.
...	can	...	...	...
...	can't	...	...	...
...	should	...	...	...
...	shouldn't	...	...	...

2 Translate the sentences into German. Be careful with *mustn't* and *needn't*.

3 Check G21 on pages 195/196 and note down how you can form questions with *must* and *should/shouldn't*, too. ▶ Grammar card | p. 179 ▶ G21 | p. 195

A4 Modal verbs ▶ DIFF Training D11, Extra D12 | p. 158

a) Copy the sentences and choose the correct modal verb. Sometimes there is more than one correct answer.

1 You **shouldn't / must / needn't** take your pet to school.
2 You **can / should / needn't** ask your parents before you buy a pet.
3 You **should / mustn't / can** check that you are not allergic to dog or cat hair.
4 You **mustn't / needn't / can't** cook special meals for your pet.

b) Copy the sentences and fill in the correct modal verb. Sometimes there is more than one correct answer. ▶ WB 9, 10 | pp. 70, 71

1 You **XXX** buy pet food in every supermarket.
2 You **XXX** leave your pet at home in your holidays.
3 You **XXX** know that you must look after your pet for a long time.
4 You **XXX** give a pet from an animal shelter a new home.

A5 A pet leaflet

Read the leaflet. Say what information is new to you.

How to take care of your dog

At home
Dogs are intelligent and they don't like to get bored. They love to play and be around people and other dogs. So don't forget to go for a walk with your dog. Dogs also need a comfortable dog bed.

Food and drink
Dogs need clean drinking water at all times.
You should give them dog food. But be careful that your dog does not get too fat! A lot of human food is not good for dogs, for example chocolate, onions and grapes.

How to travel with dogs
Make sure that you go to a dog-friendly place. Don't leave your dog in a car for a long time. It can get very hot in a car even if it is not so warm outside. Dogs sometimes even die in hot cars.

Dog training
It is important that dogs are OK with people around them. So train your dog from when it is young. Never shout or punish it. Try to be calm. You can also join training classes. Be careful when your dog's behaviour changes – maybe it is stressed or sick.

5 Part A

A6 A care sheet for a dog ▶ DIFF Extra D13 | p. 159

a) Read the leaflet on page 93 again. Match the sentence halves.

1 Don't give dogs too much food
2 Give your dog time to play
3 Don't give your food to your dog
4 Don't leave your dog in a hot car
5 Be calm and clear
6 Go to dog-training classes

A even if your dog makes mistakes.
B because they can get too fat.
C so that your dog can learn better.
D because it's often not healthy for them.
E so that it doesn't get bored.
F because it can die.

b) Make a care sheet for a dog.
Put a picture of a dog on a piece of paper and note down what you must/mustn't, should/shouldn't or can/can't do.
▶ Writing | p. 173

c)  Make a care sheet for your favourite animal.
▶ Making a page | p. 172   ▶ WB Media 6
▶ WES-149220-2

Care sheet for a dog

- You must give me dog food.
- You mustn't leave me in the car when it's hot.
- ...

A7 Gillian and her friends 🔊 L 2/4

a) Gillian talks to Caroline and Emma about Oscar.
Listen to the girls. Which statement fits best?

A Caroline and Emma think that Gillian can keep Oscar.
B Caroline and Emma don't think that Gillian can keep Oscar.
C Caroline and Emma think that Gillian's mum is unfair.

b) Listen again. Complete the grid with the friends' ideas. Note down at least two ideas for both parts of the grid. Compare your grid with a partner's.

Why it is good to have a pet	Why Gillian can't keep Oscar
– can be a friend	– his family is looking for him
– ...	– ...

A8 At home

Look at the picture.
- What can you see?
- What are Oscar, Gillian and her mother doing?
- How do they feel?

▶ Wordbank 2 | p. 199

angry • disappointed • safe • happy • scared • excited • surprised • pleased

Part A 5

A9 Gillian and her mother 🔊 L 2/5 ▶ WB 12 | p. 71

a) Now listen to Gillian and her mother. Were you right in A8?
b) Listen again. What can you say when you …

1 want somebody to listen to you?
2 are shocked?
3 really want to have something?
4 want to tell somebody that he/she can't do it?
5 want to try something with somebody?
6 think that somebody is wrong?

A I don't know what to say.
B Please listen to me for a second.
C I'm afraid it's just not possible.
D I'd love to have …
E I'm sure it's not really like that.
F Can't we give it a go?

A10 Target task Act out a dialogue ▶ Talking | p. 169 ▶ WB 13 | p. 72

Finish the dialogue from A9 and act it out.

1 Work with a partner. One of you is Mrs Collins and one of you is Gillian.
Read your role card. Think about what you can say.

Gillian
- loves Oscar
- wants to keep him
- knows that her mother doesn't want a dog in the flat
- wants a pet, but not a small pet

Mrs Collins
- is shocked and angry but understands Gillian
- only wants a small pet in the flat
- thinks that Gillian can help at an animal shelter
- is worried that Oscar's owners and the police are looking for him
- wants to take Oscar to an animal shelter

2 Take a piece of paper. Fold it in the middle. Take turns and finish the dialogue. Use phrases from A9b) and ideas from A7.

3 Cut the paper in half so that you have your part of the dialogue.
Work with two other pairs. Act out your dialogue.

4 Give feedback to the other pairs.

+	−
You use a lot of different words.	You should use different words.
It sounds like a real discussion.	It doesn't sound like a real conversation.
You sound like Gillian/Mrs Collins because you say …	It doesn't sound like Gillian/Mrs Collins when you say … because …
You have got a lot of good ideas, for example …	You should add more ideas, for example …
	Your dialogue is OK but you must practise it more.

Mrs Collins: Look, Gillian. I know you want a pet but our flat is too small for a dog. What about a rabbit?

Gillian: I don't want a small pet. Rabbits are silly. I want a dog!

5 Choose the best dialogue from your group and act it out in class.
6 Choose the best dialogue in class.
Explain why you think it is the best one.

> We believe that …'s dialogue is very good/ the best because …

Need help? Look at pages 96/97. T1 T2 T3 T4 T5 T6 T7

5 Part A: Target task tools

Target task tools for A 10: Act out a dialogue

T1 Grammar: Modal verbs ▶ G21 | p. 195

Copy the sentences and fill in the modal verbs. Sometimes there is more than one correct answer.

1 You **XXX** ask the owner of the flat before you can keep a dog there.
2 A dog **XXX** have enough room.
3 You **XXX** forget to take the dog for a walk a few times a day.
4 You **XXX** always take your dog on holiday with you. So you **XXX** find a place for it to stay.
5 There **XXX** be somebody to look after the dog when you are ill.
6 You **XXX** have your own garden, but there **XXX** be a park near your home.

T2 Grammar: Modal verbs ▶ G21 | p. 195

Work with a partner. Talk about your rules at home.

I must …   I mustn't …   I can …   I can't …

> watch TV after 9 o'clock • have a pet • wear what I like when I go to school •
> do my homework before I can … • play computer games before I do my homework •
> put on make-up • take out the rubbish • eat sweets before dinner

T3 Words: Feelings

a) Unscramble these adjectives that describe feelings. ▶ Wordbank 2 | p. 199

> anygr • haypp • sursedpri • extedci • dispointaped • woiedrr • das

b) Draw smileys for the adjectives from a). You can add more adjectives.

c) Use the words from a) or other adjectives that fit. Note down how you feel when …

1 you go on a trip with your best friend.
2 you forget your homework at home.
3 one of your friends moves to another city.
4 your grandparents forget about your birthday.
5 your results in an English test are not very good.

T4 Grammar: Questions (Revision) ▶ G15 | p. 191

Read Caroline and George's answers and write down Mr and Mrs McBride's questions:
Example: I want to go to the park **tomorrow**! → **When do you want to go to the park?**

1 Caroline is **in the garden**.
2 I want to eat **pizza**.
3 I want to watch TV now **because there's a football match on TV**.
4 I want to meet **Rajiv** this afternoon.
5 **Grandma** is on the phone.
6 I'm eating chocolate now **because I'm hungry**.

Part A: Target task tools 5

T5 Words: Discussion

a) Choose some of the phrases from the box to complete the sentences.
You needn't use all of the phrases.

That isn't true. • You're right. • Wait! I've got an idea. • Calm down. •
Don't talk to me like that. • That's not fair. • I'm your mother. •
You don't understand me. • I'm not sure. • End of discussion.

A Caroline: " **1** Why does George get an ice cream and I don't?"
   Mrs McBride: " **2** There is an ice cream for you in the kitchen, Caroline."
B George: " **3** We can go to Scotland in the summer and visit Uncle Ian."
   Mr McBride: " **4** I can ask him, but I think he wants to go away on holiday, too."
C Caroline: "Mum, I really want to go to the party!"
   Mrs McBride: "For the last time, Caroline: No, you're too young! **5** "
   Caroline: " **6** I hate you!"
   Mrs McBride: " **7** "

b) Write a short dialogue. Use the phrases from a) that are still left.

T6 Words: Discussion

What is it in German?
Match the English sentences and the German translations.

1 That's not true.   A Es ist schade, dass …
2 You see?   B Das ist nicht wahr.
3 It's a pity that …   C Warte! Ich habe eine Idee!
4 You're right.   D Verstehst du?
5 Wait! I've got an idea.   E Du hast recht.

T7 Words: Giving feedback

Match the German sentences and the English translations.

1 Euer Dialog klingt sehr überzeugend   A Your dialogue sounds very convincing.
2 Ihr habt sehr viele gute Ideen, zum Beispiel …   B Your dialogue is easy to understand.
3 Man kann euren Dialog gut verstehen.   C You should practise your dialogue more.
4 Ich finde es gut, dass ihr so viele   D There are some mistakes, for example …
   verschiedene Wörter verwendet.   E You should add more ideas to your dialogue.
5 Es wäre gut, wenn ihr noch mehr Ideen in   F You often use the same words, for example …
   eurem Dialog unterbringen würdet.   G I like your dialogue because you use a lot of
6 Ihr solltet euren Dialog öfter üben.   different words.
7 Ihr benutzt oft dieselben Wörter, zum   H You have got a lot of great ideas,
   Beispiel …   for example …
8 Ihr macht einige Fehler, zum Beispiel …

When you give feedback, always start with
positive feedback.

ninety-seven 97

5 Help the animals — Part B

B1 Stray dogs

George wants to help Gillian. He searches the internet and finds this website.
When he reads it, he is worried. Say why.

How do I report a stray dog?

- You can report a stray dog online. Please click here.
- You can contact the stray dog team. Please click here.
- We will contact the owner and return the dog or take it to the Camden animal shelter.
- Please note: You must report stray dogs. It is a criminal offence not to report a stray dog.

B2 George and Gillian L 2/6 | S 47

a) Listen to George. Find out what he is worried about.

b) Listen again and answer the questions. ▶DIFF Easy alternative D14 | p. 160

1. Where is Gillian?
2. Who is with her?
3. Why are the neighbours a problem?
4. What happens in the TV show "Help the animals"?
5. Where must Oscar stay tonight?

- Before you listen, read the questions so you know what to listen for.
- Take notes.

c) Do you think George is right? Say why/why not.

B3 At the animal shelter S 48

a) Read the dialogue and say how Gillian feels about the pets at the animal shelter. ▶DIFF Training D15 | p. 160

George and Gillian take Oscar to the animal shelter. There they meet Mike. He works at the shelter. Gillian tells him about Oscar, her mother and their neighbours.

5 **Mike:** I understand why you are upset, but we get many pets here every day and we try to find their owners. We put profiles of all the pets on our website. Many people check this website and when they read about their pets, they come
10 and take them home.
Gillian: How many owners do you find?
Mike: Oh, quite a lot.
George: So Oscar has got a chance to go back to his owners?
15 **Mike:** Sure.
Gillian: And if you can't find them?
Mike: Well, Oscar can stay at the shelter. Don't worry, we take good care of the animals here. Let me show you around.
20 **Gillian:** George, look at all these animals. Isn't it sad?
Mike: Yes, it is. Many people think it is cool to have a pet – but they don't know much about keeping a pet. I'm sure you know that a pet needs a
25 lot of care, especially dogs. There is so much information on the internet, there are books and TV programmes. But still we have got so many problems.
George: Gillian wants to have a dog. But her mum
30 says their flat is too small and they don't have enough time.
Mike: Well, I think her mum is right.
George: How many people bring pets to the shelter?
35 **Mike:** We get many animals after Christmas. And also in the summer when people want to go on holiday and just leave their pets behind. Look at these rabbits and also those guinea pigs on the right, for example.
40 **Gillian:** I just can't believe it. That dog over there looks so sad.
Mike: You really like animals. Why don't you come to the shelter and help when you have time? Maybe after school or at the weekend? Ask your
45 mum if that's OK.
George: Sounds like a great idea!
Gillian: And I can see Oscar again.

b) Read the dialogue again and complete the sentences. ▶ DIFF Training D16 | p. 160   ▶ WB 14, 15 | pp. 72, 73

1. George and Gillian take Oscar to the animal shelter where ...
2. Many people come to the shelter and take their pets home when ...
3. Many pets come to the shelter in the summer when ...
4. Gillian can't have a dog because ...
5. Gillian is happy because ...

▶ G13 | p. 189

- The word order in English sentences is:
  subject – verb – object (S – V – O)
  Gillian and George want to help Oscar.
- The word order in subordinate clauses is also S – V – O:
  Gillian and George go to the animal shelter because they want to help Oscar.

B4 Which pet?   ▶ DIFF Training D17 | p. 161   ▶ G13 | p. 189

Work with a partner.
Imagine you are at the animal shelter.
Look at the picture and talk about the animals there.
Use *this/that* and *these/those*.
Which pet would you choose?

▶ Wordbank 8 | p. 204   ▶ WB 16 | p. 73

this = diese/r/s hier (Singular)
that = der/die/das dort drüben (Singular)
these = diese hier (Plural)
those = diese dort drüben (Plural)

B5 About Oscar   L 2/7 | S 49   ▶ WB 17 | p. 74

a) What do you think happens to Oscar?
Talk to a partner. Then listen and find out.   ▶ DIFF Easy alternative D18 | p. 161

b) Choose the best title for the listening text. Explain your choice.

1. Everybody is happy
2. Oscar's new life
3. Oscar at Regent's Canal
4. A perfect day

5 Part B

B6 Pet posts ▶ DIFF Training D19, D20 | p. 161, Extra D21 | p. 162 ▶ WB 11 | p. 71

Gillian is still very sad about all the animals at the shelter. She wants to help the people at the animal shelter and posts information about the animals on social media.

a) Read the descriptions and match them to the pictures.

A
Hey there, I'm Mittens. I'm still a baby and I'm looking for a home. I'm very playful – I love toys, lots of sleep and a cuddle. My fur is super soft. My owner should give me a cosy basket, cat food and water. I also need a litter box.

#animalshelter #camden #adoptdontshop

B
My name is Spencer. I'm two years old. I love sunny and warm places. At my new home I need a big terrarium with leaves and plants and many insects to eat. I'm shy and I like to hide. Some people think I'm boring but I'm very active and I love to climb. If you take good care of me, I can become 14 years old!

#animalshelter #camden #adoptdontshop

C
Hi! We're Tim and Tony and we're looking for a new family. We are friends and we're five years old. We are very friendly and we love children! We love to run and play! You should have time for long walks because we are very energetic – even when it's cold or raining. :-) We're quite intelligent and we like to learn new tricks! Oh, and we love yummy dog food! Sometimes we try and take food from your plate!

#animalshelter #camden #adoptdontshop

D
We're Zizzi and Milly and we want to stay together. We don't like to be alone. We need a big, clean cage but we also like to fly around in a safe space. We are cute but we can be quite noisy, too! We like to eat seeds and fresh fruit. And we love a bath!

#animalshelter #camden #adoptdontshop

E
Hello there! My name is Caspar. I'm an excellent pet if you don't have much time. I'm very quiet but beautiful! You can watch me swim around in a big tank with some plants.
My owner should give me fish food every day and change the water in the tank every week.

#animalshelter #camden #adoptdontshop

b) Copy the grid and complete it with words from the pet posts. ▶ Vocabulary | p. 175

	character	food/drink	what it likes	what it needs
Mittens	playful	...	...	...
Spencer	...	...	...	...
Tim and Tony	...	...	...	...
Zizi and Milly	...	...	...	...
Caspar	...	...	...	...

B7 Pets ▶DIFF Extra D22 | p. 162 ▶ WB 18 | p. 74

a) Watch the clip. What pets have the children got?

Jake and Abby • James • Emillia (Milly)

b) Watch the clip again. What do you learn about the pets?
Pip and Jeff run around ... They like to ...
Harley sleeps ... He ...
Everlyn plays ... She ...

c) Which pet do you like best? Why?

d) Make a video of your pet or a friend's pet. Show it to your class.
▶WB Media 5   ▶ WEB-149220-2

B8 Target task **Your TV show** ▶ WB 19 | p. 75

👥 Work in groups. Act out your own TV show *Help the animals*.

1 Choose a toy pet.

2 Write a text for the TV show.
Describe your pet. Write about ...
- its character
- what it likes/doesn't like
- what it likes to eat/drink
- what it needs

▶ Wordbank 8 | p. 204   ▶ Writing | p. 173

3 Take notes on what the new owner should be like.

4 Bring your toy pet to school and act out the TV show.
- Present your pet.
- Your classmates must offer a new home for the pet.
- They must explain why they can be a good owner.
- You decide who the best owner is. Say why.

Need help? Look at pages 102/103. T1 T2 T3 T4 T5 T6

Part B: Target task tools

Target task tools for B8: Your TV show

T1 Words: Animals

Write an animal alphabet. If you can't think of an animal, ask a partner. You needn't find an animal for every letter[1]. Use the wordbank on page 204 or a dictionary for help.

A – ant
B – bear
C – ...

[1] letter – *Buchstabe*

T2 Words: Body parts

a) Work with a partner.
Choose one of the fantasy animals and describe it.
Your partner must guess it.
▶ Wordbank 2 | p. 199

1   2   3

 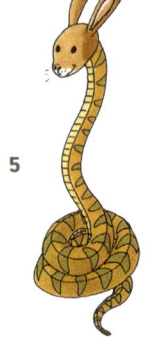  
4   5   6   7

b) Draw your own fantasy animal and label it.

T3 Words: Pets and animals

a) Write an animal quiz. Use the words in the grid.

My animal/pet is	It is	It has got	It can	It can't	It eats/drinks
big	black	four legs	swim	walk	seeds
small	brown	wings	fly	climb	leaves
...	...	...	...	...	...

b) Now read your sentences and ask your partner: What animal/pet is it?

Part B: Target task tools | **5**

T4 Words: Describing a pet
Find adjectives to describe pets and write them down.

T5 Words: What a pet needs
Write about the two pets in the pictures. The pictures and words can help you.
Example: *A hamster needs a wheel in its cage. You should …*

careful • aggressive • shy • bite • during the day • box • tank

T6 Words: A TV show
TV shows usually have a host. Here are some sentences that a host can use. Match the German sentences and the English translations. There is one German sentence that you do not need.

1 Willkommen zu unserer Show!
2 Heute haben wir fünf Tiere hier.
3 Sie suchen nach einem neuen Besitzer.
4 Ich bin sicher, wir finden ein neues Zuhause für sie.
5 Hier ist unser erster Gast mit …
6 Und damit geht *Help the animals* heute zu Ende.
7 Vielen Dank, dass Sie zugeschaut haben!

A Today we've got five pets.
B I'm sure we can find them a new home.
C Welcome to the show!
D Here is our first guest with …
E Thanks for watching!
F And that's the end of today's *Help the animals*.

5 Animals in London — Photo tour

A Did you know that there are lots of interesting animals in London? For example, there are the famous ravens[1] at the Tower. The Tower is an old castle on the River Thames. A legend says that if the ravens leave the Tower, England will[2] come to an end.
That is why there are still ravens at the Tower today.

B Do you love horses? Well, so does the Royal Family. The Queen has her own Horse Guard[3]: you can see these forty soldiers[4] parade and stand on guard[5] with their horses. Many people come to take photos with the horse guard.

C London Zoo is the place to see interesting animals – but why can you find red squirrels[6] there? Well, in England there are not many red squirrels anymore because the grey squirrel from America has taken over[7]. London parks are full of the funny animals and children love to feed them.

D There are lions in the middle of London: in Trafalgar Square. You can find them near Nelson's Column[8]. Admiral Nelson beat[9] the French and Spanish Navy so England became the most powerful nation[10] in the world at the time. The lion is the king[11] of the animals and stands for[12] power. When you walk through London, you can find many plaques or pub signs[13] with lions on them. Sometimes you can also see unicorns[14] on

Photo tour **5**

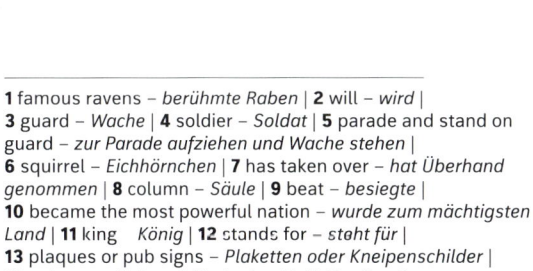

30 pub signs. Of course, they are not real animals, but they are beautiful and very special.

E There are sharks[15] in London – real ones! Not in the Thames, but just a few footsteps away[16]. Cross[17] the bridge from the Houses of Parliament
35 and Big Ben and you are at the London Aquarium. Here you can see fantastic turtles[18], colourful fish and sharks. You walk under the water through corridors of glass, so you feel like you are snorkelling[19] in a tropical underwater
40 world.

---

1 famous ravens – *berühmte Raben* | **2** will – *wird* | **3** guard – *Wache* | **4** soldier – *Soldat* | **5** parade and stand on guard – *zur Parade aufziehen und Wache stehen* | **6** squirrel – *Eichhörnchen* | **7** has taken over – *hat Überhand genommen* | **8** column – *Säule* | **9** beat – *besiegte* | **10** became the most powerful nation – *wurde zum mächtigsten Land* | **11** king – *König* | **12** stands for – *steht für* | **13** plaques or pub signs – *Plaketten oder Kneipenschilder* | **14** unicorn – *Einhorn* | **15** shark – *Hai* | **16** a few footsteps away – *wenige Schritte entfernt* | **17** cross – *überquere* | **18** turtle – *Schildkröte* | **19** to snorkel – *schnorcheln*

P1

a) Imagine you are in London. What animals would you like to see and why?
b) Read about animals in London. Match the photos to the texts.
c) Look around your town for animals on monuments, in parks, on signs etc and make a photo page for animals in your town.
▶ Making a page | p. 172   ▶ WB Media 6
▶ WES-149220-2

one hundred and five   105

5 I can ...

Was hast du alles neu gelernt? Diese Seite hilft dir dabei, das zu erkennen. Falls du Hilfe benötigst, etwas nachlesen oder noch ein paar Übungen machen möchtest, findest du hier passende Hinweise.

WORTSCHATZ

Ich kann ...	Aufgaben	Übungen/Hilfen
Tiere beschreiben *big teeth • four legs*	1-3	▶ **DIFF** D1-D3 ▶ T3 | p. 102 ▶ Wordbank 8 | p. 204 ▶ **WB** 1-3
Gefühle benennen *angry • disappointed • happy • scared • surprised • excited*	A8	▶ T3 | p. 96 ▶ Wordbank 2 | p. 199
an einer Diskussion teilnehmen *It's a pity that ... • You're right! • You see? • Wait! I've got an idea.*	A10	▶ T5, T6 | p. 97 ▶ **WB** 13
über Charaktereigenschaften sprechen *energetic • playful • friendly • intelligent*	B6, B8	▶ T4 | p. 103

SKILLS

Ich kann ...	Aufgaben	Übungen/Hilfen
die Situation verstehen, in der sich ein Tier befindet LISTENING	A1	▶ **DIFF** D5
einem Gespräch folgen, wenn ich das Thema kenne LISTENING	A7, A9, B2, B5	▶ **DIFF** D14, D18 ▶ Listening | p. 166 ▶ **WB** 12
eine Diskussion führen, wenn ich mich darauf vorbereitet habe SPEAKING	A10	▶ T1-T7 | p. 96-97 ▶ Talking | p. 169 ▶ **WB** 13
ein Bild beschreiben SPEAKING	B4	▶ **DIFF** D17 ▶ **WB** 4
Fragen zu einem Video zum Thema Haustiere beantworten VIEWING	B7	▶ **DIFF** D22 ▶ **WB** 18
mit einer Gruppe mithilfe der *mini-jigsaw*-Methode mehrere Texte gemeinsam erschließen READING	4	▶ **DIFF** D4 ▶ Mini-jigsaw | p. 178
eine Handlung zusammenfassen READING	A2	▶ **DIFF** D6 ▶ **WB** 7
die Hauptaussagen einer Broschüre verstehen READING	A5, A6	▶ **DIFF** D13 ▶ Reading | p. 167 ▶ **WB** 17
über ein Haustier schreiben WRITING	B8	▶ T1-T6 | pp. 102-103 ▶ Writing | p. 173
Informationen auf einem Plakat auf Deutsch wiedergeben MEDIATION	D7, D20	▶ Mediation | p. 177 ▶ **WB** 17

GRAMMATIK

Ich kann ...	Aufgaben	Übungen/Hilfen
Objektpronomen korrekt verwenden *Gillian sees Oscar. She talks to him.*	D8, D9	▶ G20
Sätze mit Modalverben bilden *You shouldn't take your pet to school. • Dogs mustn't eat ice cream.*	A3, A4, A6	▶ **DIFF** D10-D12 ▶ T1, T2 | p. 96 ▶ G21 ▶ **WB** 8-10
die Regeln zur Satzstellung anwenden *George and Gillian take Oscar to the animal shelter where they meet Mike.*	B3	▶ **DIFF** D16 ▶ **WB** 15

6 OPTIONAL

Holidays in Britain

In diesem *Theme* wirst du ...

- interessante Orte in Großbritannien entdecken
- Vorlieben ausdrücken
- Manchester kennenlernen
- einen Flyer gestalten
- Bilder beschreiben
- eine Geschichte schreiben
- einen Comic erstellen

6 Magical Britain — Intro

1 Your favourite place in Britain ▶ WB 1, 2 | p. 82

a) Look at these place names.

Lake District • London • Edinburgh • Manchester • Brighton • Newquay • Nottingham

Watch the video and note down the place names in the correct order.

b) Where would you like to go? ▶ DIFF Support D1 | p. 162
Watch again and take notes on your favourite place.

c) Tell a partner about your favourite place and say why you like it.
▶ Wordbank 5 | p. 202
▶ WB Media 5 ▶ WES-149220-2

> My favourite place is … because you can …

take a boat trip • relax on the beach • climb • go to a football match • go sightseeing • play arcade games • go shopping • go surfing • take a tour of … • shoot with a bow and arrow

2 The McBrides 🔊 L 2/9 | S 51 ▶ WB 3 | p. 83

a) Listen to the McBrides. Say what their dialogue is about, but don't use more than three sentences.
▶ Listening | p. 166 ▶ DIFF Easy alternative D2 | p. 162

b) Read the sentences. Then listen again and complete the sentences.

1. The McBrides can't go on holiday because Mr and Mrs McBride …
2. Gillian's mum must work and Rajiv's parents …
3. Gillian and Rajiv must stay …
4. George and Caroline can visit …
5. George wants to take …
6. Mr McBride can take …

3 Magical Britain ▶ DIFF Training D3 | p. 163 ▶ WB 4, 5 | p. 83

George and Caroline do some research for their trip and find this map of "Magical Britain".

a) Read the texts and match them to the places on the map. ▶ Reading | p. 167

(A) It is a big castle in the north of England. It is Hogwarts in the *Harry Potter* films and you can take part in classes on how to fly on a broomstick.

(B) Some people say that you can see Nessie the monster there, but we can't be sure. So some people are still looking for her in this beautiful lake.

(C) This is the capital of Scotland with a beautiful castle in the heart of the city.

(D) The ruins of this castle are on a cliff on the coast of Cornwall. People say it's King Arthur's birthplace. You can also find the cave of Merlin, the magician, nearby.

(E) This is the home of Robin Hood. There is a very big tree. It is more than 800 years old.

(F) This is a world-famous sight in the south of England. It is a huge stone circle and more than 4,000 years old.

b) Which place would you like to visit? Explain why.

> … looks like a good place to visit because …

> I'd like to visit … because …

> I like stories about … so I'd like to visit …

MAGICAL BRITAIN

Intro 6

4 Maps

a) Compare this map to the map of Britain at the back of the book.
Where are London and Manchester?

- ... is in the north/south of ...
- ... is between ... and ...
- ... is north/south of ...

b) Which place can the twins visit on their way from London to Manchester?

one hundred and nine 109

6 Manchester

Part A

A1 Welcome home! ▶ DIFF Training D4, D5 | p. 163

a) Look at the picture. Choose the caption that fits best. Say why.
 1 Caroline and George in Manchester
 2 A special welcome
 3 Happy grandparents

> I think caption … is the best because the picture shows that …

b) Read what Caroline, George, Gillian and Rajiv think. Say who thinks what.
 1 "They made the poster to show us that they are Caroline's real friends."
 2 "I'm so happy about the poster – she really is my best friend!"
 3 "Not bad! He is a cool friend really, but I'm sure she had the idea with the heart."
 4 "It's nice of them to make a poster. But I hope they want to meet us, too."

A2 The first evening 🔊 L 2/10 | S 52

a) Read about the first evening in Manchester. Why are Gillian and Rajiv quiet? ▶ DIFF Easy alternative D6 | p. 163

Caroline and George run to Sophie and Tom and the four hug each other. Sophie and Tom shout, "It's so great to see you again! You're back home!" Gillian looks at Rajiv and whispers, "Home?
5 Camden is their home now."
Before Rajiv can answer, the twins' grandmother welcomes her guests. "Hello, everyone! It's lovely to see you. Come in. Dinner's ready!" Mr McBride says, "I'm sorry, but I must be back in London
10 tonight. Bye! Enjoy your stay here."
A few minutes later, Mr McBride is on his way back to London and the twins are in the house with their old friends. Gillian and Rajiv are still outside. "Erm … OK, let's go inside, too," says Rajiv.
15 They go inside and look for George and Caroline. The twins' grandmother is happy to see them. "Come in, I hope you like pizza. I think they are all upstairs, they should be back in a minute." Gillian and Rajiv sit down at the table. They don't
20 know what to say.
When the other four come back down, they don't notice how quiet Rajiv and Gillian are.

"You must see the new sports shop in the city centre," Tom tells George. "And don't forget to
25 buy a new Man United shirt! You must show the Londoners that Manchester is the home of football." Now Gillian can't stay quiet: "There are a lot of good teams in …" But Sophie interrupts her, "Caroline, before I forget! All the girls want
30 to see you – they are all waiting for you. We've already got the perfect plan for your stay!" Gillian doesn't say anything.

Later, Sophie and Tom are on their way home. They are talking about Gillian and Rajiv. "What
35 do you think of them?", Sophie asks Tom. "I don't know," he answers. "They're very quiet. That's strange." Sophie agrees with him, "They're not very friendly. I think they're a bit arrogant because they're from London and we're 'just'
40 from Manchester."
Tom says, "Maybe they're just tired from the long journey. Anyway, it's great to have George and Caroline back."

Part A 6

b) Read about the first evening in Manchester. Correct the sentences. ▶ DIFF Training D7 | p. 163
Example: Sophie and Tom hug Rajiv and Gillian. → *They don't ..., but they ...*
1 Mr McBride stays for dinner.
2 George and Caroline's grandparents take the children to a restaurant.
3 Rajiv and Gillian talk a lot about their trip from London to Manchester.
4 Tom and Sophie ask the others about their plans for their stay.
5 Sophie and Tom talk about the twins on their way home.
▶ Reading | p. 167

c) Do you think it is a good or a bad idea that Gillian and Rajiv are in Manchester with the twins? Explain why you think so.

A3 Feelings ▶ DIFF Training D8 | p. 164 ▶ WB 6 | p. 84
Read these sentences from A2. Explain how the children feel and why they feel like this.
Example: Sophie and Tom shout, "You're back home!"
→ *Sophie and Tom are excited that Caroline and George are back in Manchester.*

1 Gillian whispers, "Camden is their home now."
2 Rajiv says, "Erm … OK, let's go inside, too."
3 Rajiv and Gillian don't know what to say.
4 Now Gillian can't stay quiet: "There are a lot of good teams in …"
5 Sophie interrupts Gillian and says, "We've already got the perfect plan for your stay!"

Rajiv	is	jealous	
Gillian	feels	angry	because …
Sophie	thinks that it is	annoyed	
		excited	
		happy	
Rajiv and Gillian	are	stupid	
Sophie and Tom	feel	puzzled	that …
	think that it is	strange	

A4 Emma's texts ▶ DIFF Easy alternative D9 | p. 164
When the friends go to bed, Gillian gets text messages from Emma in London and answers them.
Write down Emma's questions.

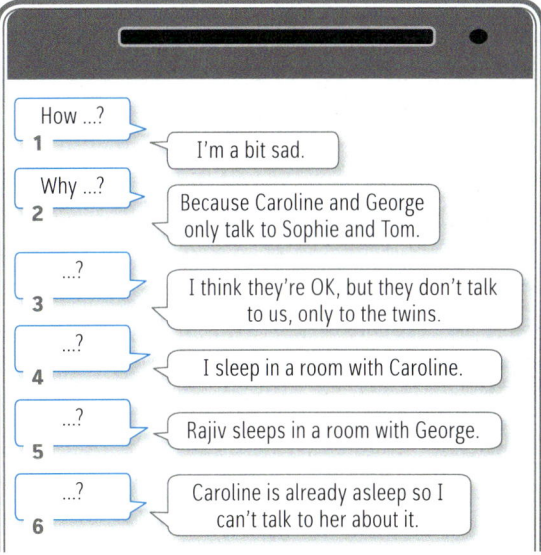

1 How …? — I'm a bit sad.
2 Why …? — Because Caroline and George only talk to Sophie and Tom.
3 …? — I think they're OK, but they don't talk to us, only to the twins.
4 …? — I sleep in a room with Caroline.
5 …? — Rajiv sleeps in a room with George.
6 …? — Caroline is already asleep so I can't talk to her about it.

6 Part A

A5 What's on in Manchester? ▶ WB 7 | p. 84

The next day, the twins and their friends plan what they want to do.
Read the flyers and choose where you would like to go. Talk about it in class. ▶ Reading | p. 167

> ... is my favourite because I like ...

> I would like to go to ... because you can do/see a lot of different things, for example ...

> ... sounds great because there is something for everybody, for example ...

> I like ... because you can try out/look at ...

NATIONAL FOOTBALL MUSEUM

Enjoy a visit to the world's best football museum. Learn about the fascinating history of the game, its teams, players and competitions, and what the football world looks like today.

5 The museum is free. Test your skills at everything from penalty kicks to clever tricks!

Get the perfect present in our shop, or eat a delicious meal with a stunning view of Manchester in the beautiful restaurant. There is even a special
10 area for younger children to join in the fun!

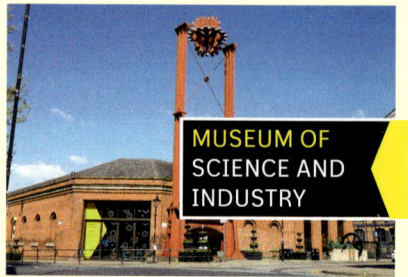

MUSEUM OF SCIENCE AND INDUSTRY

Manchester is a city of science and industry. You can find this museum in the world's first train station – this extraordinary place is really worth
5 a visit.

⇒ Learn about trains, planes and other machines.
⇒ Find out why Manchester is the home of many big factories.
10 ⇒ Take a train ride and take part in interesting workshops.

And all of this is free!

The experiment centre is an absolute must – here you can see how science
15 works, and even very small children can join in. Enjoy an extraordinary experience!

MANCHESTER CLIMBING CENTRE

Manchester Climbing Centre is very special – you can find it in an old church.

There are routes for everyone – from beginners to experts. Start in one of the training areas
5 and see if you can climb the 20-metre wall.

There is a great café with delicious food and drink – the ideal place to relax!

If you really like climbing, why not buy your own climbing kit? The shop has everything you
10 need to become an expert and impress your friends.

Come and see this spectacular centre!

Play Factore is one of Britain's best family entertainment centres for children from 6 months to 16 years old – it is fun for the whole family.

You can spend a whole day here with Europe's no. 1 indoor slide and exciting activities like a
5 laser tag arena, zip-wire ride, go-kart track and much more.

You can also take part in the Play Factore Just Dance sessions to learn dance moves to your favourite chart hits. Then take part in the dance
10 competitions and show everyone your cool skills!

The Italian café and pizza place make sure that there is fresh and healthy food for everyone. Play Factore is always an amazing trip!

Part A | 6

Manchester
Culture box

Manchester wird oft als „Hauptstadt des Nordens" *(capital of the North)* bezeichnet. Mit etwa 550.000 Einwohnern ist Manchester die sechstgrößte Stadt im Vereinigten Königreich und ein wichtiges kulturelles und wirtschaftliches Zentrum. Aus Manchester kommen bekannte Bands und Musiker wie Oasis, Take That, Harry Styles oder Bugzy Malone. Auch für ihre beiden Fußballteams Manchester United und Manchester City ist die Stadt bekannt.
Gibt es etwas, wofür dein Heimatort bekannt ist?

A6 Words and phrases ▶ WB 8 | p. 85

a) Go through the flyers again and collect words and phrases that make them sound interesting.

positive adjectives	describing interesting activities
fascinating, …	enjoy a visit to …, learn about …, …

b) Work with a partner. Think of more words and phrases to describe something as very positive. Add them to your grid. ▶ Wordbank 5 | p. 202

A7 Where do they go? 🔊 L 2/11 ▶ DIFF Extra D10 | p. 164

a) Think about Rajiv and Gillian. What do you think: Where do they want to go? Give reasons.

b) Listen to the boys and girls. Find out …
- what each girl/boy wants to do,
- which activity they choose in the end for today.

▶ Listening | p. 166

c) What do you think? How does Gillian feel about Manchester now?

A8 Target task Make a flyer

Work with a partner. Make a flyer about an exciting place in your area.
1 Choose a place that tourists find interesting.
2 Find information about it:
- What is it called?
- Where is it?
- What can you do/see there?
- What is interesting about it?
3 Write about your place. Use the words from A6 to make your text interesting.
▶ Writing | p. 173 ▶ Wordbank 5 | p. 202
4 Find pictures and add them to your text.
5 Put up your flyers in class and do a gallery walk.
▶ Gallery walk | p. 178

> You can decorate your flyer, too. Add drawings or photos to make it look more interesting. If you want, you can use a computer programme.
> ▶ Making a page | p. 172
> ▶ WB Media 6 ▶ WES-149220-2

Need help? Look at pages 114/115: T1 T2 T3 T4 T5 T6

6 Part A: Target task tools

Target task tools for A8: Make a flyer

T1 Words: Positive/negative adjectives
Copy the grid and fill in the adjectives.

+	-
fascinating	...
...	...

fascinating • boring • stupid • interesting • perfect • silly • stunning • beautiful • extraordinary • horrible • great • spectacular • amazing • cool

T2 Words: Phrases to describe places

a) Match the parts to make correct phrases. Sometimes there is more than one correct answer.

1 Enjoy ...
2 Learn about ...
3 Eat ...
4 This extraordinary place is ...
5 This place is ...
6 This is the ideal place ...
7 It is fun ...
8 It is always ...

A a delicious meal in the beautiful café/restaurant.
B an absolute must!
C a visit to ...
D to relax.
E the fascinating history of ...
F worth a visit.
G an amazing trip!
H for the whole family.

b) Use each phrase to write a sentence about the places in Manchester.

T3 Words: Phrases to describe activities

a) Look at this flyer about Old Trafford. Note down words and phrases to describe a visit.
b) Do you want to visit Old Trafford? Say why/why not.

OLD TRAFFORD

Do you love football?
Then you probably know that Manchester
5 United is one of the best football teams in the world. Come and visit their stadium, Old Trafford, and see what makes this team so great. Take a stadium tour and see where the players get ready for matches – you can even sit in 10 your favourite player's seat! The museum has information about the team's history and famous players, and you can take photos with Man United's real trophies. After the tour, you get a 15 certificate with your name on it so that you never forget the day. You don't need to be a fan to have a great time!

114 one hundred and fourteen

Part A: Target task tools 6

T4 Mediation: A website
Read the website for a tourist attraction in Manchester. Your cousin Kathrin is not so good at English and wants to know more about it. Answer her questions in German. ▶ Mediation | p. 177

1. Was ist denn so speziell an der Kletterhalle?
2. Oh, wie hoch sind denn die Kletterwände?
3. Das ist doch dann nur was für Profis. Oder haben die auch was für jemanden wie mich, der das noch nie gemacht hat?
4. Wie teuer ist denn dann eine Trainingsstunde?
5. Könnte Nathalie auch mitkommen? Die wird nächste Woche 5. Und wenn ja, wie teuer wäre das?
6. Aber das wird sowieso nichts. Ich habe ja gar keine Kletterausrüstung. Wie kann ich da denn mitmachen?
7. Vielleicht schaffen wir das noch am Wochenende. Haben die da überhaupt geöffnet?
8. Mama klettert bestimmt nicht mit. Was kann die in der Zeit machen?

COME TO THE MANCHESTER CLIMBING CENTRE!

It is very special – you can find us in an old church. There are routes for everyone on our climbing walls – easy beginner routes and some for first-class climbers. Start in one of the
5 training areas and see if you can make it to the 20-metre wall.

You can take the 205 and 206 buses from Manchester city centre to Bennett Street. But there is also a free car park at the climbing centre.

After some climbing, you can relax in our café with some cake as well as hot and
10 cold drinks. If you have already got some photos of your climbing experience, why not use our Wi-Fi to post them online?

Entry costs £ 10.
You can borrow climbing shoes for £ 3.50, helmets are free.
If you want to take part in a climbing session with a coach,
15 kids aged 7-17 pay £ 12.50, younger children aged 3-6 £ 10.

We are open every day from 10 am to 10 pm on weekdays and 10 am to 6 pm at the weekend.

T5 Words: Adjectives
Look at this text about the Manchester Museum. Copy the text, but use other adjectives for *interesting* from the box.

important • perfect • fascinating • special • wonderful • amazing

T6 Speaking: Flyers and a website
👥 Talk to a partner about the two flyers and the website on pages 114-115. What do you like about them? What is not so good? Why?

Manchester Museum

Visit the Manchester Museum to see lots of interesting animals from all over the world – from tiny insects to
5 giant bears! Come and see how interesting it is to learn about and look after our world. The museum has some interesting animals that no longer exist, and you can see
10 huge dinosaur bones! There are also some living animals, like interesting rare frogs from South America which live in the museum. At the end of
15 an interesting day make sure you visit the shop to buy a gift before you leave.

6 On the canal — Part B

B1 Holiday plans L 2/12 | S 53

a) Listen to the Butlers. What are Mr Butler's ideas for the holidays?
   ▶ Listening | p. 166   ▶ DIFF Easy alternative D11 | p. 164

b) Listen again and answer the questions:
   1 Why is Emma disappointed?
   2 What does she think about her dad's plan at first?
   3 Why does she suddenly like the idea?
   4 What does Emma's father offer to do?

B2 A canal trip ▶ WB 9–11 | pp. 86–87

Look at the map and read the information.
Say where you would like to go and why.

> I would like to visit … because …
> My favourite place is … because …
> I wouldn't like to go to … because …
> I would choose … because …

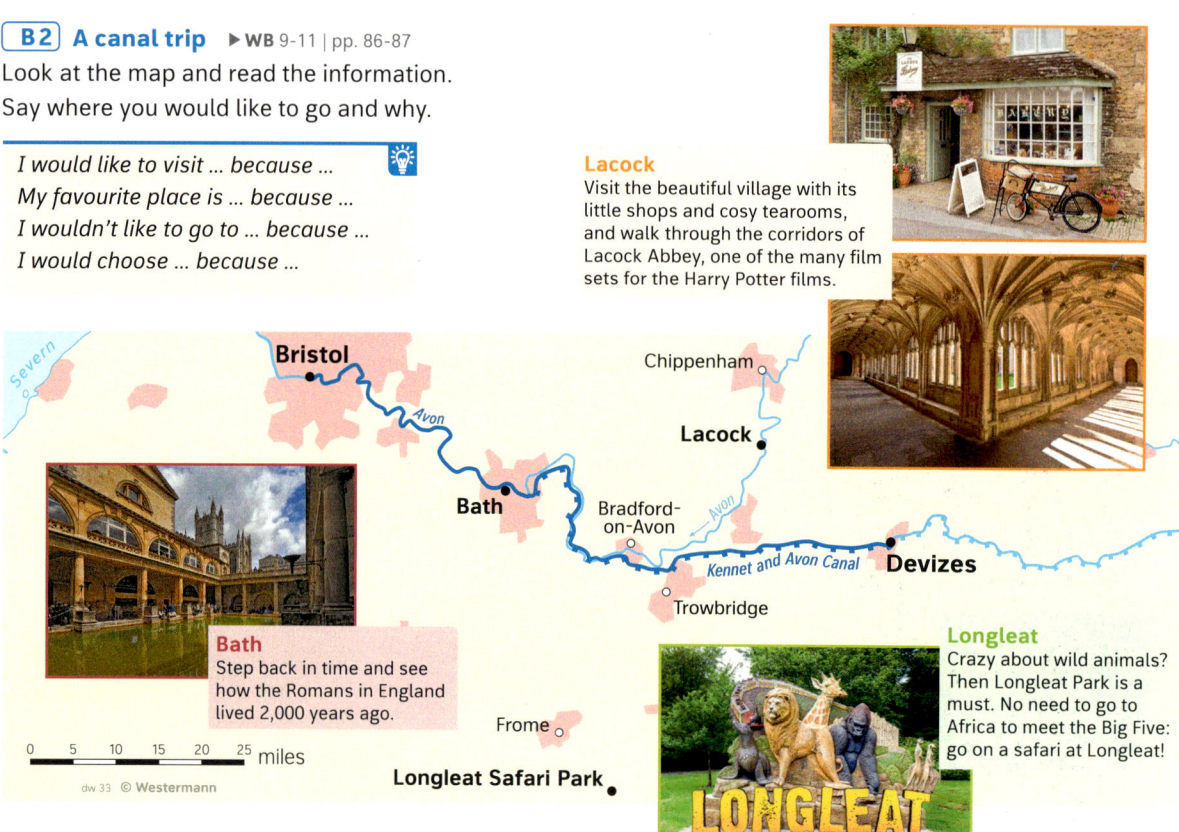

Lacock
Visit the beautiful village with its little shops and cosy tearooms, and walk through the corridors of Lacock Abbey, one of the many film sets for the Harry Potter films.

Bath
Step back in time and see how the Romans in England lived 2,000 years ago.

Longleat
Crazy about wild animals? Then Longleat Park is a must. No need to go to Africa to meet the Big Five: go on a safari at Longleat!

B3 Questions about the trip ▶ DIFF Training D12 | p. 164, Easy alternative D13 | p. 165   ▶ WB 12 | p. 87

When the Butlers get their boat in Devizes, they have got a lot of questions.
Read the answers and write down the Butlers' questions.
Example: It takes 19 hours to get to Bristol on the canal. (how long)
   → How long does it take to get to Bristol?

1 Most people arrive in Bristol after 8 to 10 days on the canal. (when)
2 It takes so long because there are many locks on the canal. (why)
3 You can stop almost everywhere. (where)
4 Tourists often visit the many interesting sights near the canal. (what)
5 You can get there by bike or by taxi. (how)
6 You can phone Mr Fox if you need help. (what)

Part B 6

B4 Day 1

Mr Butler and the children go on board. Work with a partner. Read the dialogue, then close the book and ask each other questions about the things on board.

> Is there a bathroom?
> Yes, there is.

Emma: Wow, Dad, this boat is really cool!
Mr Butler: Yes, it has got six beds. There's room for all of us.
Emma: And for Patch! He can sleep in my bed.
5 **Jack:** Dad, where's the kitchen?
Mr Butler: It's here. You can cook dinner with me tonight.
Caroline: And there's a table with seats for all of us. Great!
10 **Jack:** Look, there's even a shower in the bathroom.
Emma: And there are bikes on board!
Caroline: This is so exciting! Let's go.

B5 Day 2

a) Read the comic about day 2 and choose a title. Explain your choice.
- Too hot for Patch
- The video stars
- A dangerous adventure
- Great fun on board

> I think ... is a good title because ...

b) Imagine what happens next. Draw the last frame of the comic and add speech bubbles. Do a gallery walk and choose the best ending. ▶ Gallery walk | p. 178

c) Later that evening, Emma shows her dad the photos. Imagine you are Emma. Use the verbs from the box to describe what is happening.
Example: *In this photo, we are all sitting on deck.*
▶ G16 | p. 192   ▶ WB 13 | p. 88

sit • come • try to take it away • pull • laugh • throw • fall • shout • jump • swim

6 Part B

B6 Day 3 L 2/13 | S 54 ▶ DIFF Training D14 | p. 165

a) Read the text and say why it is Caroline's lucky day. ▶ Reading | p. 167

It is day 3 of the boat trip. The friends take the bikes to visit Lacock Abbey: Hogwarts! Caroline is excited. She feels like she is in a Harry Potter film. She is holding her phone with the new pink case:
5 "Wait, I want to take another selfie. Hey, that's a cool place!"
"Oh, Caroline," Emma sighs. "Please stop it! You've already got hundreds of photos."
"Come on, hurry up. We want to go to the tearoom
10 now. I'm really hungry," George says. "Me too," Jack adds.
"We want to buy some postcards in the village first. We can meet you at the tearoom later, OK?" Emma suggests.
15 Twenty minutes later the girls arrive at the tearoom. Caroline is very upset.

"Hey, what's wrong?", Jack asks.
"My phone … it's not in my bag. And I can't find it
20 anywhere." Caroline starts to cry.
"Perhaps it is still at the Abbey?" George suggests.
"Come on, let's go back!"

Meanwhile at the Abbey
The Barton family is walking around the Abbey.
25 Their little boy Sam is playing with a Harry Potter wand.
"OK, let's take one more photo," Mr Barton says.
"Show me your magic wand, Sam!" Sam waves his wand. Suddenly he shouts: "Daddy, look!
30 I can do magic!" He is so excited: on the floor there is a phone with a pink case.
"Oh, a phone. I'm sure somebody is looking for it," Mr Barton says.
"But how can we find the owner, Dad?" Sam asks.

35 The friends can't find Caroline's phone at the Abbey. Caroline starts to cry again. Suddenly they see a man and a woman with a little boy. He is holding a pink phone. "Hello," Caroline says. "That's my phone."
40 "Really?" Sam asks.
"Look!" Caroline takes the phone, unlocks it and shows Sam her photos. There she is on the boat and at the Abbey. "Hey, it's really you!" Sam shouts. "And you're the finder," Caroline smiles.
45 "Thank you so much!"
"Caroline, this really is your lucky day," George says. "Let's all have a big ice cream to celebrate!"

b) Read again and find out:
- Who is hungry?
- Who is upset?
- Who is excited?
- Who is happy?

B7 Who says what?

a) Read the speech bubbles. Say who the speaker is and describe the situation.

- This really is your lucky day.
- I can do magic!
- Come on, let's go back!
- Hey, what's wrong?
- Please stop it!
- We can meet you at the tearoom later, OK?

b) Read the story again and collect words you can use instead of *say*.
Example: *sigh, add, …*

Part B 6

B8 Day 4 🔊 L 2/14 | S 55

a) Listen to Mr Butler and the children and find out what place they are talking about.
Say why the friends would like to go there.

b) Listen again and explain why they aren't going today. ▶ **DIFF** Easy alternative D15 | p. 165

B9 Day 5 🔊 L 2/15 | S 56 ▶ **DIFF** Training D16, Extra D17 | p. 165

Read about the friends in Bath. Describe what they learn about the Roman baths. ▶ Reading | p. 167

It is day 5 of the boat trip. The friends are in Bath now. Mr Butler is very interested in history and takes the friends to the Roman baths in the town centre. "Here are your audio guides," Mr Butler
5 tells them. "Let's go! This is fun!"
"Not my idea of fun …," George whispers to Caroline.
The audio guide begins: "Welcome to the Roman baths. This beautiful building is almost 2,000
10 years old and gives you an idea of Roman life in England in 70 AD. You can see the hot water pool and statues of famous Romans like Caesar and Hadrian. You can even talk to 'real' Romans: today our museum guides are wearing Roman
15 costumes and can tell you their stories. You can ask them questions and take photos with them."
"Photos? Well, Caroline is happy then." George rolls his eyes. He doesn't want to listen to the guide anymore. "Roman baths! How boring!", he

20 thinks and walks away. He finds a small room and sits down to play a game on his phone. Caroline and Emma talk to the guides in Roman costumes. A soldier and a Roman lady tell them about relaxing days at the baths, interesting
25 meetings and a wishing well. It's great fun and, of course, they take some cool photos.
"Where's George?", Emma suddenly asks.
"I think he finds museums boring," Jack answers. "Perhaps he is waiting outside?"
30 "Typical!" Caroline is angry. "This is your dad's plan for the day. But George doesn't care. That's so rude!"

Meanwhile, George is still playing a game on his phone. Suddenly he hears somebody crying. He looks around and sees a little girl. She is holding
35 a teddy bear.
"What's wrong?", he asks. "Why are you crying?"
"I … I can't find my parents. What if they go home without me?", the little girl answers.
"Don't worry," George says. "I'm sure they're
40 looking for you. Why don't you call them?"
"I don't have a phone. Can you phone them?"
"Sorry, but I haven't got their number," George explains. "Oh, right, the number." The little girl starts to smile. "It's here." She points at the teddy
45 bear's T-shirt. "Wow, that's really clever!" George pulls out a piece of paper from the teddy bear's pocket. Then he takes his phone and calls the number.

Five minutes later, Jack, Emma and Caroline go
50 back to the entrance. They are surprised to see George. Caroline is still angry. George is talking to a little girl.
Suddenly they hear excited voices: "Oh, Olivia, there you are, darling! And you must be George!
55 Thank you so much," Olivia's parents say. They shake George's hand: "You're our hero!"
"I think you can be proud of your brother," Emma whispers to Caroline and winks at her.

6 Part B

B10 Freeze-frame

👥 Group work: Read the story again. Choose a scene from the story and plan a freeze-frame.
- Arrange your group members like the characters in the scene.
- Use body language to make the situation clear.
- Show your freeze-frame in class.
- Your classmates must guess who you are and what you are doing.
  ▶ Freeze-frame | p. 179

B11 Target task — Write a story OR draw a comic about day 6

What could happen at the safari park?
Collect ideas and note them down. ▶ WB 14 | p. 88

Choose: Write a story about day 6 **OR** draw a comic.

Story

1. Plan your story.

2. Write a first draft.
   - Include direct speech.
   - Use other words for *say*.
   - Use words to structure your story
     (for example *when, suddenly, at that moment, ten minutes later*).
     ▶ Writing | p. 173   ▶ Wordbank 5 | p. 202

3. Read your story to a partner. Give feedback to each other.

> I like your story because it's funny/exciting/entertaining/...

> Sometimes your story doesn't sound very interesting because ...

> There is direct speech in your story, but you should use other words for *say*, for example ...

Comic

1. Plan your comic:
   - Note down what happens in each picture,
   - write speech bubbles,
   - write captions where necessary.

> ❗ Don't put too many speech bubbles in one picture!
> The speech bubbles should be short and easy to understand.

2. Draw the pictures and add the speech bubbles.

3. Present your comic to a partner and give each other feedback.

> I like your comic because it's funny/exciting/entertaining/...

> I'm sorry, but I don't understand ...

Need help? Look at page 121:   T3   **Need help? Look at page 121:** T2

Part B: Target task tools

Target task tools for B11: Write a story OR draw a comic about day 6

T1 Words: At the safari park

a) Read the conversation about Longleat Safari Park and organize the highlighted parts in a word web.
b) Use a different colour to add ideas about what could happen.

Caroline: What's the next place on the canal?
Mr Butler: Bradford-on-Avon.
Jack: Oh, look! There's a "safari park" on the map.
Mr Butler: Yes, there's a safari park at Longleat.
5   That's a beautiful old house. More like a palace really, with a fantastic park. And they have African animals – not like in the zoo, but as wild animals in the park.
George: You mean tigers and lions?
10 **Mr Butler:** … and elephants! And even giraffes … Yes!
George: Please, Mr Butler, can we go?
Emma: Yes, Dad, that sounds like a real adventure. Let's go.
15 **Mr Butler:** Well, remember[1], we haven't got a car.

Jack: We can cycle there. It's not that far[2] from the canal.
Mr Butler: That's true. But we need a car to drive through the park. See, it says: "Close your
20 windows, put away your sandwiches and drive through."
Jack: But there are safari vans, Dad, just like on a real safari in Africa. You can see them on their website.
25 **Mr Butler:** True, too. But that is very expensive. Maybe we can do it on our way back to London. We've got our car then.
Emma and Jack: Promise?
Mr Butler: Promise!

[1] to remember – *sich erinnern; hier: daran denken*
[2] far – *weit*

T2 Connectives

Read about the day at the Roman baths in Bath. Use the connectives to link the parts of the sentences.

Caroline and Emma are excited		she is crying.
George is not interested in Roman history		he walks away.
Caroline gets angry	because	the girl's parents call George a hero.
George starts to talk to a little girl	so	she notices that George is not there.
George phones the girl's parents	when	he finds their phone number.
The friends find George		they can take photos with Roman characters.

T3 Writing

Read the sentences below. Decide what happens next. Write two more sentences for each situation.

1. Two lions are walking around near the car. George takes out his mobile. Then he opens the window.
2. Mr Butler is driving the car through the safari park. He is following[1] a safari van. Suddenly the van stops.
3. Caroline wants a really good photo of the elephants, but they are too far away. She waits for them to come near the car. For two minutes. For five minutes. Then she remembers the sandwich in her rucksack.

[1] to follow – *folgen*

6 Robin Hood — Reading tour

R1   The best title   L 2/16 | S 57

Read the story about Robin Hood. Choose the best title.

A   Late at night in Sherwood Forest
B   Robin Hood and the golden arrow
C   Maid Marian helps Robin Hood

PART 1

"We must catch[1] Robin Hood! He is taking all our money. He is a thief[2] and we must stop him! Now!"

It is the year 1157. Prince John of England and the Sheriff of Nottingham are at Nottingham Castle. Prince John is very angry. The cook is serving him delicious pancakes, his favourite breakfast. But the Prince is so angry that he doesn't want to eat anything today. His face is red and he is shouting at everybody. Somebody is stealing[3] money from rich[4] people, and Prince John knows who it is. He tells the Sheriff that he must catch Robin Hood.

"But how can we find Robin Hood?", the Sheriff asks. "He only comes to take the money at night. During the day he hides in Sherwood Forest. It's very difficult to find him there. The forest[5] is big and it's very dark. And Robin Hood is very clever. He wears green clothes so you cannot see him."

"You must find him!", shouts Prince John. "Take my dogs to help you."

"But, Prince John, you know there's another big problem. Robin Hood has got a big group of friends. They all live in the forest and call themselves "The Merry Men". Those young men and women are all very good with their bows and arrows[6]. They can kill us if we try to find them."

"We need to think of something else then. Sheriff, have you got any ideas?"

"Yes, I have a plan," the Sheriff answers. "Let's have a competition to find the best archer[7] in the land. The winner can take home a golden arrow. Robin Hood always wants to be the best. I'm sure he will love such an exciting competition – and when he comes, we can catch him!"

"That sounds like a good plan. Let's catch that thief! Tell everybody about the competition."

PART 2

It is late afternoon. In Sherwood Forest, Robin Hood and his friends are sitting around a fire. They are still tired from last night but when Robin's best friend, Little John, tells a joke[8], everybody laughs. Every night, Robin and his friends steal money from the rich, and the next morning they give it to the poor[9]. Prince John does not care about poor people. He takes everything from them so he can buy more and more horses and things for his castle and have big parties with his rich friends. Robin thinks this is unfair and he hates the Prince. The poor people call Robin a hero because he helps them. He and his friends are very brave[10].

"Look at this!", says Maid Marian, Robin Hood's girlfriend. She shows him a piece of paper. "There is a competition at Nottingham Castle. They want to find the best archer in the land."

"Let me see." Robin reads the paper. "It's tomorrow. The prize is a golden arrow. I must go!"

---

1 to catch – fangen | **2** thief – Dieb | **3** to steal – stehlen | **4** rich – reich | **5** forest – Wald | **6** bow and arrow – Pfeil und Bogen | **7** archer – Schütze | **8** joke – Witz | **9** the poor – die Armen | **10** brave – mutig

Reading tour 6

"But Robin, I think it's a trap[11]! They will arrest or even kill you! Don't go, please. It's too dangerous," Marian says. She can see how excited Robin is about the competition, but she doesn't want him to go.

"Don't worry, my darling. I have an idea," Robin answers. He kisses Marian and gets on[12] his horse.

PART 3

On the day of the competition, there are ten men with their bows and arrows. The round target[13] is so far away that it is difficult to see its black and red circles. One by one, the young men shoot their arrows. Some of the arrows land on the target, but nobody comes close to the centre.

The Prince asks the Sheriff, "Where's that thief, Robin Hood? Can you see him? Is he here yet?"

"No, he isn't here, my Lord. Robin Hood has got red hair. Nobody here has got red hair."

"Robin Hood is a coward[14]!", shouts Prince John. "He's not here. He is hiding in the forest because he's too scared! The poor call him a hero but he is nothing without his friends."

There are only two more men in the competition. The first one is William, the Sheriff's son. His arrow lands at the very centre of the target – bull's eye! The crowd cheers for William.

It is time for the last man. He is tall and has got black hair. Nobody knows him. His arrow sails through the air – and lands right in the middle of William's arrow! The man smiles and suddenly there are two more arrows in the air. They go through the Sheriff's clothes and pin[15] him to his chair.

The Sheriff is shocked! Then the man pulls off his hair – it is a black wig[16]!

"Get him, you idiots!", shouts Prince John. "It's Robin Hood!"

The Sheriff tries to get up from his chair. But … too late! Robin Hood is already on his horse and galloping away. He waves the golden arrow at the Sheriff and at Prince John. When he gets back to Sherwood Forest, his friends cheer for him. Maid Marian gives him a kiss. Robin Hood is not only the best archer in the land; he is also a very clever man.

---

11 trap – *Falle* | **12** to get on sth – *auf etw. aufsteigen* | **13** target – hier: *Zielscheibe* | **14** coward – *Feigling* | **15** to pin – *festnageln* | **16** wig – *Perücke*

R2 Write your own title
Read the story again and write titles for the three parts of the story.

R3 Choose
The Sheriff needs a "Wanted poster" to help him find Robin Hood. Make the poster. Describe
- what Robin Hood looks like,
- where he lives,
- what he is good at,
- why the Sheriff wants to find him.

▶ Making a page | p. 172   ▶ WB Media 6   ▶ WES-149220-2

OR

Draw a comic for each scene of the story. Add speech bubbles and write captions for each picture.

▶ Writing | p. 173

WANTED
Robin Hood
- he …
- …

6 I can ...

Was hast du alles neu gelernt? Diese Seite hilft dir dabei, das zu erkennen. Falls du Hilfe benötigst, etwas nachlesen oder noch ein paar Übungen machen möchtest, findest du hier passende Hinweise.

WORTSCHATZ

Ich kann ...	Aufgaben	Übungen/Hilfen
über Urlaubsaktivitäten sprechen *take a boat trip • go sightseeing • relax on the beach • climb*	1, 3	▶ DIFF D1 ▶ Wordbank 5 | p. 202 ▶ WB 1
Gefühle benennen *Sophie and Tom are excited that ...*	A3	▶ DIFF D8 ▶ Wordbank 2 | p. 199 ▶ WB 6
Orte anschaulich beschreiben *Enjoy a visit to ... • It is fun for the whole family.*	A6, A8	▶ DIFF D10 ▶ T1, T2, T4 | pp. 114-115 ▶ Wordbank 5 | p. 202

SKILLS

Ich kann ...	Aufgaben	Übungen/Hilfen
einem Gespräch folgen und Fragen dazu beantworten LISTENING	2, B1, B8	▶ DIFF D2, D11 ▶ Listening | p. 166 ▶ WB 3
Vorlieben ausdrücken SPEAKING	1, A5, B2	▶ Talking | p. 169 ▶ WB 9
meine Meinung begründen SPEAKING	A2	▶ Talking | p. 169
mein Arbeitsergebnis in einem *gallery walk* präsentieren SPEAKING	A8, B5	▶ Gallery walk | p. 178
ein Video verstehen, in dem Orte in Großbritannien beschrieben werden VIEWING	1	▶ WB 2
Ortsbeschreibungen verstehen und die Orte auf einer Karte Großbritanniens finden READING	3, 4	▶ DIFF D3 ▶ WB 4
der Handlung einer Geschichte folgen READING	A2, B6, B7, B9	▶ DIFF D6, D7, D14, D16
Broschüren die wichtigsten Informationen entnehmen READING	A5, A6	▶ Reading | p. 167 ▶ WB 7
mit einer Gruppe eine Situation in einer Geschichte mithilfe eines Standbilds darstellen (*Freeze-frame*) READING	B10	▶ Freeze-frame | p. 179
einen Chat vervollständigen WRITING • MEDIA	A4	▶ DIFF D9
eine Broschüre über einen Ort gestalten WRITING • MEDIA	A8	▶ DIFF D10 ▶ T1-T6 | pp. 114-115 ▶ Writing | p. 173
eine Geschichte über ein Urlaubserlebnis schreiben oder einen Comic dazu zeichnen WRITING	B11	▶ T1-T3 | p. 121
Fragen zu einer Broschüre auf Deutsch beantworten MEDIATION	T4 | p. 115	▶ Mediation | p. 177 ▶ WB 7

GRAMMATIK

Ich kann ...	Aufgaben	Übungen/Hilfen
entscheiden, ob ich *simple present* oder *present progressive* verwende *Sophie often texts Caroline. • Caroline is texting Emma right now.*	D4, D5	▶ G17
Fragen mit Fragewörtern im *simple present* formulieren *Why are you sad? • How long does it take to get to Bristol?*	A4, B3	▶ DIFF D9, D13 ▶ G6, G15 ▶ WB 12

Diff and train 1

Theme 1: Intro

D1 Support: *There is/there are* ▶ Before Intro 1 | p. 18

There is or *There are*?
Example: **XXX** two books. → *There are two books.*
1 **XXX** a phone.
2 **XXX** two blue pencils.
3 **XXX** a green pencil case.
4 **XXX** two elephants.
5 **XXX** a school bag.

D2 Support: Singular and plural ▶ Before Intro 1 | p. 18 ▶ G1 | p. 181

Write down the plural forms of the words.
Example: door → *doors*
1 lamp
2 cat
3 dog
4 house
5 window
6 bush
7 chair
8 bed

D3 Training: Words and phrases ▶ After Intro 1 | p. 18 ▶ Wordbank 4 | p. 201

Look at the pictures. Write down the words for the rooms.

1

2

3

4

D4 Easy alternative: Listening ▶ Instead of Intro 2b | p. 18 🔊 L 1/10 | S 6

Listen to George and read the sentences. Are they right or wrong?
1 Dad's favourite room is the dining room.
2 The TV is in the kitchen.
3 Mum is in the garden.
4 There are three bedrooms.
5 The bathroom is upstairs.
6 George's room is blue.

D5 Training: Words and phrases ▶ After Intro 2b | p. 18

Puzzle out the words.

rdgaen • nvigli oorm • ntkiche • brooedm • nindig moro • staupirs • robthaom • dnstowairs

D6 Training: Words and phrases ▶ After Intro 2b | p. 18

Find the right word.
1 You eat in this room.
2 You and your family watch TV in this room.
3 You sleep in this room.
4 It is outside. You can play there.
5 You cook in this room.
6 You clean your teeth in this room.

1 Diff and train

D7 Training: Mediation ( ) ▶ After Intro 2b | p. 18

Read Tom's message to George.
What is it in German? Use the German sentences, but not all of them. Some are wrong.

- Tom bedankt sich für das Video.
- Ihm geht es gut.
- Georges Fotos gefallen ihm gut.
- Er mag Georges neues Haus.
- Er findet Georges Zimmer sehr gut.
- Er will George auch ein Video schicken.
- George soll seine Eltern und Caroline grüßen.

> Thanks for the video! Your new house is very nice. I love your room – it's super cool! Man United is the best!!! Please say hello to Caroline and your parents.

D8 Extra: Media ▶ After Intro 2d | p. 18

What is your favourite type of media?

- I like … because they are cool/interesting.
- I like … because it's …
- I like … because I can play with/talk to my friends.

books • computers • magazines • newspapers • the radio • tablets • the TV • phones • posters • laptops

D9 Support: Prepositions ▶ Before Intro 3 | p. 19

Where is George's phone?
Complete the sentences with the prepositions in the box.
Example: 1. The phone is **XXX** the bed. → *The phone is under the bed.*

under • between • in front of • behind • next to

2 The phone is **XXX** the laptop.
3 The phone is **XXX** the chair and the bed.
4 The phone is **XXX** the football.
5 The phone is **XXX** the bed.

1

2

3

4

5

D10 Training: *There is/there are* ▶ After Intro 4a | p. 19

What can you see on your desk/in your classroom?
Write five sentences with *there is/there are*.
Use these words: book • pencil • pencil case • school bag • teacher • boys • girls

Example: *There are two books on my desk. In my classroom there is a …*

Diff and train 1

D11 Training: The article *a/an* ▶ After Intro 4a | p. 19 ▶ G2 | p. 181

Write down the words and add *a* or *an*.

Example: *a lamp, an example*

1 book
2 kitchen
3 elephant
4 apple
5 TV
6 ice cream
7 school bag
8 pencil case

D12 Training: Words and phrases ▶ After Intro 4 | p. 19

Explain in German what you have to do.

1 Say what you can see.
2 Finish the sentences.
3 Write five sentences about Caroline's room.
4 Close your books.
5 Tell your partner about your room.

Ich soll …

Wir sollen …

…

Theme 1: Part A

D13 Training: Reading ▶ After A2b | p. 20

Read the dialogue on page 20 again. Choose the right words.

1 Sophie is in **London** / **Manchester** / **Coventry** .
2 Mr and Mrs McBride aren't **in London** / **at home** / **in Camden** .
3 Caroline is **happy** / **lonely** / **excited** .
4 George is **worried** / **excited** / **lonely** .
5 Camden is a **boring** / **fantastic** / **good** place.

D14 Training: Words and phrases ▶ After A2b | p. 20

What are the words?

1 e--ited
2 lo--ly
3 fan--stic
4 s-d
5 wor--ed
6 e--y

D15 Training: Personal pronouns ▶ After A4 | p. 21 ▶ G4 | p. 183

Read the dialogue and find the right personal pronoun for **1-10**.

Emma: Mum, the family next door is from Manchester. They are the McBrides. **1** are really nice. The house is cool. And **2** is so big. There is a girl and a boy, Caroline and George. Caroline is George's twin sister. **3** is at my school. **4** can go to school together. George is a football fan, just like Jack. But **5** 's a Man United fan.
Mrs Butler: Oh, **6** 'm really happy that Caroline is your new friend. I guess **7** 're happy, too?
Emma: Yeah, **8** 'm really excited. And there is Patch and Socks.
Mrs Butler: Are **9** the family pets?
Emma: Yes, a dog and a cat. **10** 're really fun!

1 Diff and train

D16 Extra: Reading ▶ After A4 | p. 21

Read the sentences. Puzzle out who it is.

1 Hi, I'm at William Ellis School. I'm sixteen and I'm an Arsenal fan. Emma is my sister. *That's Jack.*
2 Hello, I'm from Manchester. I'm eleven. I'm Caroline's friend.
3 Hi, I'm eleven. I'm from Camden and my house is on Albert Street. I'm at Camden School for Girls. My hobby is skateboarding.
4 Hi, we're Caroline and George's friends. We're new in London. And we love the new garden!
5 Hi, we're from Manchester. We're eleven and we're twins. We're new in London.
6 Hi, I'm 38. I'm from Manchester, but I live in London with my family now. My favourite room in the new house is the kitchen.

D17 Training: Sentences with *to be* ▶ After A5 | p. 21 ▶ G3 | p. 182

a) Copy the text and fill in the missing forms of *to be*.

are (2x) • *is* (3x)

George: My friend Tom in Manchester **1** cool. Tom **2** a Man United fan, too. And he **3** on Friend Chat, too. So we **4** in contact all the time. His family is big: There is his mum and dad, two brothers and a sister. They **5** very nice.

b) Copy the text and fill in the missing forms of *to be*.

Caroline: Sophie **1** my best friend in Manchester. It **2** really funny: Her parents **3** from London. But now Sophie's family **4** in Manchester and we **5** here. Sophie **6** a very good friend. When I **7** worried or sad, she **8** there to help. But, Emma, you **9** my new best friend! I **10** really happy that your home **11** next door.[1]

---

[1] next door – *nebenan*

D18 Training: Questions and short answers with *to be* ▶ After A8 | p. 23 ▶ G5 | p. 183

Match the questions and the answers.

1 Are Caroline and George twins?
2 Is Camden in London?
3 Are Patch and Socks in Manchester?
4 Is Jack sixteen?
5 Is Camden Market a school?
6 Is George sad?

A No, he isn't.
B Yes, he is.
C Yes, they are.
D Yes, it is.
E No, they aren't.
F No, it isn't.

Diff and train 1

D19 Training: Questions and short answers with *to be* ▶ After A9 | p. 23 ▶ G5 | p. 183

a) Copy and complete the questions. Use *is* or *are*.

XXX the car blue?
XXX the small dog brown?
XXX the bus blue?
XXX the trees green?

XXX the sign blue?
XXX the girl's teddy bear grey?
XXX the shop on the left a pizza shop?

b) Add the short answers.

Yes, it is. • *No, it isn't.*

Yes, they are. • *No, they aren't.*

D20 Training: Questions and short answers with *to be* ▶ After A9 | p. 23 ▶ G5 | p. 183

a) Write down the questions.
Example: eleven – is – George – ? → *Is George eleven?*

1 on Albert Street – the – is – new house – ?
2 the McBrides – are – from Liverpool – ?
3 an Arsenal fan – George – is – ?
4 Patch and Socks – are – at Caroline's school – ?

b) Answer the questions.

1 Diff and train

D21 Training: Questions with *there is/there are* ▶ After A9 | p. 23

a) Look at the picture.
Say what you can see.

There's …

There are …

b) Work with a partner. Ask and answer questions.
Take turns.

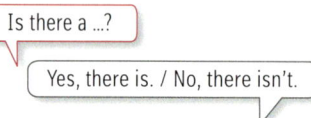

Is there a …?
Yes, there is. / No, there isn't.

Are there …?
Yes, there are. / No, there aren't.

D22 Extra: Words and phrases ▶ After A9 | p. 23
Copy the acrostic about Camden and complete it.

C
A
M *arket*
D
E
shoppi N *g*

Diff and train 1

Theme 1: Part B

D23 Easy alternative: Listening ▶ Instead of B1b | p. 26 🔊 L 1/14 | S 9
Listen to the dialogue on page 26. What is the problem? Choose the correct answer.
A Caroline and George are not friendly[1].
B There is a mouse in the shop.
C Patch is in the shop.

---
1 friendly – *freundlich*

D24 Easy alternative: Reading ▶ Instead of B1c | p. 26
Read the dialogue on page 26. Match the sentence parts.

1 Rajiv is …   A on the shelf.
2 Sheree is …   B eleven.
3 There is a noise …   C 18.
4 There is a mouse …   D behind the newspapers.

D25 Training: Words and phrases ▶ After B1c | p. 26
Look at the dialogue on page 26 again.

a) Write down the words.

1 ch-colate   4 dau--ter   7 sh--f
2 s--ter   5 ne--paper   8 sh-p
3 tw-n   6 m--se   9 bro--er

b) Write five sentences. Use words from a).

D26 Extra: Prepositions ▶ After B3 | p. 27
Where is the mouse now?
Example: *The mouse is in front of the …*

chocolate • cornflakes • newspapers

1 2 3 4

D27 Training: Questions with question words ▶ After B5 | p. 27 ▶ G6 | p. 184
Write down these questions and answer them.

1 is – your – Who – teacher – ?
2 your – is – birthday – When – ?
3 is – What – your – favourite colour – ?
4 your – is – best friend – How old – ?
5 is – pencil case – Where – your – ?

1 Diff and train

D28 Extra: Words and phrases ▶ After B7c | p. 28

a) Look at the family tree and find out about Tom's family.

> divorced – *geschieden*

1. Duncan is his father.
2. Susan is his mother.
3. Richard is her uncle.
4. Stella is her aunt.
5. Susan is her sister.
6. Tom is her brother.
7. Isabelle is her daughter.
8. Maddox is her son.

That's Eric.

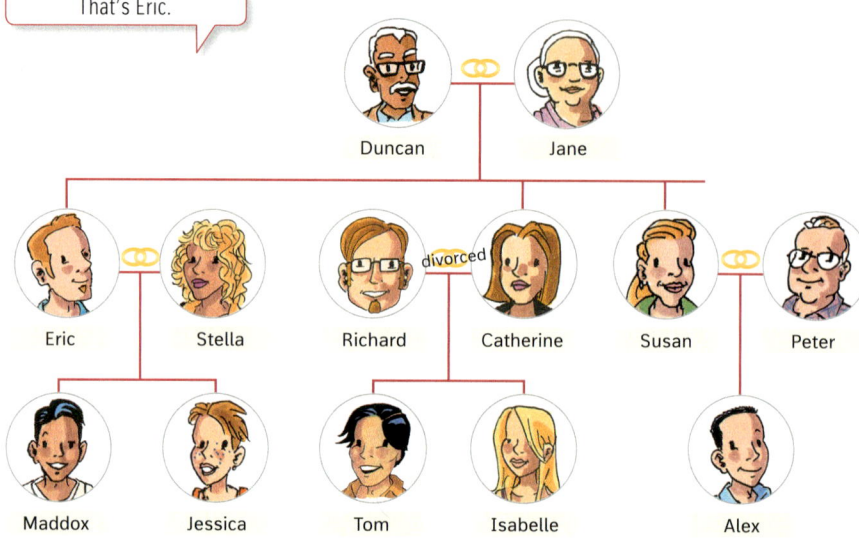

b) Draw your family tree. Then write five sentences about your family. ▶ Wordbank 2 | p. 199

D29 Easy alternative: Possessive determiners
▶ Instead of B8b | p. 29   ▶ G7 | p. 184

George writes a text message to his friend Tom.
Copy the message and fill in the correct determiner.

Hi, Tom. How are you? Camden is cool and **our / your** new house is cool, too. **His / My** room is really great. Caroline is happy now because Emma is **her / their** new friend. **Her / My** new friend is Rajiv. **Her / His** family is from India. Rajiv and **his / our** family live near **our / their** new house, on Albert Street. **My / Their** flat is above a shop. Say hi to **your / my** family. Bye! George

D30 Extra: Possessive determiners ▶ After B8b | p. 29   ▶ G7 | p. 184

Complete the sentences with the correct possessive determiners.
Example: *Jake is at Catford School. His school is in London.*

1. My parents and I like basketball.   XXX favourite team is Berlin.
2. Rajiv and Sheree speak Hindi.   XXX parents are from India.
3. I like football.   XXX favourite team is Liverpool.
4. My aunt is from Bristol.   XXX hobby is in-line skating.
5. Harry can speak German.   XXX mother is from Berlin.
6. Rosa's cat is black and white.   XXX name is Jake.

Diff and train 2

Theme 2: Intro

D1 Training: Reading ▶ After Intro 2 | p. 37

Read the comic on page 36 again. Complete the sentences.

1 George's tie is in his …
2 Charlie's team is …
3 George's old friends are in …
4 His new friends are …
5 Emma and Rajiv are Charlie's …
6 George isn't at …

D2 Extra: Listening/Reading ▶ After Intro 4b | p. 37 L 1/17 | S 12

Listen to George's phone call again.
Read the sentences and put them in the right order.

1 **Mr McBride:** Hi, George, what's wrong? Aren't you at school?
2 **Mr McBride:** Really, George! Your first day at school and you're at the wrong school. And you're late for your first lesson!
3 **Mr McBride:** Football, football, football! Listen, George, go to William Ellis, now!
4 **Mr McBride:** OK, let me check. Number 29 goes to Camden School for Girls.
5 **Mr McBride:** Wait a minute, George. Is it the 53? No, that's the bus to Hampstead Heath.
6 **Mr McBride:** Ah, here we are. First take the 93 bus to the train station and then the 214 bus to William Ellis. And hurry up, you're very late.

A **George:** OK, Dad. Thanks!
B **George:** I'm at school, but it's the wrong school. It's Acland Burghley.
C **George:** Dad, please!!
D **George:** I'm sorry, Dad, but … there is this nice boy, Charlie, and he's an Arsenal fan, and he's my new friend …
E **George:** But what's the right bus? I can't find it on the internet!
F **George:** Dad! That's not my school. It's Caroline's.

D3 Extra: Numbers ▶ After Intro 5 | p. 37 L 1/27 | S 21

a) Listen to the number quizzes and write them down. What is the result?
b) 👥 Make up two number quizzes.
   Read them out and test your partner.

+ plus / plʌs/
- minus / ˈmaɪnəs/

2 Diff and train

Theme 2: Part A

D4 Support: School things ▶ Before A3b | p. 38
Match the words to the pictures.
Example: **1: pencil case, 2: …**

exercise book • pen •
pencil case • school bag •
rubber • ruler •
pencil • glue •
folder • felt tips •
pencil sharpener

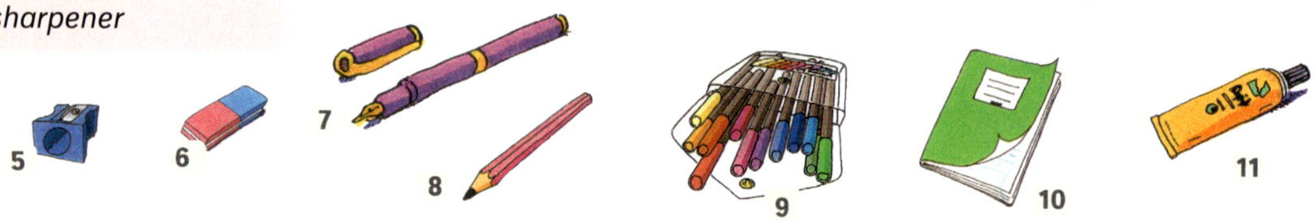

D5 Training: School things ▶ After A3b | p. 38
Make a list of the things
in your school bag.
▶ Wordbank 1 | p. 198

a blue pencil case
an exercise book
…

D6 Training: Reading ▶ After A4a | p. 39
Who says what?

That's Ms Jefferson / Joe / George.

1 "Sorry I'm late."
2 "It's your first day."
3 "Oh no! A Man United fan!"
4 "You know the rules."
5 "It's great."
6 "Where is your school tie?"

D7 Support: Reading ▶ Before A5a | p. 39
Match the English phrases with the German translations.

1 Come on time and don't be late.
2 Pay attention, sit up straight.
3 Don't forget to shut the door!
4 Put your hand up, don't call out.
5 In the classroom please just walk.
6 Do your homework, learn keywords.
7 Concentrate on what you learn.

A Konzentriere dich auf das, was du lernst.
B Vergiss nicht, die Tür zu schließen!
C Pass auf, sitz gerade.
D Melde dich und ruf nicht einfach rein.
E Sei pünktlich und komm nicht zu spät.
F Mach deine Hausaufgaben, lerne Schlüsselbegriffe.
G Im Klassenraum bitte nur gehen.

Diff and train 2

D8 Training: Mediation ▶ After A6 | p. 40
Read the sign. What is it about? Choose the best answer.

A Man darf nicht während des Unterrichts sprechen. Außerdem soll man seinen Lehrkräften und Klassenkameraden immer zuhören.
B Man soll den Lehrkräften zuhören, andere Schüler respektieren und hart arbeiten. Außerdem soll man während des Unterrichts nicht sprechen und immer pünktlich sein.
C Man soll Mitschüler respektieren, den Lehrkräften zuhören und immer pünktlich sein.

> **WILLIAM ELLIS SCHOOL FOR BOYS**
>
> **School rules**
> 1. Always listen to the teachers and don't talk in class.
> 2. Respect other pupils.
> 3. Always be on time and work hard.

D9 Training: Imperative ▶ After A7 | p. 40
a) Write down crazy rules for your home.
▶ G8 | p. 185

b) Draw signs for your rules.

Always
Don't

eat in bed.
stand on the table.
be quiet.
sleep on the table.
be late for school.
clean your room.
…

D10 Training: Words ▶ After A8 | p. 40
Look at the dialogue on page 40 again.
Write down the words.

1 pen--l ca--
2 fr--nds
3 h-mew--k
4 bas--t--ll
5 f--der
6 l--ch

D11 Training: can/can't ▶ After A11 | p. 41 ▶ G9 | p. 185
What can they do? What can't they do?
Example: 1. Lisa / play tennis → *Lisa can't play tennis.*

1 Lisa / play tennis

2 Igor / make pizza

3 Anna / swim

4 Hannah / play basketball

5 Felix / play football

6 Nick / sing

one hundred and thirty-five

2 Diff and train

D12 Easy alternative: can/can't ▶ Instead of A11b | p. 41 ▶ G9 | p. 185
Choose four questions and ask your classmates. Note down their answers.

1. Can you play basketball?
2. Can you speak French?
3. Can you make pizza?
4. Can you play hockey?
5. Can you dance?
6. Can you play tennis?

D13 Training: can/can't ▶ After A11 | p. 41 ▶ G9 | p. 185
Look at the grid. What can/can't the boys do? Talk to a partner.

Can George play the guitar?
Yes, he can./ No, he can't.

	George	Rajiv	Joe
play the guitar[1]	–	+	–
speak French	–	–	–
play football	+	+	+
make spaghetti	+	+	+

[1] play the guitar – *Gitarre spielen*

Theme 2: Part B

D14 Training: School rooms ▶ After B1 | p. 44
What are the words?

1. You can eat there.
2. It is a very big room.
3. It is the room for books.
4. You can see many computers there.
5. You can draw pictures there.
6. You can do experiments there.

D15 Training: Sentences with *to be* (Revision) ▶ After B2 | p. 44 ▶ G3 | p. 182
Write true sentences. Use the correct form of *to be*.
Example: My name **XXX** Elizabeth. → *My name isn't Elizabeth. My name is Ben.*

1. My school bag **XXX** new.
2. My eyes **XXX** blue.
3. My favourite colour **XXX** green.
4. There **XXX** a desk in my bedroom.
5. English **XXX** my favourite subject.
6. My parents **XXX** from England.

D16 Training: Sounds ▶ After B2 | p. 44 🔊 L 1/28 | S 22
Copy the grid. Then listen and fill in the words.

~~phones~~ • ~~books~~ • girls • names • lessons • shoes • maths • sandwiches • buses • seats • desks • dogs

/z/	/s/	/ɪz/
phone**s**	book**s**	...

D17 Extra: Reading ▶ After B2 | p. 44
Read the dialogue on page 44 again. Say when the girls have got the lessons.

	maths	
	French	
	music	after morning break.
They have got	geography	in the first lesson.
	PE	before morning break.
	history	in the afternoon.
	English	
	Spanish	

Diff and train 2

D18 Extra: Reading ▶ After B2 | p. 44

Look at these sentences from the dialogue on page 44. One word in each sentence is wrong.
Write down the correct sentences.
Example: Emma, where is your desk? → *Emma, where is your seat?*

1 "Next to Gillian. She's from my old school."
2 "We have got music in the first lesson."
3 "Mr May, Julia has got my school bag."
4 "And now write down the three breaks in the afternoon."
5 "Then all of you have got maths and music."

D19 Training: *have got/has got* ▶ After B4 | p. 45 ▶ G10 | p. 186

Look at the pictures and write down the sentences. Use *have got/has got*.
Example: *Elsa hasn't got a cat.*

1 Elsa
2 James
3 Michael and John
4 Sandy
5 The Browns
6 Hamida
7 Hamida's brother
8 Zoe and her sister

D20 Extra: *have got/has got* ▶ After B4 | p. 45

Look at the picture of David's classroom.
Compare your classroom to David's classroom.
Example: *In our classroom, we've got a poster of ..., but in David's classroom they've got ...*
In David's classroom they've got ..., and in our classroom, we've got ..., too.
We haven't got ..., but ...

projector = *Beamer*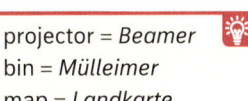
bin = *Mülleimer*
map = *Landkarte*

2 Diff and train

D21 Training: Words ▶ After B5b | p. 45

Look at these sentences from school lessons. Write down the subjects.

1 "You can still find a lot of old things from that time in England."
2 "You're too quiet. The people can't hear you. Let's do the scene again."
3 "Bonjour! Ça va?"
4 "¡Hola! ¿Qué tal?"
5 "Don't use pink. Use red and yellow here for the houses."

D22 Support: Questions with *has got* ▶ Before B6 | p. 46 ▶ G10 | p. 186

Put the words in the correct order. Write down the questions and answer them.
Example: Rajiv / got / sister / a / has / ?   → *Has Rajiv got a sister? Yes, he has.*

1 dog / Caroline / got / a / has / ?
2 French / Beebee / got / has / ?
3 Emma / brother / has / a / got / ?
4 Man United / Charlie / has / scarf / got / a / ?
5 George / got / computer / a / has / ?

D23 Training: Questions with *have got/has got* ▶ After B6 | p. 46 ▶ G10 | p. 186

a) Read this interview and write down the questions with *have got/has got*.

Miriam: Tom, can I ask you some questions?
Tom: Yes, of course.
Miriam: Have you got a brother or a sister?
Tom: Yes, I've got a brother.
5 **Miriam:** Has your brother got a hobby?
Tom: Yes, he has. In-line skating.
Miriam: And you? Have you got in-line skates?
Tom: No, but I've got a skateboard.
Miriam: Have you got a computer?
10 **Tom:** Of course! I love computer games. That's my favourite hobby!
Miriam: Has your brother got a computer, too?
Tom: No, he hasn't. He's five.

b) Add three more questions. Then work with a partner and interview him/her.

D24 Training: Genitive (*'s and s'*) ▶ After B7 | p. 46 ▶ G11 | p. 187

Look at the pictures. Write about the things.
Example: *This is Emma's computer.*

> Helen**'s** car
> Lewis**'s** pencil
> the Browns**'** house

Emma
Charlie
Rajiv
the twins

Diff and train 2

D25 Training: Genitive ▶ After B7 | p. 46 ▶ G11 | p. 187

a) Write down correct sentences. Use the *of* genitive.
Example: The (colour / house) is green. → *The colour of the house is green.*

1. The (name / school) is William Ellis.
2. There is a (picture / Camden Market) in the book.
3. The (name / Caroline's cat) is Socks.

b) Write down correct sentences. Use the *'s/s'* genitive or the *of* genitive.
Example: George is (Rajiv / friend). → *George is Rajiv's friend.*

1. This is (George / dog).
2. (Beebee / pencil case) is new.
3. What is (colour / car)?
4. This is (the twins / first day at school).
5. (My mother / favourite colour) is yellow.

D26 Easy alternative: Listening ▶ Instead of B8b | p. 46 L 1/26 | S 20
Listen to the girls and say if the sentences are right or wrong. Correct the wrong sentences.
Example: Beebee has got chicken and cheese. → *No. Beebee has got chicken and rice.*

1. Beebee has got an apple for dessert.
2. Emma has got chicken and rice for lunch.
3. Emma is a vegetarian.
4. Caroline has got macaroni for lunch.
5. Gillian has got a table for three.
6. Beebee loves animals.

D27 Training: Mediation ( ) ▶ After B10 | p. 47
An English school class is at your school. At break you talk to a boy.
He can't speak German so you speak English.
Write down what you want to say in English.

 Don't translate word for word. The highlighted words and phrases are tricky.

You: Hallo, ich heiße … Wie heißt du?
John: Hi, I'm John. You've got a great school here. How big is it?
You: Es gibt fast neunhundert Schüler. Wie groß ist deine Schule?
John: Not so big. There are about 600 pupils, I think. What's your timetable like? How many lessons have
5   you got every day?
You: Wir haben 7 oder 8 Stunden jeden Tag.
John: And what about breaks?
You: Ja, wir haben zwei kurze Pausen und eine lange Mittagspause.
John: Can you eat at school?
10 **You:** Ja. Es gibt eine gute Mensa. Hast du Hunger? Wir können jetzt essen.
John: Great!

3 Diff and train

Theme 3: Intro

D1 Support: Words ▶ Before Intro 1 | p. 54

Match the verbs and nouns.
Write down at least eight activities you can do in your free time.

do	judo
play	basketball
make	a cake
help	the cinema
sing	a film
go to	friends
surf	your family
meet	in a choir
watch	in an orchestra
talk to	the guitar
	the internet
	around the house
	TV
	the city centre
	a youth club

D2 Training: Words ▶ After Intro 5 | p. 54

Write down sentences about time.
Example: *An hour is 60 minutes.*

An hour		it is 6 o'clock in 15 minutes.
Quarter past five		60 minutes.
Half an hour		15 minutes.
Quarter to six	is	it is 8 o'clock in 30 minutes.
Ten to four	means[1]	30 minutes.
A quarter of an hour		it is 15 minutes past five.
Half past seven		it is 4 o'clock in 10 minutes.
Ten past seven		it is half past seven in 20 minutes.

[1] to mean – *bedeuten, meinen*

D3 Training: Words ▶ After Intro 5 | p. 54   L 1/41 | S 34

a) Listen and point at the right picture.

1   2   3         5

b) Look at the clocks and say the time.
Example: *1. It's half past eight.*
▶ Wordbank 3 | p. 200

Diff and train 3

Theme 3: Part A

D4 Easy alternative: Listening ▶ Instead of A1b | p. 56   🔊 L 1/31 | S 25

Listen to the dialogue. Are the sentences right or wrong?

1 There is a bake-off at Camden School for Girls.
2 The winner gets a prize for the best cake or biscuits.
3 George's cake is a banana cake.
4 George wants to bake muffins, too.
5 Grandma has got a special recipe for brownies.

That's right. *That's wrong.*

D5 Extra: Reading ▶ After A2b | p. 56

George's grandmother sends him her special muffin recipe, but it is mixed up.
Read the recipe and match the pictures to the sentences.

1 Mix together the flour[1], baking powder, salt and sugar[2].
2 Beat the egg[3] with a fork[4].
3 Mix egg with milk[5] and oil.
4 Pour[6] it all in the flour mixture.
5 Add 100 g blueberries.
6 Put the dough into muffin cups[7].
7 Bake for 20 minutes.
8 Decorate the muffins.

---
[1] flour *(no pl)* – Mehl
[2] sugar – Zucker
[3] egg – Ei
[4] fork – Gabel
[5] milk *(no pl)* – Milch
[6] to pour – gießen, schütten
[7] cup – hier: Backform

 A
 B
 C
 D
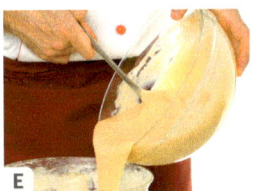 E
 F
 G
 H

D6 Training: Simple present (positive statements) ▶ After A3 | p. 57 ▶ G12 | p. 188

Everyone in the Butler family has got jobs to do around the house.
Complete the sentences with the missing verbs.
Example: *Mr Butler works in the garden.*

1 Mr Butler **XXX** in the garden. (work)
2 Mrs Butler **XXX** the bathroom. (clean)
3 Jack and Emma **XXX** the table. (lay)
4 Mr Butler **XXX** the rubbish. (take out)
5 Mrs Butler and Emma **XXX** cakes. (bake)
6 Emma **XXX** the living room. (tidy up)

3 Diff and train

D7 Training: Simple present (positive and negative statements) ▶ After A3 | p. 57 ▶ G12 | p. 188

The boys in George's class all do different jobs at home, but they don't do everything. Complete the sentences.

Example: *Harry loads the dishwasher. Yusuf doesn't …*

1 Harry **XXX** the dishwasher. (load ✔)
2 Yusuf **XXX** the table. (lay ✘)
3 Alex **XXX** his mother in the kitchen. (help ✔)
4 Aarav **XXX** shopping. (go ✔)
5 Steve and John **XXX** the car. (wash ✘)
6 Ben **XXX** his room. (tidy ✔)
7 Sanjay and Alex **XXX** the rubbish. (take out ✘)
8 James and John **XXX** their beds. (make ✔)

D8 Support: Words ▶ Before A4 | p. 57

There is something wrong with this list.
Write it down correctly.
▶ Wordbank 4 | p. 201

Things to do!
- load the table
- tidy the dishwasher
- lay the dog
- walk my room
- hoover my bed
- make the floor

D9 Training: Simple present (positive and negative statements) ▶ After A4 | p. 57 ▶ G12 | p. 188

The Camden kids have got a lot of hobbies. Write down eight sentences about what they do and don't do.
Example: *1. Charlie plays football and dances, but he doesn't play tennis.*

swim • ride a horse • play the guitar • play table tennis • …

1 Charlie
2 Caroline
3 Emma
4 George
5 Rajiv
6 Gillian

Diff and train 3

D10 Training: Simple present (positive and negative statements) ▶ After A4 | p. 57 ▶ G12 | p. 188

Look at the pictures. Say what the members of the Batson family do/don't do around the house at the weekend.

Example: *Charlie hoovers the floor at the weekend.*

1 Charlie

2 Mrs Batson

3 Mr Batson

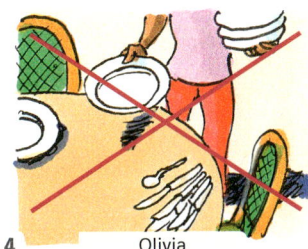
4 Olivia

5 Kayla

6 Mr Batson

D11 Training: Simple present and adverbs of frequency ▶ After A5 | p. 57 ▶ G13 | p. 189

Write eight sentences about what you and your family usually/often/sometimes/… do. Choose the correct verb form.

I		**clean/cleans** the car	at the weekend.
My brother	always	**tidy/tidies** the kitchen	in the summer.
My sister	often	**load/loads** the dishwasher	on Mondays/Tuesdays/…
My mother	usually	**take out/takes out** the rubbish	…
My father	sometimes	**watch/watches** a film	
My parents	never	**read/reads** a book	
My grandparents		**play/plays** the piano	
…		**walk/walks** the dog	
		…	

D12 Training: Simple present and adverbs of frequency ▶ After A5 | p. 57 ▶ G13 | p. 189

Write down the sentences. Add *always, usually, often* or *sometimes*.
Example: *I always go to school with my friends.*

1. I go to school with my friends. (*always*)
2. We take the bus at twenty past eight. (*always*)
3. We meet for lunch at the canteen. (*often*)
4. I am at home at ten to four. (*usually*)
5. I do my homework after school. (*always*)
6. I load the dishwasher. (*sometimes*)
7. At quarter past five I watch TV. (*sometimes*)
8. I am in bed at ten o'clock. (*usually*)

Bei *to be* steht das Häufigkeitsadverb hinter dem Verb:
Sarah is never late.

3 Diff and train

D13 **Training: Simple present (questions with *do/does*, short answers)** ▶ After A8 | p. 58 ▶ G13 | p. 189

a) Put the words in the right order to make questions. Write them down in your exercise book.

1. it / in the house / use / do / you ? – No, you don't. → *Do you use …?*
2. work / you / do / with it? – No, you don't.
3. you / play / with it / do ? – Yes, you do.
4. does / cost / it / 100 euros? – No, it doesn't.
5. in a team / play / you / with it / do ? – Yes, you do.
6. kick / it / you / do ? – Yes, you do.

b) Look at the questions and answers again. What is it?

D14 **Training: Simple present (questions with *do/does*, short answers)** ▶ After A9a | p. 58 ▶ G13 | p. 189

a) Find the right questions with *do/does* and write them down. Use the highlighted verbs.
Example: **1. *Do you play football?***

1. For my hobby I need a ball. I **play** it in the park.
2. It's from Italy. It's round and you can eat it. I **like** it very much.
3. I sometimes do it in my free time. I like *FootballWorld* best and I **play** it on my computer.
4. It's Emily's favourite subject at school. It's about numbers. She really **likes** it.

b) Now read your questions and write down your answers.
Example: Do you play football? → *Yes, I do. / No, I don't.*

D15 **Extra: Simple present (questions with *do/does*, short answers)** ▶ After A9a | p. 58 ▶ G13 | p. 189

Steve is new at William Ellis School. The other boys ask him a lot of questions.
Read Steve's answers. Find the questions with *do/does* and write them down.
Use these verbs for your questions:

eat • like (2x) • live • listen • play

Example: Yes, I do. I often play in the park, but I want to play in the school team, too.
→ *Do you play football?*

1. No, I don't. I don't really like fish.
2. Yes, I like my new school.
3. Yes, my grandmother lives in London, too.
4. No, I don't. I don't like rap music.
5. No, I don't. I want to play the guitar, but I haven't got one.
6. Yes, I like London.

D16 **Training: Words** ▶ After A10a | p. 59 ▶ English sounds | p. 265

a) What are the words?
1. /ˈmʌfɪnz/
2. /ˈdekəreɪt/
3. /ˈfəʊtəʊ/
4. /fænˈtæstɪk/
5. /ˈbeɪkə/
6. /ˈresəpi/

b) Complete the sentences with the words from a).
1. Caroline says: "George is a great **XXX**!"
2. George buys decorations and **XXX** at the supermarket.
3. George's grandmother gives him her special **XXX**.
4. George sends a **XXX** of the muffins to Rajiv.
5. Rajiv thinks the muffins look **XXX**.
6. George and Rajiv **XXX** the muffins.

Diff and train 3

D17 Extra: Reading ▶ After A10a | p. 59
Read the story on page 59 again. Talk about the friends.

		clever		George is such a good baker.
George		worried	because	she sees the muffins.
Caroline	is	surprised	when	Emma comes to their house.
Rajiv		excited	…	he buys muffins at the supermarket.
		happy		George's muffins look fantastic.

Theme 3: Part B

D18 Training: *a/an* (Revision) ▶ After B1 | p. 62   ▶ G2 | p. 181
Copy the grid and sort the words.

a	an
…	…

book • answer • exercise • kitchen • bed • shoe • aunt • uncle • school bag • elephant • club • example

D19 Easy alternative: Reading ▶ Instead of B2b | p. 62
Read the dialogue on page 62. Match the questions and the answers.
Be careful: There are more answers than you need.

1 What does Beebee say to Emma?
2 How does Beebee feel about circus clowns?
3 Why does Beebee want to take part?
4 Where do the girls want to meet?
5 When do the girls want to meet?

A She hates them.
B At Caroline's house.
C On Saturday afternoon.
D "Don't be so boring."
E She wants to wear a beautiful costume and be the star of the show.
F At Emma's house.
G This Wednesday after school.

D20 Training: Reading ▶ After B2b | p. 62
Read the dialogue on page 62. Complete the sentences.

1 Emma is good at …
2 Emma doesn't want to …
3 Beebee wants to wear …
4 Caroline and Emma sometimes …
5 Gillian is very nervous when …

3 Diff and train

D21 **Training: can/can't (Revision)** ▶ After B2d | p. 62   ▶ G9 | p. 185

a) Put the words in the correct order to form questions.
Example: your mother / can / English / speak / ?   → *Can your mother speak English?*

1. volleyball / play / you / can / ?
2. can / your dad / pizza / make / ?
3. you / do / at school / can / your homework / ?
4. in your classroom / you / open / can / the windows / ?
5. lunch / you / have / at school / can / ?

b) Choose the answers to the questions from a) that are right for you.

1. Yes, I can. / No, I can't.
2. Yes, he can. / No, he can't.
3. Yes, I can. / No, I can't.
4. Yes, we can. / No, we can't.
5. Yes, I can. / No, I can't.

D22 **Support: Simple present (questions with question words)** ▶ Before B4 | p. 63   ▶ G15 | p. 191

Match the questions and the answers.

1. What does Rajiv do at the weekend?
2. When do Caroline and George do their homework?
3. Where does Beebee watch TV?
4. Why does Charlie wear an Arsenal shirt?
5. Who do Joe and James meet at the weekend?

A   She watches it in the living room.
B   He plays football and watches TV.
C   Because they are his favourite team.
D   They meet their friends.
E   They do it after school.

D23 **Training: Simple present (questions with question words)** ▶ After B4 | p. 63   ▶ G15 | p. 191

Look at the answers. Write down the questions. There can be more than one correct question.
Example: I do my homework in the kitchen.   → *Where do you do your homework?*
   → *What do you do in the kitchen?*

1. I live in Hamburg.
2. In my free time I play the guitar.
3. I go to school at a quarter to eight.
4. I love Harry Potter because it's an exciting story.
5. I meet my friend on Saturdays.
6. I eat toast in the morning.

D24 **Extra: Simple present (questions with question words)** ▶ After B4 | p. 63   ▶ G15 | p. 191

Write down five questions with *what/when/where/why/who* and interview your partner.
Example: *What do you do at the weekend?*

Diff and train 4

D25 Training: Reading ▶ After B8a | p. 64

Match the sentence halves to tell the story. There is one more sentence part than you need.

1. Caroline and her friends
2. Grace is a bit nervous
3. There are lots of very good acts
4. George only wants to hear
5. Charlie doesn't answer
6. Rajiv is a cool guitar player
7. Then the dancers from Acland Burghley
8. Charlie is on stage
9. Claire and Rajiv and the school band
10. Charlie wins a

A. from other schools.
B. are the winners.
C. are at The Roundhouse.
D. but the girls clap a lot.
E. come on stage.
F. Rajiv and the school band.
G. and does a solo.
H. and the band is fantastic.
I. George's texts.
J. they must be the winners.
K. special prize.

Theme 4: Intro

D1 Support: Words ▶ Before Intro 2 | p. 72

Write down the answers to these questions. Then say the dates.

▶ Wordbank 3 | p. 200

1. When is your birthday?
2. What is the last day of the year?
3. What is the last day of August?
4. When is your best friend's birthday?
5. When is your mother's birthday?
6. When is your father's birthday?

You say:
Jo's birthday is on the twenty-third of May.
You can write:
Jo's birthday is on 23rd May. Or:
Jo's birthday is on May 23rd.

D2 Support: Words ▶ Before Intro 6 | p. 73

What can you do on your birthday? Match the words and the pictures.

Picture 1 is: You can eat cake.

go swimming • go bowling • ~~eat cake~~ • go to the cinema • have a sleepover • have a party • go ice skating • eat hamburgers

1

2

3

4

5

6

7

8

4 Diff and train

D3 Extra: Sounds 🔊 L 1/49 | S 42 ▶ After Intro 6 | p. 73

a) Listen to the tongue twister¹. Then say it.

> When is aunt Ethel's birthday?
> It's on Thursday.
> It's on the thirtieth of May.
> She will be² thirty-three that day.
> I'll go there³ with my father and my mother.
> Aunt Ethel is my father's sister.
> And that's the end of this tongue twister.

1 tongue twister – *Zungenbrecher*
2 she will be – *sie wird …*
3 I'll go there – *ich werde dorthin gehen*

b) Copy the grid and fill it in.

> Es gibt zwei *th*-Laute im Englischen:
> das stimmhafte *th*, z. B. in *they* (ð) und
> das stimmlose *th*, z. B. in *thanks* (θ).

/θ/	/ð/
E**th**el	**th**at

D4 Extra: Writing ▶ After Intro 6 | p. 73

Read the poems and write a birthday poem for a friend.

▶ Writing | p. 173

Let's celebrate
Enjoy your birthday party
Open your presents
Now sit down and have some cake

Birthday
Great presents
Good music
Favourite cake
Happy friends
Birthday

D5 Extra: Words 🔊 L 1/50 | S 43 ▶ After Intro 6 | p. 73

a) Combine words from the two boxes to form new words.
Example: *birth + day → birthday*

> birth · after · grand · time · some · home · super · class

> room · table · market · day · father · times · work · noon

b) Listen and check your words.

148   one hundred and forty-eight

Diff and train 4

Theme 4: Part A

D6 Easy alternative: Reading ▶ Instead of A1 | p. 74

Read A1 on page 74. Where are Mr and Mrs McBride? Where are Caroline and George?
Choose the correct answers.

1. A Mr and Mrs McBride are at home.
   B Mr and Mrs McBride are at the supermarket.
   C Mr and Mrs McBride are at the gym.

2. A Caroline and George are at the gym.
   B Caroline and George are at home.
   C Caroline and George are in the kitchen.

D7 Training: Simple present (Revision) ▶ After A3 | p. 75 ▶ G12 | p. 188

Read the text and complete it. Use the verbs in the box.

ride • come • listen • dance • eat • meet • help • play • make

Gillian usually **1** home from school at half past four. Then she often **2** to music in her room and **3** to it. Sometimes she **4** her friends in the afternoon. They **5** lots of games together and sometimes they **6** their bikes. Gillian often **7** her mum in the kitchen and **8** a salad. They usually **9** at half past six.

D8 Support: Present progressive ▶ Before A3 | p. 75 ▶ G16 | p. 192

1 Copy the grid.
2 Then look at the verbs and fill them in. Use the colours from the grid.

play • win • stop • dance • try • run • sing • drink • make • bake • tell • get • decide • give • let

read + ing = read**ing**	write + ing = writ**ing**	sit + ing = sit**ting**
play**ing**	…	…

D9 Training: Present progressive (positive statements) ▶ After A4 | p. 75 ▶ G16 | p. 192

Write down what the people are doing at the moment.

1 Tim (watch) TV.
2 Gillian (read) a book.
3 Mr Scott (sleep) in his bed.
4 Jason (sit) on the sofa.
5 Mrs Newman (talk) on the phone.
6 The boys (play) a computer game.

4 Diff and train

D10 Training: Present progressive (positive statements) ▶ After A4 | p. 75 ▶ G16 | p. 192

Look at the pictures of sports. What are the people doing?
Be careful: There are more words than you need.
Example: **1. Louise is playing volleyball.**

play basketball · ride a bike · play table tennis ·
play volleyball · swim · dance · play tennis ·
ride a horse · play hockey · play football

1 Louise

2 Katie and Nick

3 Phil

4 Penny

5 Steve

6 Jessica

7 Claire

8 Jake

D11 Training: Present progressive (positive/negative statements) ▶ After A4 | p. 75 ▶ G16 | p. 192

Look at the pictures. Write down what the people are doing and what they aren't doing.
Example: **1. Mr McBride isn't flying a plane. He is sitting at the pool.**

1 Mr McBride: fly[1] a plane[2] / sit at the pool

2 Charlie: play football / meet his friends

3 Caroline: do her homework / bake a cake

4 Mr and Mrs McBride: go to the cinema[3] / visit friends

5 Patch: wait for George / eat

6 Socks: sleep / play

1 to fly – *fliegen* | **2** plane – *Flugzeug* | **3** cinema – *Kino*

Diff and train 4

D12 Support: Present progressive (questions and short answers) ▶ Before A5 | p. 75 ▶ G16 | p. 192

Write down the questions and answers in the present progressive.
Example: Charlie / bake / muffins? – No. / He / bake / biscuits.
→ *Is Charlie baking muffins? – No, he isn't. He is baking biscuits.*

1. George / talk to / Gillian? – No. / He / talk to / Rajiv.
2. Patch / sleep / on the sofa? – No. / He / sleep / in George's room.
3. Emma / plan / a birthday party? – No. / Caroline and George / plan / a birthday party.
4. George and Rajiv / play / football? – Yes.
5. Mrs McBride / watch / TV? – No. / She / read / a book.
6. You / watch / TV? – No. / I / do / an exercise.

D13 Extra: Present progressive (questions with question words) ▶ After A5 | p. 75 ▶ G16 | p. 192

Pair work: Look at the picture. Take turns to ask and answer questions about it.
Use *who*, *what*, *where* and the verbs in the box.

~~take her dog for a walk~~ • take a photo • talk to a friend • drive a car • stand in the road • talk on the phone • skateboard • say hello to a friend • do the shopping • eat • look at his phone

4 Diff and train

D14 Training: Simple present or present progressive? ▶ After A6 | p. 76 ▶ G17 | p. 193
Read the text and fill in the correct forms.

Today Tom **1** (visit) his grandmother. He usually **2** (go) to his grandmother's house on Friday. His grandmother always **3** (bake) a cake. Right now, they **4** (play) cards. Tom's grandmother **5** (win). She **6** (be) usually very good. In the evening, Tom sometimes **7** (watch) TV with his grandmother.

D15 Training: Simple present or present progressive? ▶ After A6 | p. 76 ▶ G17 | p. 193
Choose the correct sentences.

1 Caroline and George are in the living room. They play a game. / They are playing a game.
2 Molly is in the kitchen. She bakes a cake. / She is baking a cake.
3 Socks is Caroline's cat. She usually sleeps in Caroline's bed. / She is usually sleeping in Caroline's bed.
4 At the moment Emma is at home. She reads a book. / She is reading a book.
5 We always eat at 6 o'clock. Today we have pizza. / Today we are having pizza.
6 I always read / I'm always reading before I go to bed.

D16 Easy alternative: Listening 🔊 L 1/47 | S 39 ▶ Instead of A7a | p. 76
Listen to George and Charlie. Say what their plan is.

A They want to plan the party.
B They want to play football in the park.
C They want to meet at Camden Market.

D17 Training: Words ▶ After A7d | p. 76
Use the phrases in the box to complete the telephone calls. There can be more than one answer.

> *Sure! • It's … • Why don't we …? • Great idea! • Let's … • Oh, not now. •
> OK, see you later. • Can we …? • Sounds good! • What about …? • Bye!*

A Sam: Hello?
Simon: Hi Sam! **1** Simon. What are you doing at the moment?
Sam: I'm doing my homework.
Simon: That's boring! **2** watch a film?
Sam: **3** Can I come to your house?
Simon: OK! **4**
Sam: **5** !

B Tammy: Hello!
Maria: **1** Maria. **2** meet at the shops?
Tammy: **3** I'm just washing my hair.
Maria: Well, **4** meet later?
Tammy: **5** When?
Maria: **6** 5 o'clock?
Tammy: **7**
Maria: OK! Bye!

D18 Training: Words ▶ After A9 | p. 77
Explain in German what you have to do. You can use the English-German dictionary (pp. 238-256) for help.
1 Test your partner.
2 Find examples in A1 and write them down.
3 Mime the activity to your group.
4 Imitate the way George and Charlie talk.
5 Draw a comic and write speech bubbles.

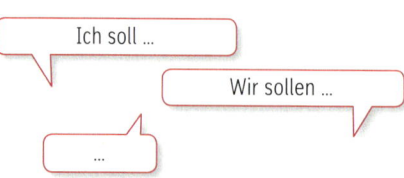

Diff and train 4

Theme 4: Part B

D19 Easy alternative: Listening 🔊 L 1/48 | S 40 ▶ Instead of B1 | p. 80

Listen to Emma and Gillian.
What do they buy?

bag with an elephant • phone case • earrings • T-shirt

D20 Training: *Some* and *any* ▶ After B3 | p. 81

👥 Work with a partner. Choose a basket. Find out what is in your partner's shopping basket. Take turns.

canned tomatoes • flour • butter • pasta • sweets • eggs • sugar

Have you got any apple juice in your basket?

Yes, I've got some. I've got two bottles. Have you got any chocolate?

No, I haven't got any. Have you got any …?

D21 Training: Listening 🔊 L 1/51 | S 44 ▶ After B4 | p. 81

a) Listen to the shopping dialogues. How much are these things?

1 The basketball is …
2 The T-shirt is …
3 The book is …
4 The posters are …
5 The jeans are …
6 The comics are …

50p • £3.50 • £4 • £7 • £8.50 • £12.50

b) 👥 Work with a partner. Ask and answer questions.

How much is the orange juice?

It's …

How much are the apples?

They're …

You write:
£1.50
50p

You say:
one pound fifty
fifty p

4 Diff and train

D22 Support: Writing a shopping dialogue ▶ Before B4 | p. 81

a) Put the two dialogues in the right order and write them down.
Start like this:

1. Shop assistant: Hi. Can I help you?
Customer: ...

1
Here you are. Bye.
It's £10.50.
Yes, please. I am looking for a pencil case.
Thanks. Have a nice day.
Hi. Can I help you?
This green one looks nice. How much is it?
Pencil cases are over there.

2
That's £1.80, please.
Can I have four of these apples, please?
No, thank you.
Thank you. Here's your change[1]. Bye.
Here you are.
Of course. Here you are. Anything else?[2]
Hello. What can I do for you?
Thank you. Bye.

b) Check your dialogues with a partner.

[1] change – *Münzgeld, Wechselgeld*
[2] Anything else? – *(Darf's) sonst noch was (sein)?*

D23 Extra: Viewing ▶ After B4 | p. 81

a) Watch the clip. What do Sam and Alex want to do?
b) Watch the clip again and find out:
- What do the friends get for Georgia?
- How much are the things?
- What do Sam and Alex want to do later?

▶ WB Media 5   ▶ WES-149220-2

D24 Extra: Mediation ( ) ▶ After B5 | p. 81

You are planning your birthday party with your mum. On the internet you find these tips.
Tell your mum about them in German.

Birthday parties – Tips

1 Ask a friend to help you. Then there isn't so much stress and you can enjoy the party.
2 Don't make too much food. Everyone is happy with some sandwiches and ice cream.
3 Send out invitations three weeks before the party.
4 Do not invite too many guests. This can be stressful for you and your guests.
5 Think about what party theme you want.
6 And finally, enjoy the party!

Diff and train 5

D25 **Training: Words** ▶ After B6 | p. 81

a) Talk about the clothes in Jasmine's wardrobe.

jumper • trousers • gloves • cap • dress • jeans • T-shirt • shoes • socks • sunglasses • skirt • ...

There is a green jumper.

There are trousers.

...

Jeans, trousers und *sunglasses* werden im Englischen nur im Plural (Mehrzahl) benutzt:
Your jeans are nice.
His trousers are yellow.
My sunglasses are black.

b) Write about what you wear.

On Mondays I usually wear ...
At the weekend ...
Today I'm wearing ...
My favourite outfit is ...

D26 **Easy alternative: Reading** ▶ Instead of B7b | p. 82

Read the story on pages 82/83 and choose a title for it.
A Party fun
B A burglar next door
C A boring party

D27 **Extra: Reading** ▶ After B9 | p. 83

Who says what in Theme 4?

1 "What about the invitation cards, George?"
2 "Bye Mum, see you soon!"
3 "Why don't you come along?"
4 "Let's find some earrings for Caroline's birthday."
5 "Have you got any elephant cases for MyPhone7?"
6 "Are you a doctor?"
7 "Don't be a baby."
8 "I think there is a burglar in the house!"

Theme 5: Intro

D1 **Training: Words** ▶ After Intro 1 | p. 90

Find the odd one out[1].

1 elephant – lion – dog – giraffe
2 hamster – cat – dog – goldfish
3 budgie – duck – chicken – lion
4 sheep – cow – elephant – pig
5 tiger – dog – lion – cat
6 budgie – hamster – cat – chicken

---
1 the odd one out – *das, was nicht dazugehört*

one hundred and fifty-five

5 Diff and train

D2 Training: Plurals (Revision) ▶ After Intro 2 | p. 90   ▶ G1 | p. 181

Write down the plural forms of these nouns. Be careful! Some of them are irregular.

sheep • foot • ear • arm • tooth • shelf • cow • mouse • house • child • woman • man • pet • fish

D3 Extra: Reading/Writing/Speaking ▶ After Intro 2 | p. 90

a) Find out what the animal is.
It is grey.
It is very big.
It has got big ears.
It lives in Africa or Asia, but you can also see it in a zoo or a circus.
It is clever and can work for its owner.

b) Write your own animal puzzle. Write down five clues¹ for each animal.
Your clues can be about …
- the animal's colour,
- its size (for example: very small, very big),
- its body parts (for example: head, ears),
- where it lives or where you can see it,
- its character or what it can do.

c) Test your classmates.

1 clue – *Hinweis, Tipp*

D4 Training: Reading ▶ After Intro 4 | p. 91

Read the flyer about Kentish Town City Farm. Some sentences are missing. Put them in the right position. Note: There are two sentences that do not fit.

KENTISH TOWN CITY FARM

1 there are a number of farms in the middle of London. Kentish Town City Farm is one of them. It is free and open from 9 am-5 pm. **2** There is something to do and see every day. You can
5 ride ponies, work in the garden and help with the animals. **3** You can join the Young Farmer Club, too. **4** But there is much more, for example meetings about healthy cooking¹ and growing² your own fruit and vegetables³. Don't
10 be surprised if you hear some noise: trains⁴ go through the farm! **5**

A You can buy a ticket for 3 pounds.
B Many people cannot believe⁵ it:
C Here you can learn more about farm animals and the environment⁶.
D The farm is over 100 years old.
E So come and visit the farm in the morning or the afternoon.
F You can feed⁷ the pigs and the chickens, for example.
G And the animals make some noise, too, of course!

1 cooking *(no pl)* – *Kochen* | **2** to grow – *anbauen* | **3** vegetable – *Gemüse* | **4** train – *Zug* | **5** to believe – *glauben* | **6** environment *(no pl)* – *Umwelt* | **7** to feed – *füttern*

Diff and train 5

Theme 5: Part A

D5 Easy alternative: Listening ◀) L 2/2 | S 45 ▶ Instead of A1a | p. 92
Listen and choose the right answers.

1 Who is Oscar?
  A A boy.
  B A dog.
  C A cat.

2 What is his situation?
  A He goes for a walk with his owner[1] Betty.
  B He goes to Betty's hot dog stand.
  C He doesn't know where his owner Betty is.

[1] owner – Besitzer/in

D6 Training: Reading ▶ After A2b | p. 92
Read the dialogue in A2 on page 92 again and find phrases with a similar[1] meaning.
Example: Isn't he sweet? → *Isn't he cute?*

1 Brilliant plan.
2 Don't get too excited
3 Don't be so scared[2].
4 It's OK, don't think about it.

[1] similar – ähnlich
[2] scared – verängstigt

D7 Training: Mediation ( ) ▶ After A2b | p. 92
You are in London and see this poster.
Your mother wants to know what it is about.

Your mother: Was ist das für ein Hund? – **You:** 1
Your mother: Und was ist mit ihm passiert? – **You:** 2
Your mother: Wann ist das denn passiert? – **You:** 3
Your mother: Steht noch mehr darüber, was an dem Hund besonders ist? – **You:** 4
Your mother: Und was soll man tun, wenn man ihn findet? – **You:** 5

LOST DOG
"Dizzee"
black labrador

Lost on Tues 24th Oct
in Hampstead Heath
Very friendly female, no collar, microchipped
PLEASE CALL FRANCES ON
0771 783 055
Substantial reward

D8 Support: Object pronouns ▶ Before A2c | p. 92 ▶ G20 | p. 195
Copy the grid. Scan the dialogue on page 92 again and fill in the grid.

Gillian sees Oscar.   She talks to him.
subject   object   subject   object
                     pronoun   pronoun

subject pronouns	object pronouns
I	me
you	...
...	him
she	...
it	it
...	us
you	you
they	...

D9 Training: Object pronouns ▶ After A2c | p. 92 ▶ G20 | p. 195
Read about Sally. Use object pronouns for the words in red.

"I've got a cat. I like **1 my cat** very much. My sister Claire has got three rabbits. She must give **2 her rabbits** food every day. Their cage gets very dirty so Claire must often clean **3 their cage**. I sometimes help **4 my sister** because she often helps me with my homework. My parents don't want to let **5 my sister and me** have a dog. They say three rabbits and a cat are enough. Susan and Sarah are my best friends. In the summer I often meet **6 Susan and Sarah** in the park. My grandparents live near the park. They are very old. So we sometimes help **7 my grandparents** and take their dog for a walk. My cousin Nick has got a horse. My sister often meets **8 Nick** at the weekend so they can go for a ride."

5 Diff and train

D10 Training: Modal verbs ▶ After A3 | p. 93

Write down one sentence for each sign.
Use different modals.

You	mustn't should shouldn't must	clean up after your dog. drink the water. sit on the stairs. ride your bike. play ball games.

D11 Training: Modal verbs ▶ After A4 | p. 93

Look at the pictures. Write down what you mustn't / needn't / should / shouldn't / must do to the animals.
Example: *1. You mustn't pull a cat's tail.*

1. pull tail
2. put a coat on
3. take for a walk
4. play
5. clean
6. give water
7. leave when it's …
8. be nice to

D12 Extra: Modal verbs ▶ After A4 | p. 93

Think about your classroom and school rules. Write down ten rules. Use modals.

1. You *mustn't/shouldn't/can* use your phones in class.
2. …

Diff and train 5

D13 Extra: Reading ▶ After A6 | p. 94

a) Read the information on good family pets at the bottom of this page. Then choose the best pet for Jessica, Phil, Meera and Bruno. Give reasons.

I think … is the best pet for … because he/she likes … and this pet is …, too. •
He/she hasn't got much room. So … is the right pet. • …

1	Jessica:	She does not like exotic animals. She likes animals with fur. She does not want to spend too much time on a pet.
2	Phil:	He wants a special pet. It should be different from a normal pet, so not a furry little friend. But he does not want to feed it other animals that look like pets.
3	Meera:	She loves animals that are clever, but her flat is too small for a dog.
4	Bruno:	He wants a pet that is not too small or too big because he has only got a small room. His pet should have fur, but must be bigger than a mouse. He is very good with all kinds of animals.

b) Read the information again and make sentences with modal verbs – two for each pet.
1 Young children **XXX** look after rabbits.
2 You **XXX** be careful with rabbits.
3 Children **XXX** keep a corn snake as a pet.
4 …

Small family pets

(1) Rabbits
Many families keep rabbits, but they are not always ideal family pets. Rabbits are often scared if
5 you are not careful with them. That is not easy for young children.

(2) Corn snakes
A corn snake is an easy pet. But it eats mice, so make sure that your family is OK with that.
10

(3) Chinchillas
They are from Chile, but are now popular as pets, too. They are very active and love a lot of room
15 to play. It is a good idea to have two chinchillas because then it is not so boring for them and it is not just your job to keep them active.

(4) Rats
Pet rats are not like street rats.
20 They are very clever and learn tricks like a dog. But they live only 2-3 years, so make sure the children in the family understand this.

(5) Geckos
25 Small geckos are good starter pets, too. They need a warm and big home, crickets to eat and water to drink.

(6) Hamsters
Hamsters are friendly and easy to
30 look after. All they need is a cage that is big enough and a little bit of time with their owners. But be careful with them – they are very small.

5 Diff and train

Theme 5: Part B

D14 Easy alternative: Listening   L 2/6 | S 47 ▶ Instead of B2b | p. 98

Read the questions and choose the correct answer.

1. Where is Gillian?
   A At home.
   B In the park.
   C At the animal shelter.

2. Who is with her?
   A George and Caroline.
   B Her mum.
   C Oscar.

3. Why are the neighbours a problem?
   A They aren't happy about Oscar.
   B They want to keep Oscar.
   C They are angry with Gillian.

4. What happens in the TV show *Help the animals*?
   A They have pets on the show and try to find new owners for them.
   B People talk about animal shelters.
   C Pet owners bring their pets to the show and talk about them.

5. Where must Oscar stay that night?
   A At George's house.
   B At an animal shelter.
   C At Gillian's flat.

D15 Training: Reading   ▶ After B3a | p. 98

Read the dialogue on page 98 again and answer the questions.
1. What does Mike do?
2. What happens to Oscar if they can't find his owner?
3. What happens after Christmas?
4. What happens in the summer?
5. What does Mike suggest to Gillian?

D16 Training: Word order in main and subordinate clauses   ▶ After B3b | p. 99

Write down the sentences in the correct order.

1. George – about stray dogs – when – on the internet – reads – he – is worried.
2. He – about the website – Gillian – calls – tells – and – her.
3. George and Gillian – Mike – to the animal shelter – and – go – meet.
4. Gillian – can't keep Oscar – sad – because – is – she.
5. Mike – their flat – is right – thinks – because – is too small – that Gillian's mum.
6. Gillian – can come – and – Mike – to the animal shelter – help.

Diff and train 5

D17 Training: Demonstrative pronouns ▶ After B4 | p. 99

this • that • these • those

Read the text and choose the correct word.

Gillian: This shop is full of baskets[1]. Look at __1__ baskets here.
Caroline: Is __2__ basket for a cat?
Assistant: No, it isn't. __3__ are baskets for dogs. All the things for cats are on __4__ shelves over there – that's our 'Cat's Corner'.
Caroline: Oh, right. Let's have a look there then, Gillian. Gillian?
Gillian: Wait, Caroline. Let me have a look at __5__ books about dogs first.
Caroline: You must have hundreds of books about dogs already. Come on, let's have a look at __6__ 'Cat's Corner'.

In the 'Cat's Corner'
Caroline: I really like __7__ basket here.
Gillian: But it is quite expensive. What about __8__ one up there on the third shelf?
Caroline: Hmm, I don't know. Hey, look at all __9__ cats' toys here. It's amazing.
Gillian: Look at __10__ posters on the wall. They are about a dog show. Maybe we can go there!
Caroline: Oh, Gillian …

---
1 basket – *Korb*

D18 Easy alternative: Listening 🔊 L 2/7 | S 49 ▶ Instead of B5a | p. 99

Listen and say what happens to Oscar.
A He must stay at the animal shelter.
B His owner comes to the animal shelter and takes him home.
C Gillian comes to the animal shelter and takes Oscar home.

D19 Training: Sounds 🔊 L 2/8 | S 50 ▶ After B6 | p. 100

Listen to the sentences. Then say them.

/z/ 	/s/
1 Budgie<u>s</u> are my favourite animal<u>s</u>.	3 Cat<u>s</u> often sleep in basket<u>s</u>.
2 Dog<u>s</u> can be really good friend<u>s</u>.	4 Elephant<u>s</u> can do funny trick<u>s</u>.

D20 Training: Mediation ( ) ▶ After B6 | p. 100

Read the text and tell a partner about it in German.

1. Read the English text and make sure you understand it.
2. Try to find the main ideas. Note them down.
3. Explain the text in German but don't include all the details. You don't need to translate every word, only the main ideas.

> **Are you an animal lover and between 11 and 15 years old? Then be a junior zoo-keeper for a day at London Zoo.**
>
> – You help our zoo-keepers to feed the animals and clean their cages. You also learn a lot about the animals.
> – You get an exclusive London Zoo T-shirt and cap.
> – You go to the restaurant for a drink and a snack.
>
> **Where:** London Zoo, Regent's Park, London NW1 4RY
> **When:** 9:15 am – 12:45 pm
> **For more information phone 0344 225 1826.**

6 Diff and train

D21 Extra: Writing a poem ▶ **After B6** | p. 100
Write an animal poem. Here is some help:

wild
long tail
black and white
can catch many mice
cat

(1 one word = an adjective)
(2 two words = looks)
(3 three words = colours)
(4 four words = likes/hates/can)
(5 one word = name of the animal)

Ears so big
Long grey tail
Eats a lot
Plays in water
Has its home in Africa
No nose, but a Trunk

D22 Extra: Viewing 🎥 6 ▶ **After B7** | p. 101 ▶ **WB** Media 5 ▶ WES-149220-2
Watch the clip and answer the questions.

1. How old are Jake and Abby's pets?
2. Where do the pets like to play?
3. What kind of pet is Harley?
4. How old is Harley?
5. Does Harley like cats?
6. How often do James and Harley go for a walk?
7. How old is Everlyn?
8. Where does she sleep?

Theme 6: Intro

D1 Support: Words ▶ **Before Intro 1b** | p. 108
Match the activities and the pictures.

take a boat trip • relax on the beach • climb •
go sightseeing • play arcade games • go surfing •
go to a football match • shoot with a bow and arrow

1 2 3 4

5 6 7 8

D2 Easy alternative: Listening 🔊 L 2/9 | S 51 ▶ **Instead of Intro 2a** | p. 108
Listen to the McBrides. Choose the sentence that sums up their dialogue best.
A George and Caroline must stay in London all summer.
B The McBrides spend their holidays at their grandparents' house.
C Caroline and George want to spend time with their old and new friends.

Diff and train 6

D3 Training: Questions (Revision) ▶ After Intro 3 | p. 108

Look at the map of "Magical Britain" on page 109 again.

a) Note down at least five questions for your partner.
Example: *What is the name of the castle from Harry Potter?*

b) 👥 Ask each other your questions.

Theme 6: Part A

D4 Training: Simple present or present progressive? (Revision) ▶ After A1 | p. 110

a) Fill in the verbs in the simple present.
Sophie often **1** (text) Caroline. They **2** (write) about their friends and what they do. Sophie **3** (hope) that they can still be very good friends. She sometimes **4** (feel) alone without Caroline.

b) Fill in the verbs in the present progressive.
Right now Sophie **1** (work) on a "Welcome!" poster for George and Caroline. She **2** (look) at a photo from the internet as an example. Her phone **3** (ring). She can't find it. Somebody **4** (try) to call her. She **5** (think) of Caroline's visit.

D5 Training: Simple present or present progressive? (Revision) ▶ After A1 | p. 110

Fill in the verbs in the correct form (simple present or present progressive).

Gillian sometimes **1** (go) on holiday with her father. But at the moment she **2** (travel[1]) to Manchester with her friends. She **3** (eat) some pakora right now. She is happy to try them because she usually **4** (have) only English or Italian food. Now she **5** (text) Emma about George and Caroline. Emma and Gillian often **6** (talk) about the twins because the twins **7** (argue[2]) all the time. But Emma can't answer Gillian's text now – she **8** (play) tennis with her cousin Sam at the moment. She isn't good at tennis, but she **9** (love) spending time with Sam.

---
1 to travel – *reisen* | **2** to argue (about) – *sich streiten (wegen)*

D6 Easy alternative: Reading ▶ Instead of A2a | p. 110

Read the story on page 110. Why are Gillian and Rajiv quiet?
- **A** They are tired because it's a long trip from Camden to Manchester.
- **B** They don't like Tom and Sophie.
- **C** They don't know what to say.

D7 Training: Reading ▶ After A2b | p. 111

Read the story on page 110 and answer the questions:
1. Why can't Mr McBride stay in Manchester?
2. Where are Tom, Sophie and the twins before dinner?
3. What are they having for dinner?
4. What docs Tom tell George about the city centre?
5. What does Tom think of Gillian and Rajiv?

6 Diff and train

D8 Training: Feelings ▶ After A3 | p. 111

a) What are the words? Note them down in a list.
   1 e--ited   3 ha--y   5 an--y   7 ann--ed
   2 j--lous   4 pu--led   6 disap--inted   8 wo--ied

b) Use the adjectives from a) and make sentences.
   Example: *I'm excited when it's my birthday.*

D9 Easy alternative: Questions ▶ Instead of A4 | p. 111

When the friends go to bed, Gillian gets text messages from Emma in London.
Read Gillian's answers and write down Emma's questions.

1 feel / do / How / you / ?   ➔ I'm a bit sad.
2 sad / Why / you / are / ?   ➔ Because Caroline and George only talk to Sophie and Tom.
3 think / do /What /of / you / Tom and Sophie / ?   ➔ I think they're OK, but they don't talk to us, only to the twins.
4 you / sleep / Where / do / ?   ➔ I sleep in a room with Caroline.
5 Rajiv / Where / does / sleep / ?   ➔ Rajiv sleeps in a room with George.
6 Caroline / you / don't / Why / talk to / ?   ➔ Caroline is already asleep so I can't talk to her.

D10 Extra: Writing ▶ After A7 | p. 113

What can you do in your town in the holidays?
a) Write a page for a holiday booklet.
   Think about your favourite activites, events, your favourite places, …
b) Ask a classmate to check your text. Then correct it.
c) Get together with other classmates who made[1] a page. Make a holiday booklet with all your pages.

---
1 made – hier: *gemacht haben*

Theme 6: Part B

D11 Easy alternative: Listening L 2/12 | S 53 ▶ Instead of B1a | p. 116
What is Mr Butler's new plan for the holidays?
A a trip to the seaside   B a trip on a canal boat   C a trip to the countryside

D12 Training: Simple present (Revision) ▶ After B3 | p. 116
Write down the correct verb forms in your exercise book.

We usually **1** our summer holidays in Devon. If the weather is good, we **2** our bikes to the beach and **3** . My father often **4** a book on the beach, and my mother **5** to music. We sometimes **6** for long walks and **7** up the hills. In the evenings we sometimes **8** to a restaurant. My brother usually **9** fish and chips and I often **10** spaghetti. Yummy! My parents **11** fish or spaghetti. But they **12** pizza. The best thing about the summer holidays is that you don't have to go to school. I **13** our summer holidays!

*love • eat (2x) • spend •
ride • go (2x) •
like • read • not like •
walk • listen •
go swimming*

Diff and train 6

D13 Easy alternative: Questions ▶ Instead of B3 | p. 116
Read the answers. Then put the words into the correct order to form the questions.

1. most people / do / When / arrive in Bristol / ? → Most people arrive in Bristol after 8 to 10 days on the canal.
2. does / Why / take / it / so long / ? → It takes so long because there are many locks on the canal.
3. you / can / Where / stop / ? → You can stop almost everywhere.
4. visit / tourists / What / do / often / ? → Tourists often visit the many interesting sights near the canal.
5. can / How / there / get / you / ? → You can get there by bike or by taxi.
6. we / can / What / do / we / if / need help / ? → You can phone Mr Fox if you need help.

D14 Training: Reading ▶ After B6 | p. 118
Read the story on page 118 again and answer the questions:
1. Where does George want to go?
2. Where do the friends meet?
3. Why is Caroline crying?
4. What does Sam find?
5. How does Caroline get her phone back?

D15 Easy alternative: Listening ▶ Instead of B8b | p. 119 L 2/14 | S 55
Listen to Mr Butler and the kids. Say why they aren't going to the park today.
A Because they need a car to drive through the park.
B Because it is too far away.
C Because the weather is bad.

D16 Training: Reading ▶ After B9 | p. 119
Read the story on page 119 again. Read the sentences and correct them.
1. The Roman baths are almost 3,000 years old.
2. George is very interested in the baths.
3. Caroline and Emma do not take any photos.
4. George talks to a little boy.
5. Olivia can't find her teddy bear.
6. Olivia's parents are not very happy.

D17 Extra: Speaking/Writing ▶ After B9 | p. 119
This was your first year with *Camden Town*.
What is your favourite story?
Who is your favourite character?
What is your favourite song?

S Skills pages

Listening (Hören)

Wenn du Gespräche und Geschichten auf Englisch hörst, brauchst du nicht jedes einzelne Wort zu verstehen. Hier sind einige Tipps, die dir beim Verstehen helfen können:

1. Vor dem Hören

- Wie lautet die Aufgabe, die du beantworten sollst? Lies sie dir gründlich durch, damit du weißt, was genau du heraushören sollst.
- Überlege: Worum könnte es im Gespräch oder der Geschichte gehen? Was weißt du schon über das Thema (z. B. Schule, Familie, Ferien)?
- Gibt es Bilder? Was ist darauf zu sehen? Vielleicht kannst du schon herausfinden, wer mit wem spricht oder wo sich die Personen befinden.

2. Während des Hörens

- Konzentriere dich während des Hörens auf die Fragen, die du beantworten sollst.
- Auch die Stimmen der Sprecher und Hintergrundgeräusche können dir helfen zu verstehen, worum es geht.
- Mache dir Notizen. Notiere nur Stichwörter, keine ganzen Sätze.
- Wenn du die Aufgabe noch nicht gleich lösen konntest, dann höre das Gespräch oder die Geschichte einfach ein weiteres Mal an.

3. Nach dem Hören

- Wenn es möglich ist, vergleiche deine Ergebnisse mit jemandem aus deiner Klasse. Habt ihr das Gleiche herausgefunden?

> **Nutze jede Gelegenheit, um Englisch zu hören!**
> - Mit den Audios zu *Camden Town 5* kannst du auch zu Hause dein Hörverstehen trainieren. Gib dazu einfach den Webcode WES-149220-1 auf www.westermann.de ins Suchfeld ein.
> - Wenn du englische Musik hörst, achte auf den Text. Was kannst du schon verstehen?
> - Sieh dir Filme, Serien oder Berichte zu Themen an, die dich interessieren. Auf DVDs oder bei Streaming-Diensten kannst du fast immer den englischen Ton wählen.

Skills pages S

Reading (Lesen)

In *Camden Town 5* begegnen dir viele unterschiedliche Texte: Dialoge, Geschichten, Comics, Gedichte, …
Hier sind einige Tipps, damit es dir leichter fällt, diese Texte zu verstehen:

1. Vor dem Lesen

- Wie lautet die Frage, die du beantworten sollst? Lies sie dir gründlich durch, damit du weißt, was du beim Lesen herausfinden sollst.
- Hat der Text eine Überschrift? Welche Hinweise gibt sie dir?
- Gibt es Bilder zum Text? Verraten sie dir vielleicht etwas über den Text?
- Überlege: Worum könnte es gehen? Weißt du schon etwas über das Thema?

2. Während des Lesens

- Versuche, beim ersten Lesen grob zu verstehen, worum es geht. Du musst nicht jedes einzelne Wort verstehen.
- Konzentriere dich auf die Leseaufgabe, die du beantworten sollst.
- Um zu prüfen, ob du einen Text wirklich verstanden hast, lies ihn noch einmal und beantworte die W-Fragen, soweit es möglich ist:

Who?	Wer ist beteiligt?
What?	Was geschieht?
Where?	Wo geschieht es?
When?	Wann geschieht es?
Why?	Warum geschieht es?

- Falls es unbekannte Wörter gibt, die du unbedingt verstehen musst, um eine Aufgabe zu lösen, hast du verschiedene Möglichkeiten, die Bedeutung herauszufinden.
  ▶ New words | p.168

3. Nach dem Lesen

- Vergleiche deine Ergebnisse mit jemandem aus deiner Klasse. Was habt ihr herausgefunden?

Unterschiedliche Aufgabentypen
Bei manchen Aufgaben musst du die richtige Antwort auswählen oder entscheiden, ob eine Aussage richtig oder falsch ist.

Choose the best title for the phone call.
A George is late
B The right bus to William Ellis
C Caroline's bus

Test your partner. Right or wrong? Correct the wrong sentences.
1 George never empties the dishwasher.
2 George always tidies his room.

That's right.
That's wrong. George never …

Skills pages

Understanding new words (Unbekannte Wörter verstehen)

1. Neue Wörter ohne Wörterbuch verstehen

Falls es Wörter in einem Text gibt, die du noch nicht kennst, aber unbedingt verstehen musst, um eine Aufgabe zu lösen, dann probiere Folgendes:
- Kennst du **ähnliche Wörter im Deutschen** oder in einer anderen Sprache? Woran erinnert dich z. B. *fantastic*?
- Vielleicht sind dir **einzelne Teile** eines englischen Wortes bekannt. Was könnte *unhappy* heißen? Denk an *happy*.
- Häufig kannst du die Bedeutung eines unbekannten Wortes aus dem **Textzusammenhang** verstehen. Sieh dir das folgende Beispiel an: *Caroline is writing invitations for the party.* Kannst du aus dem Zusammenhang verstehen, was mit *invitations* gemeint ist?

2. So arbeitest du mit einem Wörterbuch

Wenn die Tipps nicht weiterhelfen, kannst du das *dictionary* (Wörterbuch) ganz hinten im Buch verwenden. Und das geht so:
- Wenn du ein englisches Wort nicht verstehst, kannst du es im *English-German dictionary* ab Seite 238 nachschlagen. Dort findest du alle Wörter und Redewendungen aus *Camden Town 5*. Übrigens: Wenn du etwas auf Englisch sagen willst und dir ein Wort fehlt, kannst du es im *German-English dictionary* ab Seite 257 nachschlagen.
Sieh gut hin: Die Wörter sind alphabetisch geordnet. Du musst nicht nur auf den ersten Buchstaben achten, sondern auch auf den zweiten oder sogar dritten. Das Wort *cage* steht zum Beispiel vor *cake*.

> **cage** /keɪdʒ/ Käfig 5B6
> **cake** /keɪk/ Kuchen 3A1
> **calculator** /ˈkælkjʊˌleɪtə/
>   (Taschen)rechner 2A3
> **calendar** /ˈkælɪndə/ Kalender 4Intro 1

- Oft gibt es mehrere Bedeutungen für ein Wort. Sieh dir also immer alle Einträge zu einem Wort an, das du gerade nachschlägst, damit du die richtige Übersetzung findest.
- Die Einträge im *dictionary* zeigen auch, wie du ein Wort aussprichst. Eine Erklärung zu den Symbolen, die in der Lautschrift verwendet werden, findest du auf Seite 265.

Online-Wörterbuch
- Wörterbücher gibt es auch online oder als App. Du kannst ein unbekanntes Wort eingeben und bekommst Übersetzungsvorschläge. Sieh dir auch hier die Vorschläge genau an. Manchmal steht die passende Bedeutung nicht gleich an erster Stelle.
- Wenn du ein Online-Wörterbuch oder eine Wörterbuch-App verwendest, kannst du dir oft auch anhören, wie die Wörter ausgesprochen werden. Dazu gibt es meistens ein Lautsprecher-Symbol, das du auswählen musst.
- Kläre vorher, ob du ein Online-Wörterbuch oder eine App im Unterricht verwenden darfst.
  ▶ WB Media 4   ▶ WES-149220-2

Skills pages S

Talking to people (Mit anderen sprechen)

Wenn du dich auf Englisch unterhältst, ist es ganz normal, dass du nicht alles verstehst und dich nicht immer perfekt ausdrücken kannst. Hier sind einige Tipps:

1. Wenn du etwas nicht verstanden hast, dann …

… bitte darum, dass es wiederholt wird:

… bitte darum, dass es anders ausgedrückt wird und langsamer gesprochen wird:

2. Im Englischen ist man meist sehr viel höflicher als im Deutschen.

Verwende daher immer *thank you* und *please*.

Übrigens: Wenn sich jemand bei dir bedankt, dann antwortest du: *You're welcome*.

3. Wenn dir ein Wort nicht einfällt, dann …

… kannst du es umschreiben:

… kannst du Folgendes sagen, während du nachdenkst:

S Skills pages

Giving a mini-presentation (Eine Mini-Präsentation halten)

Manchmal musst du vor der Klasse etwas vortragen oder präsentieren. Hier sind ein paar Hilfen:

1. Bevor du etwas vorträgst

- Überlege: Was möchtest du zu deinem Thema sagen? Wie viel Zeit hast du für deinen Vortrag?
- Sammle deine Gedanken und schreibe sie in Stichpunkten auf, z. B. in einem *word web* oder in einer Liste. ▶Writing | p.173
- Du kannst dir eine Karteikarte mit Notizen in Stichpunkten erstellen.
- Du kannst auch ein Poster mit Bildern oder Fotos anfertigen, um deine Präsentation interessanter zu gestalten. Hast du Bilder aus dem Internet kopiert, dann vermerke immer, wo du sie gefunden hast.

> **So sieht ein gelungenes Poster aus:**
> ✓ ansprechende Überschrift
> ✓ interessante Informationen, aber nicht zu viel Text
> ✓ lesbare Schrift
> ✓ passende Bilder mit Bildunterschriften
> ▶Making a page | p.172

- Übe deinen Vortrag vor dem Spiegel, vor Freunden oder deiner Familie. Du kannst deinen Vortrag auch zur Probe mit einem Handy aufnehmen. Prüfe dann, ob du flüssig und verständlich gesprochen hast. Wenn du dir bei der Aussprache eines Wortes unsicher bist, dann kannst du die Lautschrift im Wörterbuch nachschlagen oder dir das Wort in einem Online-Wörterbuch anhören.

2. Während deines Vortrags

- Sprich langsam und deutlich.
- Sieh deine Zuhörer während des Sprechens an.
- Versuche, möglichst frei zu sprechen. Du kannst die wichtigsten Punkte von deinen Notizen oder deinem Poster ablesen.

> **Nützliche Redewendungen für deinen Vortrag:**
> - *Hello, everyone. Today I'd like to tell you about …*
> - *On my poster you can see …*
> - *This picture shows …*
> - *Thank you for listening. Have you got any questions?*

3. Nach dem Vortrag

- Wenn du Zuhörer bist, wirst du manchmal aufgefordert, nach einem Vortrag Feedback zu geben. Folge dabei dieser Regel: Nenne zunächst eine Sache, die dir besonders gut gefallen hat. Mache dann einen Vorschlag, wie der Vortrag beim nächsten Mal noch besser werden kann. Das kannst du z. B. so formulieren:

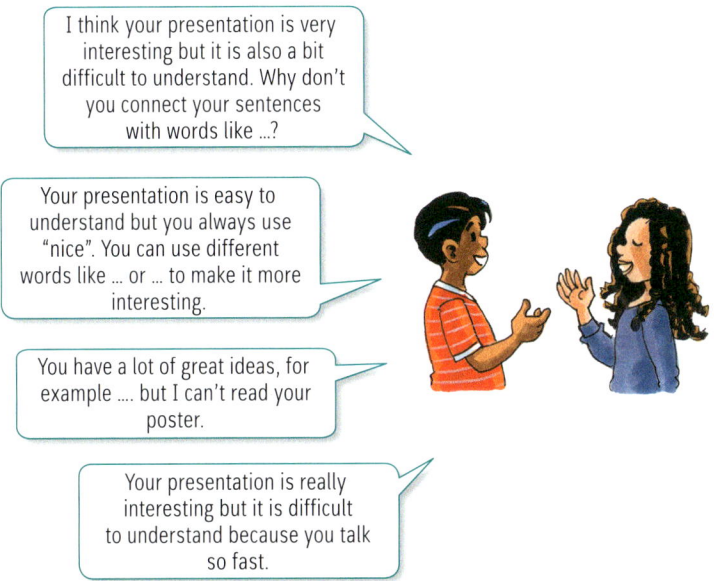

- Wenn du derjenige bist, der die Präsentation gehalten hat, dann mache dir ein paar Notizen zum Feedback deiner Zuhörer. So weißt du, was du das nächste Mal noch besser machen kannst.

Skills pages

Making a page on a computer or tablet
(Eine Seite am Computer oder auf dem Tablet gestalten)

Bei manchen Aufgaben sollst du einen Text (mit Bildern) auf einer Seite gestalten, z. B. als Broschüre, Flugblatt oder Poster. Folgende Tipps können dir dabei helfen:

1. Den Text schreiben

Zuerst musst du deine gesammelten Informationen organisieren und anschließend einen logisch aufgebauten und klar strukturierten Text schreiben. Wie das geht, kannst du auf den Seiten 173/174 nachlesen. ▶ Writing | p. 173
Denke daran, eine passende Überschrift zu finden. Nutze auch die Rechtschreib- und Grammatikkorrektur.

2. Den Text strukturieren und gestalten

Arbeitest du mit einem Textverarbeitungsprogramm am Computer, kannst du deinen Text strukturieren und gestalten:

- Verwende eine **Schriftart**, die gut zu lesen ist. Für einzelne Wörter oder eine Überschrift kannst du auch eine andere Schriftart verwenden.
- Mit Schwarz als **Schriftfarbe** liegst du immer richtig. Für wichtige Wörter oder Überschriften kannst du auch eine andere Farbe verwenden. Vermeide helle Farben, da diese auf weißem Untergrund schwer zu lesen sind.
- Wähle eine gut lesbare **Schriftgröße**: Verwende bei Broschüren 10 Punkt bis 12 Punkt. Bei Postern sollte die Schrift etwas größer sein.
- Überschriften kannst du unterstreichen oder in fetter Schrift setzen.
- **Absätze**: Mit der Eingabetaste/Return-Taste beginnst du einen neuen Absatz.
- Um Unterpunkte übersichtlich darzustellen, kannst du **Aufzählungszeichen** wie Nummerierungen, Buchstaben oder Spiegelstriche verwenden.

3. Bilder auswählen

- Überlege, welche Bilder zu deinem Text passen und wo du sie am besten auf der Seite platzierst. Die Seite sollte auf keinen Fall zu voll werden.
- Machst du Fotos selbst, dann achte darauf, dass die Qualität (Helligkeit, Kontrast, Schärfe) stimmt. Möchtest du ein Foto mit Personen aufnehmen und verwenden, dann musst du vorher ihr Einverständnis einholen.
- Bilder aus dem Internet darfst du für den Einsatz im Unterricht verwenden, aber du musst immer die Quelle (Internetadresse) angeben. Für die Verwendung von Bildern außerhalb des Unterrichts (z. B. in der Schülerzeitung) muss das Einverständnis des Urhebers eingeholt werden.

4. Seite speichern

Denke daran, die Seite immer zu speichern! Dazu klickst du normalerweise oben links auf „Datei – Speichern unter".

> Es macht Spaß, mit verschiedenen Möglichkeiten zu experimentieren. Aber denke daran, dass die Seite am Ende übersichtlich und gut lesbar sein soll.

Skills pages S

Writing (Schreiben)

Wenn du Texte schreibst, gehst du am besten Schritt für Schritt vor:

1. Planen

- Wie lautet die Aufgabe? Worüber sollst du schreiben? Was für ein Text soll es sein: ein Text über dich, eine Geschichte, ein Dialog, …?
- Sammle Ideen und Wörter zu deinem Thema. Dafür gibt es verschiedene Möglichkeiten:

Word web
Du kannst ein *word web* entweder auf Papier schreiben oder ein Computer-Programm dazu verwenden. Mit dem Computer-Programm kannst du dein *word web* speichern und jederzeit bearbeiten.

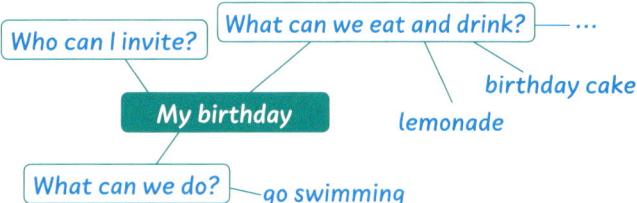

Liste
In einer Liste kannst du schnell und unkompliziert Ideen sammeln. Am einfachsten geht das auf einem Blatt Papier. Es gibt aber auch Apps, die dir helfen, deine Notizen zu organisieren. Der Vorteil ist, dass du die Liste bearbeiten und beliebig erweitern kannst.

Tabelle
In einer Tabelle kannst du deine Ideen gleich in einer Struktur ordnen. Das bietet sich zum Beispiel an, wenn du darüber schreiben willst, was du magst und was nicht. Tabellen lassen sich auf Papier oder mit einem Textverarbeitungsprogramm auf dem Computer erstellen. Das ist praktisch, wenn du noch Zeilen oder Spalten ergänzen möchtest.

- Bevor du mit dem Schreiben beginnst, überlege dir eine sinnvolle Reihenfolge: Was schreibst du zuerst, was folgt darauf und was kann am Ende stehen?

2. Einen ersten Entwurf schreiben

- Schau dir deine Planung noch einmal an und los geht's!
- Du kannst auch Texte im Buch als Muster benutzen: Übernimm passende Satzanfänge und Ausdrücke und ersetze die Wörter, die nicht zu deinem Thema passen.
- Unterteile deinen Text in verschiedene Abschnitte: Beginne für jeden neuen Gedanken einen neuen Absatz.
- Verbinde Sätze mit Wörtern wie *and, but, or, so* oder *because* (*connectives*), damit sich dein Text flüssig liest. ▶ G19 | p. 194
- Verwende nicht immer das gleiche Wort: Verwende statt *say* zum Beispiel *shout, whisper, ask* oder *answer*.
- Überlege dir eine passende Überschrift für deinen Text.

Skills pages

3. Überarbeiten

- Wenn es möglich ist, tauscht eure Texte untereinander aus. Markiert mit einem Bleistift im fremden Text, was euch gefällt, was unverständlich ist, was noch ergänzt und was verbessert werden sollte.
- Schlage Wörter, bei denen du unsicher bist, im *dictionary* ab Seite 238 nach.
- Schau auch in der Grammatik ab Seite 180 nach, wenn du dir nicht ganz sicher bist.
- Du kannst deinen Text auch am Computer oder auf einem Tablet schreiben. Das hat den Vorteil, dass du die Rechtschreib- und Grammatikkorrektur des Textverarbeitungsprogramms zur Hilfe nehmen kannst.

Checkliste:
- ✓ Wörter richtig geschrieben?
- ✓ Wörter am Satzanfang groß?
- ✓ Satzzeichen am Ende aller Sätze?
- ✓ Grammatische Formen richtig gebildet?
- ✓ Satzstellung korrekt?
- ✓ Ist der Text verständlich?
- ✓ Enthält der Text alle wichtigen Punkte?
- ✓ Überschrift passend?

4. Fertigstellen

- Jetzt kannst du deinen Text ins Reine schreiben und gestalten.   ▶ Making a page | p. 172
- Du kannst deinen Text vorlesen, aushängen oder in einem *class book* veröffentlichen.
- Sammle deine besten Texte in deiner Portfolio-Mappe.

 Audios aufnehmen:
Du kannst deinen Text auch aufnehmen, z. B. mit einem Handy oder einem Tablet. Damit deine Aufnahme gelingt, beachte Folgendes:
- Suche dir einen ruhigen Raum. Vermeide Aufnahmen im vollen Klassenzimmer oder draußen.
- Sprich laut, langsam und deutlich.
- Mache Pausen zwischen den Sätzen.
- Sprich nah am Mikrofon.
- Denke daran, die Aufnahme zu speichern.

▶ **WB** Media 3   ▶ WES-149220-2

Skills pages S

Memorizing vocabulary (Vokabeln lernen)

Je mehr Wörter und Redewendungen du kennst, desto besser kannst du dich auf Englisch verständigen. Neue Vokabeln kannst du auf ganz unterschiedliche Art und Weise lernen. Hier sind ein paar Möglichkeiten. Probiere aus, welche für dich am besten funktioniert.

Wortlisten im Buch

- In den *Wordlists* findest du im Buch ab Seite 206 alle neuen Wörter nach *Themes* geordnet.

big /bɪg/	groß	Elephants are **big** animals.
small /smɔːl/	klein	Hamsters are **small** animals.

- Links ist das englische Wort abgedruckt. Lies es laut. Die Lautschrift in eckigen Klammern zeigt dir, wie das Wort ausgesprochen wird. Auf Seite 265 werden die Symbole der Lautschrift erklärt.
- Lies dann die deutsche Übersetzung in der Mitte.
- In der rechten Spalte siehst du, wie du das neue Wort in einem Satz verwendest.
- Nun kannst du dir die Wörter einprägen, indem du die rechte und mittlere Spalte mit einem Blatt Papier abdeckst und dich Zeile für Zeile abfragst.

Vokabelordner

- Ein Vokabelordner hat gegenüber einem Vokabelheft den Vorteil, dass du ihn leicht ergänzen kannst.
- Du kannst für deinen Vokabelordner Tabellen erstellen, in denen du Wörter sammelst, die zu einem Oberbegriff passen.

SCHOOL WORDS		
subjects	things	people
French	pen	teacher
History	ruler	classmate
…	…	…

- Außerdem kannst du *word webs* zu bestimmten Themen anlegen und im Ordner abheften. Nimm ein Blatt Papier und schreibe das Thema in die Mitte. Welche Wörter passen dazu? Gibt es Oberbegriffe, unter denen du sie gliedern kannst? Füge die anderen Wörter hinzu und verbinde sie sinnvoll.

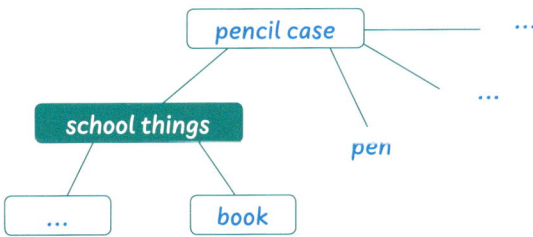

Skills pages

- Du kannst auch verschiedene Listen erstellen, zum Beispiel eine Liste für
  - Wörter, die du dir besonders schwer merken kannst,
  - Gegensatzpaare (z. B. *big – small*),
  - Wörter, die eine ähnliche Bedeutung haben (z. B. *nice, great, good*),
  - Redewendungen zu einem Thema,
  - deine Lieblingswörter.

> **Nutze den Computer**
> Tabellen, *word webs* und Listen lassen sich auch am Computer oder Tablet erstellen. Das ist praktisch, weil du sie dort speichern und beliebig erweitern und verändern kannst.

Karteikarten

- Um eine Vokabelkartei anzulegen, schreibst du das englische Wort auf die Vorderseite einer Karteikarte und die deutsche Übersetzung auf die Rückseite.
- Du kannst deine Karteikarten in einem Karton oder Kasten mit zwei Fächern aufbewahren.
- Prüfe Karte für Karte, ob du die Bedeutung der Wörter weißt. Zunächst Englisch-Deutsch, danach Deutsch-Englisch.
- Wenn du die Bedeutung ohne Zögern weißt und die englischen Wörter zügig und fehlerfrei buchstabieren kannst, ist das Wort in deinem Langzeitgedächtnis und du kannst die Karte in das hintere Fach stecken. Kannst du das noch nicht, dann behalte die Karte noch im vorderen Fach und probiere es später oder am nächsten Tag noch einmal.

Vokabeltrainer-App

- Du kannst auch verschiedene Apps nutzen, um neue Wörter zu lernen. Sprich mit deinen Eltern, bevor du eine kostenpflichtige App herunterlädst.
- Das Programm der App testet, welche Wörter du schon kennst. Oft gibt es auch kleine Aufgaben, bei denen du Wörter in Sätze einfügen oder die richtige Bedeutung eines Wortes auswählen musst.
- In den meisten Apps kannst du dir die Aussprache eines Wortes auch noch einmal anhören.

> **So erzielst du beim Vokabellernen die besten Erfolge:**
> - Trainiere regelmäßig: 10 Minuten pro Tag bringen dich ans Ziel!
> - Lerne jeweils 6-7 neue Vokabeln auf einmal. Wenn du diese sicher beherrschst, nimmst du dir die nächste Portion vor.
> - Suche dir einen Platz zum Vokabellernen, an dem du dich wohl fühlst.
> - Merke dir nicht nur einzelne Wörter, sondern auch ganze Redewendungen oder Sätze. Wie Wörter in Sätzen verwendet werden, siehst du in den Beispielsätzen in der rechten Spalte der Wortlisten. Außerdem findest du nützliche Redewendungen zu jedem *Theme* unter *Say it in English* (z. B. S. 213-214).

Skills pages S

Mediation (Sprachmittlung)

Wenn du zwischen zwei Sprachen vermittelst, nennt man das *mediation*. Damit kannst du Menschen helfen, die kaum Englisch oder Deutsch verstehen. Am besten funktioniert das so:

1. Gib den Sinn wieder

Es kommt nicht darauf an, dass du alles Wort für Wort übersetzt. Wichtiger ist es, den Sinn wiederzugeben. Es muss nur klar werden, worum es geht. Unwichtige Einzelheiten kannst du weglassen.

2. Bilde kurze Sätze

Bilde einfache, kurze Sätze.

WILLIAM ELLIS SCHOOL
At William Ellis School most of our pupils stay for our after-school activities.

Was steht denn da?

An der William-Ellis-Schule gibt es Aktivitäten am Nachmittag. Die meisten Schüler nehmen daran teil.

3. Verwende Redewendungen

Versuche, dich an Redewendungen und feststehende Formulierungen aus dem Englischunterricht zu erinnern.

4. Umschreibe Wörter

Wenn dir ein wichtiges Wort nicht einfällt, kannst du es umschreiben. Du weißt zum Beispiel nicht, was „Geschenk" auf Englisch heißt. Dann kannst du sagen:
You give it to a friend. It's for a birthday.

S Skills pages

Working with others (Mit anderen zusammenarbeiten)

Im Unterricht werdet ihr immer wieder mit anderen zusammenarbeiten. Hier sind ein paar Tipps und Methoden dafür.

Milling around

Milling around bedeutet „Umherlaufen". Damit könnt ihr euch in der Klasse zu einem Thema austauschen. Und das geht so:
1. Jede/Jeder in der Klasse geht mit Aufgabe und Stift durch den Raum, ohne dass dabei gesprochen wird.
2. Wenn deine Lehrerin/dein Lehrer ein Zeichen gibt, dann sprich mit der Person, vor der du gerade stehst. Tauscht euch über die Aufgabe aus und notiert die Ergebnisse.
3. Beim nächsten Zeichen gehst du weiter.

Dramatic reading

Wenn ihr einen Dialog mit verteilten Rollen lest, ist es wichtig, dass jeder seinen Text lebendig vorträgt. Das nennt man *dramatic reading*. Dabei können dir diese Tipps helfen:
- *Buzz reading:* Lies deinen Text mit leiser Stimme, so oft du kannst, um ihn dir zu merken.
- *Read and look up:* Schau dir jeden Satz einzeln an und präge ihn dir ein. Sieh hoch und sprich ihn möglichst natürlich nach. Arbeite so deinen ganzen Text durch.
- Überlege, wie sich die Person gerade fühlt, deren Rolle du liest. Ist sie verärgert, fröhlich, aufgeregt, überrascht, …? Versuche, deine Sätze so zu sprechen, dass diese Gefühle deutlich werden.

Mini-jigsaw

Die *mini-jigsaw*-Methode bezeichnet ein Mini-Gruppenpuzzle. Damit könnt ihr mehrere Texte oder einen längeren Text gemeinsam lesen:
1. Teilt den Text oder die Texte untereinander auf. Jeder/Jede liest einen Teil.
2. Dann tauscht ihr euch in der Gruppe über eure Teile aus, sodass zum Schluss jeder/jede über den gesamten Text oder alle Textteile Bescheid weiß.

Gallery walk

Mit einem *gallery walk* könnt ihr Arbeitsergebnisse präsentieren, z. B. ein Poster, das ihr gemeinsam in einer Gruppe erstellt habt.
1. Hängt euer Poster im Klassenzimmer auf.
2. Eine/Einer aus der Gruppe stellt das Poster einem Teil der Klasse vor. Die anderen sehen sich in der Zwischenzeit andere Poster im Klassenzimmer an.
3. Wichtig ist, dass jeder von euch mindestens einmal das Poster vorstellt, aber auch die anderen Poster sieht.

Skills pages S

Freeze-frame

Freeze-frame bedeutet „Standbild". Mit dieser Methode könnt ihr euch eine bestimmte Situation in einer Geschichte besser erarbeiten und dadurch besser verstehen. Um ein Standbild zu bauen, arbeitet ihr in einer Gruppe.

1. Sucht euch eine Szene aus dem Text aus, die ihr als Standbild nachbauen wollt.
2. Überlegt euch, in welchem Verhältnis die Personen zueinander stehen. Was denken und fühlen sie in der Situation?
3. Verteilt nun die Rollen. Probiert aus, wie ihr die Situation so nachstellen könnt, dass die Klasse nachher erraten kann, wer die Personen sind und um welche Situation es sich handelt. Im Standbild dürft ihr nicht sprechen, aber mit Körpersprache und Gesichtsausdruck könnt ihr viel ausdrücken.
4. Präsentiert euer Standbild der Klasse.

Writing a grammar card (Eine *grammar card* erstellen)

Wenn du gut Englisch sprechen willst, brauchst du dafür auch Grammatik.
Du kannst Grammatikregeln und viele Beispiele dazu im *Grammar*-Teil ab Seite 180 nachlesen.
Damit du sie dir besser merken kannst, solltest du eigene *grammar cards* schreiben.
Das geht so:

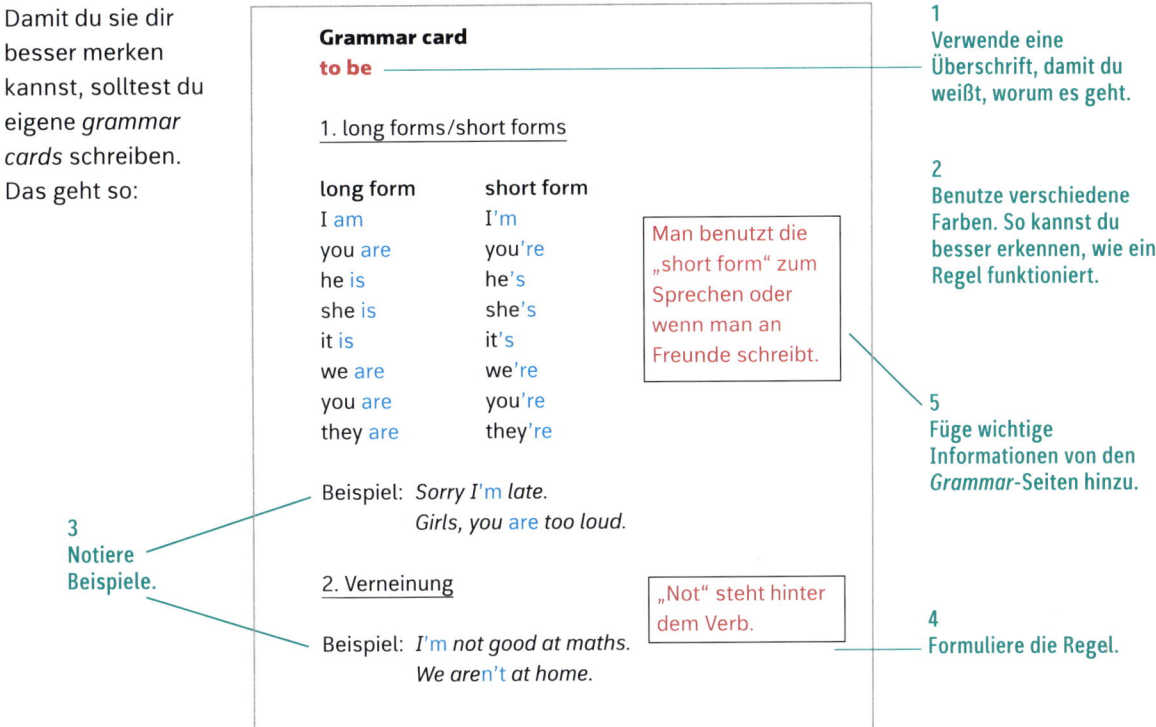

Und hier noch einige Hinweise:
- Lass Platz für Ergänzungen.
- Ergänze deine *grammar card*, wenn du neue Informationen hast.
- Du kannst deine *grammar cards* auch am Computer oder Tablet erstellen. So lassen sie sich leichter ergänzen.
- Hefte deine *grammar cards* zusammen ab, damit du keine verlierst.

G Grammar

Inhalt

> 📹 Videos zu einzelnen Grammatik-Themen findest du, indem du den Webcode
> ▶ WES-149220-4 auf www.westermann.de/webcode eingibst.

Theme 1
- **G1** Die Pluralformen der Nomen   p. 181
- **G2** Die Artikel *the, a/an*   p. 181
  - a) Der bestimmte Artikel *the*
  - b) Der unbestimmte Artikel *a/an*
- **G3** Das Verb *to be*: Kurzformen, Langformen, Verneinung   p. 182
  - a) *To be:* Kurzformen und Langformen
  - b) *To be:* Verneinung
- **G4** Personalpronomen   p. 183
- **G5** Das Verb *to be*: Entscheidungsfragen und Kurzantworten   p. 183
- **G6** Das Verb *to be*: Fragen mit Fragewörtern   p. 184
- **G7** Possessivbegleiter   p. 184

Theme 2
- **G8** Der Imperativ   p. 185
- **G9** *Can*   p. 185
- **G10** Das Verb *have got*   p. 186
  - a) *Have got:* Bejahte Aussagesätze
  - b) *Have got:* Verneinung
  - c) *Have got:* Entscheidungsfragen und Kurzantworten
- **G11** Der Genitiv   p. 187

Theme 3
- **G12** Die einfache Gegenwart: Aussagesätze   p. 188
  - a) Die einfache Gegenwart: bejahte Aussagesätze
  - b) Die einfache Gegenwart: Verneinung
- **G13** Die Satzstellung im Aussagesatz   p. 189
  - a) Satzstellung Subjekt – Verb – Objekt
  - b) Aussagesätze mit Häufigkeitsadverbien
- **G14** Die einfache Gegenwart: Entscheidungsfragen und Kurzantworten   p. 190
- **G15** Die einfache Gegenwart: Fragen mit Fragewörtern   p. 191

Theme 4
- **G16** Die Verlaufsform der Gegenwart   p. 192
  - a) Die Verlaufsform der Gegenwart: Aussagesätze
  - b) Die Verlaufsform der Gegenwart: Fragen
- **G17** Einfache Gegenwart oder Verlaufsform der Gegenwart?   p. 193
- **G18** Die Mengenwörter *some, any* und *no*   p. 194
- **G19** Verbindung von Sätzen durch Konjunktionen   p. 194

Theme 5
- **G20** Objektpronomen   p. 195
- **G21** Die Modalverben *must, mustn't, needn't, should/shouldn't*   p. 195
  - a) Das Modalverb *must*
  - b) Das Modalverb *mustn't*
  - c) Das Modalverb *needn't*
  - d) Das Modalverb *should/shouldn't*

Grammatical terms   p. 197

Grammar 1

Theme 1

G1 Die Pluralformen der Nomen — The plural forms of nouns ▶p. 18
▶D2 | p. 125, D2 | p. 156

Die meisten englischen Nomen (Hauptwörter) haben einen regelmäßigen Plural (Mehrzahl).
Du bildest ihn, indem du ein **-s** an das Nomen anhängst:

Singular (Einzahl)	Plural (Mehrzahl)
a book	two book**s**
a pen	two pen**s**
a house	two house**s**

 a girl  two girl**s**

Nomen, die auf *-s*, *-ss*, *-sh*, *-ch* oder *-x* enden, erhalten im Plural ein **-es**:, z. B. *a bus – two bus**es***.

Die Aussprache hängt von der Endung des Wortes im Singular ab:

/s/ SSS	/z/ ZZZ	/ɪz/
nach stimmlosen (harten) Konsonanten:	nach stimmhaften (weichen) Konsonanten und nach Vokalen:	nach Zischlauten:
a lamp – two lamp**s**	a hand – two hand**s**	a bus – two bus**es**
a T-shirt – two T-shirt**s**	a dog – two dog**s**	a sentence – two sentenc**es**
a book – two book**s**	a boy – two boy**s**	a page – two pag**es**

❗ Bei der Schreibung gibt es auch Ausnahmen, z. B. *a hobby – two hobb**ies***.
Es gibt auch unregelmäßige Pluralformen, die man einfach lernen muss, z. B. *a child – two child**ren***.

G2 Die Artikel *the, a/an* — The articles *the, a/an* ▶p. 19 ▶D11 | p. 127, D18 | p. 145

a) Der bestimmte Artikel *the* — The definite article *the*
Der bestimmte Artikel (der, die, das) heißt im Englischen immer **the**.
The wird /ðə/ ausgesprochen. Beginnt das folgende Wort mit einem Vokal, sagt man /ðiː/.

the /ðə/	**the** /ðiː/
the cat	**the** elephant
the big house	**the** answer

b) Der unbestimmte Artikel *a/an* — The indefinite article *a/an*
Der unbestimmte Artikel (ein, eine) heißt im Englischen **a** oder **an**.
Beginnt das folgende Wort mit einem Vokal, verwendet man **an**, sonst **a**.

a /ə/	**an** /ən/
a car	**an** apple
a house	**an** elephant

 **a** car  **an** apple

1 Grammar

G3 Das Verb *to be*: Kurzformen, Langformen, Verneinung
The verb *to be*: short forms, long forms, negation

▶ p. 21   ▶ D17 | p. 128, D15 | p. 136   Grammatik-Video zum Thema *to be* (G3, G5, G6)   ▶ WES-149220-4

a) *To be:* Kurzformen und Langformen   *To be:* short forms and long forms

To be ist ein Verb und heißt auf Deutsch „sein". Die verschiedenen Formen von *to be (am, are, is)* gibt es als Kurzformen und als Langformen:

	Langform (long form)	Kurzform (short form)			
Singular	I **am**	I**'m**	I**'m**	eleven.	*Ich bin …*
	you **are**	you**'re**	You**'re**	my friend.	*Du bist …*
	he **is**	he**'s**	He**'s**	from Manchester.	*Er ist …*
	she **is**	she**'s**	She**'s**	my sister.	*Sie ist …*
	it **is**	it**'s**	It**'s**	warm.	*Es ist …*
Plural	we **are**	we**'re**	We**'re**	hungry.	*Wir sind …*
	you **are**	you**'re**	You**'re**	nice.	*Ihr seid …*
	they **are**	they**'re**	They**'re**	in the garden.	*Sie sind …*

Die **Kurzformen** verwendet man meistens beim Sprechen und in persönlichen Briefen, E-Mails oder Chats.
Die **Langformen** verwendet man eher beim offiziellen Schreiben.

We**'re** from Manchester.

b) *To be:* Verneinung   *To be:* negation

Die Formen von **to be** kannst du verneinen, indem du **not** einfügst:
He **is** from Camden. ➡ He **is not** from Camden. Oder: He **isn't** from Camden.

	Langform (long form)	Kurzform (short form)			
Singular	I **am not**	I**'m not**	I**'m not**	from Camden.	*Ich bin nicht …*
	you **are not**	you **aren't**	You **aren't**	happy.	*Du bist nicht …*
	he **is not**	he **isn't**	He **isn't**	my brother.	*Er ist nicht …*
	she **is not**	she **isn't**	She **isn't**	eleven. She's twelve.	*Sie ist nicht …*
	it **is not**	it **isn't**	It **isn't**	a car. It's a bus.	*Es ist nicht …*
Plural	we **are not**	we **aren't**	We **aren't**	from London.	*Wir sind nicht …*
	you **are not**	you **aren't**	You **aren't**	in my class.	*Ihr seid nicht …*
	they **are not**	they **aren't**	They **aren't**	from England.	*Sie sind nicht …*

❗ In den Kurzformen wird **not** meist zu **-n't** verkürzt: She **is not** eleven ➡ She **isn't** eleven.
Nur mit *I am* kannst du *not* nicht verkürzen: I **am not** from London. ➡ I**'m not** from London.

Grammar 1

G4 Personalpronomen — Personal pronouns ▶ p. 21 ▶ D15 | p. 127

Anstatt ein Nomen (Hauptwort) mehrmals zu verwenden, kannst du es durch ein Personalpronomen ersetzen:

Emma is from Camden. Emma is eleven. Emma likes skateboarding.
➡ *Emma is from Camden.* **She** *is eleven.* **She** *likes skateboarding.*

he

she

	Personalpronomen	
Singular	I	ich
	you	du/Sie
	he	er
	she	sie
	it	es
Plural	we	wir
	you	ihr/Sie
	they	sie

it

❗ *I* wird immer großgeschrieben. **You** kann **du**, **Sie** oder **ihr** bedeuten:
You *are from London.* ➡ **Du** *bist aus London.* / **Sie** *sind aus London.* / **Ihr** *seid aus London.*

❗ Anders als im Deutschen steht *it* für alle Dinge und Tiere:
the football ➡ **It** *is new.* — der Fußball ➡ **Er** ist neu.
the school ➡ **It** *is big.* — die Schule ➡ **Sie** ist groß.
the house ➡ **It** *is very old.* — das Haus ➡ **Es** ist sehr alt.
the cat ➡ **It** *is so black.* — die Katze ➡ **Sie** ist so schwarz.

Wenn du weißt, ob das Tier männlich oder weiblich ist, kannst du **he** oder **she** sagen.

This is my cat Luna. **She**'s two years old.

G5 Das Verb *to be*: Entscheidungsfragen und Kurzantworten
The verb *to be*: yes/no questions and short answers ▶ p. 23 ▶ D18–D20 | pp. 128–129

Auf Entscheidungsfragen kann man mit „Ja" oder „Nein" antworten. Sie werden wie im Deutschen gebildet, indem das Subjekt und das Verb die Plätze tauschen:

Emma is from Camden.   Emma ist aus Camden.
      ✗   ✗
Is Emma from Camden?   Ist Emma aus Camden?

Is this your book?   Yes, it is.

Es klingt unhöflich, nur mit *yes* oder *no* auf eine Entscheidungsfrage zu antworten. Deshalb verwendet man häufig Kurzantworten:
Is Peter from London? – **Yes, he is.** / **No, he isn't.**

1 Grammar

Bei Kurzantworten mit **Yes** verwendest du die Langformen von *to be*.
Nur bei Kurzantworten mit **No** verwendet man Kurzformen.

	Entscheidungsfragen	Kurzantworten +	Kurzantworten −
Singular	**Am I** your friend?	Yes, you are.	No, you aren't.
	Are you twelve?	Yes, I am.	No, I'm not.
	Is he your dad?	Yes, he is.	No, he isn't.
	Is she your sister?	Yes, she is.	No, she isn't.
	Is it a big school?	Yes, it is.	No, it isn't.
Plural	**Are we** in team 1?	Yes, we are.	No, we aren't.
	Are you from London?	Yes, we are.	No, we aren't.
	Are they from Camden?	Yes, they are.	No, they aren't.

G6 Das Verb *to be*: Fragen mit Fragewörtern ▶ p. 27 ▶ D27 | p. 131, D3 | p. 163
The verb *to be*: questions with question words

Bei Fragen mit Fragewörtern steht das Fragewort (*who, what, …*)
am Satzanfang. Danach kommt die Form von *to be*.

Who?	Wer?
What?	Was?
When?	Wann?
Where?	Wo?
Why?	Warum?
How?	Wie?

Fragen mit Fragewörtern	
Where is my school bag?	**Wo** ist meine Schultasche?
Where are you from?	**Woher** kommst du?
What is this?	**Was** ist das?
Who is Joe?	**Wer** ist Joe?
How old are you?	**Wie** alt bist du?

Nach einem Fragewort kannst du *is* verkürzen:
Who's your friend? **Where's** my dog? **What's** your name?

! Mit **who** fragst du nach Personen, mit **where** nach Orten.

G7 Possessivbegleiter   Possessive determiners ▶ p. 29 ▶ D29, D30 | p. 132

Mit einem Possessivbegleiter kannst du sagen,
wem etwas gehört oder zu wem etwas gehört.

	Possessivbegleiter			
Singular	**my**	mein	**My** bike is blue.	*Mein Fahrrad …*
	your	dein/Ihr	**Your** uncle is very nice.	*Dein/Ihr Onkel …*
	his	sein	**His** daughter is twelve.	*Seine Tochter …*
	her	ihr	**Her** school is in Camden.	*Ihre Schule …*
	its	sein/ihr	**Its** door its brown.	*Ihre Tür …*
Plural	**our**	unser	**Our** house is very old.	*Unser Haus …*
	your	euer/Ihr	**Your** song is cool!	*Euer/Ihr Lied …*
	their	ihr	The children like **their** school.	*… ihre Schule.*

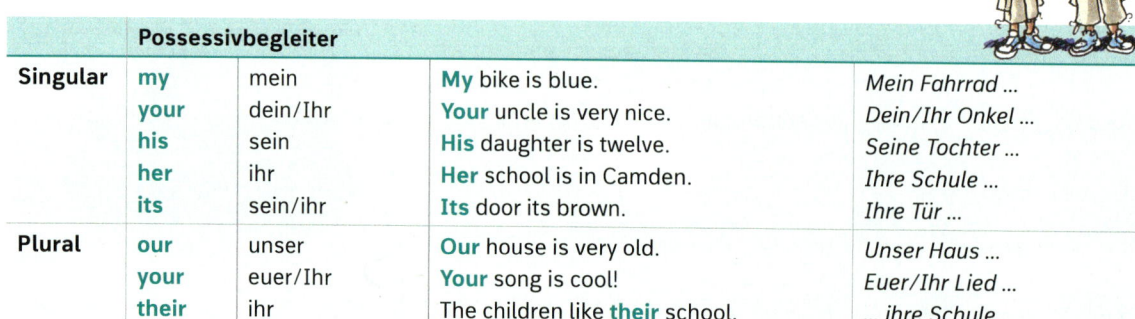

Grammar 2

Theme 2

G8 Der Imperativ — The imperative ▶ p. 40 ▶ D9 | p. 135

Mit dem Imperativ (der Befehlsform) forderst du jemanden auf, etwas zu tun oder nicht zu tun.

Please **open** the window, Lisa.	*Bitte mach das Fenster auf, Lisa.*
Sit down, Lucy and Ben.	*Setzt euch, Lucy und Ben.*

Don't talk in class, please.

Der Imperativ hat im Englischen nur eine Form. Es spielt also keine Rolle, ob du eine oder mehrere Personen ansprichst. Du verwendest immer die Grundform des Verbs:
***Help** me, please.* – *Bitte **hilf** mir. / Bitte **helfen** Sie mir. / Bitte **helft** mir.*

Wenn jemand etwas **nicht** tun soll, stellst du ***don't*** vor das Verb: ***Don't open** the window.*

Don't do your homework at school.	*Macht eure Hausaufgaben nicht in der Schule.*
Don't play in the street.	*Spielt nicht auf der Straße.*

⚠ Wenn du nur den Imperativ verwendest, kann das im Englischen sehr unhöflich klingen. Höflicher ist es, wenn du ***please*** hinzufügst.

G9 Can ▶ p. 41 ▶ D11 | p. 135, D12–D13 | p. 136, D21 | p. 146 🎬 Grammatik-Video ▶ WES-149220-4

Mit ***can*** (= können/dürfen) drückst du aus, was jemand tun kann oder tun darf. ***Can*** steht mit dem Infinitiv (der Grundform des Verbs) und bleibt in allen Personen gleich.

She **can** play football.	*Sie kann Fußball spielen.*
They **can** swim.	*Sie können schwimmen.*
You **can** go now.	*Du darfst jetzt gehen.*

She **can** play an instrument.

⚠ Im Deutschen kann man „können" auch ohne weiteres Verb verwenden. Im Englischen ist das nicht möglich: *Ich **kann** Englisch.* ➡ *I **can speak** English.*

Wenn du ausdrücken willst, dass jemand etwas nicht tun kann oder nicht tun darf, verwendest du ***can't*** oder die Langform ***cannot***:

You **can't** go now.	*Du darfst jetzt nicht gehen.*
I **can't** play an instrument.	*Ich kann kein Instrument spielen.*

Mit ***can*** kannst du auch um Erlaubnis bitten oder fragen, ob jemand etwas kann. Auf Entscheidungsfragen mit ***can*** antwortet man meist mit Kurzantworten.

Can you play an instrument? – **Yes, I can.**	*Kannst du ein Instrument spielen?*
Can I go now? – **No, you can't.**	*Darf ich jetzt gehen?*

2 Grammar

G10 Das Verb *have got*   The verb *have got*

▶ p. 45   ▶ D19–D20 | p. 137, D22–D23 | p. 138   🎬 Grammatik-Video   ▶ WES-149220-4

a) *Have got:* **Bejahte Aussagesätze**   *Have got:* positive statements

Have got ist ein Verb und bedeutet „haben". Man kann damit ausdrücken, dass jemand etwas besitzt oder etwas hat.

	Langformen		Kurzformen	
Singular	I **have got**	a dog.	I**'ve got**	a dog.
	You **have got**	a dog.	You**'ve got**	a dog.
	He **has got**	a dog.	He**'s got**	a dog.
	She **has got**	a dog.	She**'s got**	a dog.
	It **has got**	green doors.	It**'s got**	green doors.
Plural	We **have got**	a dog.	We**'ve got**	a dog.
	You **have got**	a dog.	You**'ve got**	a dog.
	They **have got**	a dog.	They**'ve got**	a dog.

Die Kurzformen von *have got* verwendet man meist beim Sprechen, die Langformen verwendet man meist, wenn man etwas schreibt – genau wie bei den Formen von *to be*.

❗ **Has** und **is** haben dieselbe Kurzform: *She's got a new book.* → *She has got a new book.*
She's my sister. → *She is my sister.*

b) *Have got:* **Verneinung**   *Have got:* negation

Die Formen von **have got** kannst du verneinen, indem du das Wort **not** zwischen **have** und **got** oder zwischen **has** und **got** einfügst. Meistens verwendet man bei der Verneinung die Kurzformen.

	Langformen		Kurzformen	
Singular	I **have not got**	a dog.	I **haven't got**	a dog.
	You **have not got**	a dog.	You **haven't got**	a dog.
	He **has not got**	a dog.	He **hasn't got**	a dog.
	She **has not got**	a dog.	She **hasn't got**	a dog.
	It **has not got**	green doors.	It **hasn't got**	green doors.
Plural	We **have not got**	a dog.	We **haven't got**	a dog.
	You **have not got**	a dog.	You **haven't got**	a dog.
	They **have not got**	a dog.	They **haven't got**	a dog.

Grammar 2

c) *Have got:* Entscheidungsfragen und Kurzantworten
Have got: yes/no questions and short answers

Entscheidungsfragen mit **have got** bildest du so:

Entscheidungsfragen	Kurzantworten	
	+	**–**
Have you **got** a computer?	Yes, I have.	No, I haven't.
Has Charlie **got** a sister?	Yes, he has.	No, he hasn't.
Has Emma **got** a new book?	Yes, she has.	No, she hasn't.
Has your school **got** a library?	Yes, it has.	No, it hasn't.
Have we **got** music now?	Yes, we have.	No, we haven't.
Have the McBrides **got** a dog?	Yes, they have.	No, they haven't.

❗ Bei den Kurzantworten lässt du **got** weg und wiederholst nur **have**:
Have you **got** time? – Yes, I **have**.

G11 Der Genitiv   The genitive   ▶ p. 46   ▶ D24 | p. 138, D25 | p. 139

Um zu sagen, wem etwas gehört (oder zu wem etwas gehört), verwendest du im Englischen den **s-Genitiv**.

Im **Singular** hängst du einen Apostroph und ein s (**'s**) an die Person.

| Jack**'s** room is great. | *Jacks Zimmer ist großartig.* |
| Dennis**'s** football is new. | *Dennis' Fußball ist neu.* |

Im **Plural** fügst du bei **regelmäßigen Pluralformen** nur einen Apostroph an das Plural-s an.

| The boys**'** room is very big. | *Das Zimmer der Jungen ist sehr groß.* |

the boy**'s** room

Bei **unregelmäßigen Pluralformen** bildest du den s-Genitiv mit **'s**:

| The children**'s** room is very big. | *Das Zimmer der Kinder ist sehr groß.* |

the boys**'** room

❗ Bei mehreren Namen hängt man **'s** nur an den letzten Namen an, z. B.: *Caroline and George's friends*.

❗ Der s-Genitiv wird meistens dann verwendet, wenn etwas (zu) einer Person oder einem Tier gehört. Wenn man ausdrücken möchte, dass etwas zu einer Sache gehört, verwendet man meistens den Genitiv mit **of**: *The name **of** the school is 'William Ellis'*. – *Der Name der Schule ist „William Ellis".*

3 Grammar

Theme 3

G12 Die einfache Gegenwart: Aussagesätze
The simple present: statements ▶ p. 57 ▶ D6 | p. 141, D7, D9 | p. 142, D10 | p. 143
Grammatik-Video zum Thema Gegenwart (G12, G14, G15) ▶ WES-149220-4

a) Die einfache Gegenwart: bejahte Aussagesätze The simple present: positive statements

Das **simple present** verwendest du, …
- um über Gewohnheiten oder regelmäßige Handlungen zu sprechen: *They **play** football every Tuesday.*
- um über aufeinander folgende Handlungen zu sprechen:
  *First Caroline **makes** her bed. Then she **loads** the dishwasher. After that she **reads** a book.*
- um über Zustände zu sprechen, die längere Zeit andauern: *Emma and Gillian **live** in London.*

	Simple present: Aussagesätze	
Singular	I often **play**	football in the park.
	You sometimes **play**	tennis.
	He **plays**	hockey.
	She **plays**	volleyball on Tuesdays.
	It always **plays**	with other dogs.
Plural	We **play**	basketball every Monday.
	You always **play**	hockey.
	They **play**	games at the weekend.

He/she/it – the **-s** must fit.

Bei **he**, **she** und **it** (in der 3. Person Singular) hängst du ein **-s** an die Grundform des Verbs an.
Bei *I*, *you*, *we* und *they* hat das *simple present* dieselbe Form wie die Grundform.

❗ Wenn das Verb auf *-ss*, *-sh*, *-ch* oder *-x* endet, hängst du bei *he*, *she*, *it* ein **-es** an:

| Linda watch**es** TV on Sundays. | *Linda sieht sonntags fern.* |
| Greg wash**es** his face in the morning. | *Greg wäscht sich morgens das Gesicht.* |

❗ Auch an die Verben *to do* und *to go* hängst du bei *he*, *she*, *it* ein **-es** an.
Achte auf die unterschiedliche Aussprache:

| She do**es** /dʌz/ her homework in the afternoon. | *Sie macht ihre Hausaufgaben nachmittags.* |
| Kate go**es** /gəʊz/ to dance classes. | *Kate nimmt Tanzunterricht.* |

❗ Bei Verben, die auf *-y* enden, gilt:
Steht ein Konsonant (Mitlaut) vor dem *-y*, so wird das *-y* zu **-ies**.
Steht ein Vokal vor dem *-y*, so bleibt das *-y* erhalten und es wird nur ein **-s** angehängt:

| Jason often tid**ies** his room. | *Jason räumt häufig sein Zimmer auf.* |
| Emily pla**ys** football. | *Emily spielt Fußball.* |

Grammar 3

b) Die einfache Gegenwart: Verneinung — The simple present: negation

Sätze im *simple present* kannst du mit **don't** (= **do not**) verneinen.
Bei *he, she, it* (also in der 3. Person Singular) verwendest du **doesn't** (= **does not**).

	Simple present: Verneinung	
Singular	I **don't**	play football.
	You **don't**	like tennis.
	He **doesn't**	wear jeans.
	She **doesn't**	live in Camden.
	It **doesn't**	look like a dog.
Plural	We **don't**	walk the dog.
	You **don't**	know Peter's sister.
	They **don't**	go to London.

Ben **doesn't like** cornflakes every day.

❗ Bei der Verneinung von Sätzen mit *to be*, *can* oder *have got* benutzt man *don't* oder *doesn't* nicht:
She **is not** from Camden. ▶ G3b
He **can't** play tennis. ▶ G9
I **haven't got** a computer. ▶ G10b

G13 Die Satzstellung im Aussagesatz
Word order in statements

▶ p. 57 ▶ D11, D12 | p. 143, D7 | p. 149, D16 | p. 160   🎥 Grammatik-Video ▶ WES-149220-4

a) Satzstellung Subjekt – Verb – Objekt — Word order subject – verb – object

Im englischen Aussagesatz ist die Satzstellung meist:
Subjekt – Verb – Objekt (S – V – O).
Im Anschluss können noch Orts-
oder Zeitangaben folgen.

Subjekt	Verb	Objekt	Ortsangabe/Zeitangabe
Tom and Leo	play	football	in the park.
Harry	plays	computer games	in the evening.
Linda and Zoe	have got	music	on Mondays.

Wenn ein Satz eine Orts- und eine Zeitangabe enthält, nennt man zuerst den Ort und dann die Zeit:
Tom and Leo play football in the park after school.

Zeitangaben können auch am Satzanfang stehen: **On Mondays** *Linda and Zoe have got music.*

3 Grammar

b) Aussagesätze mit Häufigkeitsadverbien Statements with adverbs of frequency

Die Wörter **always**, **usually**, **often**, **sometimes** und **never** nennt man Häufigkeitsadverbien. Mit ihnen kannst du ausdrücken, wie häufig etwas geschieht.

Anders als im Deutschen stehen Häufigkeitsadverbien im Englischen fast immer **vor** dem Verb:

always	– *immer*
usually	– *normalerweise*
often	– *oft*
sometimes	– *manchmal*
never	– *nie*

Subjekt	Häufigkeitsadverb	Verb		
I	sometimes	help	at home.	*Ich helfe manchmal zu Hause.*
George	never	walks	to school.	*George läuft nie zur Schule.*
They	often	eat	pizza.	*Sie essen oft Pizza.*

❗ Das Häufigkeitsadverb steht **hinter** der Form von *to be*:   Sarah **is never** late. Zoe **is always** late.

❗ Das Häufigkeitsadverb steht **zwischen** *have* und *got*:   We **have never got** the time.

❗ Das Häufigkeitsadverb steht **hinter** *can/can't*:   We **can usually** eat at school.
They **can't always** eat chocolate.

G14 Die einfache Gegenwart: Entscheidungsfragen und Kurzantworten
The simple present: yes/no questions and short answers   ▶ p. 58   ▶ D13–D15 | p. 144

Du kennst bereits Entscheidungsfragen mit *to be*, *can* und *have got*: (▶ G5, G9, G10c)

> **Are** you eleven? – **Yes, I am.** / **No, I'm not.**
> **Can** you play an instrument? – **Yes, I can.** / **No, I can't.**
> **Has** Emma **got** a new book? – **Yes, she has.** / **No, she hasn't.**

In Entscheidungsfragen mit einem anderen Verb steht **do** oder **does** am Satzanfang.
In den Kurzantworten wird **do** oder **does** aufgegriffen:

Entscheidungsfragen mit *do/does* + Verb	Kurzantworten	
	+	**−**
Do you **play** volleyball?	Yes, I do.	No, I don't.
Do they **like** pizza?	Yes, they do.	No, they don't.
Does Jack **know** Gillian?	Yes, he does.	No, he doesn't.

❗ Bei *he*, *she*, *it* (in der 3. Person Singular) verwendest du in den Entscheidungsfragen *does*.
Das Verb hat dann kein *-s* für die 3. Person Singular. Vergleiche:
*Jack know**s** Gillian.*   Aber: ***Does** Jack know Gillian?*

Grammar 3

G15 Die einfache Gegenwart: Fragen mit Fragewörtern ▶ p. 63 ▶ D22–D24 | p. 146
The simple present: questions with question words

Who, *what*, *when*, *where*, *why* und *how* sind Fragewörter.
Mit dem Fragewort fragst du nach bestimmten Informationen.

Fragen mit Fragewörtern mit *to be*, *can*, *have got*			
Where	is	George?	*Wo ist George?*
What	can	we eat?	*Was können wir essen?*
Who	has got	an idea?	*Wer hat eine Idee?*

Bei Fragen mit einem anderen Verb als *to be*, *can* oder *have got* verwendet man *do* oder *does* nach dem Fragewort:

Fragen mit Fragewörtern mit *do/does* + Verb			
What	do	you usually **do** after school?	*Was machst du normalerweise nach der Schule?*
When	do	you **play** football?	*Wann spielt ihr Fußball?*
Why	does	Caroline **like** elephants?	*Warum mag Caroline Elefanten?*
How	do	you **decorate** muffins?	*Wie dekoriert man Muffins?*

Bei Fragen mit Fragewörtern ist die Satzstellung: Fragewort – *do/does* – Subjekt – Infinitiv

Fragewort	*do/does*	Subjekt	Infinitiv
Where	do	you	live?

> ⚠ Bei Fragen mit dem Verb *to do* kommt *do* zweimal im Satz vor:
> *What **do** you **do**?*

⚠ Bei *he*, *she*, *it* (in der 3. Person Singular) verwendest du in den Fragen mit Fragewörtern *does*.
Das Verb hat dann kein *-s* für die 3. Person Singular. Vergleiche:
*He **lives** in London.* Aber: *Where **does** he **live**?*

⚠ Wenn man nach dem Subjekt fragt, verwendet man kein *do* oder *does* nach *who*:
***Who lives** in Camden?* – *Who* ist Subjekt: **Wer** lebt in Camden?
aber: ***Who** do you meet?* – *Who* ist Objekt: **Wen** triffst du?

Achte auf die **Satzmelodie**:
Bei Aussagesätzen ist die Satzmelodie am Satzende fallend:

Sue writes Charlie an email.

Bei Fragen steigt die Satzmelodie häufig an:

Why does Caroline want to make a cake?   *When is your party, Charlie?*

Where do you live?
Next door.

4 Grammar

Theme 4

G16 Die Verlaufsform der Gegenwart
The present progressive Grammatik-Video ▶ WES-149220-4
▶ p. 75   ▶ D8–D13 | pp. 149–151

a) Die Verlaufsform der Gegenwart: Aussagesätze   The present progressive: statements

Wie du schon weißt, verwendest du das *simple present*, um zum Beispiel über Gewohnheiten und regelmäßige Ereignisse zu sprechen. ▶ G12

Das **present progressive** verwendest du, wenn du sagen möchtest, was jemand gerade tut oder was gerade passiert – also für Vorgänge, die gerade ablaufen und noch nicht abgeschlossen sind.

So bildest du das **present progressive**:
Form von *be* (am, is, are) + **Grundform des Verbs** + **-ing**
She **is** drink**ing** orange juice.

Caroline **is reading** a book.

	Present progressive: Aussagesätze			
Singular	I	**am watching**	TV.	*Ich sehe (gerade) fern.*
	You	**are writing**	an email.	*Du schreibst (gerade) eine E-Mail.*
	He	**is opening**	the window.	*Er öffnet (gerade) das Fenster.*
	She	**is sitting**	on the sofa.	*Sie sitzt (gerade) auf dem Sofa.*
	Oh no, it	**is raining**	again!	*Oh nein, es regnet schon wieder!*
Plural	We	**are eating**	pizza.	*Wir essen (gerade) Pizza.*
	You	**are playing**	football.	*Ihr spielt (gerade) Fußball.*
	Listen, they	**are singing**	a song.	*Hör mal, sie singen (gerade) ein Lied.*

❗ Endet das Verb auf ein stummes *-e*, dann fällt das *-e* in der Verlaufsform weg:
to writ**e** ➡ writ**ing**, to danc**e** ➡ danc**ing**, to hav**e** ➡ hav**ing**.

❗ Endet das Verb auf einem kurzen, betonten Vokal + Konsonant, dann wird der Konsonant verdoppelt:
to sit ➡ si**tt**ing, to run ➡ ru**nn**ing.

Für die **Verneinung** fügst du einfach *not* hinter die Form von *to be* ein.
In den Kurzformen wird *not* verkürzt:

> Caroline is **not** writing a text.
> Emma is**n't** reading a book.

> 💡 Im Deutschen gibt es keine Verlaufsform.
> Mit Wörtern wie *gerade*, *im Moment* oder *jetzt* lässt sich die Verlaufsform aber gut wiedergeben:
> *Caroline is reading a book.*
> ➡ Caroline **liest gerade** ein Buch.

Grammar 4

b) Die Verlaufsform der Gegenwart: Fragen   The present progressive: questions

Entscheidungsfragen im *present progressive* bildest du, indem du die Form von *to be (am, is, are)* an den Satzanfang stellst.
Die Kurzantworten sind wie beim Verb *to be*.   ▶ G5

Is Tom **helping** his mum?	Yes, he is. / No, he isn't.
Are Alex and Sue **playing** basketball?	Yes, they are. / No, they aren't.

Bei Fragen mit Fragewörtern stellst du das Fragewort an den Satzanfang.

What are you **doing**?	I'm writing an email.
Where is she **going**?	She's going to school.

G17   Einfache Gegenwart oder Verlaufsform der Gegenwart?
Simple present or present progressive?   ▶ p. 76   ▶ D14-D15 | p. 152, D4-D5 | p. 163

Im Englischen gibt es zwei Formen der Gegenwart: die einfache Form *simple present* und die Verlaufsform *present progressive*. Sie werden unterschiedlich verwendet:

The children **usually play** football in the park.

Today, they **are playing** football at the sports ground.

Das **simple present** (▶ G12) verwendest du, …
- um über Gewohnheiten oder regelmäßige Handlungen zu sprechen:
  Signalwörter: *never, always, sometimes, often, usually, every day/morning/…*
  They **play** football every Tuesday.
- um über aufeinander folgende Handlungen zu sprechen: *First Caroline **makes** her bed. Then she **loads** the dishwasher. After that she **reads** a book.*
- um über Zustände zu sprechen, die längere Zeit andauern: *Emma and Gillian **live** in London.*

Das **present progressive** (▶ G16) verwendest du, wenn du sagen möchtest, was jemand gerade tut oder was gerade passiert – also für Vorgänge, die gerade ablaufen und noch nicht abgeschlossen sind:
Signalwörter: *(right) now, at the moment …*
Right now, Linda **is writing** a text.

4 Grammar

G18 Die Mengenwörter *some, any* und *no*   The quantifiers *some, any* and *no*
▶ p. 81   ▶ D20 | p. 153

Some oder *any* verwendest du, wenn du keine genaue Menge oder Anzahl von etwas angeben möchtest. Auf Deutsch bedeuten *some* und *any* so viel wie „etwas", „einige" oder „ein paar". *Some* und *any* werden aber oft nicht übersetzt:

Bejahte Aussagesätze mit *some*

| There are **some** apples in the kitchen. | In der Küche sind (ein paar) Äpfel. |
| I need **some** milk for my cornflakes. | Ich brauche (etwas) Milch für meine Cornflakes. |

> Have you got **any** questions?

Fragen und verneinte Aussagesätze mit *any*

Are there **any** apples?	Gibt es Äpfel?
Have you got **any** milk?	Hast du (etwas) Milch?
We have**n't** got **any** apples.	Wir haben keine Äpfel.
There is**n't any** milk.	Es gibt keine Milch.

> Statt *not any* kannst du auch *no* (deutsch „kein/e") verwenden:
> *There are **no** apples.* – Es gibt keine Äpfel.

❗ Wenn du jemanden höflich um etwas bittest oder jemandem etwas anbietest, verwendest du *some* auch in Fragen:

| Can I have **some** milk, please? | Kann ich bitte (etwas) Milch haben? |
| Would you like to eat **some** chocolate? | Möchtest du etwas Schokolade essen? |

G19 Verbindung von Sätzen durch Konjunktionen   ▶ p. 83
Linking sentences with conjunctions

Konjunktionen (Bindewörter) wie *and* oder *because* verwendest du, um Sätze miteinander zu verbinden.

Manche Konjunktionen verbinden Hauptsätze *(main clauses)* miteinander, zum Beispiel *and*, *or* und *but*:

1. Hauptsatz		2. Hauptsatz	
Mr Brown is our French teacher,	and	Mrs Thompson is our English teacher.	… und …
Carol likes ice cream,	but	she doesn't like chocolate.	… aber …

Andere Konjunktionen verbinden einen Hauptsatz mit einem Nebensatz *(subordinate clause)*, zum Beispiel *because* und *when*:

Hauptsatz	Nebensatz		
Sarah is happy	**because** she can play football.	… weil sie Fußball spielen kann.
Carl smiles	**when** he sees his dog.	… wenn er seinen Hund sieht.

Anders als im Deutschen bleibt die Satzstellung im Nebensatz unverändert **S**ubjekt – **V**erb – **O**bjekt:

| *Sam talks to Sarah because* | he | likes | her. | *Sam spricht mit Sarah, weil* | er | sie | mag. |
| | S | V | O | | S | O | V |

Grammar 5

Theme 5

G20 Objektpronomen — Object pronouns ▶ p. 92 ▶ D8-D9 | p. 157

Die Personalpronomen *I, you, he/she/it, we, you* und *they* kannst du als Subjekt eines Satzes verwenden. Man nennt sie deshalb **Subjektpronomen**.
Es gibt auch Personalpronomen, die du als Objekt verwenden kannst. Diese nennt man **Objektpronomen**.

> 💡 Nach dem Subjekt fragst du: „Wer oder was?"
>
> Nach dem Objekt fragst du: „Wem? Wen oder was?"

Subjekt-pronomen	Objektpronomen		Subjektpronomen	Objektpronomen
I	me	mir; mich	I want to write a shopping list.	Can you give **me** a pen, please?
you	you	dir; dich	You are new in class.	Jo can show **you** our school.
he	him	ihm; ihn	He needs help.	Can you help **him**, Jill?
she	her	ihr; sie	She's my friend.	I like **her**.
it	it	ihm/ihr; ihn/sie/es	This is my bike. It's new.	Do you like **it**?
we	us	uns	We want to play football.	You can come with **us**.
you	you	euch/Ihnen; euch/Sie	Jo and Jill, where are **you**?	I can't find **you**.
they	them	ihnen; sie	They are in the garden.	I can see **them**.

❗ Anders als im Deutschen gibt es im Englischen für jedes Personalpronomen nur eine Objektform. Zum Beispiel kann *him* „ihn" oder „ihm" heißen:

| I can see **him**. | – | Ich kann **ihn** sehen. |
| We can give **him** a present. | – | Wir können **ihm** ein Geschenk geben. |

G21 Die Modalverben *must, mustn't, needn't, should/shouldn't*
The modal verbs *must, mustn't, needn't, should/shouldn't*
▶ p. 93 ▶ D10-D12 | p. 158 🎬 Grammatik-Video ▶ WES-149220-4

a) Das Modalverb *must* — The modal verb *must*

Mit *must* kannst du sagen, was jemand tun muss.
Must steht mit dem **Infinitiv** zusammen und bleibt für alle Personen gleich:

| I **must go** home now. | *Ich muss jetzt nach Hause gehen.* |
| She **must walk** her dog. | *Sie muss den Hund ausführen.* |

Bei Fragen wird *must* an den Anfang gestellt:

| **Must** we **buy** dog food today? | *Müssen wir heute Hundefutter kaufen?* |

5 Grammar

b) Das Modalverb *mustn't* The modal verb *mustn't*

Mit *mustn't* kannst du sagen, was jemand **nicht tun darf**.
Mustn't steht mit dem **Infinitiv** zusammen
und bleibt für alle Personen gleich:

You **mustn't** play football.

I **mustn't go** to bed late.	*Ich **darf nicht** spät ins Bett gehen.*
She **mustn't play** computer games every day.	*Sie **darf nicht** jeden Tag Computerspiele spielen.*

❗ *Mustn't* bedeutet „nicht dürfen".
Wenn jemand etwas nicht zu tun braucht, verwendet man *needn't*. ▶ G21c

c) Das Modalverb *needn't* The modal verb *needn't*

Mit *needn't* kannst du sagen, was jemand **nicht zu tun braucht**.
Needn't steht mit dem **Infinitiv** zusammen und bleibt für alle Personen gleich:

We **needn't do** our homework now.	*Wir **brauchen** unsere Hausaufgaben **nicht** jetzt zu machen.*
Sarah **needn't buy** cornflakes. There are still two boxes here.	*Sarah **braucht keine** Cornflakes zu kaufen. Es sind noch zwei Schachteln hier.*

d) Das Modalverb *should/shouldn't* The modal verb *should/shouldn't*

Mit *should/shouldn't* kannst du sagen, was jemand **tun soll(te)/nicht tun soll(te)**.
Should/shouldn't steht mit dem **Infinitiv** zusammen und bleibt für alle Personen gleich:

The dog is hungry. You **should give** him some food.	*Der Hund hat Hunger. Du **solltest** ihm Futter geben.*
We **shouldn't go out** now. It's raining.	*Wir **sollten** jetzt nicht rausgehen. Es regnet.*

Bei Fragen wird *should/shouldn't* an den Anfang gestellt:

Let's go now! – **Shouldn't** we **wait** for George?	*Lasst uns gehen! – **Sollten** wir nicht auf George warten?*

Grammar G

Grammatical terms

Englisch		Deutsch	Beispiel
adverb of frequency	G13b	Häufigkeitsadverb	often, sometimes, never, …
article		Artikel	
definite article	G2a	bestimmter Artikel	the
indefinite article	G2b	unbestimmter Artikel	a/an
conjunction	G19	Konjunktion	and, or, because, …
genitive		Genitiv	
genitive with of/s-genitive	G11	Genitiv mit of/s-Genitiv	the name of the ship/Dan's dog
imperative	G8	Imperativ	Please sit down! Don't shout!
infinitive		Infinitiv (Grundform)	(to) walk, (to) go, (to) read, …
long form	G3a	Langform	Charlie is not from Germany.
modal verb	G21	Modalverb	can, must, needn't, should, …
noun	G1	Nomen (Hauptwort, Substantiv)	song, child, car, dog, …
personal pronoun	G4, G20	Personalpronomen (persönliches Fürwort)	
object pronoun	G20	Objektpronomen	me, you, him, her, it, us, them
subject pronoun	G20	Subjektpronomen	I, you, he, she, it, we, they
plural		Plural (Mehrzahl)	cars, numbers, … /
regular/irregular	G1	regelmäßig/unregelmäßig	children, women, …
possessive determiner	G7	Possessivbegleiter	my, your, his, her, its, our, their
present tense		Präsens (Gegenwart)	
present progressive	G16, 17	Verlaufsform der Gegenwart	It's raining.
simple present	G12–15, 17	einfache Gegenwart	I often walk to school.
question		Frage	
question word	G6	Fragewort	who, where, what, when, why, how
yes/no question	G5	Entscheidungsfrage	Are you from Germany?
short answer	G5	Kurzantwort	Yes, I am. / No, I'm not.
short form	G3	Kurzform	he's, they're, …
singular	G1	Singular (Einzahl)	dog, friend, house, …
statement	G12	Aussagesatz	She's from Camden. /
positive/negative		bejaht/verneint	I don't like football.
subject	G13	Subjekt	Our school is great. / Jo and I like football.
verb	G13	Verb	(to) look, (to) walk, (to) meet, (to) see
word order	G13	Satzstellung	Sarah is reading a book.
s – v – o (subject – verb – object)	G13a	S – V – O (Subjekt – Verb – Objekt)	s – v – o

W Wordbanks

In den *Wordbanks* sind nützliche Wörter und Redewendungen zu unterschiedlichen Themen zusammengefasst. Wenn bei einer Aufgabe vorne im Buch zum Beispiel ▶ Wordbank 1 | p. 198 steht, findest du auf Seite 198 passende Wörter zum Thema Schule.

1 Wordbank School

(Illustration of a classroom with labelled items: board, poster, clock, calendar, map, window, school bag, book, piece of paper, bin, pencil, pen, pupil, pencil case, desk, chair, exercise book, computer, teacher)

Places at school

assembly hall • canteen • classroom • IT room • library • science room • sports ground

Subjects

art • English • French • geography • German • history • IT • maths • music • PE • RE • science • Spanish • technology

In the classroom

- What's ... in English?
- Sorry, I'm late.
- Can I open the window, please?
- Can you say that again, please?
- Clean the board, please.
- Sit down, please.

198   one hundred and ninety-eight

Wordbanks

2 Wordbank People

Family and friends

mother • father • parents • daughter • son •
brother • sister • twins • husband • wife • grandparents •
grandfather • grandmother • aunt • uncle • cousin •
girlfriend • boyfriend • best friend

Making friends

Feelings

annoyed • bored • delighted • disappointed •
grumpy • jealous • nervous • optimistic •
pleased • puzzled • safe • scared • shocked •
surprised • tired • unhappy • upset

Body parts

one foot • two feet
one tooth • two teeth

one hundred and ninety-nine 199

W Wordbanks

3 Wordbank Time

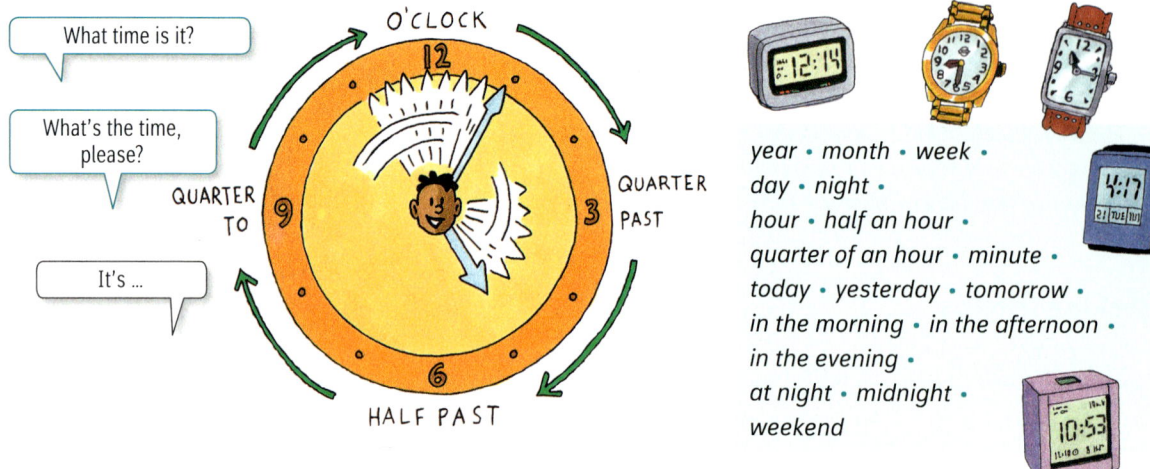

What time is it?

What's the time, please?

It's ...

O'CLOCK
12
QUARTER PAST
3
HALF PAST
6
QUARTER TO
9

12:14

year • *month* • *week* •
day • *night* •
hour • *half an hour* •
quarter of an hour • *minute* •
today • *yesterday* • *tomorrow* •
in the morning • *in the afternoon* •
in the evening •
at night • *midnight* •
weekend

4:17

10:53

The seasons

spring • *summer* • *autumn* • *winter*

When is your birthday?

My birthday is in May.

It's on the 28th of May.

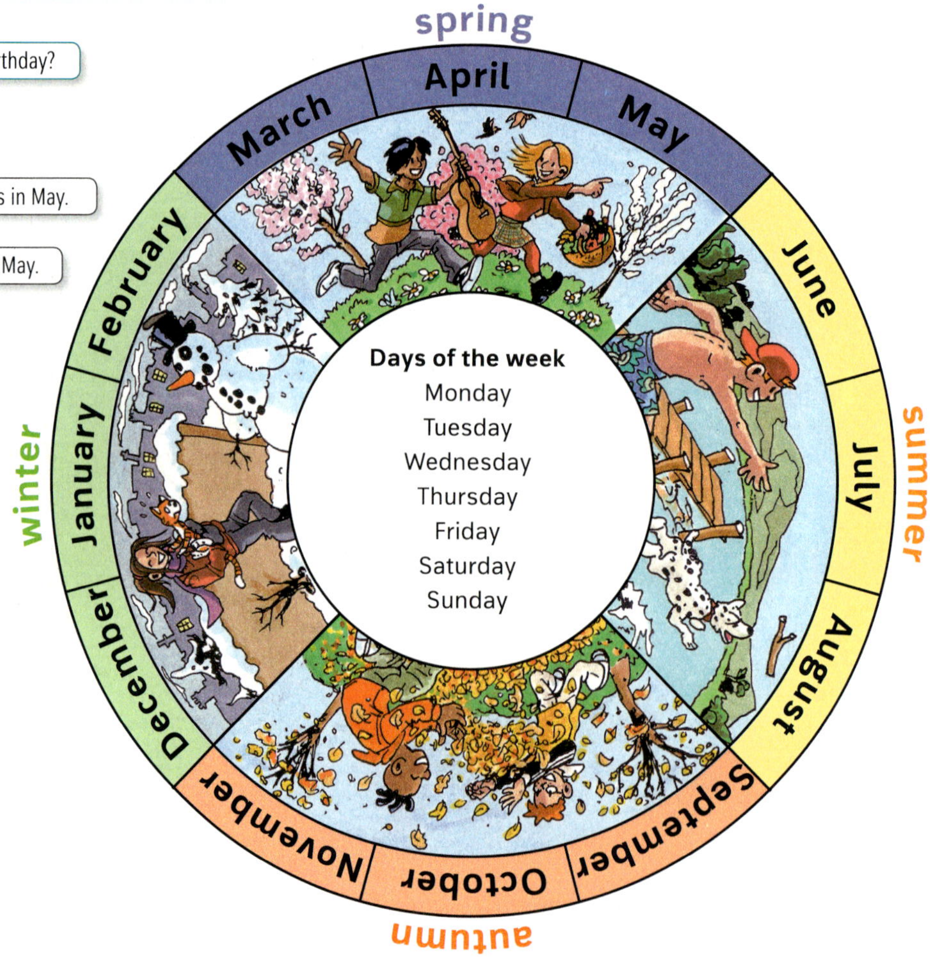

spring
March
April
May
summer
June
July
August
autumn
September
October
November
winter
December
January
February
Days of the week
Monday
Tuesday
Wednesday
Thursday
Friday
Saturday
Sunday

Wordbanks

4 Wordbank At home

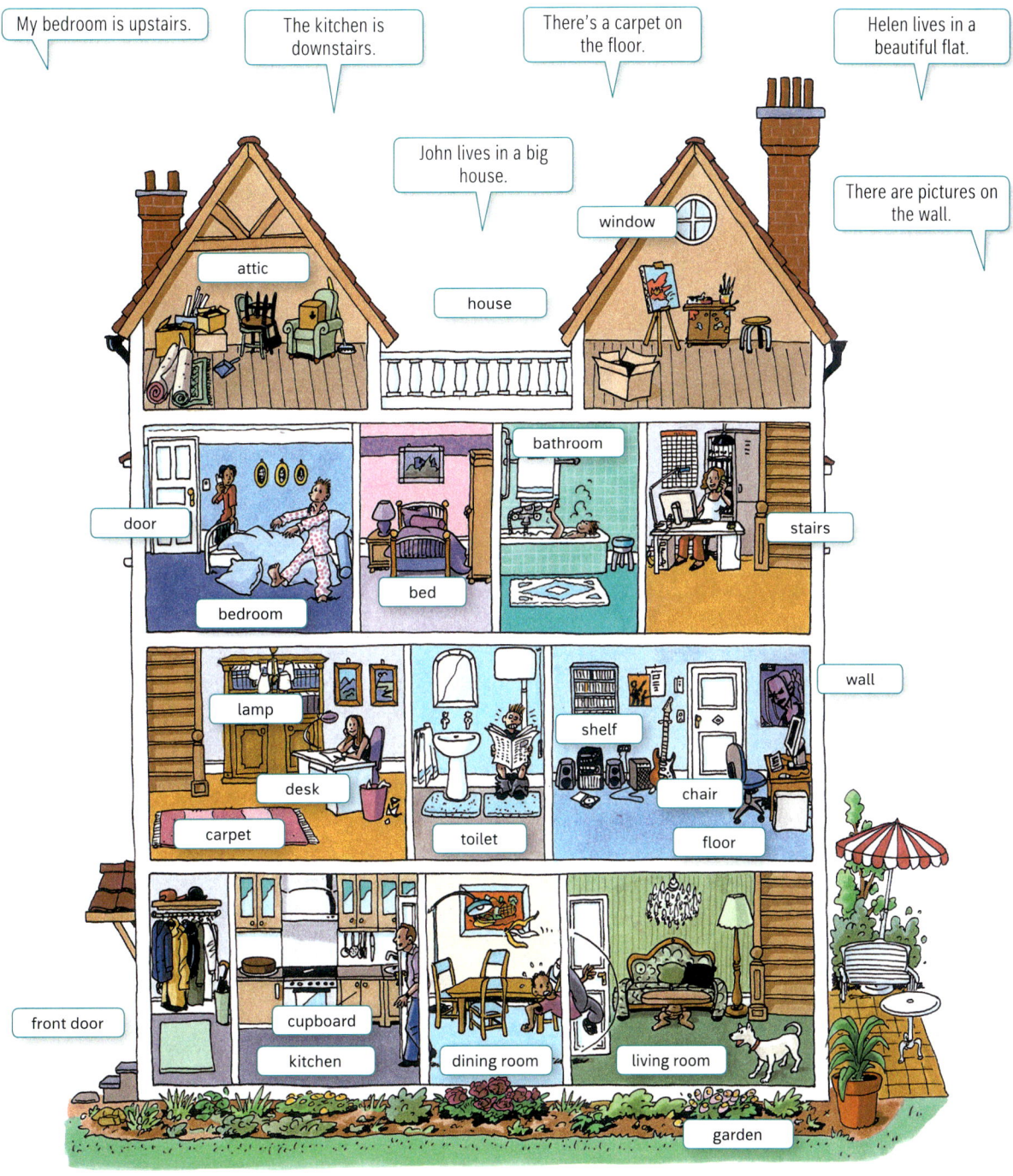

Jobs around the house

to clean the toilet • to cook • to hoover • to lay the table • to empty/load the dishwasher • to make the bed • to sweep the floor • to take out the rubbish • to tidy the room • to walk the dog

Wordbanks

5 Wordbank Things and places

Adjectives for things and places

amazing • awesome • beautiful • extraordinary • fancy •
fantastic • fascinating • interesting • important • lovely •
perfect • spectacular • stunning • wonderful

awful • boring • dark • horrible • strange • scary • terrible

Manchester is the place to go!

It's a fascinating experience!

Enjoy the amazing view!

Camden is a great place for shopping.

The museum is open from 10 to 2.

On holiday

to climb • to discover new places • to go hiking • to go sightseeing •
to go on a trip • to go surfing • to go to the beach • to take a boat trip •
to take a tour of … • to visit …

6 Wordbank Clothes

Clothes

boots • cap • cardigan • coat • dress • gloves • hat •
hiking boots • jacket • pullover • scarf • shirt • shoes • shorts •
socks • swimming trunks • swimsuit • trousers • underwear

trainers • tie • sunglasses • skirt • T-shirt

Shopping

to go shopping • to buy • to sell
to try on • to fit • size • special offer • shop assistant • customer
cheap • expensive

How much is this T-shirt?
It's £ 19.99.
How much are these jeans?
They are …

Why don't you buy it anyway?
We're just looking.
Can I try this on?

Excuse me, have you got any …?
Here you are.

Wordbanks

7 Wordbank Food and drink

Food

biscuit • bread • broccoli • cake • carrot • cereal • chicken • chips • cucumber • fish • fruit • ham • jam • lemon • meat • onion • rice • pasta • potatoes • salad • sandwich • sauce • sausage • strawberry • sugar • toast • vegetables • yogurt

an ice cream

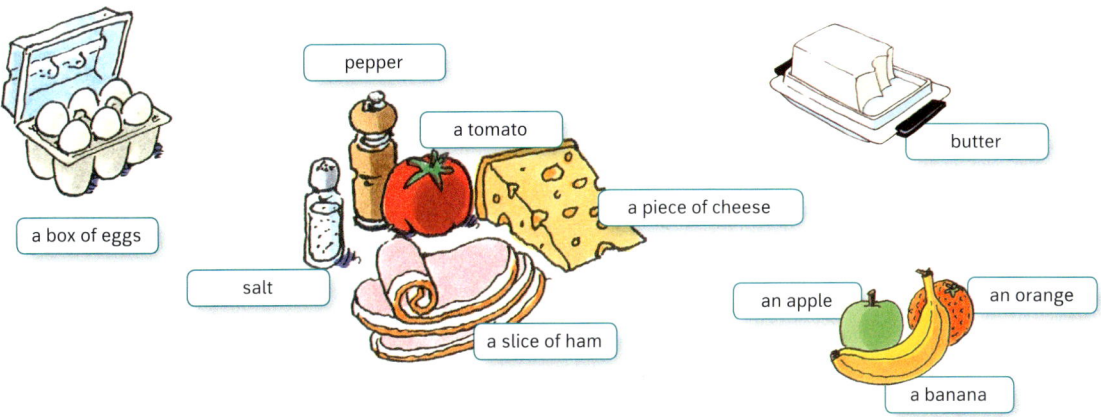

a box of eggs, pepper, a tomato, salt, a piece of cheese, butter, a slice of ham, an apple, an orange, a banana

Drinks

coke • coffee • hot chocolate • milk • water

a cup of tea

a glass of juice

to be hungry • to be thirsty • to eat • to drink • to cook • to bake a cake • to have breakfast • to have lunch • to have dinner

Mengenangaben mit *of*	
a bar of chocolate	= eine Tafel Schokolade
a bag of crisps	= eine Tüte Chips
a bottle of water	= eine Flasche Wasser
a kilo of sugar	= ein Kilo Zucker

This pizza is delicious!

Paul is a vegetarian.

Would you like some toast?

I'm allergic to peanuts.

No thanks, I'm full.

W Wordbanks

8 Wordbank Animals

to eat • to look like • to catch • to smell • to lick • to keep •
to feed • to look after • to miaow • to take ... for a walk

What's your favourite animal?

Elephants are my favourite animals.

I love ponies.

I like fish.

Have you got a pet?

Wordbanks

9 Wordbank Hobbies and free time

hockey stick

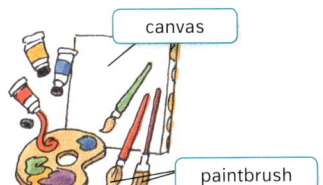
canvas
paintbrush

guitar

bike

Hobbies

to cycle • to dance • to draw • to do ballet • to do yoga • to go to the gym • to play chess • to play the piano • to ride • to sing in a choir • to swim

- My favourite hobby is playing the piano.
- I like playing hockey, because it is a fast sport.
- Swimming is great!
- I have three hobbies!
- I always have basketball training on Mondays.

Free-time activities

to play a board game

to relax

to go to a concert

- What do you do in your free time?

to listen to music • to meet friends • to go for a walk • to go shopping • to go to the cinema • to go to the theatre • to read a book • to visit a museum • to watch TV

W Word lists

So funktionieren die Wortlisten

Es gibt Wortlisten nach *Themes* und alphabetische Wortlisten *(dictionaries)*.

Wortlisten nach *Themes*
In den Wortlisten nach *Themes* ab Seite 207 findest du die Wörter in der Reihenfolge, in der sie in den *Themes* vorkommen.
Am Ende der Wortliste zu jedem *Theme* steht *Say it in English*, eine Liste mit nützlichen Redewendungen.

Dictionaries
Camden Town hat zwei *dictionaries*:
1 Im *English-German dictionary* ab Seite 238 kannst du nachschlagen, wenn du die Bedeutung von einem englischen Wort aus dem Buch wissen möchtest.
2 Im *German-English dictionary* ab Seite 257 kannst du nachschlagen, wenn dir mal ein englisches Wort nicht einfällt.

So kannst du die Wortlisten nach *Themes* und die *dictionaries* benutzen:

Fett gedruckte Wörter solltest du dir merken.	**picture** /ˈpɪktʃə/
Die /Lautschrift/ zeigt an, wie man ein Wort ausspricht. Eine Erläuterung der Lautschrift findest du auf S. 265.	**can** /kæn/
❗ weist auf wichtige Besonderheiten hin.	❗ **I** wird immer großgeschrieben.
↔ bedeutet „ist das Gegenteil von".	**right** ↔ **wrong**
In den gelb hinterlegten Kästen stehen Wörter, die du dir merken solltest, Tipps und Hinweise.	**Family** /ˈfæm(ə)li/ **parents** *(pl)* /ˈpeərənts/ Eltern **father** /ˈfɑːðə/ Vater
Pick-up bedeutet: In diesem Kasten stehen Wörter, die du vielleicht schon aus der Grundschule kennst. Diese Wörter solltest du dir merken.	**Pick-up: Colours** /ˈkʌləz/ **red orange yellow green**
(informal) bedeutet: Dieses Wort ist umgangssprachlich.	**Sure!** *(informal)* /ʃɔː/
(pl mice) bedeutet: Dieses Wort hat einen unregelmäßigen Plural *(mice)*.	**mouse** *(pl **mice**)* /maʊs, maɪs/
(no pl) bedeutet: Dieses Wort hat keinen Plural.	**people** *(no pl)* /ˈpiːp(ə)l/
(pl) bedeutet: Dieses Wort wird nur oder gewöhnlich im Plural benutzt.	**scissors** *(pl)* /ˈsɪzəz/
° bedeutet: Dieses Wort ist nur für einen bestimmten Text wichtig. Du brauchst es nicht zu lernen.	° **to knock** /nɒk/
Folgende Abkürzungen werden noch verwendet: sb = somebody sth = something	jdm/jdn = jemandem/jemanden etw = etwas

Welcome to Camden Town!

Word lists

Tipps zum Wörterlernen findest du auf der *Skills page Memorizing vocabulary* auf Seite 175.

Weitere Listen zum Nachschlagen:
1 *Names* (S. 263): Hier findest du die Namen, die in den *Themes* vorkommen, mit ihrer Lautschrift.
2 *Numbers* (S. 266): Hier findest du Zahlen und ihre Aussprache.
3 *Wörter, die im Deutschen und Englischen ähnlich sind* (S. 267)
4 *Class instructions* (S. 268): Hier kannst du die häufigsten Arbeitsanweisungen in deinem Buch nachschlagen.

Word lists

Welcome to Camden Town!

1 Welcome to Camden Town! /ˌwelkəm tʊ ˌkæmdən ˈtaʊn/ — Willkommen in Camden Town!

Arbeitsanweisungen, die häufig im Buch vorkommen, kannst du in der Liste auf Seite 266 nachschlagen. *p. 10*

° What can you see? /ˌwɒt kən jʊ ˈsiː/ — Was siehst du?
can /kæn/ — können — **can** ↔ **can't** / **cannot** /kɑːnt, ˈkænɒt/
to* **see** /siː/ — sehen — I can **see** a car.

* An dem Wort *to* erkennst du, dass es sich um den Infinitiv (die Grundform) des Verbs handelt.

a, an /ə, ən/ — ein(e) — **a** car / **an** email
car /kɑː/ — Auto
I /aɪ/ — ich — ❗ I wird immer großgeschrieben.

2 ° What can you hear? /ˌwɒt kən jʊ ˈhɪə/ — Was hörst du?

3 **Where is …? / Where are …?** /ˈweərˌɪz, ˈweərˌɑː/ — Wo ist …? / Wo sind …? — **Where's …?** = **Where is …?**
° Find the children. — Findet die Kinder.
the /ðə/ — der/die/das — /ð/ klingt ungefähr wie ein gelispeltes „s" in „Ha**s**e".

° in the road /ˌɪn ðə ˈrəʊd/ — auf der Straße
° in a car /ɪn ə ˈkɑː/ — in einem Auto
° in his room /ɪn ˌhɪz ˈruːm/ — in seinem Zimmer
° in front of a shop /ɪn ˌfrʌnt əv ə ˈʃɒp/ — vor einem Geschäft

4 to **play** /pleɪ/ — spielen

I can **play** basketball. *p. 11*

° I spy with my little eye something red. /aɪ ˌspaɪ wɪð ˌmaɪ ˌlɪt(ə)l ˈaɪ ˌsʌmθɪŋ ˈred/ — Ich sehe was, was du nicht siehst, und das ist rot.
bus /bʌs/ — Bus
yes /jes/ — ja — **yes** ↔ **no** /nəʊ/

Pick-up: Colours /ˈkʌləz/

red	orange	yellow	green	blue	purple	pink	brown	white	grey	black
/red/	/ˈɒrɪndʒ/	/ˈjeləʊ/	/griːn/	/bluː/	/ˈpɜːpl/	/pɪŋk/	/braʊn/	/waɪt/	/greɪ/	/blæk/

6 ° Spell your name. — Buchstabiere deinen Namen. *p. 12*
7 ° Play 'hangman'. — Spielt „Galgenmännchen".

Word lists

Welcome to Camden Town!

8	° on Albert Street /ɒn ˈælbət striːt/	in der Albert Street	p. 13
	and /ænd/	und	
	are /ɑː/	bist, sind, seid	
	to listen to /ˈlɪs(ə)n tə/	zuhören, (an)hören	
	to read /riːd/	lesen	**Read** the text.

Pick-up: Sich begrüßen und kennen lernen

In den *Pick-up*-Boxen stehen Wörter und Sätze, die du vielleicht schon aus der Grundschule kennst:

Hi, my name is … What's your name?	Hallo, ich heiße … Wie heißt du?
Hello, I'm … (Hello, I am)	Hallo, ich heiße / ich bin …
Where are you from? – I'm from …	Woher kommst du? – Ich komme aus …
This is my brother/sister.	Das ist mein Bruder/meine Schwester.
How old are you? – I'm eleven years old.	Wie alt bist du? – Ich bin elf Jahre alt.
We're twelve. (We are twelve.)	Wir sind zwölf.
Elephants are my favourite animals.	Elefanten sind meine Lieblingstiere.
I like … / I don't like …	Ich mag … / Ich mag … nicht.

> Hi, my name is Sarah. What's your name?

	too /tuː/	auch	I like elephants, **too**.
			⚠ **too** steht am Satzende.
	twin /twɪn/	Zwilling; Zwillings-	
	boring /ˈbɔːrɪŋ/	langweilig	/ŋ/ wird wie das „ng" in Kli**ng**el ausgesprochen.
	football /ˈfʊtˌbɔːl/	Fußball	
	° Learn "your" sentences.	Lerne „deine" Sätze.	I like **football**.
9	° Talk to a partner like this.	Sprich so mit einem Partner/ einer Partnerin.	p. 14
	What about you? /ˌwɒt əˌbaʊt ˈjuː/	Was ist mit dir?, Und du?	
	What's your favourite …? /ˌwɒts jə ˈfeɪv(ə)rət/	Was ist dein Lieblings…?	**What's your favourite** film?
	what's (= what is) /ˈwɒts, ˌwɒt ɪz/	was ist	
11	that /ðæt/	das, der/die/das	p. 15
	cat /kæt/	Katze	**cat**
	her /hɜː/	ihr(e)	
	you /juː/	du; dich; dir; Sie; Ihnen; ihr; euch	
	sweet /swiːt/	süß	
	clever /ˈklevə/	klug, gescheit, schlau	
	° Socks can do tricks.	Socks kann Kunststücke vorführen.	
	dog /dɒɡ/	Hund	**Dogs** are my favourite animals.
	° much better /ˌmʌtʃ ˈbetə/	viel besser	
	skateboarding (no pl) /ˈskeɪtˌbɔːdɪŋ/	Skateboard fahren	
	great /ɡreɪt/	groß, riesig, großartig, wunderbar	
	it's (= it is) /ɪts, ˈɪt ɪz/	es ist	

There is … / there are … /ðeər ɪz/ ðeər ɑː/

There bedeutet „da, dort". **There is …** und **there are …** bedeuten, dass etwas vorhanden ist/dass es etwas gibt. Die Kurzform **there's** (= *there is*) verwendet man vor allem beim Sprechen.

There's a skateboarding club at my school.	Es gibt eine Skateboard-AG an meiner Schule.
There is a computer in my room.	Es gibt einen Computer in meinem Zimmer.
There are 14 girls in my class.	In meiner Klasse gibt es 14 Mädchen.
There are two apples in my bag.	Es sind zwei Äpfel in meiner Tasche.

Word lists 1

Theme 1: New in Camden

school /skuːl/ — Schule
° What's the name of your school? — Wie heißt deine/eure Schule?
for /fɔː/ — für
girl /gɜːl/ — Mädchen
° We can go to school together. — Wir können zusammen zur Schule gehen.
boy /bɔɪ/ — Junge
with /wɪð/ — mit
he's (= he is) /hiːz, ˈhiˌɪz/ — er ist
right /raɪt/ — richtig
example /ɪɡˈzɑːmp(ə)l/ — Beispiel ❗ Beachte die Aussprache.
in-line skating (no pl) /ˌɪnˌlaɪn ˈskeɪtɪŋ/ — Inlineskaten

❗ Die Zahlen von 1–1000 kannst du auf Seite 264 nachschlagen.

12 house /haʊs/ — Haus   *p. 16*
in /ɪn/ — in
Listen to Caroline and look at the pictures of three houses in Manchester. — Hör Caroline zu und sieh dir die Bilder von drei Häusern in Manchester an.
big /bɪɡ/ — groß — Elephants are **big** animals.
small /smɔːl/ — klein — Hamsters are **small** animals.

Theme 1: New in Camden

1 new /njuː/ — neu — **new** ↔ old   *p. 18*
lamp /læmp/ — Lampe
door /dɔː/ — Tür
book /bʊk/ — Buch

Die meisten englischen Substantive (Nomen, Hauptwörter) haben einen regelmäßigen Plural. Du bildest ihn, indem du einfach ein **s** an das Substantiv anhängst: **one book – two books**. Es gibt aber auch Ausnahmen. Lies dir deshalb G1 auf Seite 181 durch.

Rooms

room /ruːm/ — Zimmer, Raum
kitchen /ˈkɪtʃən/ — Küche
bedroom /ˈbedruːm/ — Schlafzimmer

bathroom /ˈbɑːθˌruːm/ — Bad(ezimmer)
dining room /ˈdaɪnɪŋ ruːm/ — Esszimmer, Speisesaal
living room /ˈlɪvɪŋ ruːm/ — Wohnzimmer

garden /ˈɡɑːd(ə)n/ — Garten
window /ˈwɪndəʊ/ — Fenster
upstairs /ʌpˈsteəz/ — (nach) oben — **upstairs** ↔ **downstairs**
downstairs /ˌdaʊnˈsteəz/ — (nach) unten

2 dad (informal) /dæd/ — Papa, Vati
mum (informal) /mʌm/ — Mama, Mutti

3 thing /θɪŋ/ — Ding, Gegenstand, Sache   *p. 19*
(mobile) phone /ˌməʊbaɪl ˈfəʊn/ — (Mobil)telefon, Handy — an old **phone**
shoe /ʃuː/ — Schuh — The **shoes** are brown.

1 Word lists

Theme 1: New in Camden

Wo befindet sich was? – Präpositionen

in /ɪn/	**on** /ɒn/	**under** /ˈʌndə/	**next to** /ˈnekst tə/	**in front of** /ɪn ˈfrʌnt əv/	**behind** /bɪˈhaɪnd/	**between** /bɪˈtwiːn/

on /ɒn/	auf, an	There is a new name **on** the door.
pencil case /ˈpensl keɪs/	Federmäppchen	What is in your **pencil case**?
school bag, schoolbag /ˈskuːl bæɡ/	Schultasche	

In a room

desk /desk/	Schreibtisch	**shelf** (*pl* **shelves**) /ʃelf, ʃelvz/	(Regal)brett, Bord
chair /tʃeə/	Stuhl	**wardrobe** /ˈwɔːdrəʊb/	(Kleider)schrank, Garderobe
bed /bed/	Bett		

pencil /ˈpensl/	Bleistift	**pencil**	
4 to **write (down)** /ˌraɪt ˈdaʊn/	(auf)schreiben, (nieder)schreiben		
about /əˈbaʊt/	über, von		
to close /kləʊz/	schließen, zumachen		
° Read out your sentences to your partner.	Lest eure Sätze eurem Partner/eurer Partnerin vor.		
that's (= that is) /ðæts, ˈðæt ɪz/	das ist	**That's** right.	

Das Englische hat nur einen unbestimmten Artikel: **a car**.
Vor Vokalen verwendet man **an**. Achte auf die Bindung: **an‿elephant**

5 **it** /ɪt/	er; sie; es; ihm; ihr; ihn	the pencil → **it** = **er**	
she /ʃiː/	sie	the school → **it** = **sie**	
A1 ° Imagine you live in a new city.	Stell dir vor, du lebst in einer neuen Stadt.	the bed → **it** = **es**	
		on the desk → on **it** = auf **ihm**	p. 20
		in the school → in **it** = in **ihr**	
° Say how you feel.	Sag, wie du dich fühlst.	about my room → about **it** = über **ihn**	
to **say** /seɪ/	sagen		

You can feel ...

happy /ˈhæpi/	glücklich, zufrieden, fröhlich	**worried** /ˈwʌrid/	beunruhigt, besorgt
sad /sæd/	traurig	**lonely** /ˈləʊnli/	einsam
excited /ɪkˈsaɪtɪd/	aufgeregt		

because /bɪˈkɒz/	weil, da	Tom is sad **because** Zoe is late.
friend /frend/	Freund/in	They are **friends**.
not /nɒt/	nicht	Stephen is **not** happy.

here /hɪə/	hier	
many /ˈmeni/	viele	
A2 **word** /wɜːd/	Wort	What's the English **word** for "Bleistift"? – "pencil".

Are you OK? /ə jʊ əʊˈkeɪ/	Alles in Ordnung?
well /wel/	nun (ja), tja
a bit /ə ˈbɪt/	ein bisschen, ein wenig
grandma (*informal*) /ˈɡrænˌmɑː/	Oma, Omi
grandpa (*informal*) /ˈɡrænˌpɑː/	Opa, Opi
best /best/	beste(r, s)
now /naʊ/	jetzt, nun

Please stop **now**!

Word lists 1

Theme 1: New in Camden

at home /ət ˈhəʊm/	zu Hause	Liam is **very** happy. 
very /ˈveri/	sehr, außerordentlich	
busy /ˈbɪzi/	beschäftigt; arbeitsreich	
easy /ˈiːzi/	leicht, einfach	3 + 1 = 4. – That's **easy**!
What about …? (informal) /ˈwɒt‿əˌbaʊt/	Was ist mit …? / Wie wäre es mit …?	**What about** a game of football?
but /bʌt/	aber	 My brother is excited, **but** I'm not **really** happy.
really /ˈrɪəli/	wirklich, tatsächlich, echt	
home /həʊm/	Zuhause, Haus, Wohnung	
about /əˈbaʊt/	über, von, *hier:* wegen	
What's wrong with …? /ˌwɒts ˈrɒŋ wɪð/	Was stimmt nicht mit …?, Was fehlt …?	
fantastic (informal) /fænˈtæstɪk/	fantastisch	Frz. *la place*  Camden is a **fantastic place**!
place /pleɪs/	Ort, Platz, Stelle	
to show /ʃəʊ/	zeigen	
let's (= let us) /lets, ˈlet‿ʌs/	Lass(t) uns	
game /geɪm/	Spiel	**Let's** play a **game**!
photo (= photograph) /ˈfəʊtəʊ, ˈfəʊtəˌɡrɑːf/	Foto	
° Can I call you back in ten minutes?	Kann ich dich in zehn Minuten zurückrufen?	
people (no pl) /ˈpiːp(ə)l/	Leute, Menschen	one person – two **people**
Mr (= Mister) /ˈmɪstə/	Herr *(Anrede)*	**Mr** Scott **Mrs** Scott
Mrs /ˈmɪsɪz/	Frau *(Anrede)*	
A3 to be /biː/	sein	I **am**, you/we/they **are**, he/she/it **is** p. 21 ▶ G3, G4 | p. 181
page /peɪdʒ/	Seite	Open your books at **page** 20.
sentence /ˈsentəns/	Satz	
A4 from /frɒm/	von, aus	
nice /naɪs/	schön, angenehm, nett, freundlich	
to love /lʌv/	lieben, sehr mögen	
A5 ° What's up? (informal) /ˌwɒts‿ˈʌp/	Was ist los?, Wie geht's?	
° nothing /ˈnʌθɪŋ/	nichts	
why /waɪ/	warum	
to know /nəʊ/	wissen, kennen	I **know** the German word for "dog": "Hund".
me /miː/	mir, mich	
to come (in) /ˈkʌm‿ɪn/	(herein)kommen, *hier:* mitkommen	Let's go to the party! – Can I **come**, too?
A6 canal /kəˈnæl/	Kanal	p. 22
shop /ʃɒp/	Geschäft, Laden	shop 
sign /saɪn/	Zeichen, (Straßen-/Verkehrs)schild	
underground station /ˈʌndəˌɡraʊnd ˌsteɪʃ(ə)n/	U-Bahn-Station	
° After each dialogue, say where Caroline and George go and find the right photo.	Sag nach jedem Dialog, wohin Caroline und George gehen, und finde das passende Foto.	
to go /ɡəʊ/	gehen, fahren	
number /ˈnʌmbə/	Nummer	1 and 2 are **numbers**.
English /ˈɪŋɡlɪʃ/	Englisch, englisch	
to look /lʊk/	sehen, schauen	
° Are you serious? /ə jʊ ˈsɪərɪəs/	Meinst du das ernst?	

1 Word lists

Theme 1: New in Camden

° to be mad about sb/sth /bɪˈmæd_ə_baʊt/	nach jdm/etw verrückt sein	
shopping (no pl) /ˈʃɒpɪŋ/	Einkaufen	They like **shopping**.
to **hate** /heɪt/	hassen, verabscheuen	to **hate** ↔ to like
amazing /əˈmeɪzɪŋ/	erstaunlich, toll	
little /ˈlɪt(ə)l/	klein(e, er, es)	
Shut up! (informal) /ʃʌt_ˈʌp/	Halt den Mund!	
hungry /ˈhʌŋgri/	hungrig	
ice cream /ˌaɪs ˈkriːm/	Eiscreme, Eis	This **ice cream** looks good!
to **look** /lʊk/	aussehen	
good /gʊd/	gut	
chocolate /ˈtʃɒklət/	Schokolade	❗ Achte auf die Aussprache.
to **get** /get/	erhalten, bekommen, holen	Let's **get** more chocolate!
still /stɪl/	(immer) noch, noch immer	
I'm fine. /aɪm ˈfaɪn/	Mir geht es gut.	
A7 **answer** /ˈɑːnsə/	Antwort, Lösung	347 + 179? I don't know the **answer**. *p. 23*
boat /bəʊt/	Boot, Schiff	**boat**
A8 **question** /ˈkwestʃ(ə)n/	Frage	**question** ↔ **answer**
to /tʊ/	in, nach, zu, an, *hier:* auf	

to /tʊ/
1. go **to** the park — **in** den Park gehen
2. the bus **to** London — der Bus **nach** London
3. go **to** school — **zur** Schule gehen
4. an email **to** Emma — eine E-Mail **an** Emma
5. find the answer **to** this question — finde die Antwort **auf** diese Frage

A9 **or** /ɔː/	oder	
then /ðen/	dann	
to **ask** /bəʊθ/	fragen	
sister /ˈsɪstə/	Schwester	**sister** ↔ **brother**
A11 to **answer** /ˈɑːnsə/	(be)antworten	Please **answer** the question.
to **use** /juːz/	(be)nutzen, verwenden	Jim can **use** a computer for his homework.
feeling /ˈfiːlɪŋ/	Gefühl	
exercise /ˈeksəsaɪz/	Übung, Aufgabe	42–7 is a maths **exercise**.
How are you? /ˌhaʊ_ˈɑː jʊ/	Wie geht es dir/Ihnen/euch?	Hi, **how are you** today?
° to **miss** /mɪs/	vermissen	
please /pliːz/	bitte	**Please** come to our party!
to **send** /send/	(zu)schicken	
Bye! (= **Goodbye!**) (informal) /baɪ, gʊdˈbaɪ/	Tschüss!	Hello! ↔ **Bye!** *p. 26*
B1 **at** /æt/	auf, an, in, bei	
picture /ˈpɪktʃə/	Bild	
child (*pl* **children**) /tʃaɪld, ˈtʃɪldrən/	Kind	**child** **children**
noise /nɔɪz/	Geräusch	❗ Achte auf den Plural: **child**ren.
mouse (*pl* **mice**) /maʊs, maɪs/	Maus	
to **help** /help/	helfen	
° We'd like some white chocolate.	Wir hätten gerne weiße Schokolade.	
son /sʌn/	Sohn	**son** ↔ **daughter**
daughter /ˈdɔːtə/	Tochter	
funny /ˈfʌni/	lustig, witzig, komisch, merkwürdig	What a **funny** film!
newspaper /ˈnjuːzˌpeɪpə/	Zeitung(s-)	
who /huː/	wer	❗ **Who** bedeutet „**wer**": Who is George? Where bedeutet „**wo**": Where is my pen?

Word lists 1

Theme 1: New in Camden

to find /faɪnd/	finden	
to bring in /ˌbrɪŋ ˈɪn/	(her)einbringen, einführen	
B2 when /wen/	wenn	p. 27
to **speak** /spiːk/	sprechen	
B3 **where's** (= where is) /weəz, ˈweər ɪz/	wo ist	**Where's** the mouse?
B4 again /əˈgen/	wieder, noch einmal	
to **check** /tʃek/	überprüfen, nachsehen	
B5 to **work** /wɜːk/	arbeiten	
B6 **classmate** /ˈklɑːsˌmeɪt/	Klassenkamerad/in, Mitschüler/in	a **classmate** = a boy or girl in your class
family /ˈfæm(ə)li/	Familie	Mrs and Mr McBride, Caroline and George are a **family**.
flat /flæt/	(Etagen)wohnung, Mietwohnung	
How many ...? /ˌhaʊ ˈmeni/	Wie viele ...?	**How many** girls and boys are at your school?
B7 to look after /ˌlʊk ˈɑːftə/	sich kümmern um	p. 28
minute /ˈmɪnɪt/	Minute	
° I need a cup of tea.	Ich brauche eine Tasse Tee.	
to **live** /lɪv/	leben, wohnen	

Family /ˈfæm(ə)li/

parents (pl) /ˈpeərənts/	Eltern	**sister** /ˈsɪstə/	Schwester		
father /ˈfɑːðə/	Vater	**grandparents** (pl) /ˈgrænˌpeərənts/	Großeltern		
mother /ˈmʌðə/	Mutter	**grandfather** /ˈgrænˌfɑːðə/	Großvater		
son /sʌn/	Sohn	**grandmother** /ˈgrænˌmʌðə/	Großmutter		
daughter /ˈdɔːtə/	Tochter	**aunt** /ɑːnt/	Tante		
brother /ˈbrʌðə/	Bruder	**uncle** /ˈʌŋk(ə)l/	Onkel		

always /ˈɔːlweɪz/	immer	
day /deɪ/	Tag	1 **day** = 24 hours
° long /lɒŋ/	lang	
must /mʌst/	müssen	
° Indian /ˈɪndiən/	Inder/in, indisch	
° India /ˈɪndiə/	Indien	
° Hindi (no pl) /ˈhɪndi/	Hindi (Amtssprache in Indien)	
together /təˈgeðə/	zusammen	
like /laɪk/	wie	
his /hɪz/	sein(e)	
to **like** /laɪk/	mögen	George and Jack **like** computer games.

B8 Die Wörter **my**, **your**, **his**/**her**/**its**, **our** und **their** nennt man Possessivbegleiter. Sieh in G7 auf Seite 184 nach, um herauszufinden, wie man sie verwendet. *p. 29*

above /əˈbʌv/	über	
B9 **class** /klɑːs/	(Schul)klasse	There are 17 girls and 13 boys in my **class**.
year /jɪə/	Jahr	

Say it in English – Theme 1

So kannst du ...

jemanden begrüßen – dich verabschieden	Hi! / Hello! – Goodbye. / Bye.
dich vorstellen – jemand anderen vorstellen	I'm ... – This is ...
sagen, wo sich etwas befindet	The phone is under the bed.
	There are books on the shelf.
	There is a pink school bag on the desk.
	There is an elephant under the bed.

two hundred and thirteen

2 Word lists

Theme 2: At school

Gefühle ausdrücken	I'm happy because … I'm not really happy. I'm sad because … I'm excited because … I'm worried because … I'm (a bit) lonely.
fragen, wie es jemandem geht	How are you? Are you OK?
sagen, wie es jemandem geht	He's happy. He isn't sad. George is excited.
einen Vorschlag machen	Let's play a game!
Entscheidungsfragen stellen und mit Kurzantworten auf sie antworten	Are you hungry? – Yes, I am. / No, I'm not.
Fragen mit Fragewörtern stellen	What is your favourite book? • Where is your house? Where are you from? • Why is there a mouse in my shop? Who is Patch?
sagen, wie du etwas findest	Camden is a fantastic place! There are so many great places here in Camden! The shoe shop is amazing/so cool. The shops are great. The shop is fantastic. Camden is cool! I hate shopping!
über die Familie sprechen	My family is from … My mother and father are … My grandparents live in …

Theme 2: At school

1 at school /ət ˈskuːl/ — in der Schule
first /fɜːst/ — erste(r, s)
problem /ˈprɒbləm/ — Schwierigkeit, Problem
late /leɪt/ — (zu) spät
wrong /rɒŋ/ — falsch
tie /taɪ/ — Krawatte
scarf (*pl* scarves) /skɑːf, skɑːvz/ — Schal
uniform /ˈjuːnɪfɔːm/ — Uniform
only /ˈəʊnli/ — nur

I'm sorry. / Sorry. /ˌaɪm ˈsɒri, ˈsɒri/ — Entschuldigung. / Tut mir leid.
to have /hæv/ — haben
bus stop /ˈbʌs ˌstɒp/ — Bushaltestelle
here /hɪə/ — hier

2 of /əv/ — von

4 Choose the best title for the phone call. — Finde den passendsten Titel zu seinem Telefongespräch.

A1 rule /ruːl/ — Regel
way /weɪ/ — Weg, Art und Weise
classroom /ˈklɑːsˌruːm/ — Klassenzimmer

⚠ *at* school = *in* der Schule — *p. 36*

⚠ Achte auf die Betonung.

right ↔ wrong

You're **late**!

There is **only** one blue pencil in this pencil case.
Sorry I'm late.
George and Caroline **have** new friends.

This is a photo **of** Lisa. — *p. 37*

p. 38

Theme 2: At school

Word lists 2

A2 to **watch** /wɒtʃ/ — beobachten, zuschauen, anschauen — Let's **watch** a film!

canteen /kæn'ti:n/ — Kantine, Mensa
club /klʌb/ — Klub, Verein, *hier:* Arbeitsgemeinschaft — There's a film **club** at our school.
different /'dɪfrənt/ — anders, andere(r, s), verschieden
no /nəʊ/ — kein/e — There is **no** computer in this classroom.
A3 to **look at** /'lʊk ət/ — (sich) ansehen, anschauen — **Look at** the picture.

Pick-up: School things

 **school bag, schoolbag** /'sku:l ˌbæg/

 **pencil case** /'pensl ˌkeɪs/

 pencil /'pensl/

 **pen** /pen/

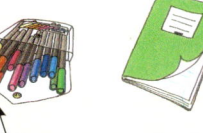 **felt tip** /'felt ˌtɪp/

 **exercise book** /'eksəsaɪz bʊk/

 **folder** /'fəʊldə/

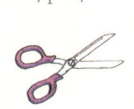 **pencil sharpener** /'pensl ˌʃɑ:p(ə)nə/

rubber /'rʌbə/

 **scissors** *(pl)* /'sɪzəz/

 **glue** /glu:/

ruler /'ru:lə/

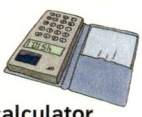 **calculator** /'kælkjʊˌleɪtə/

Viele nützliche Wörter zum Thema Schule findest du auch auf der *Wordbank School*, S. 198.
Tipps zum Wörterlernen findest du auf der *Skills page Memorizing vocabulary*, S. 175.

(only pl) bedeutet, dass dieses Wort nur oder gewöhnlich im Plural verwendet wird.

p. 39

A4 **rude** /ru:d/ — unhöflich
friendly /'frendli/ — freundlich
strict /strɪkt/ — streng, strikt, genau
quiet /'kwaɪət/ — leise, ruhig — Shh! Be **quiet**.
to **start** /stɑ:t/ — anfangen
to **open** /'əʊpən/ — öffnen, *hier:* aufschlagen — **Open** your books at page 39.
° to **knock** /nɒk/ — klopfen, stoßen
teacher /'ti:tʃə/ — Lehrer/in — **teacher**
Sorry I'm late. /ˌsɒri ˌaɪm 'leɪt/ — Entschuldigung, dass ich zu spät komme.
° Tell us about yourself. — Erzähl uns etwas über dich.
don't (= do not) /dəʊnt, du: 'nɒt/ — nicht tun, nicht machen
to **talk** (**about/to**) /'tɔ:k ə,baʊt, tə/ — sprechen, reden (über/mit) — Don't **talk in class**!
in class /ɪn 'klɑ:s/ — im Unterricht — Don't **talk in class**!
° Please go on. /ˌpli:z ˌgəʊ 'ɒn/ — Mach(t) bitte weiter.
° **loser** /'lu:zə/ — Verlierer/in
to **sit down** /ˌsɪt 'daʊn/ — sich (hin)setzen
° to **put on** /ˌpʊt 'ɒn/ — anziehen
A5 **floor** /flɔ:/ — Boden
more /mɔ:/ — (noch) mehr, weitere(r, s)
A6 to **find** /faɪnd/ — finden

p. 40

to **clean** /kli:n/ — sauber machen, reinigen, putzen — **Clean** the board, please!
board /bɔ:d/ — Brett, Tafel — The teacher writes on the **board**.
to **do** /du:/ — machen, tun — Don't do your **homework** in class.
homework *(no pl)* /'həʊmˌwɜ:k/ — Hausaufgabe(n)
lesson /'les(ə)n/ — (Unterrichts)stunde — Our first **lesson** is English.
A8 **time** /taɪm/ — Zeit, Uhrzeit — It's **time** for lunch.

2 Word lists — Theme 2: At school

I'm not sure (about that). /aɪm ˌnɒt ˈʃɔː/	Ich bin mir (dieser Sache) nicht sicher., Ich weiß nicht genau.	
idea /aɪˈdɪə/	Idee, Einfall	That's a great **idea**! Frz. *une idée*
next /nekst/	nächste(r, s)	What's our **next** lesson?
° outside /ˌaʊtˈsaɪd/	(dr)außen; außerhalb; *hier:* nach draußen	
quite /kwaɪt/	ziemlich, ganz	
sure /ʃɔː/	sicher	17 + 19 = 35. – Are you **sure**?
to fall down /ˌfɔːl ˈdaʊn/	hin(unter)fallen, (ein)stürzen	
Thanks! *(informal)* / Thank you. /θæŋks, ˈθæŋk ju/	Danke!	You can have my pen. – **Thank you**.
to help /help/	helfen	Can I **help**?
the same /ðə ˈseɪm/	der-/die-/dasselbe, der/die/das Gleiche	

diary /ˈdaɪəri/	Tagebuch, (Termin)kalender	
music /ˈmjuːzɪk/	Musik(unterricht)	
° I'm sorry for earlier.	Es tut mir leid wegen vorhin.	
to have lunch /ˌhæv ˈlʌntʃ/	zu Mittag essen	It is one o'clock. Let's **have lunch**!
to meet /miːt/	(sich) treffen	I **meet** my friends at school.
after /ˈɑːftə/	nach	
real /rɪəl/	wirklich, echt	
both /bəʊθ/	beide(s)	
A11 French /frentʃ/	Französisch(-); französisch	p. 41
to make /meɪk/	machen, erstellen	Can you **make** pizza?
A12 to think /θɪŋk/	denken, glauben, meinen	I **think** that's great!
° stupid /ˈstjuːpɪd/	dumm, blöd	
I don't think so. /aɪ ˌdəʊnt ˈθɪŋk səʊ/	Das glaube ich nicht.	
pet /pet/	Haustier	George's **pet** Patch is a dog.
B1 IT room /ˌaɪ ˈtiː ruːm/	Computerraum	p. 44
art /ɑːt/	Kunst(unterricht)	
assembly hall /əˈsembli hɔːl/	(Versammlungs)saal, Aula	
library /ˈlaɪbrəri/	Bibliothek, Bücherei	**library**
science /ˈsaɪəns/	(Natur)wissenschaft	
number /ˈnʌmbə/	Zahl, Ziffer, Nummer	1, 4, 7, 10 are **numbers**.

B2 Subjects /ˈsʌbdʒɪkts/

art /ɑːt/	Kunst(unterricht)	music /ˈmjuːzɪk/	Musik		
drama *(no pl)* /ˈdrɑːmə/	Schauspielerei, Drama, Theater(-)	science /ˈsaɪəns/	(Natur)wissenschaft		
		Spanish /ˈspænɪʃ/	Spanisch		
English /ˈɪŋglɪʃ/	Englisch	technology /tekˈnɒlədʒi/	Technologie, Technik		
French /frentʃ/	Französisch	RE (= religious education) /ˌɑːrˌiː, rəˌlɪdʒəsˌedjʊˈkeɪʃ(ə)n/	Religionslehre		
geography /dʒiˈɒgrəfi/	Erdkunde, Geografie				
history /ˈhɪst(ə)ri/	Geschichte	PE (= physical education) /ˌpiːˈiː/	Sport(unterricht)		
maths *(informal, only pl)* /mæθs/	Mathe				

face /feɪs/	Gesicht	
seat /siːt/	(Sitz)platz	
lunchbox /ˈlʌntʃˌbɒks/	Lunchbox, Brot(zeit)dose	
to have got /ˌhæv ˈgɒt/	haben	I**'ve got** a red T-shirt. He**'s got** a green T-shirt.
to call /kɔːl/	(an)rufen, nennen	
grumpy /ˈgrʌmpi/	mürrisch, schlecht gelaunt	
first /fɜːst/	zuerst, als Erstes	

Theme 2: At school

Word lists 2

timetable /ˈtaɪmˌteɪb(ə)l/	Stundenplan	
today /təˈdeɪ/	heute	It's Saturday **today**. No school!
before /bɪˈfɔː/	vor	
morning /ˈmɔːnɪŋ/	Morgen, Vormittag	Good **morning**!
break /breɪk/	Pause	
Sir /sɜː/	(Mein) Herr, *hier:* Herr Lehrer!	
some /sʌm/	einige, etwas	
in the afternoon /ɪn ði ˌɑːftəˈnuːn/	am Nachmittag	⚠ **in** the afternoon = **am** Nachmittag
B4 when /wen/	wann	*p. 45*
B5 what /wɒt/	welche(r, s)	**What** school subjects do you know?
puzzle /ˈpʌz(ə)l/	Rätsel, Fragespiel	
to understand /ˌʌndəˈstænd/	verstehen	I don't **understand** the word 'weird'. –
weird /wɪəd/	merkwürdig, seltsam, komisch	It's 'seltsam' in German.
crown /kraʊn/	Krone	
flag /flæɡ/	Fahne, Flagge	
to let /let/	lassen	
to try /traɪ/	versuchen, (aus)probieren	A puzzle? **Let** me **try**.

Pick-up: Days of the week

Monday	Tuesday	Wednesday	Thursday	Friday	Saturday	Sunday
/ˈmʌndeɪ/	/ˈtjuːzdeɪ/	/ˈwenzdeɪ/	/ˈθɜːzdeɪ/	/ˈfraɪdeɪ/	/ˈsætədeɪ/	/ˈsʌndeɪ/

to sit /sɪt/	sitzen	
B7 pupil /ˈpjuːp(ə)l/	Schüler/in	**pupil** *p. 46*
B8 menu /ˈmenjuː/	Speisekarte	What's on the **menu**?
meal /miːl/	Mahlzeit, Essen	
in German /ɪn ˈdʒɜːmən/	auf Deutsch	⚠ **in** German = **auf** Deutsch
salad /ˈsæləd/	Salat	
other /ˈʌðə/	andere(r, s)	
language /ˈlæŋɡwɪdʒ/	Sprache	Frz. *la langue*
main course /ˈmeɪn kɔːs/	Hauptgericht, Hauptgang	
vegetarian /ˌvedʒəˈteərɪən/	Vegetarier/in; vegetarisch	
dessert /dɪˈzɜːt/	Nachtisch	⚠ Achte auf die Aussprache.
fresh /freʃ/	neu, ungebraucht, frisch	
fruit (*pl* **fruit** or **fruits**) /fruːt, fruːts/	Frucht, Obst	Apples and bananas are **fruit**. Frz. *le fruit*
chicken /ˈtʃɪkɪn/	Huhn, Hähnchen, Hühnchen	
rice (*no pl*) /raɪs/	Reis	
cheese /tʃiːz/	Käse	**cheese**
tomato (*pl* **tomatoes**) /təˈmɑːtəʊ, təˈmɑːtəʊz/	Tomate	

Unregelmäßige Pluralformen

Einige englische Wörter haben einen unregelmäßigen Plural, zum Beispiel

child - children	scarf - scarves
mouse - mice	tomato - tomatoes

apple /ˈæp(ə)l/	Apfel	
sauce /sɔːs/	Soße, Sauce	
banana /bəˈnɑːnə/	Banane(n-)	
lamb /læm/	Lamm(fleisch)	
potato (*pl* **potatoes**) /pəˈteɪtəʊ, pəˈteɪtəʊz/	Kartoffel	**potato**
chips (*pl*) /tʃɪps/	Pommes frites	⚠ **chips** bedeutet auf Deutsch *Pommes frites*. Das deutsche Wort *Chips* heißt auf Englisch *crisps*.
fish and chips (*no pl*) /ˌfɪʃ ən ˈtʃɪps/	frittierter Fisch mit Pommes frites	
food /fuːd/	Essen, Nahrung, Futter	⚠ Achte auf die Aussprache: /fuːd/
B10 nice /naɪs/	schön, angenehm; nett, freundlich, *hier:* gut	*p. 47*

2 Word lists

Theme 3: Hobbies and activities

healthy /ˈhelθi/	gesund	Pizza is not very **healthy**.
B12 **short** /ʃɔːt/	kurz	
these (= *pl of* this) /ðiːz/	diese	

Say it in English – Theme 2

So kannst du …

dich entschuldigen	Sorry. / I'm (so) sorry.
dich für deine Verspätung entschuldigen	Sorry I'm late.
sagen, wie sich jemand verhält	She is funny/friendly/strict. He is rude/nice.
sagen, wie sich jemand fühlt	He is worried. She is excited.
jemanden auffordern, etwas zu tun	Clean the board, please.
jemanden auffordern, etwas nicht zu tun	Don't talk in class.
sagen, dass du dir nicht sicher bist	I'm not sure. Well, I'm not sure about that.
deine Hilfe anbieten	Can I help?
fragen, was jemand tun kann	Can you play basketball?
sagen, was du tun kannst	I can dance.
einen Vorschlag machen	Let's meet after school and play *FootballWorld*.
sagen, dass du etwas toll findest	Great! / Manchester is great.
sagen, wie du eine Regel findest	I think this rule is OK/boring/stupid. I like this rule because … I don't like this rule because …
sagen, dass du anderer Meinung bist	I don't think so.
über den Stundenplan sprechen	We have got English in the first lesson. On Friday morning we've got French.
sagen, was jemand hat/besitzt	Caroline has got a cat. I have got a dog. We have got a pony.
sagen, was dein Lieblingsessen ist	My favourite food is …
sagen, dass du etwas lecker findest	… is nice. / I like … / I love …
sagen, dass ein Gericht nicht gesund ist	… is not very healthy.

Theme 3: Hobbies and activities

1 **free time** /ˌfriː ˈtaɪm/	Freizeit	What do you do in your **free time**?	*p. 54*
piano /piˈænəʊ/	Klavier, Piano	I play the **piano**.	
activity /ækˈtɪvəti/	Aktivität, Tätigkeit		
3 to **tell** /tel/	erzählen, sagen		
4 **What's the time?** /ˌwɒts ðə ˈtaɪm/	Wie spät/Wie viel Uhr ist es?		
clock /klɒk/	Uhr		
5 **half past (seven)** /ˌhɑːf pɑːst ˈsev(ə)n/	halb (acht)		

 half past seven

Word lists 3

Theme 3: Hobbies and activities

The time

one **o'clock** | **five past** (one) | **quarter past** (one) | **twenty past** (one) | **half past** (one) | **twenty to** (two) | **quarter to** (two) | **ten to** (two)

At one o'clock /ˌwʌn_əˈklɒk/, I meet my friends. – Um ein Uhr treffe ich meine Freunde.

Im Englischen verwendet man **am** /ˌeɪˈem/ und **pm** /ˌpiːˈem/, um zu sagen, ob es sich um eine Zeit vor oder nach 12 Uhr mittags handelt:
7 am = 7 Uhr (morgens), 7 pm = 19 Uhr.

hour /ˈaʊə/	Stunde	One **hour** has 60 minutes.
later /ˈleɪtə/	später	
dance /dɑːns/	Tanz	
class /klɑːs/	(Schul)klasse; *hier:* Unterricht, Kurs	I go to yoga **class** every Sunday.
charity /ˈtʃærəti/	Barmherzigkeit, Wohltätigkeitsorganisation; *hier:* für einen guten Zweck	
bake-off /ˈbeɪkɒf/	Backwettbewerb	
gym (= gymnastics, *pl***)** /dʒɪm, dʒɪmˈnæstɪks/	Turnen	
minute /ˈmɪnɪt/	Minute	
6 **biscuit** /ˈbɪskɪt/	Keks, Biskuit	My grandma eats **biscuits** with her tea. p. 55
prize /praɪz/	(Sieg)preis, Gewinn	The winner gets a **prize**.
money *(no pl)* /ˈmʌni/	Geld	
German /ˈdʒɜːmən/	Deutsche/r, deutsch	What's 'tomorrow' in **German**?
for example /fərˌɪɡˈzɑːmp(ə)l/	zum Beispiel	
to win /wɪn/	gewinnen	Who **wins** the prize money?
A1 What a mess! /ˌwɒt_əˈmes/	Was für ein Durcheinander! p. 56	
cake /keɪk/	Kuchen	Zoe likes chocolate **cake** for her birthday.
special /ˈspeʃ(ə)l/	besondere(r, s)	Do you have a **special** talent? Frz. *spécial*
recipe /ˈresəpi/	Rezept	Can you give me the **recipe** for your banana cake?
A2 **into** /ˈɪntuː/	in	Go **into** the kitchen and get your lunch.
to want /wɒnt/	wünschen, wollen	Jack **wants** to play football in the afternoon.
difficult /ˈdɪfɪk(ə)lt/	schwierig, schwer	342 x 127? That's **difficult**.
tomorrow /təˈmɒrəʊ/	morgen	Today it is Monday. **Tomorrow** it is Tuesday.
horrible /ˈhɒrəb(ə)l/	schrecklich	My brother's cake tastes horrible. Frz. *horrible*
bad /bæd/	schlecht, schlimm, böse	**good** ↔ **bad**
must /mʌst/	müssen	You **must** read this book!
to give /ɡɪv/	geben	I can **give** you a pen.
baker /ˈbeɪkə/	Bäcker/in	
to sound /saʊnd/	klingen	
a lot (of) /əˈlɒt_əv/	viel(e), eine Menge	
this /ðɪs/	diese(r, s), das	Can we meet **this** afternoon?
everyone /ˈevriˌwʌn/	jede/r	Almost **everyone** likes chocolate.
all /ɔːl/	alle(s)	Jo, Tim, Leo – they **all** want to win.
Good luck! /ˌɡʊdˈlʌk/	Viel Glück!	
No way! *(informal)* /ˌnəʊˈweɪ/	Ausgeschlossen!	

3 Word lists

Theme 3: Hobbies and activities

job /dʒɒb/	Stelle, Job, Arbeit	
true /truː/	wahr	4 + 4 = 8. – That's **true**.

Jobs around the house

to **load/empty the dishwasher** /ləʊd, ˌempti ðə ˈdɪʃˌwɒʃə/	die Geschirrspülmaschine einräumen/ausräumen	
to **lay the table** /ˌleɪ ðə ˈteɪb(ə)l/	den Tisch decken	
to **tidy (up)** /ˌtaɪdi ˈʌp/	aufräumen	
to **take out the rubbish** /ˌteɪk ˌaʊt ðə ˈrʌbɪʃ/	den Müll hinausbringen	
to **hoover** /ˈhuːvə/	staubsaugen	
to **walk the dog** /ˌwɔːk ðə ˈdɒɡ/	den Hund ausführen	

to **empty** /ˈempti/	(ent)leeren; *hier:* ausräumen	Can you **empty** the dishwasher? – OK. You can **load** it then.
to **load** /ləʊd/	(auf)laden; *hier:* einräumen	
always /ˈɔːlweɪz/	immer	*Always, usually, often, sometimes* und *never* sind Häufigkeitsadverbien.
never /ˈnevə/	nie(mals)	
often /ˈɒf(ə)n/	oft	❗ Achte auf die Wortstellung:
sometimes /ˈsʌmtaɪmz/	manchmal	Jo **sometimes plays** basketball.
usually /ˈjuːʒəli/	gewöhnlich, normalerweise	Jo **spielt manchmal** Basketball.
A7 **supermarket** /ˈsuːpəˌmɑːkɪt/	Supermarkt	*p. 58*
when /wen/	als	
to **buy** /baɪ/	kaufen	
delicious /dɪˈlɪʃəs/	köstlich, lecker	Frz. *délicieux*
decoration /ˌdekəˈreɪʃ(ə)n/	Dekoration, Verzierung	
to **decorate** /ˈdekəreɪt/	dekorieren, verzieren	
to **need** /niːd/	müssen, brauchen	
to **bake** /ˈbeɪk/	backen	Let's **bake** a cake!
every /ˈevri/	jede(r, s)	
A9 to **eat** /iːt/	essen, fressen	My cat **eats** cat food.
night /naɪt/	Nacht, Abend	
to **watch TV** /ˌwɒtʃ ˌtiː ˈviː/	fernsehen	She **is watching TV**.
A10 **perfect** /ˈpɜːfɪkt/	perfekt	*p. 59*
story /ˈstɔːri/	Geschichte, Erzählung	Lizzy likes the **story** of Robin Hood.
back /bæk/	(wieder) zurück	George is **back** from the supermarket.
message /ˈmesɪdʒ/	Nachricht, Botschaft	
help *(no pl)* /help/	Hilfe	
to **smile (at)** /ˈsmaɪl ət/	(an)lächeln	She **smiles at** her friend.
to **taste** /teɪst/	schmecken	Lisa's biscuits **taste** great.
nothing /ˈnʌθɪŋ/	nichts	George smiles but says **nothing**.
to **begin** /bɪˈɡɪn/	anfangen, beginnen	
suddenly /ˈsʌd(ə)nli/	plötzlich	
° **doorbell** /ˈdɔːbel/	Türklingel	
° to **ring (up)** /ˌrɪŋ ˈʌp/	anrufen, klingeln, läuten	
to **shout (at)** /ˈʃaʊt ət/	(an)schreien	Don't **shout at** your teacher!
to **hide** /haɪd/	(sich) verstecken	
to **explain (sth to sb)** /ɪkˈspleɪn/	(jdm etw) erklären	I don't understand. Can you **explain** the task, please?
surprised /səˈpraɪzd/	überrascht, erstaunt	Caroline is **surprised** when she sees George's muffins.
to **happen** /ˈhæpən/	geschehen, passieren	What **happens** next?
B1 **talent show** /ˈtælənt ʃəʊ/	Castingshow, Talentwettbewerb	*p. 62*
audition /ɔːˈdɪʃ(ə)n/	Vorsprechen, Vorsingen, Vorspielen	
winner /ˈwɪnə/	Gewinner/in, Sieger/in	

Word lists 3

Theme 3: Hobbies and activities

English	German	Example
to **take part (in)** /ˌteɪk ˈpɑːt_ɪn/	teilnehmen (an), mitmachen (bei)	Our school **takes part in** a lot of competitions.
competition /ˌkɒmpəˈtɪʃ(ə)n/	Wettbewerb	
B2 to **describe** /dɪˈskraɪb/	beschreiben	
of course /əv ˈkɔːs/	natürlich	Can you help me, please?
much /mʌtʃ/	viel	
anything /ˈeniθɪŋ/	(irgend)etwas, (irgend)was	
reading (no pl) /ˈriːdɪŋ/	Lesen	She likes **reading**.
dancing (no pl) /ˈdɑːnsɪŋ/	Tanzen	
to **dance** /dɑːns/	tanzen	Come and **dance** with me. The music is great!
Come on! (informal) /ˌkʌm ˈɒn/	Komm(t) jetzt!, Mach(t) schon!	**Come on!** We're late!
to **wear** /weə/	tragen, anhaben	He **wears** a blue T-shirt.
beautiful /ˈbjuːtəf(ə)l/	schön	What a **beautiful** day!
costume /ˈkɒstjuːm/	Kostüm	
° **than** /ðæn/	als	
° **circus** /ˈsɜːkəs/	Zirkus	
just /dʒʌst/	nur, bloß, einfach	
pretty /ˈprɪti/	hübsch, nett	I like your costume. It's very **pretty**.
dance routine /ˈdɑːns ruːˌtiːn/	Tanznummer	
if /ɪf/	wenn, falls, ob	
nervous /ˈnɜːvəs/	nervös	We have a test in class today. I am very **nervous**.
stage /steɪdʒ/	Bühne	
angry /ˈæŋgri/	verärgert, zornig, wütend	She is **angry** with him.
to **agree** /əˈgriː/	zustimmen	
to **disagree** /ˌdɪsəˈgriː/	nicht übereinstimmen, nicht einverstanden sein	
suggestion /səˈdʒestʃ(ə)n/	Vorschlag	
B4 to **take place** /ˌteɪk ˈpleɪs/	stattfinden	
at /æt/	auf, an, in, bei, *hier:* um	❗ **at** 4 o'clock = **um** 4 Uhr
act /ækt/	(Show)nummer, Akt	We have a dance **act** for the show.
B5 to **imagine** /ɪˈmædʒɪn/	sich vorstellen	Frz. *imaginer*
B6 disappointed /ˌdɪsəˈpɔɪntɪd/	enttäuscht	Zoe can't come to my party. I'm very **disappointed**.
glad /glæd/	glücklich, dankbar, froh	We are friends. I'm so **glad**!
B8 reason /ˈriːz(ə)n/	Grund	Choose the best title and give **reasons**.
exciting /ɪkˈsaɪtɪŋ/	aufregend, spannend	The film is very **exciting**!
evening /ˈiːvnɪŋ/	Abend	**evening** ↔ **morning**
to **surprise** /səˈpraɪz/	überraschen	Charlie **surprises** his friends.
brilliant (informal) /ˈbrɪljənt/	brillant, strahlend; *hier:* toll, klasse	Tom is a **brilliant** singer.
to **clap** /klæp/	klatschen	
to **support** /səˈpɔːt/	(unter)stützen	Pia always **supports** her friends.

her /hɜː/
1. Lisa always helps. You can ask **her**.
   (Lisa hilft immer. Du kannst **sie** fragen.)
2. Can you give **her** a pen?
   (Kannst du **ihr** einen Stift geben?)

him /hɪm/
1. John never helps. Don't ask **him**.
   (John hilft nie. Frag **ihn** nicht.)
2. Can you give **him** your book?
   (Kannst du **ihm** dein Buch geben?)

to **laugh (at sb/sth)** /ˈlɑːf_ət/	lachen (über jdn/etw)	Gillian **laughs at** the clowns act.
too /tuː/	zu	Can your brother read? – No, he's **too** young.
to **hear** /hɪə/	hören	Don't shout. I can **hear** you.

3 Word lists

Theme 3: Hobbies and activities

unfortunately /ʌnˈfɔːtʃ(ə)nətli/	unglücklicherweise, leider	**Unfortunately**, I can't help.
text (= text message) /tekst, ˈtekst ˌmesɪdʒ/	Textnachricht, SMS	Where is Laura? Can you send her a **text** to ask?
strange /streɪndʒ/	sonderbar, merkwürdig, fremd, unheimlich	Charlie is a bit **strange** at the moment.
at the moment /ət ðə ˈməʊmənt/	im Augenblick, momentan	❗ **at** the moment = **im** Augenblick
audience /ˈɔːdiəns/	Publikum, Besucher, Zuschauer	The **audience** enjoys the show.
long /lɒŋ/	lang	The film goes on for hours. It is very **long**. 
guitar /ɡɪˈtɑː/	Gitarre	
player /ˈpleɪə/	Spieler/in	
to finish /ˈfɪnɪʃ/	(be)enden, aufhören	
to stand up /ˌstænd ˈʌp/	aufstehen	to **stand up** ↔ to **sit down**
on stage /ɒn ˈsteɪdʒ/	auf der/die Bühne	
dancer /ˈdɑːnsə/	Tänzer/in	Sarah is a good **dancer**, she can really **move**.
to move /muːv/	(sich) bewegen	
group /ɡruːp/	Gruppe	
to cheer /tʃɪə/	jubeln	
to take a bow /ˌteɪk ə ˈbaʊ/	sich (unter Applaus) verbeugen	
to find out /ˌfaɪnd ˈaʊt/	herausfinden	How old can birds get? – Let's **find out**.
to decide /dɪˈsaɪd/	entscheiden, bestimmen	
line /laɪn/	Linie, Zeile	In **line** 20 of the story it says ...
B9 **to feel** /fiːl/	(sich) fühlen	
to practise /ˈpræktɪs/	üben	Rajiv wants to be a very good guitar player. He **practises** a lot.
another /əˈnʌðə/	noch eine(r); ein(e) andere(r)	

p. 65

Say it in English – Theme 3

So kannst du ...

nach der Uhrzeit fragen	What's the time?
die Uhrzeit sagen	It's two o'clock. / It's half past seven. / It's ten to four.
sagen, wann etwas stattfindet	The audition takes place at 4 pm.
über (regelmäßige) Termine sprechen	I have got a dance class at half past four on Tuesday. I have got football training at quarter past four on Wednesday.
sagen, was du immer/nie tust	I always/never make my bed.
sagen, was du oft/manchmal tust	I often/sometimes take out the rubbish.
Vorschläge machen	Why don't you take part in a talent show? Let's meet at my house on Saturday afternoon. What do you think?
einem Vorschlag zustimmen	Of course! That's a great idea!
einen Vorschlag entschieden ablehnen (z. B. gegenüber Freunden)	No way!
sagen, dass jemand traurig/besorgt ist	He feels sad/worried.
sagen, dass jemand froh/glücklich ist	She is glad/happy.
sagen, dass jemand enttäuscht ist	He is disappointed.
sagen, dass jemand wütend ist	She is angry.
sagen, dass jemand aufgeregt ist	He is excited.

Word lists 4

Theme 4: Birthdays

1
English	German	Example
birthday /ˈbɜːθdeɪ/	Geburtstag(s-)	I like **birthday** parties. *p. 72*
calendar /ˈkælɪndə/	Kalender	
to **sing** /sɪŋ/	singen	They **are singing**.
month /mʌnθ/	Monat	

Pick-up: The year

January /ˈdʒænjuəri/	Januar
February /ˈfebruəri/	Februar
March /mɑːtʃ/	März
April /ˈeɪprəl/	April
May /meɪ/	Mai
June /dʒuːn/	Juni
July /dʒʊˈlaɪ/	Juli
August /ˈɔːɡəst/	August
September /sepˈtembə/	September
October /ɒkˈtəʊbə/	Oktober
November /nəʊˈvembə/	November
December /dɪˈsembə/	Dezember

Für **2nd May** kannst du **the second of May** oder auch **May the second** sagen.

on 23rd May – am 23. Mai
in September – im September

2 **date** /deɪt/ — Datum — Frz. *la date*

1st (= **first**), **2nd** (= **second**), **3rd** (= **third**), … – diese Zahlen nennt man Ordinalzahlen. Auf Seite 266 findest du eine Liste mit Ordinalzahlen.

first /fɜːst/	erste(r, s)	**fourth** /fɔːθ/	vierte(r, s)
second /ˈsekənd/	zweite(r, s)	**fifth** /fɪfθ/	fünfte(r, s)
third /θɜːd/	dritte(r, s)		

3
Pick-up: Seasons

(in) spring /sprɪŋ/	(im) Frühling
(in) summer /ˈsʌmə/	(im) Sommer
(in) autumn /ˈɔːtəm/	(im) Herbst
(in) winter /ˈwɪntə/	(im) Winter

My birthday is **in summer**. It's on 28th August.

4
English	German	Example
something /ˈsʌmθɪŋ/	etwas	Let's have **something** to eat. – What about pizza?
riding *(no pl)* /ˈraɪdɪŋ/	Reiten	
to **celebrate** /ˈseləˌbreɪt/	feiern	Let's **celebrate** your birthday with a party.
to **ride** /raɪd/	fahren (mit), reiten	
to **enjoy** /ɪnˈdʒɔɪ/	genießen	
horse /hɔːs/	Pferd	
to **offer** /ˈɒfə/	(an)bieten	Frz. *offrir*
each /iːtʃ/	jede(r, s)	
per /pɜː/	pro	
kayaking *(no pl)* /ˈkaɪækɪŋ/	Kajakfahren	
to **take** /teɪk/	(mit)nehmen	I **take** a lot of books to school.
lots of *(informal)* /ˈlɒts_əv/	viel(e), eine Menge	I love books. I've got **lots of** books.
up to /ˈʌp tʊ/	bis (zu)	
balloon /bəˈluːn/	(Luft)ballon	
paper chain /ˌpeɪpə ˈtʃeɪn/	Papierkette	
to **bring** /brɪŋ/	(mit)bringen	Can I **bring** my friends to your party?

4 Word lists

Theme 4: Birthdays

own /əʊn/	eigene(r, s)	
ice /aɪs/	Eis	
wonderful /ˈwʌndəf(ə)l/	wunderbar, wundervoll	
to include /ɪnˈkluːd/	beinhalten, mit einschließen, aufnehmen	
ice skating *(no pl)* /ˈaɪsˌskeɪtɪŋ/	Schlittschuhlaufen, Eislaufen	
price /praɪs/	Preis	The **price** of the book is £4.99.
free /friː/	frei, gratis	The price is £8.50. Children are **free**.
guest /gest/	Gast	
lemonade /ˌleməˈneɪd/	Limonade	
fish finger /ˌfɪʃ ˈfɪŋgə/	Fischstäbchen	
juice /dʒuːs/	Saft	Do you like orange **juice**?
° buffet /ˈbʊfeɪ/	Büfett	
paper plate /ˌpeɪpə ˈpleɪt/	Pappteller	
indoor /ˈɪndɔː/	Innen-, Haus-, Indoor-	
fireworks *(pl)* /ˈfaɪəˌwɜːks/	Feuerwerk	
present /ˈprez(ə)nt/	Geschenk	
drink /drɪŋk/	Getränk, Trinken	
5 fancy dress party /ˌfænsi ˈdres ˌpɑːti/	Kostümfest	What costume do you wear to the **fancy dress party**? *p. 73*
6 dream /driːm/	Traum(-)	
also /ˈɔːlsəʊ/	auch	
A1 to train /treɪn/	trainieren	*p. 74*
gym /dʒɪm/	Turnhalle, *hier:* Fitnesscenter	
to stay /steɪ/	bleiben	
to plan /plæn/	planen	
right now /ˌraɪt ˈnaʊ/	jetzt (gerade), sofort, gleich	
on TV /ˌɒn ˌtiː ˈviː/	im Fernsehen	They watch football **on TV**.
against /əˈgenst/	gegen	Arsenal is playing **against** Manchester United.
to **sleep** /sliːp/	schlafen	It is 9 pm. Time to **sleep**.
invitation /ˌɪnvɪˈteɪʃ(ə)n/	Einladung(s-)	Zoe has got an **invitation** to go to Karla's party.
card /kɑːd/	Karte	
to **ring (up)** /ˌrɪŋ ˈʌp/	anrufen, klingeln, läuten	I always **ring** my grandma to talk to her on her birthday.
to **answer the phone** /ˌɑːnsə ðə ˈfəʊn/	ans Telefon gehen	Can you **answer the phone**, please?
everything /ˈevriθɪŋ/	alles	
home /həʊm/	zu Hause, *hier:* nach Hause	Half past three … time to go **home** from school!
just /dʒʌst/	nur, bloß, einfach, *hier:* gerade	I'm **just** doing my homework.
to **have** /hæv/	haben, *hier:* trinken, zu sich nehmen	We always **have** cake on my birthday.
coffee /ˈkɒfi/	Kaffee	
See you soon! *(informal)* /ˌsiː jʊ ˈsuːn/	Bis bald!	Bye! See you soon!
lazy /ˈleɪzi/	faul, träge	My brother is **lazy**. He sleeps all day.
liar /ˈlaɪə/	Lügner/in	
TV (= television) /ˌtiː ˈviː, ˈteliˌvɪʒn/	Fernsehen, Fernseher	
to be over /ˌbiː ˈəʊvə/	vorbei sein	
A3 somebody /ˈsʌmbədi/	(irgend)jemand, irgendwer	Do you know **somebody** from London? *p. 75*
A4 to **wash** /wɒʃ/	(sich) waschen	**Wash** your hands before you eat, please.

Theme 4: Birthdays

Word lists 4

A5 to **put** /pʊt/	setzen, legen, stellen	**Put** your books on the table, please.
A6 **at the weekend** /ət ðə ˌwiːkˈend/	am Wochenende	Can we meet **at the weekend**? p. 76
holiday /ˈhɒlədeɪ/	Urlaub, Ferien	Let's go to Paris on **holiday**!
A7 **phone call** (= **telephone call**) /ˈfəʊn kɔːl, ˈtelɪˌfəʊn kɔːl/	Anruf, Telefongespräch	

to **look for** /ˈlʊk fɔː/	suchen nach	Tia is **looking for** her phone.
° to **imitate** /ˈɪmɪteɪt/	imitieren, nachahmen	
it's (= **it is**) /ɪts, ɪt‿ɪz/	es ist, *hier:* hier spricht	
so /səʊ/	also, deshalb	
to **come along** /ˌkʌm əˈlɒŋ/	mitgehen, (mit)kommen	
by the way /ˌbaɪ ðə ˈweɪ/	übrigens	
to **text (sb)** /tekst/	(jdm) eine Textnachricht/SMS senden	Where is Sarah? – I don't know. Why don't you **text** her?
to **be fun** /ˌbiː ˈfʌn/	Spaß machen	Reading is **fun**!
Just a minute. *(informal)* /ˌdʒʌst ə ˈmɪnɪt/	Einen Moment noch. / Moment mal.	
to **shop** /ʃɒp/	einkaufen	Jo **is shopping**. He wants to buy new shoes.
fine /faɪn/	in Ordnung, gut	
See you (later). *(informal)* /ˌsiː jʊ ˈleɪtə/	Bis später. / Bis nachher.	
Bye for now. *(informal)* /ˈbaɪ fə naʊ/	Bis bald.	
phrase /freɪz/	Satz, Ausdruck	
to **end** /end/	beenden, zu Ende bringen, enden	to begin ↔ to **end**
to **react (to sb/sth)** /riˈækt tə/	(auf jdn/etw) reagieren	
A8 **box** /bɒks/	Kiste, Schachtel, *hier:* Kästchen	p. 77
to **score (a goal)** /ˌskɔːr ə ˈɡəʊl/	(ein Tor) schießen	Charlie **scores a goal**.
to **walk off** /ˌwɔːk ˈɒf/	weggehen (von), hinuntergehen (von)	

field /fiːld/	Wiese, Feld, *hier:* Spielfeld	
to **say sorry** /ˌseɪ ˈsɒri/	sich entschuldigen	
goal /ɡəʊl/	Ziel, Tor	
A10 to **collect** /kəˈlekt/	(ein)sammeln	
B1 to **close** /kləʊz/	schließen, zumachen	**Close** the door behind you. p. 80
bag /bæɡ/	Tasche	
earring /ˈɪərɪŋ/	Ohrring	
case /keɪs/	Koffer, *hier:* Hülle	Do you like pink phone **cases**?
shop assistant /ˈʃɒp əˌsɪst(ə)nt/	Verkäufer/in	
Excuse me! /ɪkˈskjuːs mi/	Entschuldigen Sie bitte!, Entschuldigung!	
How much is/are ...? /ˈhaʊ mʌtʃ ɪz/ə/	Was kostet/kosten ...?	**How much** is the orange juice? **It's** £1.19.
it's (= **it is**) /ɪts, ˈɪt‿ɪz/	es ist, *hier:* es kostet	
expensive /ɪkˈspensɪv/	teuer	The T-shirt is £35. That's **expensive**!
any /ˈeni/	(irgend)ein(e), jede(r, s)	

some, any

Auf Deutsch bedeuten **some** und **any** so viel wie „etwas", „einige" oder „ein paar".
Sie werden aber oft nicht übersetzt (siehe G18 auf Seite 194):

There are **some** apples on the table. – Auf dem Tisch sind (ein paar) Äpfel.
Have we got **any** eggs? – Haben wir Eier?

4 Word lists

Theme 4: Birthdays

How about ...? /ˈhaʊ_ə,baʊt/	Wie wäre es mit ...?	**How about** a fancy dress party for your birthday?
over there /ˌəʊvə ˈðeə/	dort drüben	
Let me check. *(informal)* /ˌlet mi ˈtʃek/	Lass(t) mich nachsehen.	
Here you are. /ˌhɪə juˈɑː/	Hier, bitte., Bitte schön.	
cheap /tʃiːp/	billig, preiswert	**cheap** ↔ **expensive**
even /ˈiːv(ə)n/	selbst, sogar	
left /left/	übrig	
not ... any /nɒt_ˈeni/	kein, keine(r, s)	They have**n't** got **any** cards in this shop.
B4 customer /ˈkʌstəmə/	Kunde/Kundin	shop assistant ↔ **customer** *p. 81*
B6 to guess /ges/	(er)raten	
hint /hɪnt/	Spur, Andeutung, Hinweis, Tipp	
trainer /ˈtreɪnə/	Trainer/in; Turnschuh	Charlotte's **trainers** are very old.
sock /sɒk/	Socke	
trousers *(pl)* /ˈtraʊzəz/	Hose	
jumper /ˈdʒʌmpə/	Pullover, Pulli	He is wearing a **jumper**.
coat /kəʊt/	Mantel	
doctor /ˈdɒktə/	Arzt/Ärztin	
glove /glʌv/	Handschuh	These are my new **gloves**.
° ghost /gəʊst/	Geist, Gespenst	
° helmet /ˈhelmɪt/	Helm	
last /lɑːst/	letzte(r, s)	
clothes *(pl)* /kləʊðz/	Kleider, Kleidung	
B7 stormtrooper /ˈstɔːmˌtruːpə/	Figur aus Star Wars *(Krieg der Sterne)*	*p. 82*
detective /dɪˈtektɪv/	Detektiv/in	
elf *(pl* elves*)* /elf, elvz/	Elf/e	
to take /teɪk/	(mit)nehmen, *hier:* machen	Tina **is taking** a picture. 
to roll one's eyes /ˌrəʊl wʌnz_ˈaɪz/	die Augen verdrehen	
vampire /ˈvæmpaɪə/	Vampir/in	
to be upset (about sth) /ˌbiˌʌpˈset_əˌbaʊt/	(über etw) traurig/aufgebracht sein	
jealous /ˈdʒeləs/	eifersüchtig, neidisch	
glass /glɑːs/	Glas	
hand /hænd/	Hand	They are putting their **hands** up. 
move /muːv/	Bewegung	
° to spill /spɪl/	verschütten	
over /ˈəʊvə/	über, *hier:* auf	
to scream /skriːm/	schreien, kreischen	
to ruin /ˈruːɪn/	zerstören, verderben, kaputtmachen	
not ... anymore /nɒt ˌeniˈmɔː/	nicht mehr	
outside /ˌaʊtˈsaɪd/	(dr)außen, außerhalb, *hier:* nach draußen	Let's go **outside** and play football! 
ladder /ˈlædə/	(Stufen)leiter	
next door /ˌnekstˈdɔː/	nebenan, benachbart	
light /laɪt/	Licht, Lichtquelle, Lampe	
to point (at) /ˈpɔɪnt_ət/	deuten/zeigen (auf)	
torch *(BE)* /tɔːtʃ/	Taschenlampe	
burglar /ˈbɜːglə/	Einbrecher/in	
through /θruː/	durch	
fun *(no pl)* /fʌn/	Spaß	

Theme 4: Birthdays

Word lists 4

the police *(no pl)* /ðə pəˈliːs/	die Polizei	
° This is … /ˈðɪs_ɪz/	Das ist …, *hier:* Hier ist/spricht …	
quick /kwɪk/	schnell	
to **wait (for)** /ˈweɪt fɔː/	warten (auf)	They **are waiting** for the bus.
to take away /ˌteɪk_əˈweɪ/	wegnehmen, mitnehmen	
to **run** /rʌn/	rennen, laufen	Arthur **is running**.
to whisper /ˈwɪspə/	flüstern	
heavy /ˈhevi/	schwer	
away /əˈweɪ/	weg	
to get away /ˌget_əˈweɪ/	fortkommen, flüchten	
What if …? /ˌwɒt_ɪf/	Was (wäre), wenn …?	
front door /ˌfrʌnt_ˈdɔː/	Vordertür, Haustür	
around /əˈraʊnd/	umher, um, rund um, um … herum	
bike *(informal)* /baɪk/	(Fahr)rad	Ruth is riding her **bike**.
man *(pl* **men**) /mæn, men/	Mann	**man**
to climb (up) /ˌklaɪm_ˈʌp/	(hinauf)steigen, klettern (auf), besteigen	
out of /ˈaʊt_əv/	aus	
B10 ° to let out /ˌlet_ˈaʊt/	herauslassen	*p. 83*
° air *(no pl)* /eə/	Luft	
° tyre /ˈtaɪə/	Reifen	
° to hang /hæŋ/	(auf)hängen	
° to jump /dʒʌmp/	springen	
° Hurry up! /ˌhʌri_ˈʌp/	Beeil dich!, Beeilt euch!	
° to catch /kætʃ/	(auf)fangen, einfangen, ergreifen	
° hero *(pl* heroes) /ˈhɪərəʊ, ˈhɪərəʊz/	Held/in	

Say it in English – Theme 4

So kannst du …

fragen, wann jemand Geburtstag hat	When is your birthday?
sagen, wann du Geburtstag hast	My birthday is on the 31st of January.
sagen, was jemand gerade tut	Caroline is writing a shopping list. George is watching TV.
fragen, was jemand gerade tut	Are you playing tennis?
dich am Telefon melden	Hi, George, it's …
einen Vorschlag machen	Why don't you come along?
einen Vorschlag annehmen	Sounds good. / Yes, that's fine.
eine Uhrzeit vorschlagen	What about 4:30?
dich (am Telefon) verabschieden	Bye for now. / See you later.
dich entschuldigen	I'm sorry.
nach dem Preis fragen	Excuse me, how much is the elephant bag, please?
einen Preis nennen	It's £19.99.
jemandem Hilfe anbieten	Can I help you?
sagen, dass ihr euch nur umschaut	We're just looking.
sagen, dass du etwas teuer findest	That's a bit expensive.
sagen, dass du etwas günstig findest	That's cheap.
sagen, dass du einen Preis angemessen findest	That's a good price.

5 Word lists

Theme 5: Pets and animals

Theme 5: Pets and animals

1 sound /saʊnd/ — Geräusch, Klang, Laut — p. 90
fish (pl fish or fishes) /fɪʃ, fɪʃ, fɪʃɪz/ — Fisch
cow /kaʊ/ — Kuh

Auf der *Wordbank Animals* (Seite 204) findest du viele Tiernamen in einem Bildwörterbuch.

pig /pɪg/ — Schwein — **Pigs** are usually pink.
sheep (pl sheep) /ʃiːp/ — Schaf — **Sheep** live on a farm.
lion /ˈlaɪən/ — Löwe
duck /dʌk/ — Ente
budgie (= budgerigar) *(informal)* /ˈbʌdʒi, ˈbʌdʒərɪˌgɑː/ — Wellensittich
fur *(no pl)* /fɜː/ — Fell
to fly /flaɪ/ — fliegen

2 tooth (pl teeth) /tuːθ, tiːθ/ — Zahn
leg /leg/ — Bein
foot (pl feet) /fʊt, fiːt/ — Fuß
head /hed/ — Kopf

Auf Seite 199 findest du die Namen vieler Körperteile in einem Bildwörterbuch.

ear /ɪə/ — Ohr — Elephants have big **ears**.
eye /aɪ/ — Auge
mouth /maʊθ/ — Mund
nose /nəʊz/ — Nase
water *(no pl)* /ˈwɔːtə/ — Wasser
to swim /swɪm/ — schwimmen — He **is swimming**.

4 kind /kaɪnd/ — Art, Sorte — p. 91
home /həʊm/ — Zuhause, Haus, Wohnung, *hier:* Heim
° wetland /ˈwetlænd/ — Sumpfgebiet, Feuchtgebiet
famous /ˈfeɪməs/ — berühmt — Adele is a **famous** singer.
animal shelter /ˈænɪm(ə)l ˌʃeltə/ — Tierheim
open (from ... to ...) /ˈəʊpən frəm tʊ/ — offen, geöffnet (von ... bis ...) — Is the shop **open** today?
adult /ˈædʌlt/ — erwachsene(r)
to pay /peɪ/ — (be)zahlen
to visit /ˈvɪzɪt/ — besuchen, anschauen — Let's **visit** the zoo.
to become /bɪˈkʌm/ — werden
careful /ˈkeəf(ə)l/ — vorsichtig, sorgfältig
may /meɪ/ — können, dürfen, *hier:* vielleicht
to fall in love (with sb) /ˌfɔːl ɪn ˈlʌv wɪð/ — sich (in jdn) verlieben
close /kləʊs/ — nah(e)
as well /əz ˈwel/ — auch
to leave /liːv/ — verlassen, weggehen, *hier:* (zurück)lassen

weather /ˈweðə/ — Wetter — The **weather** is very hot.
bird /bɜːd/ — Vogel — **Birds** can fly.
playground /ˈpleɪˌgraʊnd/ — Spielplatz
to rain /reɪn/ — regnen
pond /pɒnd/ — Teich
ticket /ˈtɪkɪt/ — Fahrkarte, (Eintritts)karte — Can I buy a **ticket** for the football game, please?

to miss /mɪs/ — verfehlen; versäumen; verpassen

Word lists 5

Theme 5: Pets and animals

this, that

Mit **this** (diese/r/s) kann man sich auf etwas beziehen, das in der Nähe des Sprechers ist,
mit **that** (der/die/das dort drüben) auf etwas, das weiter weg ist:

> **This** is a picture and **that**'s a poster.

these, those

Im Plural verwendest du **these** (diese hier) und **those** (diese dort drüben):

> I don't like **these** CDs, but I like **those** CDs over there.

penguin /ˈpeŋgwɪn/	Pinguin	
° **unforgettable** /ˌʌnfəˈgetəb(ə)l/	unvergesslich	
zoo-keeper /ˈzuːˌkiːpə/	Tierpfleger/in	
to help out /ˌhelp ˈaʊt/	aushelfen, helfen bei	
A1 unhappy /ʌnˈhæpi/	unglücklich	p. 92
maybe /ˈmeɪbi/	vielleicht, möglicherweise	**Maybe** Linda knows the answer.
perhaps /pəˈhæps/	vielleicht	**Perhaps** the shop isn't open today.
life (pl **lives**) /laɪf, laɪvz/	Leben	I love my **life** in London.
A2 cute /kjuːt/	süß, niedlich	
to calm down /ˌkɑːm ˈdaʊn/	sich beruhigen	Don't get too excited. **Calm down**!
alone /əˈləʊn/	allein	My grandfather lives **alone**.
to hope /həʊp/	hoffen	I **hope** you can come to my party!

Objektpronomen

Die Personalpronomen *I, you, he/she/it, we, you* und *they* kannst du als Subjekt eines Satzes verwenden. Deshalb nennt man sie Subjektpronomen. Personalpronomen, die du als Objekt verwenden kannst, nennt man **Objektpronomen**. Mehr Informationen zu Objektpronomen findest du in G20 auf Seite 195.

Objektpronomen (Singular)		Objektpronomen (Plural)	
me	Are you coming with **me**?	**us**	Don't be angry with **us**.
you	He wants to talk to **you**.	**you**	I can see **you**.
him	I can help **him**.	**them**	Don't ask **them**.
her	This book is for **her**.		
it	Do you like **it**?		

sick /sɪk/	krank	My sister is not at school because she is **sick**.
should /ʃʊd/	sollen	You **should** give a dog dog food.
shouldn't (= should not) /ˈʃʊdnt, ʃʊd nɒt/	nicht sollen	You **shouldn't** give a dog ice cream.

Must, mustn't, needn't und *should/shouldn't* sind Modalverben. Mehr Informationen zu den Modalverben findest du in G21 auf Seite 195/196.

near /nɪə/	nahe, in der Nähe	Don't go **near** that dog.
dangerous /ˈdeɪndʒərəs/	gefährlich	Maybe it's **dangerous**.
to smell /smel/	riechen, duften	I can **smell** my mum's cake.
What is ... like? /ˌwɒt ɪz ˈlaɪk/	Wie ist ... (denn so)?	
to lick /lɪk/	(ab)lecken, (ab)schlecken	
collar /ˈkɒlə/	Kragen, *hier:* Halsband	
mustn't (= must not) /ˈmʌsnt, mʌst nɒt/	nicht dürfen	You **mustn't** be late to school! ⚠ **mustn't** bedeutet „nicht dürfen".
anyway /ˈeniˌweɪ/	sowieso, jedenfalls	
pet shop /ˈpet ʃɒp/	Tierhandlung	

5 Word lists

Theme 5: Pets and animals

to **keep** /kiːp/	(bei)behalten, aufbewahren	You can't **keep** the dog. Maybe the **owner** is already looking for it.
owner /ˈəʊnə/	Besitzer/in, Eigentümer/in	
already /ɔːlˈredi/	schon, bereits	
needn't (= need not) /ˈniːdnt, niːd nɒt/	nicht müssen, nicht brauchen	You **needn't worry** about the weather when you are wearing a coat.
to **worry (about)** /ˈwʌri ˌəbaʊt/	sich Sorgen machen (um)	
to **give sth to sb** /ˈgɪv ˌsʌmθɪŋ tʊ ˌsʌmbədi/	jdm etw geben	Can you **give me** a pen, please?
to **replace (with)** /rɪˈpleɪs wɪð/	ersetzen durch	
A4 to **take** /teɪk/	(mit)nehmen, *hier:* (hin)bringen	We should **take** some food to the picnic. p. 93
before /bɪˈfɔː/	bevor, ehe	You should talk to your parents **before** you buy a pet.
that /ðæt/	dass	
hair *(no pl)* /heə/	Haare	
than /ðæn/	als	
A5 **information** *(no pl)* /ˌɪnfəˈmeɪʃ(ə)n/	Information(en), Auskunft	❗ **information** steht immer im Singular.
intelligent /ɪnˈtelɪdʒ(ə)nt/	klug, intelligent	
to **get bored** /ˌget ˈbɔːd/	sich (anfangen zu) langweilen	
to **forget** /fəˈget/	vergessen	Don't **forget** to do your homework.
to **go for a walk** /ˌgəʊ fər ə ˈwɔːk/	einen Spaziergang machen	Can we **go for a walk** in the park?
walk /wɔːk/	Spaziergang	Let's go for a **walk** in the park.
also /ˈɔːlsəʊ/	auch	
comfortable /ˈkʌmftəb(ə)l/	behaglich, bequem, komfortabel	
clean /kliːn/	sauber, rein	The yellow car is **clean**.
to **get** /get/	erhalten, bekommen, holen, *hier:* werden	It can **get** very hot in a car.
fat /fæt/	dick, fett	Be careful that your pet does not get too **fat**!
to **make sure (that)** /ˌmeɪk ˈʃɔː ðət/	darauf achten, (dass)	**Make sure that** your dog doesn't get bored.
hot /hɒt/	heiß, warm	Mark's drink is **hot**.
important /ɪmˈpɔːt(ə)nt/	wichtig, wesentlich, bedeutend	Frz. *important*
young /jʌŋ/	jung	**young** ↔ old
calm /kɑːm/	ruhig, gelassen	**calm** ↔ excited
behaviour /bɪˈheɪvjə/	Benehmen, Verhalten, Betragen	
to **change** /tʃeɪndʒ/	(ver)ändern	The weather **changes** every day.
A6 °**care sheet** /ˈkeə ʃiːt/	Haltungsanleitung	p. 94
leaflet /ˈliːflət/	Flyer, Prospekt	
so that /ˈsəʊ ðæt/	sodass, damit	
to **die (of)** /ˈdaɪ əv/	sterben (an)	
clear /klɪə/	klar, deutlich	It is **clear** that she loves her dog.
even if /ˈiːv(ə)n ɪf/	selbst wenn	
mistake /mɪˈsteɪk/	Fehler, Irrtum, Versehen	Read through your work and look for **mistakes**.
to **learn** /lɜːn/	lernen	I want to **learn** how to swim.
better /ˈbetə/	besser	
piece of paper /ˌpiːs əv ˈpeɪpə/	Blatt Papier	
can't (= cannot) /kɑːnt, ˈkænɒt/	nicht können, *hier auch:* nicht dürfen	You **can't** watch TV now. It's too late.
A8 **safe** /seɪf/	sicher	I feel **safe** at home.
scared /ˈskeəd/	verängstigt	
pleased /pliːzd/	froh, zufrieden	My mother is **pleased** with her birthday present.
A9 to **be right** /ˌbi ˈraɪt/	recht haben	2 + 2 = 4 – You**'re right**. p. 95

Word lists 5

Theme 5: Pets and animals

to **want sb to do sth** /ˌwɒnt ˌsʌmbədi tə ˈduː ˌsʌmθɪŋ/	wollen, dass jd etw tut	
for a **second** /fər ə ˈsekənd/	eine Sekunde (lang), einen Augenblick	
shocked /ʃɒkt/	schockiert, entsetzt	
I'd love to have /ˌaɪd ˈlʌv tə hæv/	ich hätte gerne	**I'd love to have** a pet.
I'm afraid ... /ˌaɪm əˈfreɪd/	Leider ..., Ich fürchte ...	**I'm afraid** I cannot come to your party.
possible /ˈpɒsəb(ə)l/	möglich	We can't have a dog. It's not **possible**.
to **give sth a go** /ˌɡɪv ˌsʌmθɪŋ ə ˈɡəʊ/	etw versuchen	
to **be wrong** /bi ˈrɒŋ/	nicht stimmen, sich irren	Charlie is nine. – You**'re wrong**. He's eleven.
A10 to **think about sb/sth** /ˈθɪŋk əˌbaʊt/	an jdn/etw denken, über jdn/etw nachdenken	
to **take turns** (BE) /ˌteɪk ˈtɜːnz/	sich abwechseln	Greg and Sarah **are taking turns** to play on the computer.
part /pɑːt/	Teil	The first **part** is the best **part** of the book.
to **believe** /bɪˈliːv/	glauben	My grandfather is 122 years old. – I don't **believe** you.

p. 98

B1 ° **stray** /streɪ/	streunend, herrenlos	
to **search the internet** /ˌsɜːtʃ ði ˈɪntəˌnet/	im Internet suchen	
° to **report** /rɪˈpɔːt/	berichten, melden	
to **contact sb** /ˈkɒntækt/	sich mit jdm in Verbindung setzen	
° to **return sth** /rɪˈtɜːn/	etw zurückgeben/-senden	
° **will** /wɪl/	werden	
to **note** /nəʊt/	beachten	
° **criminal offence** /ˌkrɪmɪn(ə)l əˈfens/	strafbare Handlung	
B2 **neighbour** /ˈneɪbə/	Nachbar/in	They are **neighbours**. 
tonight /təˈnaɪt/	heute Abend, heute Nacht	Let's meet **tonight**. We can watch a film.
B3 to **feel** /fiːl/	(sich) fühlen, *hier:* denken	
profile /ˈprəʊfaɪl/	Profil, Porträt	
chance /tʃɑːns/	Möglichkeit, Gelegenheit, Chance	
Sure! *(informal)* /ʃɔː/	Natürlich!, Klar!	
to **take care of** /ˌteɪk ˈkeər əv/	sich kümmern um	
to **show sb (a)round** /ʃəʊ ˌsʌmbədi əˈraʊnd/	jdn herumführen	
to **keep** /kiːp/	(bei)behalten, aufbewahren, *hier:* halten	Many people don't know much about **keeping** a pet.
care /keə/	Betreuung, Aufsicht, Pflege	
especially /ɪˈspeʃ(ə)li/	besonders, insbesondere	I like all animals, **especially** cats.
on the internet /ˌɒn ði ˈɪntəˌnet/	im Internet	❗ **on** the internet – **im** Internet
enough /ɪˈnʌf/	genügend, ausreichend, genug	Has your cat got **enough** water? – Yes, it has.
Christmas /ˈkrɪsməs/	Weihnachten	
on holiday /ɒn ˈhɒlədeɪ/	im Urlaub, in den Ferien	We are feeding our neighbours' fish because they are **on holiday**.
to **leave sb behind** /ˌliːv ˌsʌmbədi bɪˈhaɪnd/	jdn zurücklassen	
those (= *pl of* **that**) /ðəʊz/	diese	Look at **those** animals!
to **complete** /kəmˈpliːt/	vervollständigen, ausfüllen	
B5 **everybody** /ˈevriˌbɒdi/	alle, jede/r	**Everybody** in our class can come to my party.

p. 99

B6 **post** /pəʊst/	online veröffentlichter Beitrag/ Artikel/Eintrag	The singer's **post** about her new song is very exciting.

p. 100

two hundred and thirty-one 231

5 Word lists

Theme 5: Pets and animals

to **post** /pəʊst/	posten *(einen Beitrag/Artikel online stellen)*	She **is posting** a video of the concert on her **social media** profile.
social media /ˌsəʊʃ(ə)l ˈmiːdiə/	Social Media *(Gesamtheit der digitalen Technologien/Medien, über die Nutzer/-innen sich austauschen können)*	
description /dɪˈskrɪpʃ(ə)n/	Beschreibung	The **description** of the film makes me want to watch it.
cuddle /ˈkʌd(ə)l/	Umarmung, Liebkosung, Kuscheln	
cosy /ˈkəʊzi/	gemütlich, behaglich, heimelig	
basket /ˈbɑːskɪt/	Korb	
litter box /ˈlɪtə bɒks/	Katzenklo	
sunny /ˈsʌni/	sonnig	It's very **sunny**.
shy /ʃaɪ/	schüchtern, scheu	My brother is too **shy** to answer questions at school.
active /ˈæktɪv/	aktiv	
energetic /ˌenəˈdʒetɪk/	voller Energie	
cold /kəʊld/	kalt	**cold** ↔ hot
cage /keɪdʒ/	Käfig	a bird in a **cage**
noisy /ˈnɔɪzi/	laut	**noisy** ↔ quiet
bath /bɑːθ/	(Bade)wanne, Bad(ezimmer)	
excellent /ˈeksələnt/	ausgezeichnet	Frz. *excellent*
tank /tæŋk/	(Flüssigkeits)behälter, Tank, *hier:* Aquarium	
plant /plɑːnt/	Pflanze	There are lots of **plants** in my garden.
to **change** /ˈtʃeɪndʒ/	(ver)ändern, *hier:* (aus)wechseln	
character /ˈkærɪktə/	Charakter, Figur	My favourite **character** in the film is the funny lion.
B8 to **drink** /drɪŋk/	trinken	Alex always **drinks** orange juice. *p. 101*

Say it in English – Theme 5

So kannst du ...

Vermutungen anstellen	I think ... / Perhaps ... / Maybe his owners are looking for him. I guess ...
sagen, was jemand tun sollte	We should get him some dog food.
sagen, was jemand nicht tun sollte	You shouldn't go near him.
sagen, was jemand nicht tun darf	Dogs mustn't eat ice cream.
sagen, was jemand tun muss	You must look after your pet. Make sure that you go to a dog-friendly place.
sagen, dass jemand wütend ist	She is angry.
sagen, dass jemand enttäuscht ist	He is disappointed.
sagen, dass jemand Angst hat	She is scared.
sagen, dass jemand überrascht ist	He is surprised.
sagen, dass jemand froh/zufrieden ist	She is pleased.
sagen, dass jemand aufgeregt ist	He is excited.

Word lists 6

Theme 6: Holidays in Britain

Rückmeldung geben	You use a lot of different words.
	You should use different words.
	It sounds like a real discussion.
	It doesn't sound like a real conversation.
	You have got a lot of good ideas, for example …
	You should add more ideas, for example …
	We believe that …'s dialogue is very good/the best because …
ausdrücken, dass du etwas unglaublich findest	I just can't believe it.
einem Vorschlag zustimmen	Sounds like a great idea!
sagen, wo sich etwas befindet	This … / That dog over there …
	These … / Those guinea pigs on the right …
sagen, wann ein guter Tag für einen Besuch ist	One of the best days to visit is the first Sunday in September.
	World Wetlands Day on 2nd February is a good day to visit the London Wetland Centre.
	At London Zoo every day is a great day to visit!

Theme 6: Holidays in Britain

Theme 6 ist optional. Wie in den anderen Kapiteln auch, ist der Lernwortschatz für dieses Kapitel in der folgenden Wortliste **fett gedruckt**.
Der Lernwortschatz von *Theme 6* wird in Camden Town 6 allerdings nicht vorausgesetzt.

1
to **take a trip** /ˌteɪk ə ˈtrɪp/	einen Ausflug machen	I want to **take a trip** to Birmingham. *p. 108*
to **relax** /rɪˈlæks/	entspannen	
beach /biːtʃ/	Strand	
to **go sightseeing** /ˌgəʊ ˈsaɪtˌsiːɪŋ/	auf Besichtigungstour gehen	Let's **go sightseeing** and see the London Eye.
arcade game /ɑːˈkeɪd geɪm/	Videospiel	
to **go shopping** /ˌgəʊ ˈʃɒpɪŋ/	einkaufen gehen	Can we **go shopping**? I want some apples.
to **go surfing** /ˌgəʊ ˈsɜːfɪŋ/	surfen gehen	It is so sunny! Let's **go surfing** in the sea.
to **take a tour** /ˌteɪk ə ˈtʊə/	eine Reise machen	
° to shoot with a bow and arrow /ʃuːt wɪð ə ˌbəʊ ən ˈærəʊ/	mit Pfeil und Bogen schießen	

2
to **go on holiday** /ˌgəʊ ɒn ˈhɒlədeɪ/	in Urlaub gehen/fahren	We always **go on holiday** to England. *map*

3
map /mæp/	(Land)karte, (Stadt)plan	
castle /ˈkɑːs(ə)l/	Burg, Schloss	The Queen lives in a **castle**.
north /nɔːθ/	Norden, nördlich, Nord-	Mary is from Scotland. That is in the **north**.
° broomstick /ˈbruːmˌstɪk/	Besenstiel	
lake /leɪk/	See	**lake**
capital (city) /ˌkæpɪt(ə)l ˈsɪti/	Hauptstadt	
heart /hɑːt/	Herz	
city /ˈsɪti/	(Groß)stadt(-), städtisch	Berlin is a big **city**.
ruin /ˈruːɪn/	Ruin(e), Untergang	The house is so old. It's a **ruin**.
cliff /klɪf/	Klippe, Kliff	
coast /kəʊst/	Küste	
° birthplace /ˈbɜːθˌpleɪs/	Geburtsort	
° cave /keɪv/	Höhle	
° magician /məˈdʒɪʃ(ə)n/	Zauberer/Zauberin	
tree /triː/	Baum	 tree

6 Word lists

Theme 6: Holidays in Britain

sight /saɪt/	Sehenswürdigkeit	One of the best **sights** in London is the Tower Bridge.
south /saʊθ/	Süden, südlich, Süd-	John lives in Cornwall. That's in the **south** of England.
stone /stəʊn/	Stein(-)	
circle /ˈsɜːk(ə)l/	Kreis	A **circle** has no corners.
I'd like to (= I would like to) /aɪd ˈlaɪk tʊ/	ich würde gern	**I'd like to** go to Cornwall, but Sandra wants to go to Scotland.
A2 ° to hug /hʌg/	umarmen	*p. 110*
° each other /ˌiːtʃ ˈʌðə/	einander, gegenseitig	
dinner /ˈdɪnə/	Abendessen, Mittagessen	What's for **dinner**? – Pizza.
ready /ˈredi/	fertig, bereit	She is **ready** for school.
° **stay** /steɪ/	Aufenthalt	
a few /ə ˈfjuː/	einige, wenige	How many potatoes do you want? – Not many, just **a few**.
to be on one's way /ˌbi ɒn wʌnz ˈweɪ/	auf dem Weg sein	
inside /ˈɪnˌsaɪd/	innen; in(nerhalb); (nach) drinnen	It's warm **inside**.
down /daʊn/	hinunter, herunter	
to **notice** /ˈnəʊtɪs/	bemerken, beachten	
sports /spɔːts/	Sport(-)	
shirt /ʃɜːt/	Hemd, *hier:* Trikot	
to interrupt /ˌɪntəˈrʌpt/	unterbrechen	
not ... anything /ˌnɒt ˈeniθɪŋ/	gar nichts	
tired /ˈtaɪəd/	müde	Wow! It's 11pm! I'm **tired**.
journey /ˈdʒɜːni/	Reise	The **journey** from London to Manchester is four hours long.
restaurant /ˈrestrɒnt/	Restaurant, Gaststätte	Dad doesn't want to cook so we're going to a **restaurant**.
the others /ði ˈʌðəz/	die anderen	
A3 **annoyed** /əˈnɔɪd/	verärgert	I'm so **annoyed** that we have homework. *p. 111*
stupid /ˈstjuːpɪd/	dumm, blöd	
puzzled /ˈpʌz(ə)ld/	ratlos, verwirrt, (sehr) überrascht	
A4 to **go to bed** /ˌgəʊ tə ˈbed/	ins Bett gehen	It's nearly 9pm. Time **to go to bed**.
A5 would like to /wʊd ˈlaɪk tʊ/	würde(n/st/t) gern	*p. 112*
visit /ˈvɪzɪt/	Besuch	Enjoy your **visit** to this great museum.
world /wɜːld/	Welt	world
fascinating /ˈfæsɪneɪtɪŋ/	faszinierend	
° penalty kick /ˈpen(ə)lti kɪk/	Strafstoß, Elfmeter	
stunning /ˈstʌnɪŋ/	toll, fantastisch, umwerfend	
view /vjuː/	(Aus)sicht, (Aus)blick	The view is **stunning**.
area /ˈeəriə/	Gebiet, Region, Gegend, *hier:* Bereich	We live in a nice **area** with lots of parks.
to **join in** /ˌdʒɔɪn ˈɪn/	mitmachen	When we sing happy birthday, everyone **joins in**.
industry /ˈɪndəstri/	Industrie, Branche	
train station /ˈtreɪn ˌsteɪʃ(ə)n/	Bahnhof	
extraordinary /ɪkˈstrɔːd(ə)n(ə)ri/	außerordentlich, ungewöhnlich	Leo is so clever, it's **extraordinary**.
to **be worth sth** /ˌbi ˈwɜːθ/	etw wert sein	It is a long walk up the hill, but the view is **worth it**.

Theme 6: Holidays in Britain

Word lists 6

train   plane

train /treɪn/	Zug	
plane /pleɪn/	Flugzeug	
machine /məˈʃiːn/	Maschine, Apparat	
factory /ˈfæktri/	Fabrik	
to **take a ride** /ˌteɪk ə ˈraɪd/	eine Fahrt machen	The weather is nice so we're **taking a** bike **ride**.
interesting /ˈɪntrəstɪŋ/	interessant	
centre /ˈsentə/	Zentrum, Mitte	
absolute /ˈæbsəluːt/	absolut, total	❗ Achte auf die Betonung.
a must /ə ˈmʌst/	ein Muss	A visit to Big Ben is a **must** in London.
to **work** /wɜːk/	arbeiten; *hier:* funktionieren	Oh no, my phone doesn't **work**!
experience /ɪkˈspɪəriəns/	Erfahrung; Erlebnis	
° church /tʃɜːtʃ/	Kirche	
route /ruːt/	Strecke, Route	I walk through a park on my **route** to school.
beginner /bɪˈgɪnə/	Anfänger/in	
wall /wɔːl/	Wand	
ideal /aɪˈdɪəl/	ideal	The weather is sunny. That's **ideal** for a picnic.
° climbing *(no pl)* /ˈklaɪmɪŋ/	Bergsteigen, Klettern	
° kit /kɪt/	Ausrüstung, Ausstattung	
to impress /ɪmˈpres/	beeindrucken, imponieren	
spectacular /spekˈtækjʊlə/	atemberaubend, fantastisch	She is a **spectacular** dancer.
family entertainment centre /ˈfæm(ə)li ˌentəˌteɪnmənt ˌsentə/	Indoorfreizeitpark	

whole /həʊl/	ganz, gesamt	
to **spend** /spend/	verbringen *(Zeit)*; ausgeben *(Geld)*	I want to **spend** a lot of time with my friends.
slide /slaɪd/	Rutschbahn, Rutsche	
zip wire /ˈzɪp ˌwaɪə/	Seilrutsche	
ride /raɪd/	Fahrt	
to **make sure (that)** /ˌmeɪk ˈʃɔː ðət/	darauf achten, (dass), *hier:* sicherstellen, (dass)	**Make sure** that you do your homework.
B2 wouldn't (= would not) /ˈwʊd(ə)nt, wʊd nɒt/	würde(n/st/t) nicht	*p. 116*
would /wʊd/	würde(n/st/t)	
Roman /ˈrəʊmən/	Römer/in, römisch	
England /ˈɪŋglənd/	England	We live in London. That's in **England**.
(a week) ago /ə ˌwiːk əˈgəʊ/	vor (einer Woche)	
village /ˈvɪlɪdʒ/	Dorf	
tearoom /ˈtiːˌruːm/	Teestube	
to **walk** /wɔːk/	(zu Fuß) gehen, laufen	We **walk** to school every day.
abbey /ˈæbi/	Abtei, Kloster	
to be crazy about sb/sth /ˌbiː ˈkreɪziˌəˌbaʊt/	nach jdm/etw verrückt sein	
wild /waɪld/	wild, *hier:* in freier Wildbahn lebend	
need *(no pl)* /niːd/	Bedarf, Notwendigkeit, Bedürfnis	
° the Big Five /ðə ˌbɪg ˈfaɪv/	*Bezeichnung für fünf afrikanische Großtierarten (Büffel, Elefant, Leopard, Löwe, Nashorn)*	

B3 to **take** /teɪk/	(mit)nehmen, *hier:* dauern	My walk to school **takes** 25 minutes.
to **get** /get/	erhalten, bekommen, *hier:* (hin)kommen	I **get** to the cinema at 6pm.
most /məʊst/	(die) meisten	

6 Word lists

Theme 6: Holidays in Britain

to **arrive** /əˈraɪv/	ankommen, eintreffen	We **arrive** at school at 9am.
lock /lɒk/	Schloss, *hier:* Schleuse	
to **stop** /stɒp/	stoppen, (an)halten, aufhören, beenden	The policeman tells us to **stop**.
almost /ˈɔːlməʊst/	fast, beinahe	
everywhere /ˈevriˌweə/	überall	The beach is very busy. There are people **everywhere**.
there /ðeə/	dahin, dorthin	There's a free concert in the park. Let's go **there**.
by bike /ˌbaɪ ˈbaɪk/	mit dem (Fahr)rad	My sister goes everywhere **by bike**.
by taxi /ˌbaɪ ˈtæksi/	mit dem Taxi	
to **phone** /fəʊn/	anrufen, telefonieren	She **phones** her friend to tell her the news.
B4 on board /ˌɒn ˈbɔːd/	an Bord	 *p. 117*
room /ruːm/	Zimmer, Raum, *hier:* Platz	
us /ʌs/	uns	
to cook /kʊk/	kochen	
shower /ˈʃaʊə/	Schauer, Regen, Dusche	
B5 **adventure** /ədˈventʃə/	Abenteuer, Erlebnis	Robin Hood is a man who has many **adventures**.
to **throw** /θrəʊ/	werfen	Can you **throw** a ball?
to **jump** /dʒʌmp/	springen	She **is jumping**.
to **pull** /pʊl/	ziehen	Don't **pull** the cat's tail! 
to **fall** /fɔːl/	(um)fallen, stürzen	
B6 **lucky** /ˈlʌki/	glücklich *(Glück habend/Glück bringend)*	Look, this is my new phone. – Wow, you're so **lucky**!  *p. 118*
like /laɪk/	als ob	
to hold /həʊld/	halten	
to sigh /saɪ/	seufzen	
Stop it! *(informal)* /ˈstɒp ˌɪt/	Hör(t) auf!	
Hurry up! /ˌhʌri ˈʌp/	Beeil dich!, Beeilt euch!	
Me too! /mi ˈtuː/	Ich (mir/mich) auch!	
postcard /ˈpəʊstˌkɑːd/	Postkarte	
not … anywhere /nɒt ˈeniˌweə/	nirgendwo	
to cry /kraɪ/	weinen, schreien	
to **suggest** /səˈdʒest/	vorschlagen, *hier:* andeuten, (darauf) hinweisen	Claire **suggests** we go to the park, but I want to go to the pool.
meanwhile /ˈmiːnˌwaɪl/	inzwischen, unterdessen, mittlerweile	
(magic) wand /ˌmædʒɪk ˈwɒnd/	Zauberstab	
to wave (at) /ˈweɪv ˌət/	(zu)winken, *hier:* schwingen	
° to do magic /ˌduː ˈmædʒɪk/	zaubern	
woman (*pl* **women**) /ˈwʊmən, ˈwɪmɪn/	Frau	 **woman** ↔ **man**
B7 What's wrong? /ˌwɒts ˈrɒŋ/	Was ist los?	
B9 town centre /ˌtaʊn ˈsentə/	Stadtmitte	*p. 119*
building /ˈbɪldɪŋ/	Gebäude	
° AD (= Anno Domini) /ˌeɪ ˈdiː, ˌænəʊ ˈdɒmɪnaɪ/	nach Christus	
statue /ˈstætʃuː/	Statue	
guide /gaɪd/	(Reise)führer/in, Führer/in im Museum etc.	
soldier /ˈsəʊldʒə/	Soldat/in	
lady /ˈleɪdi/	Frau, Dame	

Word lists 6

Theme 6: Holidays in Britain

relaxing /rɪˈlæksɪŋ/	entspannend, erholsam	
meeting /ˈmiːtɪŋ/	Versammlung, Sitzung, Treffen	
wishing well /ˈwɪʃɪŋ wel/	Wunschbrunnen	
to care (about) /ˈkeər_əˌbaʊt/	sich etw machen (aus)	
to look around /ˌlʊk_əˈraʊnd/	sich umsehen	
without /wɪðˈaʊt/	ohne	Would you like your pizza with or **without** cheese? – **Without**, please!
pocket /ˈpɒkɪt/	Tasche *(an Kleidungsstücken)*	
entrance /ˈentrəns/	Eingang, Einfahrt	
voice /vɔɪs/	Stimme	
to shake sb's hand /ʃeɪk ˌsʌmbədɪz ˈhænd/	jds Hand schütteln	
hero (*pl* heroes) /ˈhɪərəʊ, ˈhɪərəʊz/	Held/in	
proud /praʊd/	stolz	
to wink (at sb) /ˈwɪŋk_ət/	(jdm zu)zwinkern	

Say it in English – Theme 6

So kannst du …

sagen, wo du gerne hingehen würdest	I would like to go to … because you can do/see a lot of different things, for example …
	I like … because you can try out/look at …
	… is my favourite because I like …
	… sounds great because there is something for everybody, for example …
	I'd like to visit … because …
	My favourite place is … because …
	I would choose … because …
	… looks like a good place to visit because …
über Gefühle sprechen	… is jealous/angry/annoyed.
	… is excited/puzzled.
	I'm a bit sad.
sagen, wo du nicht gerne hingehen würdest	I wouldn't like to go to … because …

W English-German

English-German dictionary

Im *English-German dictionary* kannst du englische Wörter nachschlagen, die im Buch vorkommen.
- Die **fett gedruckten** Wörter solltest du dir merken.
- Wörter mit einem ° sind nur für einen bestimmten Text wichtig. Du brauchst sie nicht zu lernen.
- 1Intro 1 bedeutet: Dieses Wort kommt in *Theme* 1, Aufgabe 1 im Intro-Teil vor.
- 1B1 bedeutet: Dieses Wort kommt in *Theme* 1, Aufgabe B1 vor.
- 1A/T1 bedeutet: Dieses Wort kommt in Aufgabe T1 in den *Target task tools* zu *Theme* 1 Part A vor.
- Folgende Abkürzungen werden noch verwendet:
    D = *Diff and train*   R = *Reading tour*
    P = *Photo tour*   W = *Welcome to Camden Town!*

A

a/an /ə/ən/ ein(e) W1
a bit /ə ˈbɪt/ ein bisschen; ein wenig 1A2
° a cup of ... /ə ˈkʌp ˌəv/ eine Tasse/ein Becher ... 3A6
° a day /ə ˈdeɪ/ pro Tag 5A/T1
a few /ə ˈfjuː/ einige; wenige 6A2
a lot (of) /ə ˈlɒt ˌəv/ viel(e); eine Menge 3A2
a must /ə ˈmʌst/ ein Muss 6A5
° a number of /ə ˈnʌmbər ˌəv/ einige; eine Reihe (von) 5D4
abbey /ˈæbi/ Abtei; Kloster 6B2
about /əˈbaʊt/ über; von; *hier:* wegen 1A2; *hier:* an 2A4
    ° about /əˈbaʊt/ ungefähr 2B12
above /əˈbʌv/ über 1B8; oberhalb; darüber; oben; obige(r, s) 4A9
absolute /ˈæbsəluːt/ absolut; total 6A5
° acrobatic routine /ˌækrəˌbætɪk ruːˈtiːn/ Akrobatiknummer 3B6
° acrostic /əˈkrɒstɪk/ Akrostichon 1D2
act /ækt/ (Show)nummer; Akt 3B4
° to act /ækt/ (schau)spielen 3B9
    ° to act out /ˌækt ˈaʊt/ nachspielen 3A6
active /ˈæktɪv/ aktiv 5B6
activity /ækˈtɪvəti/ Aktivität; Tätigkeit 3Intro 1
° AD (= Anno Domini) /ˌeɪ ˈdiː, ˌænəʊ ˈdɒmɪnaɪ/ nach Christus 6B9
° to add (sth to sth) /ˈæd ˌsʌmθɪŋ tə ˌsʌmθɪŋ/ (etw etw) hinzufügen 1A3
° to adopt /əˈdɒpt/ adoptieren; annehmen 5B6
adult /ˈædʌlt/ Erwachsene/r 5Intro 4
adventure /ədˈventʃə/ Abenteuer; Erlebnis 6B5
° African /ˈæfrɪkən/ Afrikaner/in; afrikanisch 6B/T1
after /ˈɑːftə/ nach 2A8

° After each dialogue, say where Caroline and George go and find the right photo: Sag nach jedem Dialog, wohin Caroline und George gehen, und finde das passende Foto. 1A6
afternoon /ˌɑːftəˈnuːn/ Nachmittag 2B2
    in the afternoon /ɪn ðiˌɑːftəˈnuːn/ am Nachmittag 2B2
again /əˈgen/ wieder; noch einmal 1B4
against /əˈgenst/ gegen 4A1
° aged ... /eɪdʒd/ im Alter von ... 6A/T5
° aggressive /əˈgresɪv/ aggressiv 5B/T5
ago /əˈgəʊ/ vor 6B2
to agree /əˈgriː/ zustimmen 3B2
° air *(no pl)* /eə/ Luft 4B10
all /ɔːl/ alle(s) 3A2
    ° all kinds of /ˌɔːl ˈkaɪndz ˌəv/ alle möglichen 5D12
    ° all of you /ˌɔːl ˌəv ˈjuː/ ihr alle; Sie alle 2B2
    ° all over the world /ˌɔːl ˌəʊvə ðə ˈwɜːld/ auf der ganzen Welt 6A/T5
    ° all summer /ˌɔːl ˈsʌmə/ den ganzen Sommer 6D2
    ° all the time /ˌɔːl ðə ˈtaɪm/ die ganze Zeit 1D17
    ° at all /ˌæt ˈɔːl/ überhaupt 4R3
° allergic (to) /əˈlɜːdʒɪk tʊ/ allergisch (auf/gegen) Wordbank 7
° to allow /əˈlaʊ/ erlauben; ermöglichen 5D10
almost /ˈɔːlməʊst/ fast; beinahe 1A6
alone /əˈləʊn/ allein 5A2
along /əˈlɒŋ/ entlang 1P1
already /ɔːlˈredi/ schon; bereits 5A2
also /ˈɔːlsəʊ/ auch 4Intro 6
° alternative /ɔːlˈtɜːnətɪv/ Alternative 1D4
always /ˈɔːlweɪz/ immer 3A2
(I) am /æm/ (ich) bin W8
am (= ante meridiem) /ˌeɪ ˈem, ˌænti məˈrɪdiəm/ morgens; vormittags *(nur hinter Uhrzeit zwischen Mitternacht und 12 Uhr mittags)* 3Intro 4 (Box *The time* S. 219)
amazing /əˈmeɪzɪŋ/ erstaunlich; toll 1A6
and /ænd/ und W8
angry /ˈæŋgri/ verärgert; zornig; wütend 3B2
animal /ˈænɪm(ə)l/ Tier W8
    ° animal lover /ˈænɪm(ə)lˌlʌvə/ Tierfreund/in 5D20
    animal shelter /ˈænɪm(ə)l ˌʃeltə/ Tierheim 5Intro 4
° ankle /ˈæŋk(ə)l/ (Fuß)knöchel Wordbank 2
annoyed /əˈnɔɪd/ verärgert 6A3
another /əˈnʌðə/ noch eine(r, s); ein(e) andere(r) 3B9
answer /ˈɑːnsə/ Antwort; Lösung 1A7
    to **answer** /ˈɑːnsə/ (be)antworten 1A11
    to **answer the phone** /ˌɑːnsə ðə ˈfəʊn/ ans Telefon gehen 4A1
° ant /ænt/ Ameise 5B/T1
any /ˈeni/ (irgend)ein(e); jede(r, s) 4B1 (Box *some, any* S. 225)
anything /ˈeniθɪŋ/ (irgend)etwas; (irgend)was 3B2
anyway /ˈeniˌweɪ/ sowieso; jedenfalls 5A2
apple /ˈæp(ə)l/ Apfel 2B8
April /ˈeɪprəl/ April 4Intro 1 (Box *The year* S. 223)
arcade game /ɑːˈkeɪd geɪm/ Videospiel 6Intro 1; Videospiel *(in Spielhallen)* 6D1
are /ɑː/ bist; sind; seid W8
    aren't (= are not) /ɑːnt, əˈnɒt/ bist nicht; seid nicht; sind nicht 1A3
    Are you OK? /ə jʊˌəʊˈkeɪ/ Alles in Ordnung? 1A2
    ° Are you serious? /ə jʊ ˈsɪəriəs/ Meinst du das ernst? 1A6
area /ˈeəriə/ Gebiet; Region; Gegend; *hier:* Bereich 6A5
° to argue (about) /ˈɑːgjuː əˌbaʊt/ sich streiten (wegen) 6D5

238 two hundred and thirty-eight

English-German W

° arm /ɑːm/ Arm 5D2
around /əˈraʊnd/ umher; um; rund um; um … herum 4B7
to look around /ˌlʊk‿əˈraʊnd/ sich umsehen 6B9
to show sb (a)round /ˌʃəʊ ˌsʌmbədi‿əˈraʊnd/ jdn herumführen 5B3
° to arrange /əˈreɪndʒ/ arrangieren; (an)ordnen 6B10
° to arrest /əˈrest/ verhaften 6R1
to arrive /əˈraɪv/ ankommen; eintreffen 6B3
art /ɑːt/ Kunst(unterricht) 2B1 (Box *Subjects* S. 216)
° as /æz/ als; *hier:* wie 3P2
° as … as /æz æz/ so … wie 2A/T1
as well /əz ˈwel/ auch 5Intro 4
° as well as /əz ˈwel‿əz/ sowohl … als auch … 6A/T4
° Asia /ˈeɪʒə/ Asien 5D3
to ask /ɑːsk/ fragen 1A9
° to ask (for sth) /ˈɑːsk fɔː/ (um etw) bitten 4D24
° to be asleep /ˌbi‿əˈsliːp/ schlafen 6A4
° assembly /əˈsembli/ Versammlung; *hier:* Schulversammlung 2A2
assembly hall /əˈsembli hɔːl/ (Versammlungs)saal; Aula 2B1
at /æt/ auf; an; in; bei 1B; um 3B4
° at all /æt‿ˈɔːl/ überhaupt 4R3
° at all times /ət‿ˌɔːl ˈtaɪmz/ immer; jederzeit 5A5
° at first /ət ˈfɜːst/ zuerst 6B1
at home /ət ˈhəʊm/ zu Hause 1A2
° at last /ət ˈlɑːst/ endlich W10
° at least /ət ˈliːst/ mindestens; wenigstens 2A2
° at night /ət‿ˈnaɪt/ nachts 2A/T3
at school /ət ˈskuːl/ in der Schule 2Intro 1
° at the back (of) /ət ðə ˈbæk‿əv/ hinten; *hier:* am Ende (von) 6Intro 4
° at the end /ət ðɪ‿ˈend/ am Ende 2Intro 2
at the moment /ət ðə ˈməʊmənt/ im Augenblick; momentan 3B8
at the weekend /ət ðə ˌwiːkˈend/ am Wochenende 4A6
° to pay attention /ˌpeɪˈtenʃ(ə)n/ Acht geben; aufpassen 2A5
° attic /ˈætɪk/ Dachboden; Speicher Wordbank 4
° attractive /əˈtræktɪv/ attraktiv; verlockend 1P1
audience /ˈɔːdiəns/ Publikum; Besucher; Zuschauer 3B8
audition /ɔːˈdɪʃ(ə)n/ Vorsprechen; Vorsingen; Vorspielen 3B1
August /ˈɔːɡəst/ August 4Intro 1 (Box *The year* S. 223)

aunt /ɑːnt/ Tante 1B7 (Box *Family* S. 213)
autumn /ˈɔːtəm/ Herbst 4Intro 3 (Box *Seasons* S. 223)
away /əˈweɪ/ weg 4B7
° awesome *(informal, AE)* /ˈɔːs(ə)m/ spitze; super Wordbank 5
° awful /ˈɔːf(ə)l/ furchtbar; schrecklich Wordbank 5

B

back /bæk/ (wieder) zurück 3A10
° back /bæk/ Rücken; Rückseite Wordbank 2
° at the back (of) /ət ðə ˈbæk‿əv/ hinten; *hier:* am Ende (von) 6Intro 4
bad /bæd/ schlecht; schlimm; böse 3A2
bag /bæɡ/ Tasche 4B1
to bake /ˈbeɪk/ backen 3A7
bake-off /ˈbeɪkɒf/ Backwettbewerb 3Intro 5
baker /ˈbeɪkə/ Bäcker/in 3A2
° baking powder *(no pl)* /ˈbeɪkɪŋ ˌpaʊdə/ Backpulver 3D5
° ball /bɔːl/ Ball 2B/T3
° ballet /ˈbæleɪ/ Ballett 1B9
balloon /bəˈluːn/ (Luft)ballon 4Intro 4
banana /bəˈnɑːnə/ Banane(n-) 2B8
° banana pudding /bəˌnɑːnə ˈpʊdɪŋ/ Dessert aus Vanillepudding, Keksen und geschnittenen Bananen 2B8
° bar /bɑː/ Stange; Stab; *hier:* Riegel Wordbank 7
basket /ˈbɑːskɪt/ Korb 5B6
° bat /bæt/ Fledermaus Wordbank 8
bath /bɑːθ/ (Bade)wanne; Bad(ezimmer) 5B6
bathroom /ˈbɑːθruːm/ Bad(ezimmer) 1Intro 1 (Box *Rooms* S. 209)
to be /biː/ sein 1A3
° to be a pity /ˌbi‿ə ˈpɪti/ schade/ bedauerlich sein 5A/T6
° to be allergic to sth /ˌbi‿əˈlɜːdʒɪk tʊ/ auf etw allergisch reagieren; gegen etw allergisch sein 5A4
° to be asleep /ˌbi‿əˈsliːp/ schlafen 6A4
° to be called /ˌbi: ˈkɔːld/ genannt werden; heißen 1B/T6
to be crazy about sb/sth /ˌbi: ˈkreɪzi‿əˌbaʊt/ nach jdm/etw verrückt sein 6B2
° to be full of … /ˌbi: ˈfʊl‿əv/ voll mit/von … sein 5D17
to be fun /ˌbi: ˈfʌn/ Spaß machen 4A7

° to be interested (in) / ˌbiːˈɪntrəstɪd‿ɪn/ sich interessieren (für); interessiert sein (an) 3B9
° to be mad about sb/sth /ˌbi: ˈmæd‿əˌbaʊt/ nach jdm/etw verrückt sein 1A6
° to be missing /ˌbi: ˈmɪsɪŋ/ fehlen 4R4
° to be on /ˌbi‿ˈɒn/ auf dem Programm stehen; laufen 6A5
to be on one's way /ˌbi‿ɒn wʌnz ˈweɪ/ auf dem Weg sein 6A2
° to be over /ˌbi:‿ˈəʊvə/ vorbei sein 4A1
to be right /ˌbi: ˈraɪt/ recht haben 5A9
° to be stressed (out) /ˌbi: ˌstrest‿ˈaʊt/ gestresst sein 5A5
to be upset (about sth) /ˌbi: ʌpˈset‿əˌbaʊt/ (über etw) traurig/aufgebracht sein 4B7
to be worth sth /ˌbi: ˈwɜːθ/ etw wert sein 6A5
to be wrong /ˌbi: ˈrɒŋ/ nicht stimmen; sich irren 5A9
beach /biːtʃ/ Strand 6Intro 1
° bear /beə/ Bär 5B/T1
° to beat /biːt/ schlagen; übertreffen 3D5
beautiful /ˈbjuːtəf(ə)l/ schön 3B2
because /bɪˈkɒz/ weil; da 1A1
° because of /bɪˈkɒz‿əv/ wegen 1A5
to become /bɪˈkʌm/ werden 5Intro 4
bed /bed/ Bett 1Intro 3 (Box *In a room* S. 210)
bedroom /ˈbedruːm/ Schlafzimmer 1Intro 1 (Box *Rooms* S. 209)
before /bɪˈfɔː/ bevor; ehe 5A4
before /bɪˈfɔː/ vor 2B2
to begin /bɪˈɡɪn/ anfangen; beginnen 3A10
beginner /bɪˈɡɪnə/ Anfänger/in 6A5
behaviour /bɪˈheɪvjə/ Benehmen; Verhalten; Betragen 5A5
behind /bɪˈhaɪnd/ hinter 1Intro 3 (Box *Präpositionen* S. 210)
to leave sb behind /ˌliːv ˌsʌmbədi bɪˈhaɪnd/ jdn zurücklassen 5B3
to believe /bɪˈliːv/ glauben 5A10
° belly /ˈbeli/ Bauch Wordbank 2
° below /bɪˈləʊ/ unten; darunter 6B/T3
best /best/ beste(r, s) 3A11
° best /best/ am besten; am liebsten; am meisten 3D14
° the best thing (about) /ðə ˈbest ˌθɪŋ‿əˌbaʊt/ das Beste (an) 6D12
better /ˈbetə/ besser 5A6
between /bɪˈtwiːn/ zwischen 1Intro 3 (Box *Präpositionen* S. 210)
big /bɪɡ/ groß W12

two hundred and thirty-nine 239

English-German

° the Big Five /ðə ˌbɪɡ ˈfaɪv/ *Bezeichnung für fünf afrikanische Großtierarten (Büffel, Elefant, Leopard, Löwe, Nashorn)* 6B2
bike *(informal)* /baɪk/ (Fahr)rad 4B7
° bin /bɪn/ Mülleimer; Mülltonne Wordbank 1
bird /bɜːd/ Vogel 5Intro 4
birthday /ˈbɜːθdeɪ/ Geburtstag(s-) 4Intro 1
° birthplace /ˈbɜːθˌpleɪs/ Geburtsort 6Intro 3
biscuit /ˈbɪskɪt/ Keks; Biskuit 3Intro 6
a bit /ə ˈbɪt/ ein bisschen; ein wenig 1A2
° to bite /baɪt/ beißen 5B/T5
black /blæk/ schwarz W4
blue /bluː/ blau W4
° blueberry /ˈbluːb(ə)ri/ Heidelbeere; Blaubeere 3D5
board /bɔːd/ Brett; Tafel 2A6
° board game /ˈbɔːd ɡeɪm/ Brettspiel Wordbank 9
boat /bəʊt/ Boot; Schiff 1A7
° body /ˈbɒdi/ Körper 5D3
° body language *(no pl)* /ˈbɒdi ˌlæŋɡwɪdʒ/ Körpersprache 6B10
° body part /ˈbɒdi pɑːt/ Körperteil 5D3
° bone /bəʊn/ Knochen 6A/T5
book /bʊk/ Buch 1Intro 1
° booklet /ˈbʊklət/ Broschüre 6D10
° boot /buːt/ Stiefel Wordbank 6
° bored /bɔːd/ gelangweilt Wordbank 2
boring /ˈbɔːrɪŋ/ langweilig W8
° to borrow /ˈbɒrəʊ/ (aus)leihen 6A/T4
both /bəʊθ/ beide(s) 2A8
° bottle /ˈbɒt(ə)l/ Flasche 4D20
° bottom /ˈbɒtəm/ Boden; (unteres) Ende; *hier*: Hinterteil Wordbank 2
° to shoot with a bow and arrow /ʃuːt wɪð ə ˌbəʊ ən ˈærəʊ/ mit Pfeil und Bogen schießen 6Intro1
to take a bow /ˌteɪk ə ˈbaʊ/ sich (unter Applaus) verbeugen 3B8
° box /bɒks/ Kiste; Schachtel; Kästchen 4A8
boy /bɔɪ/ Junge W11
° boyfriend /ˈbɔɪˌfrend/ Freund Wordbank 2
° bread /bred/ Brot(sorte) Wordbank 7
break /breɪk/ Pause 2B2
° breakfast /ˈbrekfəst/ Frühstück 3D8
° bridge /brɪdʒ/ Brücke 5P1
brilliant *(informal)* /ˈbrɪljənt/ brillant; strahlend; *hier*: toll, klasse 3B8
to bring /brɪŋ/ (mit)bringen 4Intro 4
to bring in /ˌbrɪŋ ˈɪn/ (her)einbringen; einführen 1B1
° Britain /ˈbrɪt(ə)n/ Großbritannien 2A2
° British /ˈbrɪtɪʃ/ britisch 2A2

° broomstick /ˈbruːmˌstɪk/ Besenstiel 6Intro 3
brother /ˈbrʌðə/ Bruder W8 (Box *Family* S. 213)
brown /braʊn/ braun W4
budgie (= budgerigar) *(informal)* /ˈbʌdʒi, ˈbʌdʒəriˌɡɑː/ Wellensittich 5Intro 1
° buffet /ˈbʊfeɪ/ Büfett 4Intro 4
building /ˈbɪldɪŋ/ Gebäude 6B9
° bull's eye /ˈbʊlz ˌaɪ/ Zentrum der Zielscheibe 6R1
burglar /ˈbɜːɡlə/ Einbrecher/in 4B7
bus /bʌs/ Bus W4
bus stop /ˈbʌs ˌstɒp/ Bushaltestelle 2Intro 1
° bush /bʊʃ/ Busch; Gebüsch W12
busy /ˈbɪzi/ beschäftigt; arbeitsreich 1A2
but /bʌt/ aber 1A2
° butter /ˈbʌtə/ Butter 4D20
to buy /baɪ/ kaufen 3A7
° by /baɪ/ von; mit 1P1
by bike /ˌbaɪ ˈbaɪk/ mit dem (Fahr)rad 6B3
° by bus /ˌbaɪ ˈbʌs/ mit dem Bus 3B/T5
by taxi /ˌbaɪ ˈtæksi/ mit dem Taxi 6B3
by the way /ˌbaɪ ðə ˈweɪ/ übrigens 4A7
Bye! (= Goodbye!) *(informal)* /baɪ, ɡʊdˈbaɪ/ Tschüss! 1A11
Bye for now. *(informal)* /ˈbaɪ fə naʊ/ Bis bald. 4A7

C

cage /keɪdʒ/ Käfig 5B6
cake /keɪk/ Kuchen 3A1
calculator /ˈkælkjʊˌleɪtə/ (Taschen)rechner 2A3 (Box *School things* S. 215)
calendar /ˈkælɪndə/ Kalender 4Intro1
phone call (= telephone call) /ˈfəʊn kɔːl, ˈteliˌfəʊn kɔːl/ Anruf; Telefongespräch 4A7
to call /kɔːl/ (an)rufen; nennen 2B2
° to call out /ˌkɔːl ˈaʊt/ (aus)rufen; aufschreien 2A5
calm /kɑːm/ ruhig; gelassen 5A5
to calm down /ˌkɑːm ˈdaʊn/ sich beruhigen 5A2
can /kæn/ können W1
can't (= cannot) /kɑːnt, ˈkænɒt/ nicht können W1; nicht dürfen 5A6
° Can I call you back in ten minutes?: Kann ich dich in zehn Minuten zurückrufen? 1A2
canal /kəˈnæl/ Kanal 1A6
° canned /kænd/ Dosen-; aus der Dose 4D20

canteen /kænˈtiːn/ Kantine; Mensa 2A2
° canvas /ˈkænvəs/ Leinwand Wordbank 9
° cap /kæp/ Mütze; Haube; Kappe 4D25
capital (city) /ˌkæpɪt(ə)l ˈsɪti/ Hauptstadt 6Intro 3
° caption /ˈkæpʃ(ə)n/ Überschrift; Titel; Bildunterschrift 1P2
car /kɑː/ Auto W1
° car park /ˈkɑː pɑːk/ Parkplatz 6A/T4
card /kɑːd/ Karte 4A1
° cardigan /ˈkɑːdɪɡən/ Strickjacke Wordbank 6
care /keə/ Betreuung; Aufsicht; Pflege 5B3
° care sheet /ˈkeə ʃiːt/ Haltungsanleitung 5A6
to take care of /ˌteɪk ˈkeər əv/ sich kümmern um 5B3
to care (about) /ˈkeər əˌbaʊt/ sich etw machen (aus) 6B9
careful /ˈkeəf(ə)l/ vorsichtig; sorgfältig 5Intro 4
° Caroline can't find her things. Can you help her?: Caroline kann ihre Sachen nicht finden. Kannst du ihr helfen? 1Intro 3
° carpet /ˈkɑːpɪt/ Teppich Wordbank 4
° carrot /ˈkærət/ Möhre; Karotte Wordbank 7
° to carry /ˈkæri/ tragen 5Intro 2
case /keɪs/ Koffer; *hier*: Hülle 4B1
castle /ˈkɑːs(ə)l/ Burg; Schloss 6Intro 3
cat /kæt/ Katze W11
° to catch /kætʃ/ (auf)fangen; einfangen; ergreifen 4B10
° cave /keɪv/ Höhle 6Intro 3
to celebrate /ˈseləˌbreɪt/ feiern 4Intro 4
centre /ˈsentə/ Zentrum; Mitte 6A5
° cereal /ˈsɪəriəl/ Getreide(sorten); *hier*: Frühstückscerealien *(Cornflakes, Müsli)* Wordbank 7
° certificate /səˈtɪfɪkət/ Urkunde; Bescheinigung 6A/T3
chair /tʃeə/ Stuhl 1Intro 3 (Box *In a room* S. 210)
° champion /ˈtʃæmpiən/ Champion; Sieger/in W10
chance /tʃɑːns/ Möglichkeit; Gelegenheit; Chance 5B3
to change /tʃeɪndʒ/ (ver)ändern 5A5; (aus)wechseln 5B6
° to change places /ˌtʃeɪndʒ ˈpleɪsɪz/ die Plätze tauschen 4Intro 3
° chant /tʃɑːnt/ (Sprech)gesang; Sprechchor 3A6

English-German

character /ˈkærɪktə/ Charakter; Figur 5B6
charity /ˈtʃærəti/ Barmherzigkeit; Wohltätigkeitsorganisation; *hier:* für einen guten Zweck 3Intro 5
° **chat** /tʃæt/ Unterhaltung; Chat 1A11
cheap /tʃiːp/ billig; preiswert 4B1
to **check** /tʃek/ überprüfen; nachsehen 1B4
  ° Let me check. *(informal)* /ˌlet mi ˈtʃek/ Lass(t) mich nachsehen. 2D2
° **cheeky** /ˈtʃiːki/ frech; dreist 4A2
to **cheer** /tʃɪə/ jubeln 3B8
cheese /tʃiːz/ Käse 2B8
° **chess** /tʃes/ Schach(spiel) Wordbank 9
chest /tʃest/ Brust(korb) Wordbank 2
chicken /ˈtʃɪkɪn/ Huhn; Hähnchen; Hühnchen 2B8
child (*pl* **children**) /tʃaɪld, ˈtʃɪldrən/ Kind 1B1
° **Chile** /ˈtʃɪli/ Chile 5D13
° **chinchilla** /tʃɪnˈtʃɪlə/ Chinchilla (*südamerikanisches Pelztier*) 5D13
chips *(pl)* /tʃɪps/ Pommes frites 2B8
chocolate /ˈtʃɒklət/ Schokolade 1A6
° **choice** /tʃɔɪs/ (Aus)wahl 5B5
° **choir** /ˈkwaɪə/ Chor 3D1
to **choose** /tʃuːz/ (aus)wählen 1A4
° **chorus** /ˈkɔːrəs/ Refrain; Chor 2A5
Christmas /ˈkrɪsməs/ Weihnachten 5B3
° **church** /tʃɜːtʃ/ Kirche 6A5
° **cinema** /ˈsɪnəmə/ Kino 3D1
circle /ˈsɜːk(ə)l/ Kreis 6Intro 3
° **circus** /ˈsɜːkəs/ Zirkus 3B2
city /ˈsɪti/ (Groß)stadt(-); städtisch 6Intro 3
  ° **city centre** /ˌsɪti ˈsentə/ Innenstadt; Stadtzentrum 3D1
to **clap** /klæp/ klatschen 3B8
class /klɑːs/ (Schul)klasse 1B9; Unterricht, Kurs 3Intro 5
  in **class** /ɪn ˈklɑːs/ im Unterricht 3A9
classmate /ˈklɑːsˌmeɪt/ Klassenkamerad/in; Mitschüler/in 1B6
classroom /ˈklɑːsˌruːm/ Klassenzimmer 2A1
clean /kliːn/ sauber; rein 5A5
  to **clean** /kliːn/ sauber machen; reinigen; putzen 2A6
  ° to **clean up** /ˌkliːn ˈʌp/ sauber machen; reinigen; putzen; *hier:* hinterherräumen 5D10
clear /klɪə/ klar; deutlich 5A6
clever /ˈklevə/ klug; gescheit; schlau W11
cliff /klɪf/ Klippe; Kliff 6Intro 3
to **climb (up)** /ˌklaɪm ˈʌp/ (hinauf)steigen; klettern (auf); besteigen 4B7

° **climber** /ˈklaɪmə/ Bergsteiger/in; Kletterer/Kletterin 6A/T4
° **climbing** *(no pl)* /ˈklaɪmɪŋ/ Bergsteigen; Klettern 6A5
clock /klɒk/ Uhr 3Intro 4 (Box *The time* S. 219)
to **close** /kləʊz/ schließen; zumachen 4B1
close /kləʊs/ nah(e) 5Intro 4
clothes *(pl)* /kləʊðz/ Kleider; Kleidung 4B6
club /klʌb/ Klub; Verein; *hier:* Arbeitsgemeinschaft 2A2
coast /kəʊst/ Küste 6Intro 3
coat /kəʊt/ Mantel 4B6
coffee /ˈkɒfi/ Kaffee 4A1
cold /kəʊld/ kalt 5B6
collar /ˈkɒlə/ Kragen; *hier:* Halsband 5A2
to **collect** /kəˈlekt/ (ein)sammeln 4A10
colour /ˈkʌlə/ Farbe W4
° **colourful** /ˈkʌləf(ə)l/ farbenfroh 5P1
° to **combine** /kəmˈbaɪn/ verbinden; kombinieren 4D5
to **come** /kʌm/ kommen; *hier:* mitkommen 1A5
  to **come along** /ˌkʌm əˈlɒŋ/ mitgehen; (mit)kommen 4A7
  to **come in** /ˌkʌm ˈɪn/ hereinkommen 1A5
  ° to **come to an end** /ˌkʌm tʊ ən ˈend/ zu Ende gehen 5P1
  Come on! *(informal)* /ˌkʌm ˈɒn/ Komm(t) jetzt!; Mach(t) schon! 3B2
  ° **Come on!** *(informal)* /ˌkʌm ˈɒn/ *hier:* Auf geht's! W5
° **comedy** /ˈkɒmədi/ Comedy(show); humoristische Sendung; Komödie 3B6
comfortable /ˈkʌmftəb(ə)l/ behaglich; bequem; komfortabel 5A5
° to **communicate** /kəˈmjuːnɪkeɪt/ kommunizieren, Kontakt haben 4A/T5
° to **compare** /kəmˈpeə/ vergleichen 2D20
competition /ˌkɒmpəˈtɪʃ(ə)n/ Wettbewerb 3B1
to **complete** /kəmˈpliːt/ vervollständigen; ausfüllen 5B3
° to **concentrate** /ˈkɒns(ə)nˌtreɪt/ (sich) konzentrieren 2A5
° **concert** /ˈkɒnsət/ Konzert Wordbank 9
° **Congratulations!** /kənˌɡrætʃʊˈleɪʃ(ə)nz/ Gratuliere!; (Herzlichen) Glückwunsch! 3B9
° to **connect** /kəˈnekt/ verbinden; anschließen 3A11
° **connective** /kəˈnektɪv/ Bindeglied; Bindewort 3A11

° **contact** /ˈkɒntækt/ Kontakt 1D17
  to **contact sb** /ˈkɒntækt/ sich mit jdm in Verbindung setzen 5B1
° **conversation** /ˌkɒnvəˈseɪʃ(ə)n/ Gespräch; Unterhaltung 4A/T3
° **convincing** /kənˈvɪnsɪŋ/ überzeugend 5A/T7
to **cook** /kʊk/ kochen 6B4
° **cook** /kʊk/ Koch/Köchin 6R1
° to **copy** /ˈkɒpi/ abschreiben; kopieren 1A3
° **corn snake** /ˈkɔːn sneɪk/ Kornnatter 5D13
° **corner** /ˈkɔːnə/ Ecke 5D17
° **corner shop** /ˈkɔːnə ʃɒp/ Eckladen 1B
° to **correct** /kəˈrekt/ korrigieren 2A6
° **correctly** /kəˈrektli/ korrekt; richtig 3D8
° to **cost** /kɒst/ kosten 3D13
costume /ˈkɒstjuːm/ Kostüm 3B2
cosy /ˈkəʊzi/ gemütlich; behaglich; heimelig 5B6
° to **count** /kaʊnt/ (ab)zählen; mitzählen; auszählen 2B7
° **country** /ˈkʌntri/ Land 1P1
° **countryside** *(no pl)* /ˈkʌntriˌsaɪd/ Land(schaft) 6D11
of course /əv ˈkɔːs/ natürlich 3B2
° **cover** /ˈkʌvə/ Einband; Titelseite 4R1
cow /kaʊ/ Kuh 5Intro 1
° **crazy** /ˈkreɪzi/ verrückt 2A6
  to be **crazy about sb/sth** /ˌbiː ˈkreɪzi əˌbaʊt/ nach jdm/etw verrückt sein 6B2
° **cricket** /ˈkrɪkɪt/ Grille 5D13
° **criminal offence** /ˌkrɪmɪn(ə)l əˈfens/ strafbare Handlung 5B1
° **crisps** *(pl, BE)* /krɪsps/ Chips Wordbank 7
° **crowd** /kraʊd/ (Menschen)menge; Zuschauermenge 1P1
crown /kraʊn/ Krone 2B5
to **cry** /kraɪ/ weinen; schreien 6B6
° **cucumber** /ˈkjuːˌkʌmbə/ (Salat)gurke Wordbank 7
cuddle /ˈkʌd(ə)l/ Umarmung; Liebkosung; Kuscheln 5B6
° **culture** /ˈkʌltʃə/ Kultur 2A1
° **cupboard** /ˈkʌbəd/ Schrank Wordbank 4
customer /ˈkʌstəmə/ Kunde/Kundin 4B4
° to **cut in half** /ˌkʌt ɪn ˈhɑːf/ in der Mitte durchschneiden 5A10
cute /kjuːt/ süß; niedlich 5A2
° **cycle** (= **bicycle**) /ˈsaɪk(ə)l/ (Fahr)rad 5D10
° to **cycle** /ˈsaɪk(ə)l, ˈbaɪsɪk(ə)l/ Rad fahren; radeln 6B/T1

English-German

D

dad *(informal)* /dæd/ Papa; Vati 1Intro 2
° daddy *(informal)* /'dædi/ Vati; Papi; Papa 6B6
dance /dɑːns/ Tanz 3Intro 5
dance routine /'dɑːns ruːˌtiːn/ Tanznummer 3B2
to dance /dɑːns/ tanzen 3B2
dancer /'dɑːnsə/ Tänzer/in 3B8
dancing *(no pl)* /'dɑːnsɪŋ/ Tanzen 3B2
dangerous /'deɪndʒərəs/ gefährlich 5A2
° dark /dɑːk/ dunkel 6R1
° darling /'dɑːlɪŋ/ Liebling; Schatz; Schätzchen 6B9
date /deɪt/ Datum 4Intro 2
° date /deɪt/ *hier:* Verabredung 3Intro 3
daughter /'dɔːtə/ Tochter 1B1 (Box *Family* S. 213)
day /deɪ/ Tag 1B7
December /dɪ'sembə/ Dezember 4Intro 1 (Box *The year* S. 223)
to decide /dɪ'saɪd/ entscheiden; bestimmen 3B8
to decorate /'dekəreɪt/ dekorieren; verzieren 3A7
decoration /ˌdekə'reɪʃ(ə)n/ Dekoration; Verzierung 3A7
delicious /dɪ'lɪʃəs/ köstlich; lecker 3A7
° delighted /dɪ'laɪtɪd/ hocherfreut; begeistert Wordbank 2
° delivery service /dɪ'lɪv(ə)ri ˌsɜːvɪs/ Lieferdienst 4A/T5
to describe /dɪ'skraɪb/ beschreiben 3B2
description /dɪ'skrɪpʃ(ə)n/ Beschreibung 5B6
desk /desk/ Schreibtisch 1Intro 3 (Box *In a room* S. 210)
dessert /dɪ'zɜːt/ Nachtisch 2B8
° detail /'diːteɪl/ Detail; Einzelheit 5D20
detective /dɪ'tektɪv/ Detektiv/in 4B7
diary /'daɪəri/ Tagebuch; (Termin)kalender 2A8
° dictionary /'dɪkʃən(ə)ri/ Wörterbuch 3Intro 3
to die (of) /'daɪ ˌəv/ sterben (an) 5A6
different /'dɪfrənt/ anders; andere(r, s); verschieden 2A2
difficult /'dɪfɪk(ə)lt/ schwierig; schwer 3A2
dining room /'daɪnɪŋ ruːm/ Esszimmer; Speisesaal 1Intro 1 (Box *Rooms* S. 209)
dinner /'dɪnə/ Abendessen; Mittagessen 6A2
° dinosaur /'daɪnəˌsɔː/ Dinosaurier(-) 6A/T5
° direct speech /dɪˌrekt 'spiːtʃ/ direkte Rede 3A11
° dirty /'dɜːti/ dreckig; schmutzig 5D9
to disagree /ˌdɪsə'griː/ nicht übereinstimmen; nicht einverstanden sein 3B2
disappointed /ˌdɪsə'pɔɪntɪd/ enttäuscht 3B6
° to discover /dɪ'skʌvə/ herausfinden; entdecken Wordbank 5
° discovery /dɪ'skʌv(ə)ri/ (Neu)entdeckung 5Intro 4
° discussion /dɪ'skʌʃ(ə)n/ Diskussion 2A/T5
dishwasher /'dɪʃˌwɒʃə/ Geschirrspülmaschine 3A2 (Box *Jobs around the house* S. 220)
° to divide into /dɪ'vaɪd ˌɪntʊ/ (auf)teilen in 5Intro 1
° divorced /dɪ'vɔːst/ geschieden 4B/T5
to do /duː/ machen; tun 2A6
° to do /duː/ *hier:* ausführen 2Intro 3
° to do magic /ˌduː 'mædʒɪk/ zaubern 6B6
° to do research /ˌduː rɪ'sɜːtʃ/ (er)forschen; recherchieren 6Intro 3
° to do sth to sb /'duː ˌsʌmθɪŋ tʊ ˌsʌmbədi/ jdm etw (an)tun 5D11
° Do you agree? /ˌduː ju ə'griː/ Stimmst du zu? W10
doctor /'dɒktə/ Arzt/Ärztin 4B6
dog /dɒg/ Hund W11
to walk the dog /ˌwɔːk ðə 'dɒg/ den Hund ausführen 3A2 (Box *Jobs around the house* S. 220)
don't (= do not) /dəʊnt, duː 'nɒt/ nicht tun; nicht machen 2A4
door /dɔː/ Tür 1Intro 1
front door /ˌfrʌntˈdɔː/ Vordertür; Haustür 4B7
° doorbell /'dɔːbel/ Türklingel 3A10
° dough /dəʊ/ Teig 3D5
down /daʊn/ hinunter; herunter 6A2
° face down /ˌfeɪs 'daʊn/ (mit etw) nach unten zeigend 4A5
downstairs /ˌdaʊn'steəz/ (nach) unten 1Intro 1
° draft /drɑːft/ Entwurf 6B11
drama *(no pl)* /'drɑːmə/ Schauspielerei; Drama; Theater(-) 2B2 (Box *Subjects* S. 216)
° dramatic reading *(no pl)* /drə,mætɪk 'riːdɪŋ/ theatralisches Lesen 1B2
to draw /drɔː/ zeichnen 1Intro 5
° drawing /'drɔːɪŋ/ Zeichnung 6A8
dream /driːm/ Traum(-) 4Intro 6
° dress /dres/ Kleid 4D25
fancy dress party /ˌfænsi 'dres ˌpɑːti/ Kostümfest 4Intro 5
to drink /drɪŋk/ trinken 5B8
drink /drɪŋk/ Getränk; Trinken 4Intro 4
° drinking water /'drɪŋkɪŋ ˌwɔːtə/ Trinkwasser 5D10
° to drive /draɪv/ fahren 6B/T1
duck /dʌk/ Ente 5Intro 1
° during /'djʊərɪŋ/ während 5B/T5

E

each /iːtʃ/ jede(r, s) 4Intro 4; jeweils 1B2
° each other /ˌiːtʃ 'ʌðə/ einander; gegenseitig 6A2
ear /ɪə/ Ohr 5Intro 2
earring /'ɪərɪŋ/ Ohrring 4B1
easy /'iːzi/ leicht; einfach 1A2
to eat /iːt/ essen; fressen 3A9
° to edit /'edɪt/ redigieren; bearbeiten 4B10
° egg /eg/ Ei 4D20
eight /eɪt/ acht 1Intro 1
° elbow /'elbəʊ/ Ell(en)bogen Wordbank 2
elephant /'elɪfənt/ Elefant W8
eleven /ɪ'lev(ə)n/ elf W8
elf *(pl* elves) /elf, elvz/ Elf/e 4B7
to empty /'empti/ (ent)leeren; *hier:* ausräumen 3A2 (Box *Jobs around the house* S. 220)
° encyclopedia /ɪnˌsaɪklə'piːdiə/ Enzyklopädie *(Nachschlagewerk)* 4R2
to end /end/ beenden; zu Ende bringen; enden 4A7
° end /end/ Ende; Schluss 4D3
° at the end /ət ðɪ 'end/ am Ende 3B8
° ending /'endɪŋ/ Ende; Schluss 3A11
energetic /ˌenə'dʒetɪk/ voller Energie 5B6
England /'ɪŋglənd/ England 6B2
English /'ɪŋglɪʃ/ Englisch(-); englisch 1A6 (Box *Subjects* S. 216)
to enjoy /ɪn'dʒɔɪ/ genießen 4Intro 4
enough /ɪ'nʌf/ genügend; ausreichend; genug 5B3
° entertaining /ˌentə'teɪnɪŋ/ unterhaltsam 6B11
° entertainment /ˌentə'teɪnmənt/ Unterhaltung 3B/T4
entrance /'entrəns/ Eingang; Einfahrt 6B9
° entry /'entri/ Eintrag; Eintritt 6A/T5
° environment /ɪn'vaɪrənmənt/ Umwelt; Umgebung 5D4
° especially /ɪ'speʃ(ə)li/ besonders; insbesondere 5B3
° etc (= et cetera) /et 'set(ə)rə/ usw.; etc. 5P1
° Europe /'jʊərəp/ Europa 6A5

English-German

even /ˈiːv(ə)n/ selbst; sogar 4B1
even if /ˈiːv(ə)n ɪf/ selbst wenn 5A6
evening /ˈiːvnɪŋ/ Abend 3B8
° that evening /ˌðæt ˈiːvnɪŋ/ an diesem Abend 6B5
° event /ɪˈvent/ Ereignis; Veranstaltung; Event 2B/T6
every /ˈevri/ jede(r, s) 3A7
everybody /ˈevribɒdi/ alle; jede/r 5B5
everyone /ˈevriwʌn/ jede/r 3A2
everything /ˈevriθɪŋ/ alles 4A1
everywhere /ˈevriˌweə/ überall 6B3
° exactly /ɪɡˈzæktli/ genau 3A11
example /ɪɡˈzɑːmp(ə)l/ Beispiel W11
excellent /ˈeksələnt/ ausgezeichnet 5B6
excited /ɪkˈsaɪtɪd/ aufgeregt 1A1 (Box *You can feel …* S. 210)
exciting /ɪkˈsaɪtɪŋ/ aufregend; spannend 3B8
° exclusive /ɪkˈskluːsɪv/ exklusiv 5D20
Excuse me! /ɪkˈskjuːs miː/ Entschuldigen Sie bitte!; Entschuldigung! 4B1
exercise /ˈeksəsaɪz/ Übung; Aufgabe 1A11
exercise book /ˈeksəsaɪz bʊk/ Heft 2A3 (Box *School things* S. 215)
° to exist /ɪɡˈzɪst/ existieren; bestehen; leben; vorkommen 6A/T4
° exotic /ɪɡˈzɒtɪk/ exotisch 5D13
expensive /ɪkˈspensɪv/ teuer 4B1
experience /ɪkˈspɪəriəns/ Erfahrung; Erlebnis 6A5
° expert /ˈekspɜːt/ Experte; Expertin 6A5
to explain (sth to sb) /ɪkˈspleɪn/ (jdm etw) erklären 3A10
extraordinary /ɪkˈstrɔːd(ə)n(ə)ri/ außerordentlich; ungewöhnlich 6A5
eye /aɪ/ Auge 5Intro 2
to roll one's eyes /ˌrəʊl wʌnz ˈaɪz/ die Augen verdrehen 4B7

F

face /feɪs/ Gesicht 2B2
° face down /ˌfeɪs ˈdaʊn/ (mit etw) nach unten zeigend 4A5
factory /ˈfæktri/ Fabrik 6A5
to fall /fɔːl/ (um)fallen; stürzen 6B5
to fall down /ˌfɔːl ˈdaʊn/ hin(unter)fallen; (ein)stürzen 2A8
to fall in love (with sb) /ˌfɔːl ɪn ˈlʌv wɪð/ sich (in jdn) verlieben 5Intro 4
family /ˈfæm(ə)li/ Familie DG (Box *Family* S. 213)

family entertainment centre /ˈfæm(ə)li ˌentəˌteɪnmənt ˌsentə/ Indoorfreizeitpark 6A5
° family tree /ˌfæm(ə)li ˈtriː/ Familienstammbaum 1D28
famous /ˈfeɪməs/ berühmt 5Intro 4
° fancy /ˈfænsi/ aufwändig; ausgefallen; *hier:* schick Wordbank 5
fancy dress party /ˌfænsi ˈdres ˌpɑːti/ Kostümfest 4Intro 5
fantastic (informal) /fænˈtæstɪk/ fantastisch 1A2
° fantasy /ˈfæntəsi/ Vorstellung; Fantasie(-) 5B/T2
° far /fɑː/ weit 6D12
° farm /fɑːm/ Bauernhof 5D4
° farm animal /ˈfɑːm ˌænɪm(ə)l/ Nutztier; Tier auf dem Bauernhof 5Intro 1
° farmer /ˈfɑːmə/ Bauer/Bäuerin 5D4
fascinating /ˈfæsɪneɪtɪŋ/ faszinierend 6A5
° fast /fɑːst/ schnell W10
fat /fæt/ dick; fett 5A5
father /ˈfɑːðə/ Vater 1B7 (Box *Family* S. 213)
favourite /ˈfeɪv(ə)rət/ Liebling(s-); Favorit/in W8
February /ˈfebruəri/ Februar 4Intro 1 (Box *The year* S. 223)
° to feed /fiːd/ (zu) essen geben; füttern 5D12
to feel /fiːl/ (sich) fühlen; *hier:* denken 5B3
feeling /ˈfiːlɪŋ/ Gefühl 1A11
felt tip /ˈfelt tɪp/ Filzstift 2A3 (Box *School things* S. 215)
° female /ˈfiːmeɪl/ Weibchen; weiblich 5D7
field /fiːld/ Wiese; Feld; *hier:* Spielfeld 4A8
fifth /ˈfelt tɪp/ fünfte(r, s) 4Intro 2 (Box *1st, 2nd, 3rd,…* S. 223)
° to fill in /ˌfɪl ˈɪn/ (aus)füllen; eintragen 6D4
° finally /ˈfaɪn(ə)li/ schließlich; endlich 4D24
to find /faɪnd/ finden 2A6
to find out /ˌfaɪnd ˈaʊt/ herausfinden 3B8
° Find the best title for his phone call.: Finde den passendsten Titel zu seinem Telefongespräch. 2Intro 4
fine /faɪn/ in Ordnung; gut 4A7
He's fine. /ˌhiːz ˈfaɪn/ Es geht ihm gut. 1A2
to finish /ˈfɪnɪʃ/ (be)enden; aufhören 3D8
° finisher /ˈfɪnɪʃə/ Zieleinläufer/in 5D3
° fire /ˈfaɪə/ Feuer; Brand 6R1

° fireworks (pl) /ˈfaɪəˌwɜːks/ Feuerwerk 4Intro 4
first /fɜːst/ erste(r, s) 4Intro 2; zuerst; als Erstes 5B2 (Box *1st, 2nd, 3rd, …* S. 223)
° at first /ət ˈfɜːst/ zuerst 6B1
° first-class /ˌfɜːst ˈklɑːs/ erstklassig; Spitzen- 6A/T4
fish (pl fish or fishes) /fɪʃ, fɪʃ, fɪʃɪz/ Fisch 5Intro 1
fish and chips (no pl) /ˌfɪʃ ən ˈtʃɪps/ frittierter Fisch mit Pommes frites 2B8
fish finger /ˌfɪʃ ˈfɪŋɡə/ Fischstäbchen 4Intro 4
° to fit /fɪt/ passen (zu) 5D4
five /faɪv/ fünf 1Intro 1
° the Big Five /ðə ˌbɪɡ ˈfaɪv/ *Bezeichnung für fünf afrikanische Großtierarten (Büffel, Elefant, Leopard, Löwe, Nashorn)* 6B2
° fizz /fɪz/ sprudeln; zischen 2Intro 5
flag /flæɡ/ Fahne; Flagge 2B5
flat /flæt/ (Etagen)wohnung; Mietwohnung 1B6
floor /flɔː/ Boden 2A5
° flour (no pl) /ˈflaʊə/ Mehl 4D20
to fly /flaɪ/ fliegen 5Intro 1
° to fold /fəʊld/ (zusammen)falten 5A10
folder /ˈfəʊldə/ Mappe; Schnellhefter; Ordner 2A3 (Box *School things* S. 215)
° to follow /ˈfɒləʊ/ folgen 1P1
° following /ˈfɒləʊɪŋ/ folgende(r, s) 1A8
food /fuːd/ Essen; Nahrung; Futter 2B8
foot (pl feet) /fʊt, fiːt/ Fuß 5Intro 2
football /ˈfʊtbɔːl/ Fußball W8
for /fɔː/ für W11
° for /fɔː/ *hier:* auf 1B9; *hier:* bei 2Intro 5 *hier:* zu 4B/T6
for a second /fər ə ˈsekənd/ eine Sekunde (lang); einen Augenblick 5A9
° for dessert /fə dɪˈzɜːt/ als/zum Nachtisch 2D26
° for dinner /fə ˈdɪnə/ zum Essen (zu Abend oder Mittag) 6A2
for example /fər ɪɡˈzɑːmp(ə)l/ zum Beispiel 3Intro 6
° for help /fə ˈhelp/ *hier:* als Hilfe 2B5
° for lunch /fə ˈlʌntʃ/ zum Mittagessen 2B8
° for the first/last time /fə ðə ˌfɜːst/ ˌlɑːst ˈtaɪm/ zum ersten/letzten Mal 6A/T6
to forget /fəˈɡet/ vergessen 5A5

English-German

° to forget about sth/sb / fəˈgetˌəˌbaʊt/ etw/jdn vergessen 5A/T3
° to form /fɔːm/ formen; bilden 1B4
four /fɔː/ vier 1Intro 1
fourth /fɔːθ/ vierte(r, s) 4Intro 2 (Box 1st, 2nd, 3rd, ... S. 223)
° fox /fɒks/ Fuchs Wordbank 8
° frame /freɪm/ (Bilder)rahmen 6B5
free /friː/ frei; gratis 4Intro 4
free time /ˌfriːˈtaɪm/ Freizeit 3Intro 1
° freeze-frame /ˈfriːzˌfreɪm/ Standbild 6B10
French /frentʃ/ Französisch(-); französisch 2A11 (Box Subjects S. 216)
fresh /freʃ/ neu; ungebraucht; frisch 2B8
Friday /ˈfraɪdeɪ/ Freitag 2B5 (Box Days of the week S. 217)
friend /frend/ Freund/in 1A1
friendly /ˈfrendli/ freundlich 2A4
° frog /frɒɡ/ Frosch 6A/T5
from /frɒm/ von; aus 1A4
in front of /ɪn ˈfrʌntˌəv/ vor 3B2 (Box Präpositionen S. 210)
front door /ˌfrʌntˈdɔː/ Vordertür; Haustür 4B7
fruit (pl fruit or fruits) /fruːt, fruːts/ Frucht; Obst 2B8
° full /fʊl/ voll(ständig) Wordbank 7
° to be full of ... /ˌbiː ˈfʊlˌəv/ voll mit von ... sein 5D17
to be fun /ˌbiː ˈfʌn/ Spaß machen 4A7
° This is fun. /ˌðɪsˌɪz ˈfʌn/ Das macht Spaß. W10
funny /ˈfʌni/ lustig; witzig; komisch; merkwürdig 1B1
fur (no pl) /fɜː/ Fell 5Intro 1
° furry /ˈfɜːri/ pelzig; wollig 5D13

G

° g (= gramme) /ɡræm/ Gramm 3D5
° to gallop /ˈɡæləp/ galoppieren 6R1
game /ɡeɪm/ Spiel 1A2
garden /ˈɡɑːd(ə)n/ Garten 1Intro 1
° gecko /ˈɡekəʊ/ Gecko (tropische Eidechse) 5D13
geography /dʒiˈɒɡrəfi/ Erdkunde; Geografie 2B2 (Box Subjects S. 216)
° George makes a video for his friends in Manchester.: George macht ein Video für seine Freunde in Manchester. 1Intro 2
German /ˈdʒɜːmən/ Deutsche/r; deutsch; Deutsch(unterricht) 3Intro 6
in German /ɪn ˈdʒɜːmən/ auf Deutsch 3Intro 4

° Germany /ˈdʒɜːməni/ Deutschland 3P2
to get /ɡet/ erhalten; bekommen; holen 1A6; werden 5A5; (hin)kommen 6B3
to get away /ˌɡetˌəˈweɪ/ fortkommen; flüchten 4B7
° to get back /ˌɡet ˈbæk/ zurückkommen 6R1
to get bored /ˌɡet ˈbɔːd/ sich (anfangen zu) langweilen 5A5
° to get out /ˌɡetˌˈaʊt/ aussteigen 1P1
° to get ready (for sth) /ˌɡet ˈredi fɔː/ sich (für etw) fertig machen 6A/T3
° to get up /ˌɡetˌˈʌp/ aufstehen 6R1
° ghost /ɡəʊst/ Geist; Gespenst 4B6
° giant /ˈdʒaɪənt/ Riese(n-); Gigant; riesig 6A/T5
° gift /ɡɪft/ Geschenk; Spende 6A/T5
girl /ɡɜːl/ Mädchen W11
° girlfriend /ˈɡɜːlˌfrend/ Freundin 4B/T5
to give /ɡɪv/ geben 3A2
to give sth a go /ˌɡɪv ˌsʌmθɪŋˌə ˈɡəʊ/ etw versuchen 5A9
to give sth to sb /ɡɪv/ jdm etw geben 5A2
glad /ɡlæd/ glücklich; dankbar; froh 3B6
glass /ɡlɑːs/ Glas 4B7
glove /ɡlʌv/ Handschuh 4B6
glue /ɡluː/ Klebstoff; Kleber 2A3 (Box School things S. 215)
to go /ɡəʊ/ gehen; fahren 1A6
to go to bed /ˌɡəʊ təˈbed/ ins Bett gehen 6A4
° to go bowling /ˌɡəʊ ˈbəʊlɪŋ/ Bowlen gehen 4D2
° to go for a ride /ˌɡəʊ fərˌə ˈraɪd/ eine Fahrt machen; hier: ausreiten 5D9
to go for a walk /ˌɡəʊ fərˌə ˈwɔːk/ einen Spaziergang machen 5A5
° to go hiking /ˌɡəʊ ˈhaɪkɪŋ/ wandern gehen Wordbank 5
° to go on a trip /ˌɡəʊˌɒnˌə ˈtrɪp/ einen Ausflug/eine Reise machen 5A/T3
to go on holiday /ˌɡəʊˌɒn ˈhɒlədeɪ/ in Urlaub gehen/fahren 6Intro 2
to go shopping /ˌɡəʊ ˈʃɒpɪŋ/ einkaufen gehen 6Intro 1
to go sightseeing /ˌɡəʊ ˈsaɪtˌsiːɪŋ/ auf Besichtigungstour gehen 6Intro 1
to go surfing /ˌɡəʊ ˈsɜːfɪŋ/ surfen gehen 6Intro 1
° to go swimming /ˌɡəʊ ˈswɪmɪŋ/ schwimmen gehen 4D2
° to go through /ˌɡəʊ ˈθruː/ durchgehen 6A6

° to go together /ˌɡəʊ təˈɡeðə/ zusammengehören; passen 2R3
° to go with /ˈɡəʊ wɪð/ zu ... gehören; zu ... passen 2Intro 3
° go-kart track /ˈɡəʊkɑːt træk/ Gokartbahn 6A5
goal /ɡəʊl/ Ziel; Tor 4A8
to score (a goal) /ˌskɔːrˌə ˈɡəʊl/ (ein Tor) schießen 4A8
° goalkeeper /ˈɡəʊlˌkiːpə/ Torhüter/in 3Intro 2
° goldfish (pl goldfish) /ˈɡəʊldˌfɪʃ/ Goldfisch 5D1
good /ɡʊd/ gut 1A6
Good luck! /ˌɡʊd ˈlʌk/ Viel Glück! 3A2
grandfather /ˈɡrænˌfɑːðə/ Großvater 1B7 (Box Family S. 213)
grandma (informal) /ˈɡrænˌmɑː/ Oma; Omi 1A2
grandmother /ˈɡrænˌmʌðə/ Großmutter 1B7 (Box Family S. 213)
grandpa (informal) /ˈɡrænˌpɑː/ Opa; Opi 1A2
grandparents (pl) /ˈɡrænˌpeərənts/ Großeltern 1B7 (Box Family S. 213)
° grape /ɡreɪp/ (Wein)traube 5A5
° grass (no pl) /ɡrɑːs/ Gras 5Intro 2
great /ɡreɪt/ groß; riesig; großartig; wunderbar W11
° Greece /ɡriːs/ Griechenland 1B9
green /ɡriːn/ grün W4
° grey /ɡreɪ/ grau W4
group /ɡruːp/ Gruppe 3B8
grumpy /ˈɡrʌmpi/ mürrisch; schlecht gelaunt 2B2
to guess /ɡes/ (er)raten 4B6; annehmen 5A1
guest /ɡest/ Gast 4Intro 4
guide /ɡaɪd/ (Reise)führer/in; Führer/in im Museum etc. 6B9
° guinea pig /ˈɡɪni pɪɡ/ Meerschweinchen 5B3
guitar /ɡɪˈtɑː/ Gitarre 3B8
gym /dʒɪm/ Turnhalle; hier: Fitnesscenter 4A1
gym (= gymnastics, pl) /dʒɪm, dʒɪmˈnæstɪks/ Turnen 3Intro 5
° gymnasium /dʒɪmˈneɪziəm/ Turnhalle; Sporthalle 3P2

H

hair (no pl) /heə/ Haare 5A4
° half /hɑːf/ halb 3D2
° half an hour /ˌhɑːfˌənˈaʊə/ eine halbe Stunde 3D2
half past (seven) /ˌhɑːf pɑːst ˈsev(ə)n/ halb (acht) 3Intro 4 (Box The time S. 219)
° half (pl halves) /hɑːf, hɑːvz/ Hälfte 3D25

English-German

° ham /hæm/ Schinken Wordbank 7
hand /hænd/ Hand 4B7
to shake sb's hand /ˌʃeɪk ˌsʌmbədɪz ˈhænd/ jds Hand schütteln 6B9
° handbag /ˈhændˌbæɡ/ Handtasche 1P1
° to hand (over) /ˌhændˈəʊvə/ (über)geben; (über)reichen 4R2
° to hang /hæŋ/ (auf)hängen 4B10
° hangman /ˈhæŋmən/ *hier:* Galgenmännchen *(Buchstabenspiel)* W7
to happen /ˈhæpən/ geschehen; passieren 3A10
happy /ˈhæpi/ glücklich; zufrieden; fröhlich 1A1
(Box *You can feel …* S. 210)
° Happy birthday (to you!) /ˌhæpi ˈbɜːθdeɪ tʊ juː/ Alles Gute zum Geburtstag! 4A/T5
° hard /hɑːd/ hart; schwer; schwierig; fest; kräftig 2D8
° hat /hæt/ Hut Wordbank 6
to hate /heɪt/ hassen; verabscheuen 1A6
to have /hæv/ haben 2Intro 1; trinken, zu sich nehmen 4A1
° to have /hæv/ *hier:* essen 6B6
° to have a great time /ˌhæv ə ˌɡreɪt ˈtaɪm/ (sich) amüsieren 4A/T1
° to have a look at … /ˌhæv ə ˈlʊk/ nachsehen; sich ansehen; nachschauen 5D17
° Have a nice day! /ˌhæv ə ˌnaɪs ˈdeɪ/ Einen schönen Tag noch! 4D22
° to have a party /ˌhæv ə ˈpɑːti/ eine Party geben Intro 5
° to have a picnic /ˌhæv ə ˈpɪknɪk/ ein Picknick machen 1P1
° to have a sleepover /ˌhæv ə ˈsliːpˌəʊvə/ zu mehreren bei einer Person übernachten 4D2
° to have a vote (on sth) /ˌhæv ə ˈvəʊt ɒn/ (über etw) abstimmen 2A8
° to have breakfast /ˌhæv ˈbrekfəst/ frühstücken Wordbank 7
° to have dinner /ˌhæv ˈdɪnə/ zu Abend/Mittag essen Wordbank 7
to have got /ˌhæv ˈɡɒt/ haben 2B2
to have lunch /ˌhæv ˈlʌntʃ/ zu Mittag essen 2A8
° have to /ˈhæv tə/ müssen 1D12
he /hiː/ er W11
he's (= he is) /hiːz, ˈhiˌɪz/ er ist W11
head /hed/ Kopf 5Intro 2
healthy /ˈhelθi/ gesund 2B10
to hear /hɪə/ hören 3B8
heart /hɑːt/ Herz 6Intro 3
° heaven /ˈhev(ə)n/ Himmel(reich) W10

heavy /ˈhevi/ schwer 4B7
° hedgehog /ˈhedʒˌhɒɡ/ Igel Wordbank 8
Hello! /həˈləʊ/ Hallo! W8
° helmet /ˈhelmɪt/ Helm 4B6
to help /help/ helfen 3A10
to help out /ˌhelp ˈaʊt/ aushelfen; helfen bei 5Intro 4
help *(no pl)* /help/ Hilfe 2B12
° for help /fə ˈhelp/ *hier:* als Hilfe 2B5
her /hɜː/ ihr(e) 1B8; ihr; sie 3B8 (Box *Objektpronomen* S. 229)
here /hɪə/ hier 2Intro 1
Here you are. /ˌhɪə juˈɑː/ Hier, bitte.; Bitte schön. 4B1
° Here we are. /ˌhɪə wiˈɑː/ Da sind wir.; *hier:* Da haben wir's .2D2
hero *(pl* heroes) /ˈhɪərəʊ, ˈhɪərəʊz/ Held/in 6B9
° Hey there! *(informal)* /ˈheɪ ðeə/ Hallo! 5B6
Hi! *(informal)* /haɪ/ Hi! W8
to hide /haɪd/ (sich) verstecken 3A10
° to highlight /ˈhaɪˌlaɪt/ hervorheben; markieren 2D27
° hiking boots *(pl)* /ˈhaɪkɪŋ buːts/ Wanderschuhe Wordbank 6
° hill /hɪl/ Hügel; Berg 6D12
him /hɪm/ ihm; ihn 3B8 (Box *Objektpronomen* S. 229)
° Hindi *(no pl)* /ˈhɪndi/ Hindi *(Amtssprache in Indien)* 1B7
hint /hɪnt/ Spur; Andeutung; Hinweis; Tipp 4B6
his /hɪz/ sein(e) 1B8
history /ˈhɪst(ə)ri/ Geschichte 2A4 (Box *Subjects* S. 216)
to hold /həʊld/ halten 6B6
holiday /ˈhɒlədeɪ/ Urlaub; Ferien 4A6
on holiday /ɒn ˈhɒlədeɪ/ im Urlaub; in den Ferien 5B3
home /həʊm/ Zuhause; Haus; Wohnung 1A2; zu Hause; nach Hause 4A1; Heim 5Intro 4
at home /ət ˈhəʊm/ zu Hause 1A2
homework *(no pl)* /ˈhəʊmˌwɜːk/ Hausaufgabe(n) 2A6
to hoover /ˈhuːvə/ staubsaugen 3A2 (Box *Jobs around the house* S. 220)
to hope /həʊp/ hoffen 5A2
horrible /ˈhɒrəb(ə)l/ schrecklich 3A2
horse /hɔːs/ Pferd 4Intro 4
° host /həʊst/ Gastgeber/in; *hier:* Moderator/in 5B/T6
hot /hɒt/ heiß; warm 5A5
° hot chocolate /ˌhɒt ˈtʃɒklət/ (heißer) Kakao Wordbank 7
hour /ˈaʊə/ Stunde 3Intro 4
house /haʊs/ Haus W12

° Houses of Parliament /ˌhaʊzɪz əv ˈpɑː(r)ləmənt/ das Parlament *(von Großbritannien)* 5P1
how /haʊ/ wie W8
° How to … /ˈhaʊ tə/ Wie man … 1B4
How about …? /ˈhaʊ əˌbaʊt/ Wie wäre es mit …? 4B1
How are you? /ˌhaʊ ˈɑː jə/ Wie geht es dir/Ihnen/euch? 1A11
° How is it going? *(informal)* /ˌhaʊ ɪz ɪt ˈɡəʊɪŋ/ Wie geht's (denn so)? 4A/T4
How many …? /ˌhaʊ ˈmeni/ Wie viele …? 1B6
How much is/are …? /ˌhaʊ ˈmʌtʃ ɪz/ə/ Was kostet/kosten …? 4B1
How old are you? /ˌhaʊ ˈəʊld ə jə/ Wie alt bist du?; Wie alt seid ihr? W8
° to hug /hʌɡ/ umarmen 6A2
° huge /hjuːdʒ/ riesig; riesengroß 6A/T5
° human /ˈhjuːmən/ Mensch; menschlich 5A5
° hundred /ˈhʌndrəd/ Hundert 5D17
hungry /ˈhʌŋɡri/ hungrig 1A6
Hurry up! /ˌhʌriˈʌp/ Beeil dich!; Beeilt euch! 6B6
° to hurt (sb) /hɜːt/ (jdm) wehtun; (jdn) verletzen 3A6
° husband /ˈhʌzbənd/ (Ehe)mann Wordbank 2

I

I /aɪ/ ich W1
I don't like … /aɪ ˈdəʊnt laɪk/ Ich mag … nicht. W8
I don't think so. /aɪ ˌdəʊnt ˈθɪŋk səʊ/ Das glaube ich nicht. 2A12
° I guess … /aɪ ˈɡes/ Ich schätze … 1D15
I like… /aɪ ˈlaɪk/ Ich mag… W8
° I need a cup of tea.: Ich brauche eine Tasse Tee. 1B7
° I spy with my little eye something red. /aɪ ˌspaɪ wɪð ˌmaɪ ˌlɪt(ə)l ˌaɪ ˌsʌmθɪŋ ˈred/ Ich sehe was, was du nicht siehst, und das ist rot. W4
° I'd like … (= I would like …) /ˌaɪd ˈlaɪk/ Ich hätte gern … 2B9
I'd like to (= I would like to) /ˌaɪd ˈlaɪk tʊ/ ich würde gern 6Intro 3
I'd love to have /ˌaɪd ˈlʌv tə hæv/ ich hätte gerne 5A9
I'm (= I am) /aɪm, ˈaɪˌəm/ ich bin; *auch:* ich heiße W8
I'm afraid … /ˌaɪm əˈfreɪd/ Leider …; Ich fürchte … 5A9

English-German

I'm fine. /aɪm 'faɪn/ Mir geht es gut. 1A6
I'm from ... /'aɪm frəm/ Ich komme aus ... W8
I'm not sure (about that). /aɪm ˌnɒt 'ʃɔː/ Ich bin mir (dieser Sache) nicht sicher.; Ich weiß nicht genau. 2A8
I'm sorry. /ˌaɪm 'sɒri/ Entschuldigung.; Tut mir leid. 2Intro 1
° I'm sorry for earlier.: Es tut mir leid wegen vorhin. 2A8
ice /aɪs/ Eis 4Intro 4
ice cream /ˌaɪs 'kriːm/ Eiscreme; Eis 1A6
ice skating (no pl) /'aɪsˌskeɪtɪŋ/ Schlittschuhlaufen; Eislaufen 4Intro 4
idea /aɪ'dɪə/ Idee; Einfall 2A8
° idea /aɪ'dɪə/ hier: Gedanke 5D20
ideal /aɪ'dɪəl/ ideal 6A5
if /ɪf/ wenn; falls; ob 3B2
What if ...? /wɒt ˌɪf/ Was (wäre), wenn ...? 4B7
° ill /ɪl/ krank 5A/T1
° illustrate /'ɪləstreɪt/ illustrieren 2R3
° image /'ɪmɪdʒ/ (Eben)bild; Abbild; Vorstellung 6R3
to imagine /ɪ'mædʒɪn/ sich vorstellen 3B5
° Imagine you live in a new city.: Stell dir vor, du lebst in einer neuen Stadt. 1A1
° to imitate /'ɪmɪteɪt/ imitieren; nachahmen 4A7
important /ɪm'pɔːt(ə)nt/ wichtig; wesentlich; bedeutend 5A5
to impress /ɪm'pres/ beeindrucken; imponieren 6A5
in /ɪn/ in W8
° in a car /ɪnˌə 'kɑː/ in einem Auto W3
° in bed /ɪn 'bed/ im Bett 2D9
in class /ɪn 'klɑːs/ im Unterricht 2A4
° in English /ɪnˌ'ɪŋglɪʃ/ auf Englisch Worbank 10
in front of /ɪn 'frʌntˌəv/ vor 1Intro 3
° in front of a shop /ɪnˌfrʌntˌəvˌə 'ʃɒp/ vor einem Geschäft W3
in German /ɪn 'dʒɜːmən/ auf Deutsch 2B8
° in his room /ɪnˌhɪz 'ruːm/ in seinem Zimmer W3
° in pairs /ɪn 'peəz/ paarweise 1B7
in the afternoon /ɪn ðiˌˌɑːftə'nuːn/ am Nachmittag 2B2
° in the end /ɪn ðiˌ'end/ letzten Endes; schließlich; zum Schluss 6A7
° in the evening /ɪn ðiˌ'iːvnɪŋ/ am Abend 3B/T5
° in the morning /ɪn ðə 'mɔːnɪŋ/ morgens; am Morgen; am Vormittag 3B/T5
° in the road /ɪn ðə 'rəʊd/ auf der Straße W3
in-line skating (no pl) /ˌɪnˌlaɪn 'skeɪtɪŋ/ Inlineskaten W11
to include /ɪn'kluːd/ beinhalten; mit einschließen; aufnehmen 4Intro 4
° India /'ɪndɪə/ Indien 1B7
° Indian /'ɪndɪən/ Inder/in; indisch 1B7
° individual /ˌɪndɪ'vɪdʒuəl/ Einzelne/r; Individuum; einzeln; individuell 3P2
indoor /'ɪndɔː/ Innen-; Haus-; Indoor- 4Intro 4
industry /'ɪndəstri/ Industrie; Branche 6A5
information (no pl) /ˌɪnfə'meɪʃ(ə)n/ Information(en); Auskunft 5A5
° insect /'ɪnsekt/ Insekt(en-) 5B6
inside /'ɪnˌsaɪd/ innen; in(nerhalb); (nach) drinnen 6A2
° instead of /ɪn'stedˌəv/ (an)statt 3A10
° instrument /'ɪnstrəmənt/ Instrument 3B/T3
intelligent /ɪn'telɪdʒ(ə)nt/ klug; intelligent 5A5
° to be interested (in) /ˌbiˌ'ɪntrəstɪdˌɪn/ sich interessieren (für); interessiert sein (an) 3B9
interesting /'ɪntrəstɪŋ/ interessant 6A5
on the internet /ˌɒn ðiˌ'ɪntəˌnet/ im Internet 5B3
to search the internet /ˌsɜːtʃ ðiˌ'ɪntəˌnet/ im Internet suchen 5B1
to interrupt /ˌɪntə'rʌpt/ unterbrechen 6A2
° interview /'ɪntəˌvjuː/ Interview 2D23
° to interview /'ɪntəˌvjuː/ interviewen; befragen 1B9
into /'ɪntuː/ in 3A2
invitation /ˌɪnvɪ'teɪʃ(ə)n/ Einladung(s-) 4A1
° to invite /ɪn'vaɪt/ einladen 4B5
° irregular /ɪ'regjələ/ unregelmäßig 5D2
is /ɪz/ ist W3
isn't (= is not) /'ɪznt, ɪz 'nɒt/ ist nicht 1A3
° Is there ...?/Are there ...? /'ɪz ðeəˌ'ɑː ðeə/ Gibt es ...? W7
it /ɪt/ er; sie; es; ihm; ihr; ihn 1Inro 5 (Box Objektpronomen S. 229)
it's (= it is) /ɪts, 'ɪtˌɪz/ es ist W11; hier spricht 4A7; es kostet 4B1
° it says /ɪt 'sez/ darauf steht; hier heißt es 6B/T1
° IT (no pl) (= information technology) /ˌaɪ 'tiː, ˌɪnfə'meɪʃ(ə)n tek,nɒlədʒi/ Informationstechnologie 2R3
IT room /ˌaɪ 'tiː ruːm/ Computerraum 2B1
° Italian /ɪ'tælɪən/ Italiener/in; Italienisch; italienisch 6D5
° Italy /'ɪtəli/ Italien 1B9
its /ɪts/ sein(e); ihr(e) 1B8

J

° jacket /'dʒækɪt/ Jacke Wordbank 6
° jam /dʒæm/ Marmelade Wordbank 7
January /'dʒænjuəri/ Januar 4Intro 1
jealous /'dʒeləs/ eifersüchtig; neidisch 4B7
° jewellery (no pl) /'dʒuːəlri/ Schmuck 1P1
° jigsaw /'dʒɪgsɔː/ Puzzle(spiel) 5Intro 4
job /dʒɒb/ Stelle; Job; Arbeit 3A2
° to join /dʒɔɪn/ verbinden; sich anschließen; hier: mitmachen 3B7; Mitglied werden 5D4
to join in /ˌdʒɔɪnˌ'ɪn/ mitmachen 6A5
journey /'dʒɜːni/ Reise 6A2
° judo (no pl) /'dʒuːdəʊ/ Judo 4D9
juice /dʒuːs/ Saft 4Intro 4
July /dʒʊ'laɪ/ Juli 4Intro 1 (Box The year S. 223)
to jump /dʒʌmp/ springen 6B5
jumper /'dʒʌmpə/ Pullover; Pulli 4B6
June /dʒuːn/ Juni 4Intro 1 (Box The year S. 223)
° junior /'dʒuːnɪə/ junior; Junioren-; Jugend- 5D20
just /dʒʌst/ nur; bloß; einfach; hier: gerade 4A1
° just /dʒʌst/ hier: genau 1D15
Just a minute. (informal) /ˌdʒʌstˌə 'mɪnɪt/ Einen Moment noch.; Moment mal. 4A7

K

kayaking (no pl) /'kaɪækɪŋ/ Kajakfahren 4Intro 4
to keep /kiːp/ (bei)behalten; aufbewahren 5A2; halten 5B3
° keyword /'kiːˌwɜːd/ Schlüsselwort; Stichwort 2A5
° to kick /kɪk/ treten; schießen 3D13
° kid (informal) /kɪd/ Kind; Jugendliche/r 3D9
° to kill /kɪl/ töten; umbringen 6R1
kind /kaɪnd/ Art; Sorte 5Intro 4
° kiss /kɪs/ Kuss 6R1
° to kiss /kɪs/ küssen 6R1
° kit /kɪt/ Ausrüstung; Ausstattung 6A5

English-German

kitchen /ˈkɪtʃən/ Küche **1Intro 1** (Box *Rooms* S. 209)
°**knee** /niː/ Knie **Wordbank 2**
° to **knock** /nɒk/ klopfen; stoßen **2A4**
to **know** /nəʊ/ wissen; kennen **1A5**

L

° to **label** /ˈleɪb(ə)l/ etikettieren; beschriften **5B/T2**
ladder /ˈlædə/ (Stufen)leiter **4B7**
lady /ˈleɪdi/ Frau; Dame **6B9**
lake /leɪk/ See **6Intro 3**
lamb /læm/ Lamm(fleisch) **2B8**
lamp /læmp/ Lampe **1Intro 1**
° to **land** /lænd/ landen **6R1**
language /ˈlæŋgwɪdʒ/ Sprache **2B8**
° **large** /lɑːdʒ/ groß **4R2**
° **last** /lɑːst/ letzte(r, s) **B6**
° **last name** /ˈlɑːst neɪm/ Familienname **W6**
late /leɪt/ (zu) spät **2Intro 1**
later /ˈleɪtə/ später **3Intro 4**
to **laugh (at sb/sth)** /ˈlɑːf ˌət/ lachen (über jdn/etw) **3B8**
to **lay the table** /ˌleɪ ðə ˈteɪb(ə)l/ den Tisch decken **3A2** (Box *Jobs around the house* S. 220)
lazy /ˈleɪzi/ faul; träge **4A1**
° **leaf** (*pl* **leaves**) /liːf, liːvz/ Blatt **5B6**
leaflet /ˈliːflət/ Flyer; Prospekt **5A6**
to **learn** /lɜːn/ lernen **5A6**
° to **learn** /lɜːn/ *hier:* erfahren **5D4**
to **leave** /liːv/ verlassen; weggehen; *hier:* (zurück)lassen **5Intro 4**
to **leave sb behind** /ˌliːv ˌsʌmbədi bɪˈhaɪnd/ jdn zurücklassen **5B3**
left /left/ übrig **4B1**
leg /leg/ Bein **5Intro 2**
° **legend** /ˈledʒ(ə)nd/ Sage; Legende **5P1**
° **lemon** /ˈlemən/ Zitrone **Wordbank 7**
lemonade /ˌleməˈneɪd/ Limonade **4Intro 4**
lesson /ˈles(ə)n/ (Unterrichts)stunde **2A6**
to **let** /let/ lassen **2B5**
Let me check. (*informal*) /ˌlet mi ˈtʃek/ Lass(t) mich nachsehen. **4B1**
° to **let out** /ˌletˈaʊt/ herauslassen **4B10**
let's (= **let us**) /lets, ˌletˌʌs/ Lass(t) uns **1A2**
liar /ˈlaɪə/ Lügner/in **4A1**
library /ˈlaɪbrəri/ Bibliothek; Bücherei **2B1**
to **lick** /lɪk/ (ab)lecken; (ab)schlecken **5A2**
life (*pl* **lives**) /laɪf, laɪvz/ Leben **5A1**
light /laɪt/ Licht; Lichtquelle; Lampe **4B7**
to **like** /laɪk/ mögen **1B7**

like /laɪk/ wie **1B7**; als ob **6B6**
What is … like? /ˌwɒtˌɪz ˈlaɪk/ Wie ist … (denn so)? **5A2**
° **like that** /ˌlaɪk ˈðæt/ so; auf diese Weise **5A/T5**
° **like this** /ˌlaɪk ˈðɪs/ so; auf diese Weise **3B9**
line /laɪn/ Linie; Zeile **3B8**
° **line** /laɪn/ *hier:* Reihe **4Intro 3**
° to **link** /lɪŋk/ verbinden **6B/T2**
lion /ˈlaɪən/ Löwe **5Intro 1**
° **list** /lɪst/ Liste **2B5**
to **listen to** /ˈlɪs(ə)n tə/ zuhören; (an)hören **W8**
litter box /ˈlɪtə bɒks/ Katzenklo **5B6**
little /ˈlɪt(ə)l/ klein(e, er, es) **1A6**
to **live** /lɪv/ leben; wohnen **1B7**
° **living** /ˈlɪvɪŋ/ lebend; lebendig **6A/T5**
living room /ˈlɪvɪŋ ruːm/ Wohnzimmer **1Intro 1** (Box *Rooms* S. 209)
to **load** /ləʊd/ (auf)laden; *hier:* einräumen **3A2**
° **local** /ˈləʊk(ə)l/ hiesig; örtlich **3B7**
lock /lɒk/ Schloss; *hier:* Schleuse **6B3**
° **locker** /ˈlɒkə/ Schließfach; Spind **2A2**
° **Londoner** /ˈlʌndənə/ Einwohner/in Londons **6A2**
lonely /ˈləʊnli/ einsam **1A1** (Box *You can feel …* S. 210)
long /lɒŋ/ lang **3B8**
to **look** /lʊk/ sehen; aussehen; schauen **1A6**
to **look after** /ˌlʊkˈɑːftə/ sich kümmern um **1B7**
to **look around** /ˌlʊkˌəˈraʊnd/ sich umsehen **6B9**
to **look at** /ˈlʊkˌət/ (sich) ansehen; anschauen **2A3**
to **look for** /ˈlʊk fə/ suchen nach **4A7**
° to **look up sth** /ˌlʊkˌˈʌp ˌsʌmθɪŋ/ etw nachschlagen; etw heraussuchen **4R4**
° **looks** (*pl*) /lʊks/ Aussehen **5D21**
° **Lord** /lɔːd/ Lord; Herr **6R1**
° **loser** /ˈluːzə/ Verlierer/in **2A4**
° **lost** /lɒst/ verlaufen; verloren; *hier:* entlaufen **5D7**
lots of (*informal*) /ˈlɒtsˌəv/ viel(e); eine Menge **4Intro 4**
° **loud** /laʊd/ laut **W5**
to **love** /lʌv/ lieben; sehr mögen **1A4**
to **fall in love (with sb)** /ˌfɔːlˌɪn ˈlʌv wɪð/ sich (in jdn) verlieben **5Intro 4**
° **Love** /lʌv/ Liebe; *hier:* alles Liebe (Briefschlussformel) **3P3**
° **lovely** /ˈlʌvli/ schön; hübsch; nett **1P1**
Good luck! /ˌgʊd ˈlʌk/ Viel Glück! **3A2**

lucky /ˈlʌki/ glücklich (*Glück habend/Glück bringend*) **6B6**
lunch /lʌntʃ/ Mittagessen **2A8**
to **have lunch** /ˌhæv ˈlʌntʃ/ zu Mittag essen **2A8**
lunchbox /ˈlʌntʃˌbɒks/ Lunchbox; Brot(zeit)dose **2B2**
° **lunchtime** /ˈlʌntʃˌtaɪm/ Mittagszeit; Mittagspause **3P2**

M

machine /məˈʃiːn/ Maschine; Apparat **6A5**
° **magazine** /ˌmægəˈziːn/ Zeitschrift; Magazin **1Intro 2**
° to **do magic** /ˌduː ˈmædʒɪk/ zaubern **6B6**
° **magic trick** /ˌmædʒɪk ˈtrɪk/ Zaubertrick **3B6**
(**magic**) **wand** /ˌmædʒɪk ˈwɒnd/ Zauberstab **6B6**
° **magical** /ˈmædʒɪk(ə)l/ magisch; zauberhaft **6Intro 1**
° **magician** /məˈdʒɪʃ(ə)n/ Zauberer/Zauberin **6Intro 3**
° **main** /meɪn/ Haupt-; *hier:* der/das/die wichtigste(n) … **5D20**
° **main clause** /ˌmeɪn ˈklɔːz/ Hauptsatz **5D16**
main course /ˈmeɪn kɔːs/ Hauptgericht; Hauptgang **2B8**
to **make** /meɪk/ machen; erstellen **2A11**
° to **make a phone call** /ˌmeɪkˌə ˈfəʊn kɔːl/ telefonieren **4A/T4**
° to **make friends (with sb)** /ˌmeɪk ˈfrendz wɪð/ (mit jdm) Freundschaft schließen **Wordbank 2**
° to **make sb do sth**: jdn zu etwas bringen; jdn etwas tun lassen **6A6**
° to **make sth**: etw schaffen **6A/T4**
to **make sure (that)** /ˌmeɪk ˈʃɔː ðət/ darauf achten, (dass) **5A5**, sicherstellen, (dass) **6A5**
° to **make up** /ˌmeɪkˌˈʌp/ erfinden; (sich) ausdenken **2D3**
man (*pl* **men**) /mæn, men/ Mann **4B7**
many /ˈmeni/ viele **1A1**
How many …? /ˌhaʊ ˈmeni/ Wie viele …? **3B4**
map /mæp/ (Land)karte; (Stadt)plan **6Intro 3**
March /mɑːtʃ/ März **4Intro 1**
° **market** /ˈmɑːkɪt/ Markt **1D22**
° **match** /mætʃ/ Spiel; Partie **4A1**
maths (*informal, pl*) /mæθs/ Mathe(unterricht) **2B2** (Box *Subjects* S. 216)
May /meɪ/ Mai **4Intro 1** (Box *The year* S. 223)

English-German

may /meɪ/ können; dürfen; *hier:* vielleicht **5Intro 4**
maybe /ˈmeɪbi/ vielleicht; möglicherweise **5A1**
me /miː/ mir; mich **5A2** (Box *Objektpronomen* S. 229)
  Me too! /miːˈtuː/ Ich (mir/mich) auch! **6B6**
meal /miːl/ Mahlzeit; Essen **2B8**
° to **mean** /miːn/ bedeuten; meinen **6B/T1**
° **meaning** /ˈmiːnɪŋ/ Bedeutung **3Intro 6**
meanwhile /ˈmiːnˌwaɪl/ inzwischen; unterdessen; mittlerweile **6B6**
° **meat** *(no pl)* /miːt/ Fleisch **Wordbank 7**
° **mediation** *(no pl)* /ˌmiːdiˈeɪʃ(ə)n/ (sprachliche) Vermittlung **4D24**
° **medium** *(pl media)* /ˈmiːdiəm/ (Informations)medium **1Intro 2**
to **meet** /miːt/ (sich) treffen **2A8**
  ° to **meet up (with sb)** /ˌmiːtˈʌp wɪð/ (jdn) treffen **3P1**
meeting /ˈmiːtɪŋ/ Versammlung; Sitzung; Treffen **6B9**
° **member** /ˈmembə/ Mitglied **2A5**
° **memory** /ˈmem(ə)ri/ Gedächtnis; Andenken; Erinnerung **2A/T1**
menu /ˈmenjuː/ Speisekarte **2B8**
° **merry** /ˈmeri/ fröhlich; *hier:* treu, tapfer **6R1**
mess *(no pl)* /mes/ Unordnung; Durcheinander **3A1**
message /ˈmesɪdʒ/ Nachricht; Botschaft **3A10**
  text message /ˈtekst ˌmesɪdʒ/ Textnachricht; SMS **4A7**
° **metre** /ˈmiːtə/ Meter **6A5**
° to **miaow** /mjaʊ/ miauen **Wordbank 8**
° **microchipped** /ˈmaɪkrəʊˌtʃɪpt/ mit Chip gekennzeichnet **5D7**
° **middle** /ˈmɪd(ə)l/ Mitte **5D4**
° **midnight** *(no pl)* /ˈmɪdˌnaɪt/ Mitternacht **Wordbank 3**
° **mile** /maɪl/ Meile (=1,609 km) **6B2**
° **milk** *(no pl)* /mɪlk/ Milch **4B/T2**
° to **mime** /maɪm/ pantomimisch darstellen; mimen **4A5**
minute /ˈmɪnɪt/ Minute **3Intro 4**
  Just a minute. *(informal)* /ˌdʒʌstəˈmɪnɪt/ Einen Moment noch.; Moment mal. **4A7**
  ° Wait a minute. *(informal)* /ˈweɪtəˌmɪnɪt/ Moment mal.; Warte(t) mal. **2D2**
to **miss** /mɪs/ vermissen **1A11**; verfehlen; versäumen; verpassen **5Intro 4**
° **missing** /ˈmɪsɪŋ/ verschwunden; fehlend **1A3**

mistake /mɪˈsteɪk/ Fehler; Irrtum; Versehen **5A6**
° to **mix** /mɪks/ (miteinander) (ver)mischen **3D5**
  ° to **mix up** /ˌmɪksˈʌp/ verwechseln; durcheinanderbringen **3D5**
° **mixture** /ˈmɪkstʃə/ Mischung **3D5**
mobile phone /ˌməʊbaɪlˈfəʊn/ (Mobil)telefon; Handy **1Intro3**
° **model** /ˈmɒd(ə)l/ Modell(-) **1P1**
at the moment /ət ðə ˈməʊmənt/ im Augenblick; momentan **3B8**
Monday /ˈmʌndeɪ/ Montag **2B5** (Box *Days of the week* S. 217)
money *(no pl)* /ˈmʌni/ Geld **3Intro 6**
° **monkey** /ˈmʌŋki/ Affe **Wordbank 8**
° **monster** /ˈmɒnstə/ Monster; *hier:* Ungeheuer **6Intro 3**
month /mʌnθ/ Monat **4Intro 1**
° **monument** /ˈmɒnjʊmənt/ Denkmal; Monument **5P1**
more /mɔː/ (noch) mehr; weitere(r, s) **2A5**
morning /ˈmɔːnɪŋ/ Morgen; Vormittag **2B2**
most /məʊst/ (die) meisten **6B3**; am meisten **3Intro 2**
mother /ˈmʌðə/ Mutter **1B7** (Box *Family* S. 213)
mouse *(pl mice)* /maʊs, maɪs/ Maus **1B1**
mouth /maʊθ/ Mund **5Intro 2**
move /muːv/ Bewegung **4B7**
to **move** /muːv/ (sich) bewegen **3B8**
  ° to **move** /muːv/ *hier:* (um)ziehen **5A/T3**
Mr (= Mister) /ˈmɪstə/ Herr *(Anrede)* **1A2**
Mrs /ˈmɪsɪz/ Frau *(Anrede)* **1A2**
° **Ms** /məz/ Fr.; Frau *(Alternativbezeichnung zu Mrs und Miss, die sowohl für verheiratete wie unverheiratete Frauen zutrifft)* **2A4**
much /mʌtʃ/ viel **3B2**
  How much is/are …? /ˌhaʊ ˈmʌtʃ ɪz/ə/ Was kostet/kosten …? **4B1**
  ° **much better** /ˌmʌtʃˈbetə/ viel besser **W11**
mum *(informal)* /mʌm/ Mama; Mutti **1Intro 2**
music /ˈmjuːzɪk/ Musik(unterricht) **2A8** (Box *Subjects* S. 216)
° **musical** /ˈmjuːzɪk(ə)l/ musikalisch; Musik- **3B/T3**
a must /ə ˈmʌst/ ein Muss **6A6**
must /mʌst/ müssen **3A2**
  mustn't (= must not) /ˈmʌsnt, ˌmʌst ˈnɒt/ nicht dürfen **5A2**
my /maɪ/ mein(e) **W8**

My name is … /ˈmaɪ neɪm ɪz/ Ich heiße … **W8**

N

name /neɪm/ Name **W8**
  What's your name? /ˌwɒts jə ˈneɪm/ Wie heißt du? **5A2** (Box *Sich begrüßen* S. 208)
° to **name** /neɪm/ (be)nennen **2A2**
° **navy** /ˈneɪvi/ Marine; (See)flotte **5P1**
near /nɪə/ nahe; in der Nähe **5A2**
  ° **nearby** /ˌnɪəˈbaɪ/ in der Nähe (gelegen); nahe gelegen **1P1**
° **necessary** /ˈnesəs(ə)ri/ nötig; notwendig; erforderlich **4B10**
need *(no pl)* /niːd/ Bedarf; Notwendigkeit; Bedürfnis **6B2**
to **need** /niːd/ müssen; brauchen **3A7**
  needn't (= need not) /ˈniːdnt, niːd ˈnɒt/ nicht müssen; nicht brauchen **5A2**
° **negative** /ˈneɡətɪv/ negativ; ablehnend **3A/T6**
neighbour /ˈneɪbə/ Nachbar/in **5B2**
° **nervous** /ˈnɜːvəs/ nervös **3B2**
° **netball** *(no pl)* /ˈnetˌbɔːl/ Korbball **3P2**
never /ˈnevə/ nie(mals) **3A2**
new /njuː/ neu **1Intro1**
newspaper /ˈnjuːzˌpeɪpə/ Zeitung(s-) **1B1**
° **next** /nekst/ als Nächste(r, s) **W10**
  next /nekst/ nächste(r, s) **2A8**
  ° **the next day** /ðə ˈnekstˌdeɪ/ am nächsten Tag **6A5**
  next door /ˌnekstˈdɔː/ nebenan; benachbart **4B7**
  next to /ˈnekstˌtə/ neben **1Intro 3** (Box *Präpositionen* S. 210)
nice /naɪs/ schön; angenehm; nett; freundlich **1A4**; *hier*: gut **2B10**
night /naɪt/ Nacht; Abend **3A9**
nine /naɪn/ neun **1Intro 1**
no /nəʊ/ nein **W4**; kein/e **2A2**
  ° **no longer** /nəʊ ˈlɒŋɡə/ nicht mehr **6A/T5**
  No way! *(informal)* /ˌnəʊ ˈweɪ/ Ausgeschlossen! **3A2**
° **no. (= number)** /ˈnʌmbə/ Nummer **4A5**
° **nobody** /ˈnəʊbɒdi/ niemand; keiner **6R1**
noise /nɔɪz/ Geräusch **1B1**
  ° **noise** *(no pl)* /nɔɪz/ Lärm; Krach **5D4**
noisy /ˈnɔɪzi/ laut **5B6**
north /nɔːθ/ Norden; nördlich; Nord- **6Intro 3**
° **the Northern Line** /ðə ˈnɔːðən laɪn/ *U-Bahn-Linie in London* **1P1**

English-German

nose /nəʊz/ Nase 5Intro 2
not /nɒt/ nicht 1A1
not ... any /ˌnɒt ˈeni/ kein; keine(r, s) 4B1
° **not ... anymore** /ˌnɒt ˌeniˈmɔː/ nicht mehr 4B7
° **not ... anything** /ˌnɒt ˈeniθɪŋ/ gar nichts 6A2
° **not ... anywhere** /ˌnɒt ˈeniˌweə/ nirgendwo 6B6
° **note** /nəʊt/ Notiz; Mitteilung 3A9
° **to note** /nəʊt/ beachten 5D4
° **to note down** /ˌnəʊtˈdaʊn/ (sich) notieren 2A/T2
nothing /ˈnʌθɪŋ/ nichts 3A10
to notice /ˈnəʊtɪs/ bemerken; beachten 6A2
November /nəʊˈvembə/ November 4Intro 1 (Box *The year* S. 223)
now /naʊ/ jetzt; nun 1A2
Bye for now. *(informal)* /ˈbaɪ fə naʊ/ Bis bald. 4A7
right now /ˌraɪt ˈnaʊ/ jetzt (gerade); sofort; gleich 4A1
number /ˈnʌmbə/ Nummer 1A6; Zahl; Ziffer 2B1

O

October /ɒkˈtəʊbə/ Oktober 4Intro 1 (Box *The year* S. 223)
of /əv/ von 2Intro 2
of course /əv ˈkɔːs/ natürlich 3B2
° **criminal offence** /ˌkrɪmɪn(ə)l əˈfens/ strafbare Handlung 5B1
to offer /ˈɒfə/ (an)bieten 4Intro 4
often /ˈɒf(ə)n/ oft 3A2
° **oil** /ɔɪl/ (Erd)öl 3D5
old /əʊld/ alt W8
on /ɒn/ auf; an 1Intro 3 (Box *Präpositionen* S. 210)
° **on** /ɒn/ *hier:* in 1A6; *hier:* zu 3A8; *hier:* zu, mit 5D13
on board /ˌɒn ˈbɔːd/ an Bord 6B4
° **on deck** /ˌɒn ˈdek/ an Deck 6B5
on holiday /ɒn ˈhɒlədeɪ/ im Urlaub; in den Ferien 5B3
on stage /ɒn ˈsteɪdʒ/ auf der/die Bühne 3B/T8
° **on the beach** /ˌɒn ðə ˈbiːtʃ/ am Strand 6D12
on the internet /ˌɒn ðiˈɪntəˌnet/ im Internet 5B3
° **on the left** /ˌɒn ðə ˈleft/ links; auf der linken Seite 1D19
° **on the right** /ˌɒn ðə ˈraɪt/ rechts; auf der rechten Seite 5B3
° **on time** /ɒn ˈtaɪm/ pünktlich 2D7
on TV /ˌɒn ˌtiː ˈviː/ im Fernsehen 4A1
one /wʌn/ eins; ein(e, er, es) 1Intro 1
° **one by one** /ˌwʌn baɪ ˈwʌn/ ein(e, er, es) nach dem anderen 6R1
(one) o'clock /ˌwʌn əˈklɒk/ (ein) Uhr 3Intro 4
° **onion** /ˈʌnjən/ Zwiebel 5A5
° **online dictionary** /ˌɒnˌlaɪn ˈdɪkʃən(ə)ri/ Onlinewörterbuch 3Intro 3
only /ˈəʊnli/ nur 2Intro 1
° **Oops!** /uːps/ Ups!; Hoppla! 4B7
to open /ˈəʊpən/ öffnen; *hier:* aufschlagen 2A4
open (from ... to ...) /ˈəʊpən frəm tʊ/ offen; geöffnet (von ... bis ...) 5Intro 4
° **optimistic** /ˌɒptɪˈmɪstɪk/ optimistisch Wordbank 2
or /ɔː/ oder A9
orange /ˈɒrɪndʒ/ orange; orange(farben) W4
° **orchestra** /ˈɔːkɪstrə/ Orchester 3D1
° **order** /ˈɔːdə/ Ordnung; Reihenfolge 2D22
° **to organize** /ˈɔːɡənaɪz/ organisieren 6B/T1
other /ˈʌðə/ andere(r, s) 2B8
the others /ðiˈʌðəz/ die anderen 6A2
our /aʊə/ unser(e) 1B8
° **out** /aʊt/ außen; draußen; *hier:* nach draußen 4Inro 3
° **out loud** /ˌaʊt ˈlaʊd/ laut 2A5
out of /ˈaʊt əv/ aus 4B7
° **outfit** /ˈaʊtfɪt/ Kleidung; Kleider; Outfit 4D25
outside /ˌaʊtˈsaɪd/ (dr)außen; außerhalb 6A2; *hier:* nach draußen 4B7
to be over /ˌbiːˈəʊvə/ vorbei sein 4A1
over /ˈəʊvə/ über; *hier:* auf 4B7
over there /ˌəʊvə ˈðeə/ dort drüben 4B1
own /əʊn/ eigene(r, s) 4Intro 4
owner /ˈəʊnə/ Besitzer/in; Eigentümer/in 5A2

P

page /peɪdʒ/ Seite 1A3
° **paintbrush** /ˈpeɪntˌbrʌʃ/ (Farb)pinsel Wordbank 9
° **pair** /peə/ Paar 3B9
° **in pairs** /ɪn ˈpeəz/ paarweise 1B7
° **pakora** /pəˈkɔːrə/ *indisches Gericht* 6D5
° **palace** /ˈpæləs/ Palast; Palais 6B/T1
° **paper** *(no pl)* /ˈpeɪpə/ Papier 1A2
piece of paper /ˌpiːs əv ˈpeɪpə/ Blatt Papier 5A6
paper chain /ˈpeɪpə ˌtʃeɪn/ Papierkette 4Intro 4
° **paper plate** /ˌpeɪpə ˈpleɪt/ Pappteller 4Intro 4
° **paradise** /ˈpærədaɪs/ Paradies 5A2
° **paragraph** /ˈpærəˌɡrɑːf/ Absatz; Abschnitt 3P2
parents *(pl)* /ˈpeərənts/ Eltern 1B7 (Box *Family* S. 213)
° **parrot** /ˈpærət/ Papagei Wordbank 8
part /pɑːt/ Teil 5A10
° **part** /pɑːt/ *hier:* Rolle 1B2
past /pɑːst/ nach 3Intro 4 (Box *The time* S. 219)
to pay /peɪ/ (be)zahlen 5Intro 4
° **to pay attention** /ˌpeɪ əˈtenʃ(ə)n/ Acht geben; aufpassen 2A5
PE (= physical education) /ˌpiːˈiː, ˌfɪzɪk(ə)lˌedjʊˈkeɪʃ(ə)n/ Sport *(als Schulfach)* 2B2 (Box *Subjects* S. 216)
° **peanut** /ˈpiːnʌt/ Erdnuss(-) Wordbank 7
pen /pen/ Stift 2A3 (Box *School things* S. 215)
° **pen friend** /ˈpen frend/ Brieffreund/in 3P3
° **penalty kick** /ˈpen(ə)lti kɪk/ Strafstoß; Elfmeter 6A5
° **pence** /pens/ Plural von Penny *(Untereinheit des brit. Pfund)* 4B1
pencil /ˈpensl/ Bleistift 1Intro 3 (Box *School things* S. 215)
pencil case /ˈpensl keɪs/ Federmäppchen 1Intro 3 (Box *School things* S. 215)
pencil sharpener /ˈpensl ˌʃɑːp(ə)nə/ (Bleistift)spitzer 2A3 (Box *School things* S. 215)
penguin /ˈpeŋɡwɪn/ Pinguin 5Intro 4
people *(no pl)* /ˈpiːp(ə)l/ Leute; Menschen 1A2
° **per** /pɜː/ pro 4Intro 4
perfect /ˈpɜːfɪkt/ perfekt 3A10
° **to perform** /pəˈfɔːm/ vorführen; aufführen; auftreten 3P2
° **performance** /pəˈfɔːməns/ Vorführung; Darbietung; Vorstellung 3B/T2
perhaps /pəˈhæps/ vielleicht 5A1
° **person** /ˈpɜːs(ə)n/ Person 1B2
pet /pet/ Haustier 2A12
pet shop /ˈpet ʃɒp/ Tierhandlung 5A2
photo (= photograph) /ˈfəʊtəʊ, ˈfəʊtəˌɡrɑːf/ Foto 1A2
(mobile) phone (= telephone) /ˈfəʊn, ˈteliˌfəʊn/ Telefon 1Intro 3
to answer the phone /ˌɑːnsə ðə ˈfəʊn/ ans Telefon gehen 4A1
phone call (= telephone call) /ˈfəʊn kɔːl, ˈteliˌfəʊn kɔːl/ Anruf; Telefongespräch 4A7
to phone /fəʊn/ anrufen; telefonieren 6B3
phrase /freɪz/ Satz; Ausdruck 4A7
piano /piˈænəʊ/ Klavier; Piano

English-German

picture /ˈpɪktʃə/ Bild 1B1 3Intro 1
° **piece** /piːs/ Stück Wordbank 7
  piece of paper /ˌpiːs‿əv ˈpeɪpə/ Blatt Papier 5A6
pig /pɪɡ/ Schwein 5Intro 1
° **pigeon** /ˈpɪdʒ(ə)n/ Taube Wordbank 8
° **pilot** /ˈpaɪlət/ Pilot/in 1B/T4
pink /pɪŋk/ rosa; pink W4
place /pleɪs/ Ort; Platz; Stelle 1A2
° **to change places** /ˌtʃeɪndʒ ˈpleɪsɪz/ die Plätze tauschen 4Intro 3
to plan /plæn/ planen 4A1
plane /pleɪn/ Flugzeug 6A5
° **planner** /ˈplænə/ Kalender *(zur Arbeits- oder Terminplanung)* 3Intro 3
plant /plɑːnt/ Pflanze 5B6
° **plate** /pleɪt/ Teller 5B6
to play /pleɪ/ spielen W4
player /ˈpleɪə/ Spieler/in 3B8
° **playful** /ˈpleɪf(ə)l/ spielerisch; scherzhaft; verspielt 5B6
playground /ˈpleɪˌɡraʊnd/ Spielplatz 5Intro 4
° **playing field** /ˈpleɪɪŋ fiːld/ Sportplatz; Spielfeld 3P2
please /pliːz/ bitte 1A11
  ° **Please go on.** /ˌpliːz ˌɡəʊ ˈɒn/ Mach(t) bitte weiter. 2A4
pleased /pliːzd/ froh; zufrieden 5A8
pm (= post meridiem) /ˌpiːˈem, ˌpəʊst məˈrɪdiəm/ nachmittags; abends *(nur hinter Uhrzeit zwischen 12 Uhr mittags und Mitternacht)* 3Intro 4 (Box *The time* S. 219)
pocket /ˈpɒkɪt/ Tasche *(an Kleidungsstücken)* 6B9
° **poem** /ˈpəʊɪm/ Gedicht 4D4
° **poetry** *(no pl)* /ˈpəʊɪtri/ Dichtung; Lyrik; Gedichte 3P2
° **poetry slam** /ˈpəʊɪtri slæm/ Poetry-Slam *(öffentlicher „Dichterwettstreit", bei dem die Teilnehmer/-innen selbst verfasste Texte vortragen)* 3P2
to point (at) /ˈpɔɪnt‿ət/ deuten/zeigen (auf) 4B7
° **polar bear** /ˈpəʊlə beə/ Eisbär Wordbank 8
the police *(no pl)* /ðə pəˈliːs/ die Polizei 4B7
° **polite** /pəˈlaɪt/ höflich 2A7
pond /pɒnd/ Teich 5Intro 4
° **popular** /ˈpɒpjʊlə/ beliebt; populär 1P1
° **position** /pəˈzɪʃ(ə)n/ Platz; Stelle; Position 5D4
° **positive** /ˈpɒzətɪv/ positiv 3A/T6
° **possible** /ˈpɒsəb(ə)l/ möglich 5A9

post /pəʊst/ online veröffentlichter Beitrag/Artikel/Eintrag 5B6
to post /pəʊst/ posten *(einen Beitrag/Artikel online stellen)* 5B6
postcard /ˈpəʊstˌkɑːd/ Postkarte 6B6
° **potato** *(pl* **potatoes)** /pəˈteɪtəʊ, pəˈteɪtəʊz/ Kartoffel 2B8
° **pound** /paʊnd/ Pfund *(britische Währung)* 4B1
° **power** /ˈpaʊə/ Macht 5P1
to practise /ˈpræktɪs/ üben 3B9
° **to prepare** /prɪˈpeə/ vorbereiten; erstellen 3B9
° **preposition** /ˌprepəˈzɪʃ(ə)n/ Verhältniswort; Präposition 1D26
present /ˈprez(ə)nt/ Geschenk 4Intro4
° **to present (sth to sb)** /prɪˈzent/ (jdm etw) präsentieren 2A5
pretty /ˈprɪti/ hübsch; nett 3B2
price /praɪs/ Preis 4Intro 4
prize /praɪz/ (Sieg)preis; Gewinn 3Intro 6
° **probably** /ˈprɒbəbli/ wahrscheinlich 6A/T3
problem /ˈprɒbləm/ Schwierigkeit; Problem 2Intro 1
profile /ˈprəʊfaɪl/ Profil; Porträt 5B3
° **promise** /ˈprɒmɪs/ Versprechen 6B/T1
proud /praʊd/ stolz 6B9
to pull /pʊl/ ziehen 6B5
  ° **to pull out** /ˌpʊlˈaʊt/ herausziehen 6B9
° **pullover** /ˈpʊləʊvə/ Pullover Wordbank 6
° **to punish** /ˈpʌnɪʃ/ (be)strafen 5A5
pupil /ˈpjuːp(ə)l/ Schüler/in 2B7
purple /ˈpɜːpl/ violett; lila W4
° **to push in** /ˌpʊʃˈɪn/ sich vordränge(l)n 2D7
to put /pʊt/ setzen; legen; stellen 4A5
  ° **to put away** /ˌpʊt‿əˈweɪ/ wegräumen; beiseitelegen 6B/T1
  ° **to put on** /ˌpʊtˈɒn/ anziehen 2A4
  ° **to put on make-up** /ˌpʊt‿ɒn ˈmeɪk ʌp/ sich schminken 5A/T2
  ° **to put together** /ˌpʊt təˈɡeðə/ zusammensetzen; zusammenbauen; zusammenstellen 5Intro 4
  ° **to put up** /ˌpʊtˈʌp/ aufhängen; hochheben 2A5
puzzle /ˈpʌz(ə)l/ Rätsel; Fragespiel 2B5
  ° **to puzzle out** /ˌpʌz(ə)lˈaʊt/ herausfinden; entschlüsseln 1D5
puzzled /ˈpʌz(ə)ld/ ratlos; verwirrt; (sehr) überrascht 6A3

Q

quarter (past/to) /ˈkwɔːtə pɑːst/tə/ Viertel (nach/vor) 3Intro 4 (Box *The time* S. 219)
  ° **quarter of an hour** /ˌkwɔːtər‿əv‿ənˈaʊə/ Viertelstunde 3D2
° **the Queen** /ðə ˈkwiːn/ die Queen 5P1
question /ˈkwestʃ(ə)n/ Frage 1A8
quick /kwɪk/ schnell 4B7
quiet /ˈkwaɪət/ leise; ruhig 2A4
quite /kwaɪt/ ziemlich; ganz 2A8
° **quiz** *(pl* **quizzes)** /kwɪz, ˈkwɪzɪz/ Quiz; Ratespiel 2D3

R

° **rabbit** /ˈræbɪt/ Kaninchen 2B/T6
to rain /reɪn/ regnen 5Intro 4
° **to raise** /reɪz/ (hoch)heben 2B5
° **to rap** /ræp/ rappen W10
° **rare** /reə/ rar; selten 6A/T5
° **rat** /ræt/ Ratte 5D13
° **RE (= religious education)** /ˌɑːrˈiː, rəˌlɪdʒəsˌedjʊˈkeɪʃ(ə)n/ Religionslehre 2B2
to react (to sb/sth) /rɪˈæktˌtə/ (auf jdn/etw) reagieren 4A7
to read /riːd/ lesen W8
  ° **to read out** /ˌriːdˈaʊt/ laut vorlesen 1Intro 4
reading *(no pl)* /ˈriːdɪŋ/ Lesen 3B2
ready /ˈredi/ fertig; bereit 6A2
real /rɪəl/ wirklich; echt 2A8
° **to realize** /ˈrɪəlaɪz/ sich einer Sache bewusst sein/werden; bemerken 6B/T2
really /ˈrɪəli/ wirklich; tatsächlich; echt 1A2
reason /ˈriːz(ə)n/ Grund 3B8
recipe /ˈresəpi/ Rezept 3A1
° **to record** /rɪˈkɔːd/ aufzeichnen; aufnehmen 1B2
° **recording** /rɪˈkɔːdɪŋ/ Aufnahme; Aufzeichnen 2A5
red /red/ rot W4
° **registration** /ˌredʒɪˈstreɪʃ(ə)n/ Anmeldung; *hier:* Überprüfung der Anwesenheit 2A2
to relax /rɪˈlæks/ entspannen 6Intro 1
relaxing /rɪˈlæksɪŋ/ entspannend; erholsam 6B9
religious education /rəˌlɪdʒəsˌedjʊˈkeɪʃ(ə)n/ Religionslehre 2B2 (Box *Subjects* S. 216)
° **to remember** /rɪˈmembə/ sich erinnern; *hier:* sich merken 2A/T1; daran denken 3A11

English-German

to **replace (with)** /rɪˈpleɪs wɪð/ ersetzen (durch) 5A2
° to **report** /rɪˈpɔːt/ berichten; melden 5B1
 ° to **report back (to sb)** /rɪˌpɔːt ˈbæk/ (jdm) Bericht erstatten 2B7
° to **respect** /rɪˈspekt/ respektieren 2D8
restaurant /ˈrestrɒnt/ Restaurant; Gaststätte 6A2
° **result** /rɪˈzʌlt/ Folge; Ergebnis 2B7
° to **return sth** /rɪˈtɜːn/ etw zurückgeben/-senden 5B1
° **reunion** /riːˈjuːniən/ Treffen; Wiedersehen; Wiedervereinigung 5Intro 4
reward /rɪˈwɔːd/ Belohnung 5D7
° **rhino/rhinoceros** /ˈraɪnəʊ/ raɪˈnɒs(ə)rəs/ Nashorn 6B/T1
° to **rhyme** /raɪm/ (sich) reimen 5B6
rice (no pl) /raɪs/ Reis 2B8
° **the rich** (pl) /ðə rɪtʃ/ die Reichen 6R1
to **ride** /raɪd/ fahren (mit); reiten 4Intro 4
ride /raɪd/ Fahrt 6A5
riding (no pl) /ˈraɪdɪŋ/ Reiten 4Intro 4
right /raɪt/ richtig Wordbank 11
 ° **right** /raɪt/ gleich; direkt 6R1
 ° to **be right** /ˌbiː ˈraɪt/ recht haben 4A8
 ° **You're right.** /jɔː ˈraɪt/ Du hast recht.; Ihr habt recht.; Sie haben recht. 2A12
 right now /ˌraɪt ˈnaʊ/ jetzt (gerade); sofort; gleich 4A1
° **ring** /rɪŋ/ Ring 4D23
to **ring (up)** /ˌrɪŋ ˈʌp/ anrufen; klingeln; läuten 4A1
° **river** /ˈrɪvə/ Fluss 5P1
° **on the road** /ˌɒn ðə ˈrəʊd/ auf der Straße Wordbank 3
° **role** /rəʊl/ Rolle 5A10
to **roll one's eyes** /ˌrəʊl wʌnz ˈaɪz/ die Augen verdrehen 4B7
Roman /ˈrəʊmən/ Römer/in; römisch 6B2
room /ruːm/ Zimmer; Raum 1Intro 1; Platz 6B4 (Box *Rooms* S. 209)
° **round** /raʊnd/ rund 3D14
route /ruːt/ Strecke; Route 6A5
° **routine** /ruːˈtiːn/ Routine; Gewohnheit(en) 4A6
° **the Royal Family** /ðə ˌrɔɪəl ˈfæm(ə)li/ die Königsfamilie 5P1
rubber /ˈrʌbə/ Radiergummi 2A3 (Box *School things* S. 215)
to **take out the rubbish** /ˌteɪk ˌaʊt ðə ˈrʌbɪʃ/ den Müll hinausbringen 3A2
rude /ruːd/ unhöflich 2A4
° **rugby** (no pl) /ˈrʌɡbi/ Rugby 2B/T6
ruin /ˈruːɪn/ Ruin(e); Untergang 6Intro 3

to **ruin** /ˈruːɪn/ zerstören; verderben; kaputtmachen 4B7
rule /ruːl/ Regel 2A1
ruler /ˈruːlə/ Lineal 2A3 (Box *School things* S. 215)
to **run** /rʌn/ rennen; laufen 4B7

S

sad /sæd/ traurig 1A1 (Box *You can feel ...* S. 210)
safe /seɪf/ sicher 5A8
° to **sail** /seɪl/ (auf dem Wasser) fahren/reisen; segeln 6R1
salad /ˈsæləd/ Salat 2B8
° **salt** /sɔːlt/ Salz 3D5
the same /ðə ˈseɪm/ der-/die-/dasselbe; der/die/das Gleiche 2A8
Saturday /ˈsætədeɪ/ Samstag 2B5 (Box *Days of the week* S. 217)
sauce /sɔːs/ Soße; Sauce 2B8
° **sausage** /ˈsɒsɪdʒ/ Wurst; Würstchen Wordbank 7
to **say** /seɪ/ sagen 1A1
 ° **Say hi/hello to ... (for me)!** /ˌseɪ ˈhaɪ/həˈləʊ tə fɔː mi/ Grüß (mir) bitte ...! 1D7
 ° **Say how you feel.**: Sag, wie du dich fühlst. 1A1
 to **say sorry** /ˌseɪ ˈsɒri/ sich entschuldigen 4A8
° to **scan (for)** /ˈskæn fə/ absuchen (nach); überfliegen; (ein)scannen 3A10
scared /skeəd/ verängstigt 5A8
scarf (pl **scarves**) /skɑːf, skɑːvz/ Schal 2Intro 1
° **scary** /ˈskeəri/ furchterregend Wordbank 5
° **scene** /siːn/ Szene 2Intro 3
school /skuːl/ Schule; Schul- W11
 school bag, schoolbag /ˈskuːl bæɡ/ Schultasche 1Intro 3
 science /ˈsaɪəns/ (Natur)wissenschaft 2B1 (Box *Subjects* S. 216)
 scissors (pl) /ˈsɪzəz/ Schere 2A3 (Box *School things* S. 215)
to **score (a goal)** /ˌskɔːr ə ˈɡəʊl/ (ein Tor) schießen 4A8
° **Scotland** /ˈskɒtlənd/ Schottland 1B/T6
° **Scout** /skaʊt/ Pfadfinder; Pfadfinderin 3Intro 2
to **scream** /skriːm/ schreien; kreischen 4B7
to **search the internet** /ˌsɜːtʃ ðiˌ ˈɪntəˌnet/ im Internet suchen 5B1
° **seaside** (no pl) /ˈsiːˌsaɪd/ (Meeres)küste 6D11
° **season** /ˈsiːz(ə)n/ Jahreszeit Wordbank 3

seat /siːt/ (Sitz)platz 2B2
° **second** /ˈsekənd/ Sekunde 2A/T1; zweite(r, s) 4Intro 2 (Box *1st, 2nd, 3rd, ...* S. 223)
° **secret** /ˈsiːkrət/ Geheimnis; geheim; Geheim- 3D4
to **see** /siː/ sehen W1
 See you (later). (informal) /ˌsiː jʊ ˈleɪtə/ Bis später.; Bis nachher. 4A7
 See you soon! (informal) /ˌsiː jʊ ˈsuːn/ Bis bald! 4A1
° **seed** /siːd/ Same(n); Saat 5B6
° to **sell** /sel/ verkaufen 3Intro 4
to **send** /send/ (zu)schicken 1A11
 ° to **send out** /ˌsend ˈaʊt/ verschicken; aussenden 4D24
sentence /ˈsentəns/ Satz 1A3
September /sepˈtembə/ September 4Intro 1 (Box *The year* S. 223)
° **serious** /ˈsɪəriəs/ ernst 1A6
 ° **Are you serious?** /ə jʊ ˈsɪəriəs/ Meinst du das ernst? 1A6
° to **serve** /sɜːv/ servieren; dienen 6R1
° **session** /ˈseʃ(ə)n/ Sitzung; Stunde; Session 6A5
seven /ˈsev(ə)n/ sieben 1Intro 1
° **shake** /ʃeɪk/ (Milch)shake 2D7
to **shake sb's hand** /ˌʃeɪk ˌsʌmbədiz ˈhænd/ jds Hand schütteln 6B9
she /ʃiː/ sie 1Intro 5
 she's (= **she is**) /ʃiːz, ʃɪ_ɪz/ sie ist 1A3
sheep (pl **sheep**) /ʃiːp/ Schaf 5Intro 1
° **care sheet** /ˈkeə ʃiːt/ Haltungsanleitung 5A6
shelf (pl **shelves**) /ʃelf, ʃelvz/ (Regal)brett; Bord 1Intro 3 (Box *In a room* S. 210)
animal shelter /ˈænɪm(ə)l ˌʃeltə/ Tierheim 5B1
shirt /ʃɜːt/ Hemd; *hier*: Trikot 6A2
shocked /ʃɒkt/ schockiert; entsetzt 5A9
shoe /ʃuː/ Schuh 1Intro 3
° to **shoot** /ʃuːt/ schießen 6R1
 ° to **shoot with a bow and arrow** /ˌʃuːt wɪð ə ˌbəʊ ən ˈærəʊ/ mit Pfeil und Bogen schießen 6Intro 1
shop /ʃɒp/ Geschäft; Laden 1A6
shop assistant /ˈʃɒp əˌsɪst(ə)nt/ Verkäufer/in 4B1
to **shop** /ʃɒp/ einkaufen 4A7
shopping (no pl) /ˈʃɒpɪŋ/ Einkaufen 1A6
short /ʃɔːt/ kurz 2B12
° **shorts** (pl) /ʃɔːts/ kurze Hose; Shorts Wordbank 6
° **should** /ʃʊd/ sollen 5A2
° **shoulder** /ˈʃəʊldə/ Schulter Wordbank 2

two hundred and fifty-one 251

English–German

shouldn't (= should not) /ˈʃʊdnt, ʃʊdˈnɒt/ nicht sollen 5A2
to shout (at) /ˈʃaʊt ət/ (an)schreien 3A10
talent show /ˈtælənt ʃəʊ/ Castingshow; Talentwettbewerb 3B4
to show /ʃəʊ/ zeigen 1A2
   to show sb (a)round /ʃəʊ ˌsʌmbədi əˈraʊnd/ jdn herumführen 5B3
shower /ˈʃaʊə/ Schauer; Regen; Dusche 6B4
° to shut /ʃʌt/ (ver)schließen 2A5
   Shut up! (informal) /ʃʌt ˈʌp/ Halt den Mund! 1A6
shy /ʃaɪ/ schüchtern; scheu 5B6
sick /sɪk/ krank 5A2
to sigh /saɪ/ seufzen 6B6
sight /saɪt/ Sehenswürdigkeit 6Intro 3
sign /saɪn/ Zeichen; (Straßen-/Verkehrs)schild 1A6
silly /ˈsɪli/ albern; dumm 5A10
to sing /sɪŋ/ singen 4Intro 1
   ° to sing along /ˌsɪŋ əˈlɒŋ/ mitsingen W5
   ° sing it out /ˌsɪŋ ɪt ˈaʊt/ singt aus voller Kehle W5
° singer /ˈsɪŋə/ Sänger/in 1B/T1
singing (no pl) /ˈsɪŋɪŋ/ Singen; Gesang 3B7
Sir /sɜː/ (Mein) Herr; hier: Herr Lehrer! 2B2
sister /ˈsɪstə/ Schwester W8 (Box Family S. 213)
to sit /sɪt/ sitzen 2B5
   ° to sit /sɪt/ hier: sich (hin)setzen 2A7
   to sit down /ˌsɪt ˈdaʊn/ sich (hin)setzen 2A4
   ° to sit up straight /ˌsɪt ʌp ˈstreɪt/ sich gerade hinsetzen 2A5
six /sɪks/ sechs 1Intro 1
° size /saɪz/ Größe 5D3
° to skateboard /ˈskeɪtˌbɔːd/ Skateboard fahren 4D13
skateboarding (no pl) /ˈskeɪtbɔːdɪŋ/ Skateboard fahren W11
° skill /skɪl/ Geschick; Fähigkeit; Fertigkeit 6A5
° skirt /skɜːt/ Rock 4D25
to sleep /sliːp/ schlafen 4A1
° sleep (no pl) /sliːp/ Schlaf 5B6
° slice /slaɪs/ Scheibe; Stück Wordbank 7
slide /slaɪd/ Rutschbahn; Rutsche 6A5
small /smɔːl/ klein W12
to smell /smel/ riechen; duften 5A2
to smile (at) /ˈsmaɪl ət/ (an)lächeln 3A10

° snack /snæk/ Snack; Imbiss 5D20
so /səʊ/ also; deshalb 4A7; so; sehr 1A1; damit 5B2
   ° so does … /ˈsəʊ dʌz/ das tut auch … 5P1
   so that /ˈsəʊ ðæt/ sodass; damit 5A6
social media /ˌsəʊʃ(ə)l ˈmiːdiə/ Social Media (Gesamtheit der digitalen Technologien/Medien, über die Nutzer/innen sich austauschen können) 5B6
sock /sɒk/ Socke 4B6
   ° Socks can do tricks.: Socks kann Kunststücke vorführen. W11
soldier /ˈsəʊldʒə/ Soldat/in 6B9
° solution /səˈluːʃ(ə)n/ (Auf)lösung 4B/T1
some /sʌm/ einige; etwas 2B2 (Box some, any S. 225)
somebody /ˈsʌmbədi/ (irgend)jemand; irgendwer 4A3
something /ˈsʌmθɪŋ/ etwas 4Intro 4
   ° something else /ˌsʌmθɪŋ ˈels/ etwas anderes 6R1
sometimes /ˈsʌmtaɪmz/ manchmal 3A2
son /sʌn/ Sohn 1B1 (Box Family S. 213)
Sorry! /ˈsɒri/ Entschuldigung!; Tut mir leid! 2Intro 1
   I'm sorry. /ˌaɪm ˈsɒri/ Entschuldigung.; Tut mir leid. 2Intro 1
   to say sorry /ˌseɪ ˈsɒri/ sich entschuldigen 4A8
   Sorry I'm late. /ˌsɒri aɪm ˈleɪt/ Entschuldigung, dass ich zu spät komme. 2A4
° to sort /sɔːt/ sortieren 1A/T1
sound /saʊnd/ Geräusch; Klang; Laut 5Intro 1
to sound /saʊnd/ klingen 3A2
° sour /ˈsaʊə/ sauer; hier: mürrisch 4R2
south /saʊθ/ Süden; südlich; Süd- 6Intro 3
° South America /ˌsaʊθ əˈmerɪkə/ Südamerika 6A/T5
° space /speɪs/ Raum; Platz 5B6
Spanish /ˈspænɪʃ/ Spanisch(-); spanisch 2B2 (Box Subjects S. 216)
to speak /spiːk/ sprechen 1B2
° speaker /ˈspiːkə/ Redner/in; Sprecher/in 6B7
special /ˈspeʃ(ə)l/ besondere(r, s) 3A1
° special offer /ˌspeʃ(ə)l ˈɒfə/ Sonderangebot Wordbank 6
spectacular /spekˈtækjʊlə/ atemberaubend; fantastisch 6A5

° speech bubble /ˈspiːtʃ ˌbʌb(ə)l/ Sprechblase 4A9
° to spell /spel/ buchstabieren 1B9
° spelling /ˈspelɪŋ/ Rechtschreibung; Rechtschreib- 1B9
to spend /spend/ verbringen (Zeit); ausgeben (Geld) 6A5
° to spill /spɪl/ verschütten 4B7
° sporting /ˈspɔːtɪŋ/ Sport- 3P2
sports /spɔːts/ Sport(-) 6A2
° sports field /ˈspɔːts fiːld/ Sportplatz 2B/T6
° sports ground /ˈspɔːts graʊnd/ Sportplatz Wordbank 1
spring /sprɪŋ/ Frühling 4Intro 3 (Box Seasons S. 223)
° squirrel /ˈskwɪrəl/ Eichhörnchen Wordbank 8
° stadium /ˈsteɪdiəm/ Stadion 6A/T3
stage /steɪdʒ/ Bühne 3B2
   on stage /steɪdʒ/ auf der/die Bühne 3B8
stairs (pl) /steəz/ Treppe 5D10
° stand /stænd/ (Verkaufs)stand 5D5
to stand /stænd/ stehen 2D9
   to stand up /ˌstænd ˈʌp/ aufstehen 3B8
to start /stɑːt/ anfangen 2A4
° starter /ˈstɑːtə/ Starter; für den Anfang 5D13
° statement /ˈsteɪtmənt/ Äußerung; Aussage W11
train station /ˈtreɪn ˌsteɪʃ(ə)n/ Bahnhof 6A5
statue /ˈstætʃuː/ Statue 6B9
° stay /steɪ/ Aufenthalt 6A2
to stay /steɪ/ bleiben 4A1
° steel drum /ˈstiːl drʌm/ Steeldrum (Schlaginstrument) 3P1
° to step back in time /ˌstep ˌbæk ɪn ˈtaɪm/ sich in die Vergangenheit zurückversetzen 6B2
° stick /stɪk/ Zweig; Stock; hier: Schläger Wordbank 9
still /stɪl/ (immer) noch; noch immer 1A6
stone /stəʊn/ Stein(-) 6Intro 3
to stop /stɒp/ stoppen; (an)halten; aufhören; beenden 6B3
   Stop it! (informal) /ˈstɒp ɪt/ Hör(t) auf! 6B6
stormtrooper /ˈstɔːmˌtruːpə/ Figur aus Star Wars (Krieg der Sterne) 4B7
story /ˈstɔːri/ Geschichte; Erzählung 3A10
strange /streɪndʒ/ sonderbar; merkwürdig; fremd; unheimlich 3B8
° strawberry /ˈstrɔːb(ə)ri/ Erdbeere; Erdbeer- Wordbank 7

English-German

° stray /streɪ/ streunend; herrenlos 5B1
° street /striːt/ Straße W12
° stress /stres/ Stress 4D24
° stressful /ˈstresf(ə)l/ stressig; anstrengend; aufreibend 4D24
strict /strɪkt/ streng; strikt; genau 2A4
° to structure /ˈstrʌktʃə/ strukturieren 6B11
° student /ˈstjuːd(ə)nt/ Student/in; Schüler/in 3P1
stunning /ˈstʌnɪŋ/ toll; fantastisch; umwerfend 6A5
° stunt /stʌnt/ Stunt (gefährliches, akrobatisches Kunststück) 5Intro 4
stupid /ˈstjuːpɪd/ dumm; blöd 6A3
° subject /ˈsʌbdʒɪkt/ (Schul)fach 2B2
° substantial /səbˈstænʃ(ə)l/ beträchtlich; hier: hoch 5D7
° such /sʌtʃ/ solch(er/es) 3D17
  ° such as /ˈsʌtʃ‿æz/ wie (zum Beispiel) 3P2
suddenly /ˈsʌd(ə)nli/ plötzlich 4D20
° sugar /ˈʃʊɡə/ Zucker 3D5
to suggest /səˈdʒest/ vorschlagen; hier: andeuten, (darauf) hinweisen 6B6
suggestion /səˈdʒestʃ(ə)n/ Vorschlag 3B2
° to sum up /ˌsʌm‿ˈʌp/ resümieren; zusammenfassen 6D2
summer /ˈsʌmə/ Sommer 4Intro 3 (Box Seasons S. 223)
Sunday /ˈsʌndeɪ/ Sonntag 2B5 (Box Days of the week S. 217)
° sunglasses (pl) /ˈsʌnˌɡlɑːsɪz/ Sonnenbrille 1P1
sunny /ˈsʌni/ sonnig 5B6
° superhero (pl superheroes) /ˈsuːpəˌhɪərəʊ, ˈsuːpəˌhɪərəʊz/ Superheld 4B5
supermarket /ˈsuːpəˌmɑːkɪt/ Supermarkt 3A7
to support /səˈpɔːt/ (unter)stützen 3B8
sure /ʃɔː/ sicher 2A8
  Sure! (informal) /ʃɔː/ Natürlich!; Klar! 5B3
  I'm not sure (about that). /aɪm ˌnɒt ˈʃɔː/ Ich bin mir (dieser Sache) nicht sicher.; Ich weiß nicht genau. 2A8
° to surf /sɜːf/ surfen 3D1
° surprise /səˈpraɪz/ Überraschung 3A/T5
to surprise /səˈpraɪz/ überraschen 3B8
surprised /səˈpraɪzd/ überrascht; erstaunt 3A10
° to sweep the floor /ˌswiːp ðə ˈflɔː/ den Boden fegen Wordbank 4

sweet /swiːt/ süß W11
° sweets (pl) /swiːts/ Süßigkeiten 4D20
to swim /swɪm/ schwimmen 5Intro 2
° swimming (no pl) /ˈswɪmɪŋ/ Schwimmen Wordbank 9
° swimming trunks (pl) /ˈswɪmɪŋ trʌŋks/ Badehose Wordbank 6
° swimsuit /ˈswɪmˌsuːt/ Badeanzug; Badehose Wordbank 6
° symbol /ˈsɪmb(ə)l/ Symbol; Zeichen 5P1

T

table /ˈteɪb(ə)l/ Tisch 3A2
  to lay the table /ˌleɪ ðə ˈteɪb(ə)l/ den Tisch decken 3A2
° table tennis /ˈteɪb(ə)l tenɪs/ Tischtennis 3P2
° tail /teɪl/ Schwanz 5D11
° tall /tɔːl/ groß; hoch (gewachsen) 6R1
to take /teɪk/ (mit)nehmen 4Intro 4; machen 4B7; (hin)bringen 5A4; dauern 6B3
  ° to take ... for a walk /ˌteɪk fər‿ə ˈwɔːk/ ... spazieren führen; hier: Gassi gehen mit ... 4D13
  to take a bow /ˌteɪk‿ə ˈbaʊ/ sich (unter Applaus) verbeugen 3B8
  to take a ride /ˌteɪk‿ə ˈraɪd/ eine Fahrt machen 6A5
  to take a tour /ˌteɪk‿ə ˈtʊə/ eine Reise machen 6Intro 1
  ° to take a tour /ˌteɪk‿ə ˈtʊə/ hier: eine (Besichtigungs)tour machen 6A/T3
  to take a trip /ˌteɪk‿ə ˈtrɪp/ einen Ausflug machen 6Intro 1
  to take away /ˌteɪk‿əˈweɪ/ wegnehmen; mitnehmen 4B7
  to take care of /ˌteɪk ˈkeər‿əv/ sich kümmern um 5B3
  ° to take out /ˌteɪk ˈaʊt/ herausnehmen; hinausbringen 6B/T3
  to take out the rubbish /ˌteɪk ˌaʊt ðə ˈrʌbɪʃ/ den Müll hinausbringen 3A2 (Box Jobs around the house S. 220)
  to take part (in) /ˌteɪk ˈpɑːt ɪn/ teilnehmen (an); mitmachen (bei) 3B1
  to take place /ˌteɪk ˈpleɪs/ stattfinden 3B4
  to take turns (BE) /ˌteɪk ˈtɜːnz/ sich abwechseln 5A10
talent show /ˈtælənt ʃəʊ/ Castingshow; Talentwettbewerb 3B1
° talented /ˈtæləntɪd/ talentiert; begabt 3B/T3

to talk (about/to) /ˈtɔːk ˌəˌbaʊt/tə/ sprechen; reden (über/mit) 2A4
tank /tæŋk/ (Flüssigkeits)behälter; Tank; hier: Aquarium 5B6
to taste /teɪst/ schmecken 3A10
° tea /tiː/ Tee 3A6
teacher /ˈtiːtʃə/ Lehrer/in 2A4
tearoom /ˈtiːˌruːm/ Teestube 6B2
technology /tekˈnɒlədʒi/ Technologie; Technik 2B2 (Box Subjects S. 216)
telephone (= phone) /ˈtelɪˌfəʊn, ˈfəʊn/ Telefon 1Intro 3
to tell /tel/ erzählen; sagen 3Intro 5
  ° Tell us about yourself.: Erzähl uns etwas über dich. 2A4
ten /ten/ zehn 1Intro 1
° tennis (no pl) /ˈtenɪs/ Tennis 1B/T5
° tennis court /ˈtenɪs kɔːt/ Tennisplatz 2B/T6
° terrible /ˈterəb(ə)l/ schrecklich; furchtbar Wordbank 5
text (= text message) /tekst, ˈtekst ˌmesɪdʒ/ Textnachricht; SMS 3B8
to text (sb) /tekst/ (jdm) eine Textnachricht/SMS senden 4A7
° the River Thames /ðə ˌrɪvə ˈtemz/ die Themse (Fluss in England) 5P1
than /ðæn/ als 5A4
Thank you. /ˈθæŋk ju/ Danke. 2A8
Thanks! (informal) /θæŋks/ Danke! 2A8
that /ðæt/ das; der/die/das W11 (Box this, that, these, those S. 229)
  ° that /ðæt/ dass 5A4; so 6B/T1
  ° that day /ˌðæt ˈdeɪ/ an diesem Tag 4D3
  ° that evening /ˌðæt ˈiːvnɪŋ/ an diesem Abend 6B5
  ° that is why /ˈðæt ɪz waɪ/ deshalb; darum; deswegen 1P1
that's (= that is) /ðæts, ˈðæt‿ɪz/ das ist 1Intro 4
  ° that's (= that is) /ðæts, ˈðæt‿ɪz/ hier: das macht 4D22
  ° That's right. /ˌðæts ˈraɪt/ Das stimmt. 1A5
  ° That's the alphabet. /ˌðæts ði‿ˈælfəˌbet/ Das ist das Alphabet. W5
the /ðə/ der/die/das W3
  ° The cats in the street like... /ðə ˈkæts ɪn ðə ˈstriːt laɪk/ Die Katzen in der Straße mögen... W12
  ° the Queen /ðə ˈkwiːn/ die Queen 5P1
  ° the rich (pl) /ðə rɪtʃ/ die Reichen 6R1
  ° the River Thames /ðə ˌrɪvə ˈtemz/ die Themse (Fluss in England) 5P1

English-German

° the Royal Family /ðə ˌrɔɪəl ˈfæm(ə)li/ die Königsfamilie **5P1**
° theatre /ˈθɪətə/ Theater **2B/T6**
their /ðeə/ ihr(e) **1B8**
them /ðem/ sie; ihnen **5A2** (Box *Objektpronomen* S. 229)
° theme /θiːm/ Thema(tik); Motto **4Intro 4**
° themselves /ðəmˈselvz/ sich; sie selbst; (sich) selbst **6R1**
then /ðen/ dann; danach; darauf **1A9**
there /ðeə/ dort; da **W11**; dahin; dorthin **6B3**
there is/are /ˈðeərˌɪz/ə/ es gibt, da ist; da sind **W11**
there's (= there is) /ðeəz, ˈðeərˌɪz/ es gibt; da ist **W11** (Box *There is … / there are …* S. 208)
° There you are! /ˈðeə juːˌɑː/ Da bist du ja!; Da seid ihr ja! **6B9**
these (= *pl of* this) /ðiːz/ diese **2B12** (Box *this, that, these, those* S. 229)
they /ðeɪ/ sie **1A3**
they're (= they are) /ðeə, ˈðeɪˌə/ sie sind **1A3**
° they're (= they are) /ðeə, ˈðeɪˌə/ *hier:* sie kosten **4D21**
thing /θɪŋ/ Ding; Gegenstand; Sache **1Intro 3**
to think /θɪŋk/ denken; glauben; meinen **2A12**
I don't think so. /aɪ ˌdəʊnt ˈθɪŋk səʊ/ Das glaube ich nicht. **2A12**
to think about sb/sth /ˈθɪŋkˌəˌbaʊt/ an jdn/etw denken; über jdn/etw nachdenken **5A10**
° to think of /ˈθɪŋkˌəv/ denken an; sich ausdenken **2Intro 3**; *hier:* halten von **4R3**
third /θɜːd/ dritte(r, s) **4Intro 2** (Box *1st, 2nd, 3rd, …* S. 223)
° thirsty /ˈθɜːsti/ durstig **Wordbank 7**
this /ðɪs/ diese(r, s), das **3A2** (Box *this, that, these, those* S. 229)
This is … /ˈðɪsˌɪz/ Das ist … **W8**
° This is … /ˈðɪsˌɪz/ Hier ist/spricht … **4B7**
° This is fun. /ˌðɪs ɪz ˈfʌn/ Das macht Spaß. **W10**
° this one /ˈðɪs wʌn/ diese(r, s) hier **5D17**
those (= *pl of* that) /ðəʊz/ diese **5B3** (Box *this, that, these, those* S. 229)
three /θriː/ drei **W12**
through /θruː/ durch **4B7**
to throw /θrəʊ/ werfen **6B5**
Thursday /ˈθɜːzdeɪ/ Donnerstag **2B5** (Box *Days of the week* S. 217)
ticket /ˈtɪkɪt/ Fahrkarte; (Eintritts)karte **5Intro 4**

to tidy (up) /ˌtaɪdiˈˌʌp/ aufräumen **3A2** (Box *Jobs around the house* S. 220)
tie /taɪ/ Krawatte **2Intro 1**
time /taɪm/ Zeit; Uhrzeit **2A8** (Box *The time* S. 219)
° time /taɪm/ Mal **5A/T1**
° to step back in time /ˌstepˌbækˌɪn ˈtaɪm/ sich in die Vergangenheit zurückversetzen **6B2**
timetable /ˈtaɪmˌteɪb(ə)l/ Stundenplan **2B2**
° tiny /ˈtaɪni/ winzig **6A/T5**
tired /ˈtaɪəd/ müde **6A2**
° title /ˈtaɪt(ə)l/ Titel **3B8**
to /tʊ/ in; nach; zu; an; *hier:* auf **1A8**; *hier:* vor **3Intro 4**
° to /tʊ/ *hier:* vor **3D2**; *hier:* mit **5D15**; *hier:* mit **6B3**
today /təˈdeɪ/ heute **2B2**
° toe /təʊ/ Zeh(e) **Wordbank 2**
together /təˈɡeðə/ zusammen **1B7**
° toilet /ˈtɔɪlət/ Toilette; Klo **Wordbank 4**
tomato (*pl* tomatoes) /təˈmɑːtəʊ, təˈmɑːtəʊz/ Tomate **2B8**
tomorrow /təˈmɒrəʊ/ morgen **3A2**
tonight /təˈnaɪt/ heute Abend; heute Nacht **5B2**
too /tuː/ auch **W8**; zu **3B8**
tooth (*pl* teeth) /tuːθ, tiːθ/ Zahn **5Intro 2**
° top /tɒp/ oberste(r, s); *hier:* beste(r, s) **2A12**
torch (BE) /tɔːtʃ/ Taschenlampe **4B7**
tour /tʊə/ Reise; Tour; Tournee; Führung **2B1**
° tourist attraction /ˈtʊərɪstˌəˌtrækʃ(ə)n/ Touristenattraktion **6A/T4**
° tower /ˈtaʊə/ Turm **5P1**
° town /taʊn/ Stadt **6D10**
town centre /ˌtaʊn ˈsentə/ Stadtmitte **6B9**
° toy /tɔɪ/ Spielzeug(-) **2B/T3**
train /treɪn/ Zug **6A5**
train station /ˈtreɪnˌsteɪʃ(ə)n/ Bahnhof **6A5**
to train /treɪn/ trainieren **4A1**
trainer /ˈtreɪnə/ Trainer/in; Turnschuh **4B6**
° trampolining (*no pl*) /ˈtræmpəˌliːnɪŋ/ Trampolinspringen **3P1**
° to translate /trænsˈleɪt/ übersetzen **2D27**
° translation /trænsˈleɪʃ(ə)n/ Übersetzung **2D7**
° to travel /ˈtræv(ə)l/ reisen **5A5**
tree /triː/ Baum **6Intro 3**
° trendy /ˈtrendi/ modisch **1P1**
° trick /trɪk/ Trick; *hier:* Streich; Kunststück **5D13**
° tricky /ˈtrɪki/ schwierig; kompliziert; knifflig **2D27**
trip /trɪp/ Ausflug; Reise **6Intro 3**

° trophy /ˈtrəʊfi/ Trophäe; Pokal **6A/T3**
° tropical /ˈtrɒpɪk(ə)l/ Tropen-; tropisch **5P1**
trousers (*pl*) /ˈtraʊzəz/ Hose **4B6**
true /truː/ wahr **3A2**
° trunk /trʌŋk/ Rüssel **5Intro 2**
to try /traɪ/ versuchen; (aus)probieren **2B5**
° to try on /ˌtraɪˌˈɒn/ anprobieren **Wordbank 6**
° to try out /ˌtraɪˌˈaʊt/ ausprobieren **6A5**
° tube /tjuːb/ Röhre; *hier:* die (Londoner) U-Bahn **1P1**
Tuesday /ˈtjuːzdeɪ/ Dienstag **2B5** (Box *Days of the week* S. 217)
TV (= television) /ˌtiːˈviː, ˈteliˌvɪʒn/ Fernsehen; Fernseher **4A1**
on TV /ˌɒnˌtiːˈviː/ im Fernsehen **4A1**
to watch TV /ˌwɒtʃˌtiːˈviː/ fernsehen **4A1**
twelve /twelv/ zwölf **W8**
° twig /twɪɡ/ Zweig **5Intro 2**
twin /twɪn/ Zwilling; Zwillings- **W8**
two /tuː/ zwei **1Intro 1**
° type /taɪp/ Art; Typ; Sorte **1D8**
° Typical! (*informal*) /ˈtɪpɪk(ə)l/ Typisch! **6B9**
° tyre /ˈtaɪə/ Reifen **4B10**

U

uncle /ˈʌŋk(ə)l/ Onkel **1B7** (Box *Family* S. 213)
under /ˈʌndə/ unter **1Intro 3** (Box *Präpositionen* S. 210)
underground station /ˈʌndəˌɡraʊndˌsteɪʃ(ə)n/ U-Bahn-Station **1A6**
to understand /ˌʌndəˈstænd/ verstehen **2B5**
° underwater /ˌʌndəˈwɔːtə/ Unterwasser-; unter Wasser **5Intro 4**
° underwear (*no pl*) /ˈʌndəˌweə/ Unterwäsche **Wordbank 6**
° unforgettable /ˌʌnfəˈɡetəb(ə)l/ unvergesslich **5Intro 4**
unfortunately /ʌnˈfɔːtʃ(ə)nətli/ unglücklicherweise; leider **3B8**
° unfriendly /ʌnˈfrendli/ unfreundlich **4R3**
unhappy /ʌnˈhæpi/ unglücklich **5A1**
uniform /ˈjuːnɪfɔːm/ Uniform **2Intro 1**
° to unlock /ʌnˈlɒk/ aufschließen; entsperren **6B6**
° to unscramble /ʌnˈskræmb(ə)l/ wieder ordnen **4B/T4**
° up /ʌp/ nach oben; hoch **2Intro 3**; oben **5D17**
° up till /ˈʌp tɪl/ bis (zu) **W10**
up to /ˈʌp tʊ/ bis (zu) **4Intro 4**

English–German W

upstairs /ʌpˈsteəz/ (nach) oben **1Intro 1**

us /ʌs/ uns **5A2** (Box *Objektpronomen* S. 229)

° **USA** (= United States of America) /ˌjuː_esˈeɪ, juːˌnaɪtɪd ˌsteɪts_əv_əˈmerɪkə/ Vereinigte Staaten von Amerika **1B/T4**

to use /juːz/ (be)nutzen; verwenden **1A11**

usually /ˈjuːʒʊəli/ gewöhnlich; normalerweise **3A2**

V

vampire /ˈvæmpaɪə/ Vampir/in **4B7**

° **van** /væn/ Transporter; Kleinbus **6B/T1**

° **vegetable** /ˈvedʒtəb(ə)l/ Gemüse **Wordbank 7**

vegetarian /ˌvedʒəˈteəriən/ Vegetarier/in; vegetarisch **2B8**

° **veggie** (=vegetable) *(informal)* /ˈvedʒi/ Gemüse **2B8**

° **vehicle** /ˈviːɪk(ə)l/ Fahrzeug; Vehikel **6B/T1**

° **verse** /vɜːs/ Strophe **2A5**

very /ˈveri/ sehr; außerordentlich **1A2**

° **very** /ˈveri/ *hier:* genau **6R1**

view /vjuː/ (Aus)sicht; (Aus)blick **6A5**

° **viewing** *(no pl)* /ˈvjuːɪŋ/ Anschauen **4D23**

village /ˈvɪlɪdʒ/ Dorf **6B2**

° **violin** /ˌvaɪəˈlɪn/ Violine; Geige **3P1**

visit /ˈvɪzɪt/ Besuch **6A5**

to visit /ˈvɪzɪt/ besuchen; anschauen **5Intro 4**

voice /vɔɪs/ Stimme **6B9**

° **voice message** /ˈvɔɪs ˌmesɪdʒ/ Sprachnachricht **4A/T5**

W

to wait (for) /ˈweɪt fɔː/ warten (auf) **4B7**

° **Wait a minute.** *(informal)* /ˈweɪt_ə ˌmɪnɪt/ Moment mal.; Warte(t) mal. **2D2**

walk /wɔːk/ Spaziergang **5A5**

to go for a walk /ˌɡəʊ fər_əˈwɔːk/ einen Spaziergang machen **5A5**

to walk /wɔːk/ (zu Fuß) gehen; laufen **6B2**

to walk off /ˌwɔːk_ˈɒf/ weggehen (von); hinuntergehen (von) **4A8**

to walk the dog /ˌwɔːk ðəˈdɒɡ/ den Hund ausführen **3A2** (Box *Jobs around the house* S. 220)

wall /wɔːl/ Wand **6A5**

to want /wɒnt/ wünschen; wollen **3A2**

° **wanted** /ˈwɒntɪd/ gesucht **6R3**

to want sb to do sth: wollen, dass jd etw tut **5A9**

wardrobe /ˈwɔːdrəʊb/ (Kleider)schrank; Garderobe **1Intro 3** (Box *In a room* S. 210)

to wash /wɒʃ/ (sich) waschen **4A4**

to watch /wɒtʃ/ beobachten; zuschauen; anschauen **2A2**

to watch TV /ˌwɒtʃ ˌtiːˈviː/ fernsehen **4A1**

water *(no pl)* /ˈwɔːtə/ Wasser **5Intro 2**

° **waterbus** /ˈwɔːtəbʌs/ Wasserbus **1P1**

to wave (at) /ˈweɪv_ət/ (zu)winken; *hier:* schwingen **6B6**

way /weɪ/ Weg; Art und Weise **2A1**

to be on one's way /weɪ/ auf dem Weg sein **6A2**

by the way /ˌbaɪ ðəˈweɪ/ übrigens **4A7**

No way! *(informal)* /ˌnəʊˈweɪ/ Ausgeschlossen! **3A2**

we /wiː/ wir **W8**

° **We can go to school together.:** Wir können zusammen zur Schule gehen. **W11**

° **We'd like some white chocolate.:** Wir hätten gerne weiße Schokolade. **1B1**

we're (= we are) /wɪə, ˈwi_ə/ wir sind **W8**

° **We're doing fine.** /wɪə ˌduːɪŋˈfaɪn/ Uns geht's gut.; Wir machen es gut. **W10**

to wear /weə/ tragen; anhaben **3B2**

weather /ˈweðə/ Wetter **5Intro 4**

Wednesday /ˈwenzdeɪ/ Mittwoch **2B5** (Box *Days of the week* S. 217)

week /wiːk/ Woche **2B5**

° **weekday** /ˈwiːkdeɪ/ Wochentag **6A/T4**

° **weekend** /ˌwiːkˈend/ Wochenende **3Intro 2**

at the weekend /ət ðə ˌwiːkˈend/ am Wochenende **4A6**

weird /wɪəd/ merkwürdig; seltsam; komisch **2B5**

° **to welcome** /ˈwelkəm/ willkommen heißen; begrüßen **6A2**

° **welcome** /ˈwelkəm/ willkommen **5Intro 4**; Willkommen; Begrüßung **6A1**

Welcome to /ˈwelkəm tʊ/ Willkommen in **W1**

well /wel/ nun (ja); tja **1A2**

° **wetland** /ˈwetlænd/ Sumpfgebiet; Feuchtgebiet **5Intro 4**

what /wɒt/ was **W9**; welche(r, s) **2B5**

What a/an ...! Was für ein(e) ...! **3A1**

What about ...? *(informal)* /ˈwɒt_əˌbaʊt/ Was ist mit ...?; Wie wäre es mit ...? **1A2**

What about you? /ˌwɒt_əˌbaʊtˈjuː/ Was ist mit dir?; Und du? **W9**

° **What can you hear?** /ˌwɒt kən jʊˈhɪə/ Was hörst du? **W2**

° **What can you see?** /ˌwɒt kən jʊˈsiː/ Was siehst du? **W1**

° **What do you say?** /ˌwɒt du ju ˈseɪ/ Wie sagt man? *(wenn man „Danke" erwartet)* **4R2**

What if ...? /ˈwɒt_ɪf/ Was (wäre), wenn ...? **4B7**

° **What is ... about?** /ˌwɒt_ɪz əˈbaʊt/ Worum geht es in/bei ...? **2D8**

What is ... like? /ˌwɒt_ɪzˈlaɪk/ Wie ist ... (denn so)? **5A2**

what's (= what is) /ˈwɒts, ˈwɒt_ɪz/ was ist **W9**

° **What's the name of your school?** /ˌwɒts ðəˈneɪm_əv jə skuːl/ Wie heißt deine/eure Schule? **W11**

What's the time? /ˌwɒts ðəˈtaɪm/ Wie spät/Wie viel Uhr ist es? **3Intro 4**

° **What's up?** *(informal)* /ˌwɒts_ˈʌp/ Was ist los?; Wie geht's? **1A5**

What's wrong with ...? /ˌwɒtsˈrɒŋ wɪð/ Was stimmt nicht mit ...?; Was fehlt ...? **1A2**

What's wrong? /ˌwɒtsˈrɒŋ/ Was ist los? **6B7**

What's your favourite ...? /ˌwɒts jəˈfeɪv(ə)rət/ Was ist dein Lieblings...? **W9**

What's your name? /ˌwɒts jəˈneɪm/ Wie heißt du? **W8**

° **What time is it?** /ˌwɒt_ˈtaɪm_ɪz_ɪt/ Wie spät/Wie viel Uhr ist es? **Wordbank 3**

° **wheel** /wiːl/ Rad **5B/T5**

when /wen/ wenn **1B2**; wann **2B4**; als **3A7**

° **When you hear your word, stand up and show it.:** Steh auf, wenn du dein Wort hörst, und zeige es. **1A2**

where /weə/ wo **W3**

Where are you from? /ˌweər_ə jʊˈfrɒm/ Woher kommst du?; Woher kommt ihr? **W8**

Where is ...? / Where are ...? /ˈweər_ɪz, ˈweər_ɑː/ Wo ist ...? / Wo sind ...? **W3**

where's (= where is) /weəz, ˈweər_ɪz/ wo ist **1B3**

° **which** /wɪtʃ/ welche(r, s) **2B5**; der/die/das **6A/T5**

to whisper /ˈwɪspə/ flüstern **4B7**

white /waɪt/ weiß **W4**

who /huː/ wer **1B1**

# English-German

° who /huː/ der/die/das 1P1
whole /həʊl/ ganz; gesamt 6A5
° Whose things are they?: Wessen Dinge sind das? 2D25
why /waɪ/ warum 1A5
° wife (pl wives) /waɪf, waɪfz/ (Ehe)frau Wordbank 2
° Wi-Fi /ˈwaɪ faɪ/ WLAN (Computernetzwerk mit Funktechnik) 6A/T4
wild /waɪld/ wild; hier: in freier Wildbahn lebend 6B2
° will /wɪl/ werden 5B1
to win /wɪn/ gewinnen 3Intro 6
window /ˈwɪndəʊ/ Fenster 1Intro 1
° wing /wɪŋ/ Flügel 5B/T3
to wink (at sb) /ˈwɪŋk ət/ (jdm zu)zwinkern 6B9
winner /ˈwɪnə/ Gewinner/in; Sieger/in 3B1
winter /ˈwɪntə/ Winter 4Intro 3 (Box *Seasons* S. 223)
wishing well /ˈwɪʃɪŋ wel/ Wunschbrunnen 6B9
° witch /wɪtʃ/ Hexe 4B5
with /wɪð/ mit W11
without /wɪðˈaʊt/ ohne 6B9
woman (pl women) /ˈwʊmən, ˈwɪmɪn/ Frau 6B6
wonderful /ˈwʌndəf(ə)l/ wunderbar; wundervoll 4Intro 4
word /wɜːd/ Wort 1A2
° word order /ˈwɜːd ˌɔːdə/ Wortstellung; Satzstellung 5D16
° word web /ˈwɜːd web/ Wortnetz 2A9
° work /wɜːk/ Arbeit 1B9
to work /wɜːk/ arbeiten; hier: funktionieren 6A5
° to work out /ˌwɜːk ˈaʊt/ lösen; verstehen; herausfinden 2B8
world /wɜːld/ Welt 6A5
° World Wetlands Day /ˌwɜːld ˈwetləndz deɪ/ Welttag der Feuchtgebiete 5Intro 4
° world-famous /ˌwɜːldˈfeɪməs/ weltberühmt 6Intro 3
worried /ˈwʌrid/ beunruhigt; besorgt 1A1 (Box *You can feel ...* S. 210)
to worry (about) /ˈwʌri ə ˌbaʊt/ sich Sorgen machen (um) 5A2
would /wʊd/ würde(n/st/t) 6B2
would like to /wʊd ˈlaɪk tə/ würde(n/st/t) gern 6A5
° would you like /wʊd ju ˈlaɪk/ möchtest du; möchtet ihr; möchten Sie Wordbank 7
wouldn't (= would not) /ˈwʊd(ə)nt, wʊd ˈnɒt/ würde(n/st/t) nicht 6B2
to write /raɪt/ schreiben 1Intro 4

to write down /ˌraɪt ˈdaʊn/ aufschreiben; niederschreiben 1Intro 4
wrong /rɒŋ/ falsch 2Intro 1
What's wrong with ...? /ˌwɒts ˈrɒŋ wɪð/ Was stimmt nicht mit ...?; Was fehlt ...? 1A2
° What's wrong? /ˌwɒts ˈrɒŋ/ Was ist los? 2D2

Y

year /jɪə/ Jahr 1B9
yellow /ˈjeləʊ/ gelb W4
yes /jes/ ja W4
° yesterday /ˈjestədeɪ/ gestern Wordbank 3
° yet /jet/ bis jetzt; schon; noch 6R1
° yogurt /ˈjɒɡət/ Joghurt Wordbank 7
you /juː/ du; dich; dir; Sie; Ihnen; ihr; euch W11 (Box *Objektpronomen* S. 229)
° You see? /ju ˈsiː/ Verstehst du?; Versteht ihr?; Verstehen Sie? 5A/T6
you're (= you are) /jɔː, ˈjuː ə/ du bist; ihr seid; Sie sind 1A3
° You're right. /ˌjɔː ˈraɪt/ Du hast recht.; Ihr habt recht.; Sie haben recht. 2A12
° You're welcome. /ˌjɔː ˈwelkəm/ Bitte schön.; Gern geschehen. 3B/T4
° You're wrong. /ˌjɔː ˈrɒŋ/ Du irrst dich.; Ihr irrt euch.; Sie irren sich. 2A/T5
young /jʌŋ/ jung 5A5
your /jɔː/ dein(e); euer/eure; Ihr(e) W8
° youth club /ˈjuːθ klʌb/ Jugendzentrum 3D1
° yummy (informal) /ˈjʌmi/ lecker 5B6

Z

zip wire /ˈzɪp ˌwaɪə/ Seilrutsche 6A5
° zoo /zuː/ Zoo 5D3
zoo-keeper /ˈzuːˌkiːpə/ Tierpfleger/in 5Intro 4

German-English

German-English dictionary

A

Abend evening; night
Abendessen dinner
abends *(nur hinter Uhrzeit zwischen 12 Uhr mittags und Mitternacht)* pm (= post meridiem)
Abenteuer adventure
aber but
absolut absolute
sich abwechseln to take turns
sich irren to be wrong
Akt act
aktiv active
Aktivität activity
alle everybody
allein alone
alle(s) all
als when
als Erstes first
alt old
am Nachmittag in the afternoon
am Wochenende at the weekend
an at; to
an jdn/etw denken to think about sb/sth
(an)bieten to offer
(an)dauern to go on
andere(r, s) other; different
anders different
andeuten to suggest
anfangen to start; to begin
angenehm nice
anhaben to wear
(an)halten to stop
(an)hören to listen to
ankommen to arrive
(an)lächeln to smile (at)
Anruf phone call (= telephone call)
anrufen to ring (up); to phone
ans Telefon gehen to answer the phone
anschauen to look at; to visit; to watch
(an)schreien to shout (at)
(sich) ansehen to look at
Antwort answer
Apfel apple
Apparat machine
April April
Aquarium tank
Arbeit job
arbeiten to work
Arbeitsgemeinschaft club
Art und Weise way
Arzt/Ärztin doctor
atemberaubend spectacular
auch too
auf on; at
auf Besichtigungstour gehen to go sightseeing
auf Deutsch in German
(auf jdn/etw) reagieren to react (to sb/sth)
aufbewahren to keep
Aufgabe exercise
aufgeregt excited
aufhören to stop
(auf)laden to load
aufräumen to tidy (up)
aufregend exciting
aufschlagen to open
aufschreiben to write down
Aufsicht care
aufstehen to stand up
Auge eye
im Augenblick at the moment
August August
aus from
(Aus)blick view
Ausdruck phrase
einen Ausflug machen to take a trip
ausgeben *(Geld)* to spend
ausgezeichnet excellent
Auskunft information *(no pl)*
(aus)probieren to try
ausräumen to empty
ausreichend enough
aussehen to look
außerhalb outside
außerordentlich extraordinary; very
(Aus)sicht view
(aus)wechseln to change
Auto car

B

backen to bake
(Bade)wanne bath
Bad(ezimmer) bathroom; bath
Banane banana
Baum tree
beachten to notice
(be)antworten to answer
bedeutend important
beenden to end; to stop
beginnen to begin
bei at
(bei)behalten to keep
Bein leg
Beispiel example
bekommen to get
bemerken to notice
(be)nutzen to use
beobachten to watch
Bereich area
bereit ready
sich beruhigen to calm down
berühmt famous
Beschreibung description
Besitzer/in owner
besondere(r, s) special
besonders especially
besorgt worried
besser better
beste(r, s) best
bestimmen to decide
Besuch visit
besuchen to visit
Besucher audience
Betreuung care
Bett bed
ins Bett gehen to go to bed
beunruhigt worried
bevor before
(sich) bewegen to move
(be)zahlen to pay
Bibliothek library
Bild picture
billig cheap
Bis bald! See you soon! *(informal)*
Bis bald. Bye for now. *(informal)*
Bis nachher. / Bis später. See you (later). *(informal)*
Biskuit biscuit
bitte please
Bitte schön. Here you are.
Blatt Papier piece of paper
blau blue
Bleistift pencil
(Bleistift)spitzer pencil sharpener
bloß just
Boden floor
Boot boat
Bord shelf *(pl shelves)*
böse bad
brauchen to need
braun brown
Brett board
brillant brilliant *(informal)*
Bruder brother
Buch book
Bücherei library
Burg castle
Bus bus

C

Chance chance
Charakter character

D

da there; because
da ist there's (= there is)
da sind there is/are
dahin there

two hundred and fifty-seven 257

German-English

danach then
dankbar glad
Danke! Thanks! *(informal)*, Thank you.
dann, darauf then
darauf achten, (dass) to make sure (that)
das the; that; this
das ist that's (= that is)
Datum date
dauern to take
dein(e) your
den Hund ausführen to walk the dog
den Müll hinausbringen to take out the rubbish
den Tisch decken to lay the table
denken to think; to feel
der the; that
deutlich clear
Deutsche/r; deutsch German
Deutsch(unterricht) German
Dezember December
dich you
dick fat
die the; that
Dienstag Tuesday
diese(r, s) this
diese *(Plural)* these
Ding thing
dir you
Donnerstag Thursday
dort there
dorthin there
Drama drama *(no pl)*
draußen outside
drinnen inside
dritte(r, s) third
du you
duften to smell

E

echt really
ehe before
Eigentümer/in owner
ein(e) a/an
einfach easy; just
Einfall idea
einige a few
Einkaufen shopping *(no pl)*
einkaufen to shop
einkaufen gehen to go shopping
Einladung(s-) invitation
einräumen to load
einsam lonely
eintreffen to arrive
Eis ice; ice cream
Eiscreme ice cream
Elefant elephant
Eltern parents *(pl)*
enden to end

England England
Englisch(-); englisch English
Ente duck
(ent)leeren to empty
entscheiden to decide
sich entschuldigen to say sorry
Entschuldigen Sie bitte! Excuse me!
Entschuldigung! Sorry!; Excuse me!; I'm sorry.
entsetzt shocked
entspannen to relax
enttäuscht disappointed
er he
Erdkunde geography
erhalten to get
(jdm etw) erklären to explain (sth to sb)
Erlebnis adventure
erstaunlich amazing
erstaunt surprised
erstellen to make
erste(r, s) first
erzählen to tell
Erzählung story
es it
es gibt there's (= there is)
es gibt, da ist there is/are
es kostet it's (= it is)
Essen food
essen to eat
Esszimmer dining room
etw wert sein to be worth sth
etwas something
euch you
euer/eure your

F

fahren to go
fahren (mit) to ride
Fahrkarte ticket
(Fahr)rad bike *(informal)*
mit dem (Fahr)rad by bike
eine Fahrt machen to take a ride
fallen to fall
falsch wrong
Familie family
fantastisch fantastic *(informal)*; stunning; spectacular
Farbe colour
faszinierend fascinating
faul lazy
Favorit/in favourite
Februar February
Federmäppchen pencil case
Fehler mistake
feiern to celebrate
Fenster window
Ferien holiday
in den Ferien on holiday
fernsehen to watch TV
Fernsehen TV (= television)

im Fernsehen on TV
Fernseher TV (= television)
fertig ready
fett fat
Figur character
Filzstift felt tip
finden to find
Fisch fish *(pl fish or fishes)*
fliegen to fly
Flugzeug plane
(Flüssigkeits)behälter tank
Foto photo (= photograph)
Frage question
fragen to ask
Französisch(-); französisch French
Frau woman
Frau *(Anrede)* Mrs
frei free
Freitag Friday
Freizeit free time
fremd strange
fressen to eat
Freund/in friend
freundlich friendly; nice
frisch fresh
froh pleased; glad
fröhlich happy
Frucht fruit *(pl fruit or fruits)*
Frühling spring
funktionieren to work
(sich) fühlen to feel
fünfte(r, s) fifth
für for
Fuß foot *(pl feet)*
Fußball football
Futter food

G

Garderobe wardrobe
Garten garden
Gaststätte restaurant
geben to give
jdm etw geben to give sth to sb
Gebiet area
Geburtstag(s-) birthday
gefährlich dangerous
Gefühl feeling
gegen against
Gegend area
Gegenstand thing
gehen to go
gelassen calm
gelb yellow
Geld money *(no pl)*
Gelegenheit chance
genau strict
genießen to enjoy
genug enough
genügend enough
geöffnet (von ... bis ...) open (from ... to ...)

German-English

Geografie geography
gerade just
Geschäft shop
geschehen to happen
Geschichte story
Geschichte history
Geschirrspülmaschine dishwasher
Gesicht face
gesund healthy
Gewinn prize
gewinnen to win
gewöhnlich usually
glauben to believe; to think
glücklich happy; glad
glücklich *(Glück habend/Glück bringend)* lucky
gratis free
grau grey
groß big
Großeltern grandparents *(pl)*
Großmutter grandmother
(Groß)stadt(-) city
Großvater grandfather
grün green
Grund reason
gut good

H

Haare hair *(no pl)*
haben to have; to have got
Hähnchen chicken
halb (acht) half past (seven)
Hallo! Hello!
halten to keep
Hand hand
Handschuh glove
Handy (mobile) phone
hassen to hate
Haus house; home
ins Haus inside
Hausaufgabe(n) homework *(no pl)*
Haustier pet
Heft exercise book
Heim home
heiß hot
helfen to help
herausfinden to find out
Herbst autumn
hereinkommen to come in
Herr *(Anrede)* Mr (= Mister)
herunter down
Herz heart
heute today
heute Abend tonight
heute Nacht tonight
hier here
Hier, bitte. Here you are.
Hilfe help *(no pl)*
(hin)bringen to take
(hin)kommen to get
sich (hin)setzen to sit down

hinter behind
hinunter down
hoffen to hope
holen to get
hören to hear
Hose trousers *(pl)*
hübsch pretty
Huhn chicken
Hühnchen chicken
Hülle case
Hund dog
hungrig hungry

I

ich I
ich bin I'm (= I am)
Ich fürchte ... I'm afraid ...
ich hätte gerne I'd love to have
Ich heiße ... My name is ...
Ich komme aus ... I'm from ...
Ich mag ... I like ...
Ich mag ... nicht. I don't like ...
ich würde gern I'd like to (= I would like to)
ideal ideal
Idee idea
ihm him; it
ihn him; it
ihnen them
Ihnen you
ihr you; her; it
ihr seid you're (= you are)
ihr(e) her; their; its
Ihr(e) your
immer always
in in; to; at
Information(en) information *(no pl)*
Inlineskaten in-line skating *(no pl)*
innen inside
insbesondere especially
intelligent intelligent
interessiert interested
im Internet on the internet
(irgend)ein(e) any
(irgend)jemand, irgendwer somebody
Irrtum mistake
ist is
ist nicht isn't (= is not)

J

ja yes
Jahr year
Januar January
jede/r everyone; everybody
jede(r, s) any
jetzt now
Job job
Jonglieren juggling *(no pl)*
Juli July

jung young
Junge boy
Juni June

K

Käfig cage
Kajakfahren kayaking *(no pl)*
Kalender calendar
kalt cold
Kantine canteen
Karte card
Kartoffel potato *(pl potatoes)*
Käse cheese
Kästchen box
Katze cat
kaufen to buy
kein/e no
Keks biscuit
kennen to know
Kind child *(pl children)*
Kiste box
klar clear
Klar! Sure! *(informal)*
klasse brilliant *(informal)*
Klassenkamerad/in classmate
Klassenzimmer classroom
Klavier piano
Kleber glue
Klebstoff glue
Kleider clothes *(pl)*
(Kleider)schrank wardrobe
Kleidung clothes *(pl)*
klein small
klingeln to ring (up)
Klub club
klug intelligent
Koffer case
komisch funny
kommen to come
Komm(t) jetzt! Come on! *(informal)*
können can
Kopf head
köstlich delicious
Kostümfest fancy dress party
krank sick
Kreis circle
Küche kitchen
Kuchen cake
Kuh cow
Kunde/Kundin customer
Kunst(unterricht) art
Kurs class
kurz short
Küste coast

L

lachen (über jdn/etw) to laugh (at sb/sth)
Laden shop
Lampe lamp

W German-English

(Land)karte map
lang long
langweilig boring
lassen to let
Lass(t) uns let's (= let us)
laufen to run; to walk
laut noisy
läuten to ring (up)
Leben life *(pl lives)*
leben to live
lecker delicious
legen to put
Lehrer/in teacher
leicht easy
leider unfortunately
Leider ... I'm afraid ...
leise quiet
lernen to learn
lesen to read
Lesen reading *(no pl)*
Leute people *(no pl)*
lieben to love
Liebling(s-) favourite
lila purple
Limonade lemonade
Lineal ruler
Linie line
Lösung answer
Löwe lion
Lügner/in liar
lustig funny

M

machen to do; to make
Mach(t) schon! Come on! *(informal)*
Mädchen girl
Mai May
Mama mum *(informal)*
manchmal sometimes
Mann man *(pl men)*
Mantel coat
Mappe folder
März March
Maschine machine
Mathe(unterricht) maths *(informal, pl)*
Maus mouse *(pl mice)*
mein(e) my
meinen to think
eine Menge lots of *(informal)*
Mensa canteen
Menschen people *(no pl)*
merkwürdig strange; funny
Minute minute
mit with
(mit)bringen to bring
mitkommen to come
mitmachen to join in
mitmachen (bei) to take part (in)
(mit)nehmen to take
Mitschüler/in classmate

Mittagessen lunch; dinner
Mittwoch Wednesday
(Mobil)telefon (mobile) phone
mögen to like
möglich possible
möglicherweise maybe
Möglichkeit chance
momentan at the moment
Monat month
Montag Monday
Morgen morning
morgen tomorrow
morgens *(nur hinter Uhrzeit zwischen Mitternacht und 12 Uhr mittags)* am (= ante meridiem)
müde tired
Mund mouth
Musik(unterricht) music
ein Muss a must
müssen to need; must
Mutter mother
Mutti mum *(informal)*

N

nach after; past; to
nach draußen outside
nach Hause home
(nach) oben upstairs
(nach) unten downstairs
Nachbar/in neighbour
Nachmittag afternoon
nachmittags *(nur hinter Uhrzeit zwischen 12 Uhr mittags und Mitternacht)* pm (= post meridiem)
nachsehen to check
nächste(r, s) next
Nacht night
Nachtisch dessert
nahe near
in der Nähe near
Nahrung food
Name name
Nase nose
natürlich of course
Natürlich! Sure! *(informal)*
(Natur)wissenschaft science
neben next to
nein no
nervös nervous
nett pretty; nice
neu new; fresh
nicht not
nicht stimmen to be wrong
nichts nothing
niederschreiben to write down
nie(mals) never
noch einmal again
(noch) mehr more
Nord- north
Norden north
nördlich north

normalerweise usually
November November
Nummer number
nun now
nur only; just

O

Obst fruit *(pl fruit or fruits)*
oder or
offen (von ... bis ...) open (from ... to ...)
öffnen to open
oft often
ohne without
Ohr ear
Oktober October
Oma grandma *(informal)*
Omi grandma *(informal)*
Onkel uncle
Opa, Opi grandpa *(informal)*
orange(farben) orange
Ordner folder
Ort place

P

Papa dad *(informal)*
passieren to happen
perfekt perfect
Pferd horse
Pflanze plant
Pflege care
Piano piano
Pinguin penguin
pink pink
Platz place; room
Pommes frites chips *(pl)*
posten *(einen Beitrag/Artikel online stellen)* to post
Preis price
preiswert cheap
Problem problem
Publikum audience
Pulli, Pullover jumper
putzen to clean

R

Radiergummi rubber
ratlos puzzled
Raum room
recht haben to be right
reden (über/mit) to talk (about/to)
(Regal)brett shelf *(pl shelves)*
Regel rule
Region area
rein clean
reinigen to clean
Reis rice *(no pl)*
Reise journey
eine Reise machen to take a tour

German-English

reiten to ride
Religionslehre religious education
rennen to run
Restaurant restaurant
Rezept recipe
richtig right
riechen to smell
Römer/in Roman
römisch Roman
rosa pink
rot red
Route route
ruhig calm; quiet
Ruin(e) ruin

S

Sache thing
Saft juice
sagen to say; to tell
Salat salad
Samstag Saturday
Satz phrase
sauber clean
sauber machen to clean
Sauce sauce
Schachtel box
Schaf sheep (pl sheep)
schauen to look
Schauspielerei drama (no pl)
Schere scissors (pl)
scheu shy
Schiff boat
(ein Tor) schießen to score (a goal)
schlafen to sleep
Schlafzimmer bedroom
schlecht bad
schließen to close
schlimm bad
Schloss castle
schmecken to taste
Schnellhefter folder
schockiert shocked
Schokolade chocolate
schön nice; beautiful
schrecklich horrible
schreiben to write
Schreibtisch desk
schüchtern shy
Schuh shoe
Schule, Schul- school
in der Schule at school
Schüler/in pupil
(Schul)fach subject
(Schul)klasse class
Schultasche school bag
schwarz black
Schwein pig
schwer difficult
Schwester sister
schwierig difficult
Schwierigkeit problem

schwimmen to swim
See lake
sehen to see; to look
Sehenswürdigkeit sight
sehr very
sehr mögen to love
sein to be
sein(e) its; his
Seite page
September September
setzen to put
(Show)nummer act
sicher sure; safe
sicherstellen, (dass) to make sure (that)
sie she; they; her; it; them
Sie you
sie ist she's (= she is)
sie sind they're (= they are)
Sie sind you're (= you are)
(Sieg)preis prize
singen to sing
sitzen to sit
Skateboard fahren skateboarding (no pl)
SMS text (= text message); text message
Socke sock
Sohn son
sollen should
Sommer summer
sonderbar strange
sonnig sunny
Sonntag Sunday
sich Sorgen machen (um) to worry (about)
Soße sauce
Spanisch(-); spanisch Spanish
spannend exciting
Spaß machen to be fun
(zu) spät late
Spaziergang walk
einen Spaziergang machen to go for a walk
Speisekarte menu
Speisesaal dining room
Spiel game
spielen to play
Sport (als Schulfach) PE (= physical education)
Sport(-) sports
Sprache language
sprechen to speak; to talk (about/to)
springen to jump
städtisch city
(Stadt)plan map
staubsaugen to hoover
stehen to stand
Stein(-) stone
Stelle job; place
stellen to put

Stift pen
stoppen to stop
strahlend brilliant (informal)
Strand beach
Strecke route
streng strict
strikt strict
Stuhl chair
Stunde hour
Stundenplan timetable
stürzen to fall
suchen nach to look for
Süd-; Süden; südlich south
Supermarkt supermarket
surfen gehen to go surfing

T

Tafel board
Tag day
Tank tank
Tante aunt
Tanz dance
tanzen to dance
Tanzen dancing (no pl)
Tänzer/in dancer
Tasche bag
(Taschen)rechner calculator
Tätigkeit activity
tatsächlich really
Technik, Technologie technology
Teil part
teilnehmen (an) to take part (in)
Telefongespräch phone call (= telephone call)
telefonieren to phone
teuer expensive
Textnachricht text (= text message)
(jdm) eine Textnachricht/SMS senden to text (sb)
Theater(-) drama (no pl)
Tier animal
Tisch table
Tochter daughter
toll stunning; amazing; brilliant (informal)
Tomate tomato (pl tomatoes)
Tor goal
total absolute
träge lazy
tragen to wear
Trainer/in trainer
Traum(-) dream
traurig sad
(sich) treffen to meet
trinken to drink
trinken, zu sich nehmen to have
Tschüss! Bye! (= Goodbye!) (informal)
tun to do
Tür door
Turnen gym (= gymnastics, pl)

W German-English

Turnschuh trainer
Tut mir leid! (I'm) sorry!

U

üben to practise
über about
über jdn/etw nachdenken to think about sb/sth
überall everywhere
überprüfen to check
überraschen to surprise
überrascht surprised
(sehr) überrascht puzzled
Übung exercise
(ein) Uhr (one) o'clock
Uhrzeit time
um at
umfallen to fall
umwerfend stunning
und and
Und du? What about you?
ungebraucht fresh
ungewöhnlich extraordinary
unglücklich unhappy
unglücklicherweise unfortunately
unheimlich strange
Uniform uniform
uns us
unser(e) our
unter under
Untergang ruin
Unterricht class
im Unterricht in class
(Unterrichts)stunde lesson
(unter)stützen to support
Urlaub holiday
im Urlaub on holiday
in Urlaub gehen/fahren to go on holiday

V

Vater father
Vati dad (informal)
Vegetarier/in;
  vegetarisch vegetarian
verabscheuen to hate
(ver)ändern to change
verängstigt scared
verärgert angry; annoyed
verbringen (Zeit) to spend
Verein club
vergessen to forget
Verkäufer/in shop assistant
verschieden different
Versehen mistake
verstehen to understand
versuchen to try
verwenden to use
verwirrt puzzled
viel much

viel(e) lots of (informal)
viele many
vielleicht perhaps; maybe
vierte(r, s) fourth
Viertel (nach/vor) quarter (past/to)
violett purple
Vogel bird
von from; of; about
vor in front of
Vormittag morning
vormittags (nur hinter Uhrzeit zwischen Mitternacht und 12 Uhr mittags) am (= ante meridiem)
vorschlagen to suggest
sich vorstellen to imagine

W

wahr true
wann when
warm hot
warten (auf) to wait (for)
warum why
was what
was ist what's (= what is)
Was ist dein Lieblings...? What's your favourite ...?
Was ist mit ...? What about ...? (informal)
Was ist mit dir? What about you?
Was kostet/kosten ...? How much is/are ...?
(sich) waschen to wash
Wasser water (no pl)
Weg way
wegen about
weil because
weiß white
weitere(r, s) more
welche(r, s) what
Wellensittich budgie (= budgerigar) (informal)
Welt world
wenige a few
wenn when
wer who
werden to get
werfen to throw
wesentlich important
Wetter weather
wichtig important
wie how
Wie alt bist du? How old are you?
Wie alt seid ihr? How old are you?
Wie geht es dir/Ihnen/euch? How are you?
Wie heißt du? What's your name?
Wie spät/Wie viel Uhr ist es? What's the time?
Wie viele ...? How many ...?
Wie wäre es mit ...? How about ...?; What about ...? (informal)

wieder again
(wieder) zurück back
Winter winter
wir we
wir sind we're (= we are)
wirklich really
wissen to know
witzig funny
wo where
wo ist where's (= where is)
Wo ist ...? / Wo sind ...? Where is ...? / Where are ...?
Woche week
Woher kommst du? Where are you from?
Woher kommt ihr? Where are you from?
wohnen to live
Wohnung home
Wohnzimmer living room
wollen to want
Wort word
wunderbar wonderful
wundervoll wonderful
wünschen to want
wütend angry

Z

Zahl number
Zahn tooth (pl teeth)
Zeile line
Zeit time
ziehen to pull
Ziel goal
Ziffer number
Zimmer room
zornig angry
zu to
zu (sehr) too
zu Ende bringen to end
(zu Fuß) gehen to walk
zu Hause at home; home
zu Mittag essen to have lunch
zuerst first
zufrieden happy; pleased
Zug train
Zuhause home
zuhören to listen to
zum Beispiel for example
zumachen to close
zuschauen to watch
Zuschauer audience
zweite(r, s) second
zwischen between

Words W

Names

Girls/women
Abby /ˈæbi/
Aisha /aɪˈiːʃə/
Alex /ˈæliks/
Alexa /əˈleksə/
Alice /ˈælɪs/
Amy /ˈeɪmi/
Anne /æn/
Beatrice /ˈbɪətrɪs/
Beebee /ˈbiːbi/
Betty /ˈbeti/
Brianna /briˈænə/
Cara /ˈkɑːrə/
Carol /ˈkærəl/
Caroline /ˈkærəlaɪn/
Catherine /ˈkæθ(ə)rɪn/
Claire /kleə/
Elizabeth /ɪˈlɪzəbəθ/
Elsa /ˈelsə/
Emillia /eˈmiːliə/
Emily /ˈeməli/
Emma /emə/
Ethel /ˈeθ(ə)l/
Frances /ˈfrɑːnsɪs/
Gillian /ˈdʒɪliən/
Grace /ɡreɪs/
Gracie /ˈɡreɪsi/
Hamida /həˈmiːdə/
Helen /ˈhelən/
Isabelle /ˈɪzəbel/
Jane /dʒeɪn/
Jasmine /ˈdʒæzmɪn/
Jennie /ˈdʒeni/
Jessica /ˈdʒesɪkə/
Jo /dʒəʊ/
Julia /ˈdʒuːliə/
Kate /keɪt/
Katie /ˈkeɪti/
Kayla /ˈkeɪlə/
Kemi /ˈkemi/
Kira /ˈkɪərə/
Lara /ˈlɑːrə/
Lea /liːə/
Lizzie /ˈlɪzi/
Lizzy /ˈlɪzi/
Louise /luˈiːz/
Maria /məˈriːə/
Mary /ˈmeəri/
Maya /ˈmeɪə/
Meera /ˈmɪərə/
Miriam /ˈmɪriəm/
Mo /məʊ/
Molly /ˈmɒli/
Olivia /əˈlɪviə/
Penny /ˈpeni/
Rosa /ˈrəʊzə/
Sally /ˈsæli/
Sam /sæm/
Sandy /ˈsændi/
Sarah /ˈseərə/
Sheree /ˈʃeri/
Sophia /səˈfaɪə/
Sophie /ˈsəʊfi/
Stella /ˈstelə/
Susan /ˈsuːz(ə)n/
Tammy /ˈtæmi/
Taylor /ˈteɪlə/
Zoe /ˈzəʊi/

Boys/men
Aarav /ˈɑːrɑv/
Alex /ˈæliks/
Ben /ben/
Bertie /ˈbɜːti/
Bruno /ˈbruːnəʊ/
Charlie /ˈtʃɑːli/
Christopher /ˈkrɪstəfə/
Daniel /ˈdænjəl/
Danny /ˈdæni/
David /ˈdeɪvɪd/
Duncan /ˈdʌŋk(ə)n/
Eric /ˈerɪk/
George /dʒɔːdʒ/
Harry /ˈhæri/
Henry /ˈhenri/
Ian /ˈiːən/
Jack /dʒæk/
Jake /dʒeɪk/
James /dʒeɪmz/
Jason /ˈdʒeɪs(ə)n/
Joe /dʒəʊ/
John /dʒɒn/
Maddox /ˈmædəks/
Mel /mel/
Merlin /ˈmɜːlɪn/
Michael /ˈmaɪk(ə)l/
Mike /maɪk/
Nick /nɪk/
Oscar /ˈɒskə/
Peter /ˈpiːtə/
Phil /fɪl/
Rajiv /rɑːˈdʒiːv/
Ralph /rælf/
Richard /ˈrɪtʃəd/
Rob /rɒb/
Rocco /ˈrɒkəʊ/
Sam /sæm/
Sanjay /ˈsændʒeɪ/
Simon /ˈsaɪmən/
Steve /stiːv/
Tim /tɪm/
Tom /tɒm/
Tony /ˈtəʊni/
William /ˈwɪljəm/
Yusuf /ˈjʊsʊf/

Family names
Barton /ˈbɑːt(ə)n/
Batson /ˈbæts(ə)n/
Brown /braʊn/
Butler /ˈbʌtlə/
Collins /ˈkɒlɪnz/
Dean /diːn/
Fox /fɒks/
Fung /fʌŋ/
Green /ɡriːn/
Jackson /ˈdʒæks(ə)n/
Jefferson /ˈdʒefəs(ə)n/
Khan /kɑːn/
May /meɪ/
McBride /məkˈbraɪd/
Miller /ˈmɪlə/
Nelson /ˈnels(ə)n/
Newman /ˈnjuːmən/
Rice /raɪs/
Rudd /rʌd/
Scott /skɒt/
Smith /smɪθ/
Spencer /ˈspensə/
Swift /swɪft/
Wells /welz/
Woolf /wʊlf/

Other names
Acland Burghley /ˌæklənd ˈbɜːli/
Alexandra Palace /ˌælɪɡˌzɑːndrə ˈpæləs/
Alnwick Castle /ˌænɪk ˈkɑːs(ə)l/
Arsenal /ˈɑːs(ə)n(ə)l/
Battersea Dogs and Cats Home /ˌbætəsi ˌdɒɡz ən ˈkæts həʊm/
Bennett Street /ˈbenɪt striːt/
Big Ben /ˌbɪɡ ˈben/
Big Jake /ˌbɪɡ ˈdʒeɪk/
Caesar /ˈsiːzə/
Camden School for Girls /ˌkæmdən ˌskuːl fə ˈɡɜːlz/
Caspar /ˈkæspə/
Catford School /ˌkætfəd ˈskuːl/
Chess /tʃes/
Discovery Centre /dɪˈskʌv(ə)ri ˌsentə/
Dizzee /ˈdɪzi/
Dog Reunion Day /ˌdɒɡ riˈjuːniən deɪ/
Everlyn /ˈevəlɪn/
Foxhill School /ˌfɒkshɪl ˈskuːl/

two hundred and sixty-three 263

Words

Friend Chat /ˈfrend tʃæt/
Hadrian /ˈheɪdriən/
Hadrian's Wall /ˌheɪdriənz ˈwɔːl/
Hampstead Heath /ˌhæmstɪd ˈhiːθ/
Harley /ˈhɑːli/
Harry Potter /ˌhæri ˈpɒtə/
Hoover /ˈhuːvə/
Jeff /dʒef/
Kentish Town City Farm /ˌkentɪʃ ˌtaʊn ˈsɪti fɑːm/
King Arthur /ˌkɪŋ ˈɑːθə/
Lacock Abbey /ˌleɪkɒk ˈæbi/
Langdon School /ˌlæŋdən ˈskuːl/
Little John /ˌlɪt(ə)l ˈdʒɒn/
Liverpool /ˈlɪvəpuːl/
Llyn Llydaw /ˌlɪn ˈlɪdɔː/
Loch Ness /ˌlɒk ˈnes/
London Aquarium /ˌlʌndən əˈkweəriəm/
London Zoo /ˌlʌndən ˈzuː/
Maid Marian /ˌmeɪd ˈmæriən/
Manchester Climbing Centre /ˌmænˌtʃestə ˈklaɪmɪŋ ˌsentə/
Manchester Museum /ˌmænˌtʃestə mjuːˈziːəm/
Manchester United /ˌmænˌtʃestə juːˈnaɪtɪd/
Man United (= Manchester United) /ˈmænjuː, ˌmænˌtʃestə juːˈnaɪtɪd/
Milly /ˈmɪli/
Mittens /ˈmɪt(ə)nz/
Museum of Science and Industry /mjuːˌziːəm əv ˌsaɪəns ən ˈɪndəstri/
MyPhone /ˈmaɪfəʊn/
National Football Museum /ˌnæʃ(ə)nəl ˈfʊtˌbɔːl mjuːˌziːəm/
Nessie /ˈnesi/
Neymar /ˈneɪmɑː/
Nottingham Castle /ˌnɒtɪŋəm ˈkɑːs(ə)l/
Old Trafford /ˌəʊld ˈtræfəd/
Patch /pætʃ/
Penguin Beach /ˌpeŋgwɪn ˈbiːtʃ/
Pet Paradise /ˌpet ˈpærədaɪs/
Pip /pɪp/
Play Factore /ˈpleɪ ˌfækt(ə)ri/
Prince John /ˌprɪns ˈdʒɒn/
Regent's Canal /ˌriːdʒ(ə)nts kəˈnæl/
Regent's Park /ˌriːdʒ(ə)nts ˈpɑːk/
Rex /reks/

Robin Hood /ˌrɒbɪn ˈhʊd/
Rufus /ˈruːfəs/
Scrabble /ˈskræb(ə)l/
Sheriff of Nottingham /ˌʃerɪf əv ˈnɒtɪŋəm/
Sherwood Forest /ˌʃɜːwʊd ˈfɒrɪst/
Simple Simon /ˌsɪmp(ə)l ˈsaɪmən/
Socks /sɒks/
Spencer /ˈspensə/
Stonehenge /ˌstəʊnˈhendʒ/
Super Soaker 2000 /ˌsuːpə ˌsəʊkə tuːˈθaʊz(ə)nd/
Super Sylvio /ˌsuːpə ˈsɪlviəʊ/
The London Wetland Centre /ðə ˌlʌndən ˈwetlænd ˌsentə/
the Merry Men /ðə ˌmeri ˈmen/
The Old Man of Storr /ðiˌ əʊld mæn əv ˈstɔː/
the River Thames /ðə ˌrɪvə ˈtemz/
The Roundhouse /ðə ˈraʊndˌhaʊs/
the Tower /ðə ˈtaʊə/
Tintagel Castle /tɪnˌtædʒ(ə)l ˈkɑːs(ə)l/
Tintern Abbey /ˌtɪntən ˈæbi/
Tottenham /ˈtɒtnəm/
Trent Park /ˌtrent ˈpɑːk/
William Ellis School /ˌwɪljəm ˈelɪs ˌskuːl/
Young Farmer Club /jʌŋ ˈfɑːmə klʌb/
Zizzi /ˈzɪzi/

Geographical names
Africa /ˈæfrɪkə/
Albert Street /ˈælbət striːt/
America /əˈmerɪkə/
Asia /ˈeɪʒə/
Avon /ˈeɪv(ə)n/
Bath /bɑːθ/
Berlin /bɜːˈlɪn/
Bradford-on-Avon /ˌbrædfəd ɒn ˈeɪv(ə)n/
Brighton /ˈbraɪt(ə)n/
Bristol /ˈbrɪst(ə)l/
Britain /ˈbrɪt(ə)n/
Camden /ˈkæmdən/
Camden High Street /ˌkæmdən ˈhaɪ striːt/
Camden Market /ˌkæmdən ˈmɑːkɪt/
Camden Town /ˌkæmdən ˈtaʊn/
Chile /ˈtʃɪli/
Chippenham /ˈtʃɪp(ə)nəm/
Cornwall /ˈkɔːnwɔːl/

Coventry /ˈkɒv(ə)ntri/
Devizes /dɪˈvaɪzɪz/
Devon /ˈdev(ə)n/
Dover /ˈdəʊvə/
Edinburgh /ˈedɪnb(ə)rə/
England /ˈɪŋglənd/
Europe /ˈjʊərəp/
Frome /fruːm/
Germany /ˈdʒɜːməni/
Ghana /ˈgɑːnə/
Greece /griːs/
Hogwarts /ˈhɒgwɔːts/
India /ˈɪndiə/
Kennet and Avon Canal /ˌkenɪt ən ˌeɪv(ə)n kəˈnæl/
Inverness Street /ˌɪnvəˈnes striːt/
Italy /ˈɪtəli/
Lacock /ˈleɪkɒk/
Lake District /ˈleɪk ˌdɪstrɪkt/
Lavenham /ˈlæv(ə)nəm/
Little Venice /ˌlɪt(ə)l ˈvenɪs/
Liverpool /ˈlɪvəpuːl/
London /ˈlʌndən/
Longleat Safari Park /ˌlɒŋliːt səˈfɑːri pɑːk/
Manchester /ˈmænˌtʃestə/
Mumbai /ˌmʊmˈbaɪ/
Newquay /ˈnjuːkiː/
Nottingham /ˈnɒtɪŋəm/
Rye /raɪ/
Scotland /ˈskɒtlənd/
Severn /ˈsev(ə)n/
South America /ˌsaʊθ əˈmerɪkə/
Trafalgar Square /trəˌfælgə ˈskweə/
Trowbridge /ˈtrəʊbrɪdʒ/
USA (= United States of America) /ˌjuː es ˈeɪ, juːˌnaɪtɪd ˌsteɪts əv əˈmerɪkə/
Wales /weɪlz/
York /jɔːk/

Words

The English alphabet

a /eɪ/	h /eɪtʃ/	o /əʊ/	v /viː/
b /biː/	i /aɪ/	p /piː/	w /ˈdʌbljuː/
c /siː/	j /dʒeɪ/	q /kjuː/	x /eks/
d /diː/	k /keɪ/	r /aː/	y /waɪ/
e /iː/	l /el/	s /es/	z /zed/
f /ef/	m /em/	t /tiː/	
g /dʒiː/	n /en/	u /juː/	

English sounds

Im Englischen spricht man Wörter oft anders aus, als man sie schreibt.
Deshalb ist die Lautschrift sehr nützlich: Sie gibt an, wie ein Wort ausgesprochen wird.
Hier ist eine Liste der Lautschriftzeichen zusammen mit Beispielwörtern:

Vokale
- /ɑː/ **arm**
- /ʌ/ b**u**t
- /e/ d**e**sk
- /ə/ **a**, **a**n
- /ɜː/ g**ir**l, b**ir**d
- /æ/ **a**pple
- /ɪ/ **i**n, **i**t
- /i/ ever**y**
- /iː/ **ea**sy, **ea**t
- /ɒ/ **o**range
- /ɔː/ **a**ll, st**o**ry
- /ʊ/ l**oo**k
- /u/ Febr**u**ary
- /uː/ f**oo**d

Doppellaute
- /aɪ/ **ey**e, b**uy**
- /aʊ/ h**ou**se
- /eə/ th**ere**
- /eɪ/ t**a**ke, th**ey**
- /ɪə/ h**ere**
- /ɔɪ/ b**oy**
- /əʊ/ g**o**, **o**ld
- /ʊə/ y**ou're**

Konsonanten
- /b/ **b**ag, clu**b**
- /d/ **d**uck, car**d**
- /f/ **f**ish, lau**gh**
- /g/ **g**et, do**g**
- /h/ **h**ot
- /j/ **y**ou
- /k/ **c**an, du**ck**
- /l/ **l**ot, smal**l**
- /m/ **m**ore, **m**u**m**
- /n/ **n**ow, su**n**
- /ŋ/ so**ng**, lo**ng**
- /p/ **p**resent, to**p**
- /r/ **r**ed, **r**ight
- /s/ **s**ister, cla**ss** (scharfes s)
- /t/ **t**ime, ca**t**
- /z/ no**s**e, dog**s** (weiches s)
- /ʒ/ televi**si**on
- /dʒ/ oran**ge**
- /ʃ/ **s**ure, Engli**sh**
- /tʃ/ **ch**ild, **ch**eese
- /ð/ **th**ese, mo**th**er (weicher Laut)
- /θ/ mou**th**, **th**ink (harter Laut)
- /v/ **v**ery, ha**v**e
- /w/ **wh**at, **w**ord

Betonungszeichen für die folgende Silbe
- /ˈ/ Hauptbetonung
- /ˌ/ Nebenbetonung

Words

Numbers

Cardinal numbers

0	zero /ˈzɪərəʊ/	11	eleven /ɪˈlevn/	30	thirty /ˈθɜːti/
1	one /wʌn/	12	twelve /twelv/	40	forty /ˈfɔːti/
2	two /tuː/	13	thirteen /ˌθɜːˈtiːn/	50	fifty /ˈfɪfti/
3	three /θriː/	14	fourteen /ˌfɔːˈtiːn/	...	
4	four /fɔː/	15	fifteen /ˌfɪfˈtiːn/	90	ninety /ˈnaɪnti/
5	five /faɪv/	16	sixteen /ˌsɪksˈtiːn/	100	one hundred /ˈwʌn ˌhʌndrəd/
6	six /sɪks/	17	seventeen /ˌsevnˈtiːn/	...	
7	seven /ˈsevn/	18	eighteen /ˌeɪˈtiːn/	900	nine hundred /ˈnaɪn ˌhʌndrəd/
8	eight /eɪt/	19	nineteen /ˌnaɪnˈtiːn/	1,000	one thousand /ˈwʌn ˌθauznd/
9	nine /naɪn/	20	twenty /ˈtwenti/		
10	ten /ten/	21	twenty-one /ˌtwentiˈwʌn/		
		...			

Ordinal numbers

1st	first /fɜːst/	14th	fourteenth /ˌfɔːˈtiːnθ/	30th	thirtieth /ˈθɜːtiəθ/
2nd	second /ˈsekənd/	15th	fifteenth /ˌfɪfˈtiːnθ/	31st	thirty-first /ˌθɜːtiˈfɜːst/
3rd	third /θɜːd/	16th	sixteenth /ˌsɪksˈtiːnθ/	...	
4th	fourth /fɔːθ/	...		40th	fortieth /ˈfɔːtiəθ/
5th	fifth /fɪfθ/	20th	twentieth /ˈtwentiəθ/	50th	fiftieth /ˈfɪftiəθ/
6th	sixth /sɪksθ/	21st	twenty-first /ˌtwentiˈfɜːst/	60th	sixtieth /ˈsɪkstiəθ/
7th	seventh /ˈsevnθ/	22nd	twenty-second /ˌtwentiˈsekənd/	70th	seventieth /ˈsevntiəθ/
8th	eighth /eɪtθ/	23rd	twenty-third /ˌtwentiˈθɜːd/	80th	eightieth /ˈeɪtiəθ/
9th	ninth /naɪnθ/	24th	twenty-fourth /ˌtwentiˈfɔːθ/	90th	ninetieth /ˈnaɪntiəθ/
10th	tenth /tenθ/	...		100th	hundredth /ˈhʌndrədθ/
11th	eleventh /ɪˈlevnθ/				
12th	twelfth /twelfθ/				
13th	thirteenth /ˌθɜːˈtiːnθ/				

Words W

Ähnliche Wörter

Es gibt viele Wörter, die im Englischen und im Deutschen gleich sind. Sie unterscheiden sich oft nur darin, wie sie geschrieben werden. Viele dieser Wörter sprechen wir gleich aus.
Diese Wörter stehen nicht in den Wortlisten, weil sie dir ja nicht neu sind. Bei denen, die ein bisschen anders ausgesprochen werden als im Deutschen, ist die Lautschrift farbig hervorgehoben.

ABC /ˌeɪ biː ˈsiː/
action /ˈækʃ(ə)n/
admiral /ˈædm(ə)rəl/
Africa /ˈæfrɪkə/
alphabet /ˈælfəˌbet/
aquarium /əˈkweəriəm/
arena /əˈriːnə/
arrogant /ˈærəgənt/
audio guide /ˈɔːdiəʊ ˌgaɪd/
baby /ˈbeɪbi/
badminton (no pl) /ˈbædmɪntən/
ball /bɔːl/
band /bænd/
basketball /ˈbɑːskɪtˌbɔːl/
broccoli (no pl) /ˈbrɒkəli/
brownie /ˈbraʊni/
burger /ˈbɜːgə/
café /ˈkæfeɪ/
camera /ˈkæm(ə)rə/
CD /ˌsiː ˈdiː/
chart hit /ˈtʃɑːt hɪt/
clown /klaʊn/
coach /kəʊtʃ/
comic /ˈkɒmɪk/
computer /kəmˈpjuːtə/
conversation /ˌkɒnvəˈseɪʃ(ə)n/
cornflakes /ˈkɔːnˌfleɪks/
cool /kuːl/
correct /kəˈrekt/
corridor /ˈkɒrɪdɔː/
cousin /ˈkʌz(ə)n/
cricket (no pl) /ˈkrɪkɪt/
crocodile /ˈkrɒkədaɪl/
digital /ˈdɪdʒɪt(ə)l/
DJ (= disc jockey) /ˈdiːˌdʒeɪ, ˌdɪsk ˈdʒɒki/
email /ˈiːmeɪl/
emoji /ɪˈməʊdʒi/
euro /ˈjʊərəʊ/

experiment /ɪkˈsperɪmənt/
extra /ˈekstrə/
fair /feə/
fan /fæn/
feedback (no pl) /ˈfiːdbæk/
film /fɪlm/
finger /ˈfɪŋgə/
flyer /ˈflaɪə/
form /fɔːm/
giraffe /dʒəˈrɑːf/
golden /ˈgəʊld(ə)n/
golf (no pl) /gɒlf/
hall /hɔːl/
hamburger /ˈhæmˌbɜːgə/
hamster /ˈhæmstə/
high-tech /ˌhaɪˈtek/
hip hop /ˈhɪp hɒp/
hobby /ˈhɒbi/
hockey (no pl) /ˈhɒki/
hot dog /ˌhɒt ˈdɒg/
idiot /ˈɪdiət/
in-line skate /ˌɪnˌlaɪn ˈskeɪt/
internet /ˈɪntəˌnet/
interview /ˈɪntəˌvjuː/
jeans (only pl) /ˈdʒiːnz/
job /dʒɒb/
jogging (no pl) /ˈdʒɒgɪŋ/
judo (no pl) /ˈdʒuːdəʊ/
kebab /kɪˈbæb/
kilo /ˈkɪlə/
kindergarten /ˈkɪndəˌgɑːt(ə)n/
kiwi /ˈkiːwiː/
labrador /ˈlæbrədɔː/
land (no pl) /lænd/
laptop /ˈlæpˌtɒp/
lasagne /ləˈzænjə/
laser tag /ˈleɪzə tæg/
layout /ˈleɪaʊt/
list /lɪst/
macaroni /ˌmækəˈrəʊni/

million /ˈmɪljən/
mini /ˈmɪni/
moment /ˈməʊmənt/
muffin /ˈmʌfɪn/
museum /mjuːˈziːəm/
ninja /ˈnɪndʒə/
normal /ˈnɔːm(ə)l/
OK (informal) /əʊˈkeɪ/
online /ˌɒnˈlaɪn/
otter /ˈɒtə/
park /pɑːk/
partner /ˈpɑːtnə/
party /ˈpɑːti/
pasta (no pl) /ˈpæstə/
pizza /ˈpiːtsə/
plan /plæn/
pony /ˈpəʊni/
pool /puːl/
positive /ˈpɒzətɪv/
poster /ˈpəʊstə/
problem /ˈprɒbləm/
programme /ˈprəʊgræm/
pudding /ˈpʊdɪŋ/
pyjamas (pl) /pəˈdʒɑːməz/
quiz (pl quizzes) /kwɪz, ˈkwɪzɪz/
radio /ˈreɪdiəʊ/
rap /ræp/
reporter /rɪˈpɔːtə/
rucksack /ˈrʌkˌsæk/
safari /səˈfɑːri/
sandwich /ˈsænwɪdʒ/
selfie /ˈselfi/
set /set/
sheriff /ˈʃerɪf/
show /ʃəʊ/
situation /ˌsɪtʃuˈeɪʃ(ə)n/
skateboard /ˈskeɪtˌbɔːd/
smiley /ˈsmaɪli/
so /səʊ/
sofa /ˈsəʊfə/

soft /sɒft/
solo /ˈsəʊləʊ/
song /sɒŋ/
spaghetti (no pl) /spəˈgeti/
sport /spɔːt/
star /stɑː/
steak /steɪk/
super (informal) /ˈsuːpə/
T-shirt /ˈtiːˌʃɜːt/
tablet /ˈtæblət/
talent /ˈtælənt/
team /tiːm/
teddy bear /ˈtedi beə/
teenager /ˈtiːnˌeɪdʒə/
tennis (no pl) /ˈtenɪs/
terrarium (pl terrariums or terraria) /təˈreəriəm, təˈreəriəmz, təˈreəriə/
test /test/
text /tekst/
ticket /ˈtɪkɪt/
tiger /ˈtaɪgə/
tip /tɪp/
toast /təʊst/
tour /tʊə/
tourist /ˈtʊərɪst/
training (no pl) /ˈtreɪnɪŋ/
trick /trɪk/
TV (= television) /ˌtiː ˈviː, ˈteliˌvɪʒn/
TV show /ˌtiː ˈviː ʃəʊ/
unfair /ʌnˈfeə/
vegan /ˈviːgən/
video (clip) /ˈvɪdiəʊ klɪp/
volleyball (no pl) /ˈvɒliˌbɔːl/
warm /wɔːm/
website /ˈwebˌsaɪt/
workshop /ˈwɜːkˌʃɒp/
yoga (no pl) /ˈjəʊgə/
zoo /zuː/

Words

Class instructions

Act out the dialogue.	**Spielt** den Dialog **nach**.
Add phrases from the box.	**Füge** Ausdrücke aus dem Kästchen **hinzu**.
Ask and answer questions.	**Stellt und beantwortet (euch gegenseitig) Fragen.**
Check G 1 on page 181.	**Sieh** bei G 1 auf Seite 181 **nach**.
Choose the best answer.	**Wähle** die passendste Antwort **aus**.
Close your books and listen.	**Schließt eure Bücher und hört zu.**
Collect words and phrases for your story.	**Sammle** Wörter und Ausdrücke für deine Geschichte.
Combine words from the two boxes to form new words.	**Verbinde** Wörter aus den zwei Kästchen zu neuen Wörtern.
Compare your grid with a partner's.	**Vergleiche** deine Tabelle mit der eines Partners/einer Partnerin.
Complete the grid.	**Vervollständige die Tabelle.**
Copy the text.	**Schreibe** den Text **ab**.
Correct the wrong sentences.	**Korrigiere** die falschen Sätze.
Describe it to your partner.	**Beschreibe** es deinem Partner/deiner Partnerin.
Explain in German what you have to do.	**Erkläre** auf Deutsch, was du tun sollst.
Fill in the correct words.	**Trage die richtigen Wörter ein.**
Find more examples in B2.	**Finde** weitere Beispiele in B2.
Find out more about …	**Finde mehr** über … **heraus**.
Finish the dialogue.	**Beende** den Dialog.
Guess the meaning of these words: …	**Errate** die Bedeutung dieser Wörter: …
Imagine what happens next.	**Stell dir vor**, was als Nächstes passiert.
Keep your list for later.	**Heb dir deine Liste für später auf.**
Listen and choose the right answers.	**Hör zu** und wähle die richtigen Antworten aus.
Listen to the dialogue and answer the questions.	**Hör dir** den Dialog **an** und beantworte die Fragen.
Look at p. 1 **Look at** pp.1-3. / **Look at** pages 1-3.	**Sieh dir Seite 1 an.** **Sieh dir Seite 1–3 an.**
Look at the picture/the text/the dialogue.	**Sieh dir** das Bild/den Text/den Dialog **an**.
Make a list/a quiz/a word web.	**Erstelle** eine Liste/ein Quiz/ein Wortnetz.
Match the words **to** the pictures.	**Ordne** die Wörter den Bildern **zu**.
Note down your ideas.	**Notiere** deine Ideen.

Words W

Present the story in class. — **Präsentiert** die Geschichte im Unterricht.

Read the dialogue. / **Read out** your sentences. — **Lies** den Dialog. / **Lest** eure Sätze **vor**.

Scan the dialogue. — **Überfliege** den Dialog.

Take notes (on …) — **Mach dir Notizen zu …**

Take turns. — **Wechselt euch ab.**

Talk about your favourite food. — **Sprecht über** euer Lieblingsessen.

Translate the sentences into German. — **Übersetze** die Sätze ins Deutsche.

Use your list/your notes. — **Verwende** deine Liste/deine Notizen.

Watch the video about Camden. — **Sieh** dir das Video über Camden **an**.

Write a short dialogue. / **Write about** … — **Schreibe** einen kurzen Dialog. / **Schreibe über** …

Write down your answers. — **Schreibe** deine Antworten **auf**.

Q Quellen

Bildquellen

|alamy images, Abingdon/Oxfordshire: 89, 91, 91, 93, 112, 116, 116, 156, 157, 159, 159, 159, 159, 159; Alex Segre 105; Aparicio, Juanma 33; Aroon Vater 105; Ashmore, Matthew 32; Bagnall, David 35; Barker, Andrew 112; Bond, Martin 107; Brabiner, David 114; British Retail Photography 69; Calvo, Nano 100; Chuck Pefley 165; Corbishley, Guy 91; Dagnall, Ian 116, 120; David Grossmann 140; De Rueda Roige, Jordi 32; deWitt, Kathy 68; Doyle, Paul 69; Education & Exploration 4 53; Ferrari, Cornelio 141, 141; ffotoCymru - Images of Wales 104; Fotomaton 22; Goldberg, Jonathan 68, 73; Grossman, David 162; imageBROKER 47, 100; Juniors Bildarchiv GmbH 100; Kerrison, Mark 90; Kirby, Joe 44; Lander, Douglas 22; Lane, Peter 17, 132; Morley, Caroline 156; Novarc Images 33; Peter Rauter / Art Directors 104; Peter Jordan 104; Pets, Perky 159; Phillips, Patricia 73; Pilchards 104; platz, szene, skelett, mammut, museum 115; Prisma by Dukas Presseagentur GmbH 140; Reed, David 91; Reed, Ellie 22; Scammell, Gordon 22; Science Photo Library 44; Sherratt, Adrian 73; Shironosov, Dmitriy 68; South West Images Scotland 69; Stephen Barnes/Educatio 44; tbkmedia.de 90; Tony Gwynne 105; Trask, Derek 140; Turner, Simon 44, 44; Veryan, Dale 91; Vidler, Steve 114; Viitanen, Juhani 100; Warwick, Michael 116; Waugh, Mark 113; Wavebreak Media ltd 69; Williams, John 100; Williams, Rod 90; Woods, Gary 158; workingwales 44. |Amortegui, Miguel, Saltdean - Rottingdean: 101, 154. |Dean, Finn, Robertsbridge, Eas Sussex: 109. |Dr. Heike Michaelis-Jankowski, Braunschweig: 50. |Eckart-Scheurig, Jutta, Wiesbaden: 158. |fotolia.com, New York: graphixmania 23; Schuermann, Frank 94; Stephen Bonk 158; © oskanov 98. |Hammersen-Schiffner, Bettina, Braunschweig: 158. |Hanus, Pamela, Hamburg: 26, 26, 32, 33. |iStockphoto.com, Calgary: 141, 141; coward_lion 112; gbh007 162; georgeclerk 80; Imgorthand 162; irene_k 141; martinedoucet Titel; monkeybusinessimages 112; ZoltanGabor Titel. |Jeyabalasingham, Denis, Braunschweig: 50. |Orion Publishing Group, London: 86, 86, 86, 87, 87. |Shutterstock.com, New York: 141, 141, 162; chrisdorney 162; flower travelin' man 25; Hurst Photo 29; Jorba, Josep Perianes 112; Laszlo Szirtesi 162; Prostock-studio 71; Syda Productions 14; UfaBizPhoto 112, 115, 162; Van Lennep, Chris 68. |stock.adobe.com, Dublin: Cherkasov, Andrey N. 141; iamtui7 158; Mirko 64; Ryzhov, Sergey 162; Sven Bähren 140. |Wefringhaus, Klaus, Braunschweig: 12, 27, 47, 75, 101, 103. |Zwick, Joachim, Gießen: 2.

Wir arbeiten sehr sorgfältig daran, für alle verwendeten Abbildungen die Rechteinhaberinnen und Rechteinhaber zu ermitteln. Sollte uns dies im Einzelfall nicht vollständig gelungen sein, werden berechtigte Ansprüche selbstverständlich im Rahmen der üblichen Vereinbarungen abgegolten.

Textquellen

S. 12 „Rock around the alphabet", Text: Kriwaneck, Wolle / Kienzler, Jürgen © Jürgen Kienzler
S. 86/87 „Horrid Henry's Birthday Party" © Francesca Simon 1995, Orion Children's Books, an imprint of the Orion Publishing Group London.

Solution (4R2b, p. 87)

D – B – A – C

Wortschatzerfasser

Yücel Özyürek, Lektor und Sprachtrainer, Eresing, www.language-expert.de